UBUNTU MADE EASY

UBUNTU MADE EASY

A Project-Based Introduction to Linux

by Rickford Grant with Phil Bull

no starch
press

San Francisco

16 15 14 13 12   1 2 3 4 5 6 7 8 9

First printing

ISBN-10: 1-59327-425-4
ISBN-13: 978-1-59327-425-2

Publisher: William Pollock
Production Editor: Alison Law
Cover Illustration: Charlie Wylie
Interior Design: Octopod Studios
Developmental Editor: Keith Fancher
Technical Reviewer: Milo Casagrande
Copyeditor: Paula L. Fleming
Compositor: Susan Glinert Stevens
Proofreader: Ward Webber

For information on book distributors or translations, please contact No Starch Press, Inc. directly:

No Starch Press, Inc.
38 Ringold Street, San Francisco, CA 94103
phone: 415.863.9900; fax: 415.863.9950; info@nostarch.com; www.nostarch.com

Library of Congress Cataloging-in-Publication Data
A catalog record of this book is available from the Library of Congress.

In loving memory of my mother, Angelina Pavlovich,
for whom the original version of this book was written.
She was sweet, fun, and made a mean dish of chilaquiles.
I miss her always.

—Rickford

To mum and dad:
For everything

—Phil

BRIEF CONTENTS

CONTENTS IN DETAIL

6
ROUNDING OUT THE BIRD
Downloading, Installing, and
Updating Programs the Easy Way
77

7
A TIDY NEST
File and Disc Handling in Ubuntu
95

8
SIMPLE KITTEN WAYS
Getting to Know the Linux Terminal and Command Line . . . and the Cool Things It Can Do 125

9
DRESSING UP THE BIRD
Customizing the Look and Feel of Your System
159

10
GUTENBIRD
Setting Up and Using Your Printer and Scanner   179

11
POLYGLOT PENGUINS
Linux Speaks Your Language   199

12
PENGUINS AT WORK
Getting Down to Business in Linux   213

13
RIGHT-BRAIN PENGUINS
Linux Does Art   229

14
TUX ROCKS
Music à la Linux   245

15
PLUGGIN' IN THE PENGUIN
Working with Your iPod, iPhone, and
Other Digital Media Devices 263

16
COUCH PENGUINS
Video and DVD Playback in Ubuntu 275

17
FEATHERED FLIPPERS
Linux Gaming

289

18
SWEET HOME ANTARCTICA
Linux Around the House

309

19
PENGUINS AT THE GATES
Working with Ubuntu in a Windows World

321

20
DEFENDING THE NEST
Security

339

21
A COLONY OF PENGUINS
The Ubuntu Community

351

22
WOUNDED WINGS
Fixing Common Problems

373

A
INSTALLING UBUNTU FROM A USB FLASH DRIVE   403

B
UBUNTU DESKTOP 64-BIT DISCS   407

C
MANUALLY PARTITIONING YOUR HARD DISK   411

ABOUT THE AUTHORS

Rickford Grant

My computing life began long ago, in the Commodore/Atari days. No doubt inspired by Alan Alda's television commercials at the time, I purchased my first machine, an Atari 600XL with a cassette drive for storage and 16KB of RAM—more than I thought I would ever need. Most of my time on that machine, I must admit, was spent playing cartridge-based games and transcribing pages and pages of machine code from the now-defunct magazine *Antic* to create even more games. Eventually, my interest in computers increased, especially after seeing my first (and actually *the* first) Macintosh at the UCLA bookstore. The very in-your-face nature of the Mac's operating system caused me to become an operating system maniac. To date, I have worked with a lot of different operating systems, including Mac OS up to and including OS X, every Windows version from 3.1 onward, and even IBM's mostly forgotten OS/2.

Though tempted to join the Linux fray, I continued to steer away from it for a long time because I could not help but see it, as so many others do, as a system for never-seen-the-light-of-day-faced, late-night Dr Pepper–drinking, Domino's pizza–eating compu-geeks. However, when I moved to Japan and was suddenly surrounded by machines loaded with Japanese versions of Windows, I encountered numerous problems, especially language constraints. Since everything, including Help files, was written in Japanese and my reading skills in Japanese were less than spectacular, I ended up using only a fraction of the full potential of most software. Then there were those annoying Windows-type problems that were especially prevalent back then, such as the constant freezes and restarts and the gradual system slowdowns, which were eventually remedied only by reinstalling the system. Getting the software I needed to do the things I wanted to do also took a toll on my wallet, and I began to rethink my initial resistance to Linux. With Linux's multilingual support, system stability, and extensive and free software packages, there were plenty of incentives for me to get over my preconceived notions about the typical Linux user.

After a few failed attempts at getting Linux to work on the oddball, Frankenstein-like collection of junk that was my computer, I finally succeeded with a live-CD distribution called Knoppix, which worked well enough to reel me in. I eventually tried and used a number of distributions that appeared, before eventually making my way to Fedora and then, ultimately, Ubuntu.

I started off with my three desktop machines at work and home set up as dual-boot systems running both Linux and Windows, but I gradually found myself using only Linux. Although I had expected to encounter numerous limitations in Linux that would force me to return often to Windows, I actually increased my productivity. Despite a lack of native support for Windows streaming media, I was able to do more because of the extensive software base that was now installed on my machine. Without having to fork out money that I could ill afford to spend, I was able to manipulate my digital images, rip songs from CDs, create vector drawings, generate PDF files, and do a variety of other things that I wasn't able to do under Windows. It was only a matter of time before my dual-boot setups became full Linux-only setups. I ceased to be a Windows user.

To be sure, a bit more hands-on tinkering had to be done back then to get all the things you wanted to work in Linux working, but I am happy to report that things have continued to get easier and better, and those early frustrations I suffered trying to get things to work with this machine or that piece of hardware are mostly a thing of the past. Best of all, with even more distributions being available as live CDs, which allow you to try Linux before you actually install it, you usually don't even have to take a leap of faith to get started. Ubuntu, quite fortunately, is one such distribution.

Of course, getting started in the world of Linux, no matter which distribution you are using, can be a bit intimidating, especially when you don't have anyone around to help you out when you have questions. In fact, I actually started writing this book as a Linux primer for my mother, to whom I had just given one of my extra computers with Red Hat installed. At that time, I was not planning on writing a book at all; it was just that there really weren't any books out there written with average users in mind. The books available were all more or less geek oriented, and as such, they would not do for the *mater*. I thus created a somewhat elaborate instruction set that would tell her how to do everything she might want to do in a way she could understand. Since I was in Japan and she in the United States at the time, I tried to make it as user-friendly as possible.

My auntie caught hold of the "manuscript" and decided that I must try to publish it. I responded with the obligatory, "Yeah, right," before putting it out of my mind. My auntie, being a rather persistent character, did not relent, so I moved to quiet her by submitting the book for publication. Surely a rejection slip would do the trick; however, I did not get a rejection slip, and instead my first book, *Linux for Non-Geeks*, based on Fedora Core I, was born. I later switched to Ubuntu, and the *Non-Geeks* line followed along with *Ubuntu for Non-Geeks*.

I continued with two subsequent editions of the Ubuntu books, but my new day job was making it harder and harder to devote the time necessary to keep the whole book up-to-date and up-to-snuff and get it all written by when it was needed. It seemed time to bring in a co-author to keep things moving. Enter Phil Bull. Phil was the technical editor on the third edition of *Ubuntu for Non-Geeks*, and because of his familiarity with the book, in addition to his work on Ubuntu documentation, he seemed a perfect candidate for the job. The fact that he lives closer than I to Stanage Edge, where I still imagine myself one day standing, pulling the Keira Knightley *Pride and Prejudice* pose, didn't hurt matters either.

Such *rêves de vacances* aside, having Phil on the project allowed us not only to update the book so as to reflect changes in the system and bundled applications but also to expand it to cover changes in available technology and hardware and to address suggestions from readers of past editions. These changes, I believe, made for an even more well-rounded volume than before— a book that even better served the original purpose of the series: helping you get into the world of Linux easily and comfortably.

The collaboration with Phil continues with this follow-up edition, *Ubuntu Made Easy*, and though the title is new, the book continues to improve and expand upon the previous *Non-Geeks* editions. It attempts, as did its predecessors, to make your transition into the world of Linux a smooth and easy one.

Phil Bull

As my illustrious co-author already mentioned, I've worked on two previous editions of this book, both as a writer and technical reviewer. It turned out to be so much fun (Rickford and the folks at No Starch are *really* great to work with) that I've come back for more!

So, what's my background? Well, computers have taken up most of my free time since I was eight years old. I started off playing games on my uncle's old DOS machine, and I soon found myself ripping apart our home PC and putting it back together again just to see how it worked. The geekiness doesn't stop there; I taught myself to program using Microsoft Word and Visual Basic for Applications (ugh) when I was 14, and I even worked in technical support for a while in my teens. At the end of high school, however, I realized that physics was my calling in life, and now I'm a grad student in astrophysics at the University of Oxford in the UK. I haven't completely forsaken computers, though—far from it, in fact. It turns out that numerical simulations are pretty important in my line of work, and I currently spend a lot of time studying the Universe from the comfort of my laptop (running Ubuntu, of course).

My Linux journey started off with an old copy of *PC Pro* magazine from 1999. There was an article on this weird, alien-looking operating system, and I just knew I had to try it out. Unfortunately, my dial-up modem balked at the prospect of downloading a 650MB file, so I had to wait until sometime around 2004, when a friend sent me a Xandros Linux CD. The rest, as they say, is history: I rapidly migrated to Fedora, and then settled down with Ubuntu in 2006. Not long after, I started writing documentation for Ubuntu, and then for GNOME, a pastime that I've kept up ever since. I just love to figure out problems, and writing clear, understandable instructions for people felt more productive (and, often, more challenging!) than doing the crossword.

Writing this book with Rickford is, in many ways, the culmination of the last decade or so of my computing life, and I hope you'll find my contributions to this volume fun, easy to read, and—above all—useful. The Ubuntu operating system itself is an interesting phenomenon, with much that you'll love and a few things that may frustrate you. We've highlighted lots of the good stuff, the cool features and satisfying "it just works" moments that make Ubuntu my favorite OS, but we haven't shied away from providing detailed advice about where things can sometimes go wrong. My hope is that after reading *Ubuntu Made Easy*, you'll feel confident and in control of your computer; familiar with all of the bells and whistles that are there to help you get things done, and ready to take in stride any problems that come up. I hope you enjoy reading it. Oh, and one last thing . . . welcome to Ubuntu!

ACKNOWLEDGMENTS

There are a good number of people who deserve thanks for the help and support they provided either while or before this book was written, and there are still others whose help will come after the book is released. I (Rickford) would like to acknowledge all of them now.

To start at home, so to speak, I'd like to thank my auntie and uncle, Danica Lucia and David Zollars, and the rest of my family here, for encouraging me in my various endeavors, such as this, while also watching over me when things get tough. Thanks also to all of my family in Bosnia-Herzegovina, who helped remind me that I was not alone as the world around me seemed to be vanishing. Before moving on, I'd also like to thank a few friends who had an impact on this continuing project. First I'd like to thank Setsu Uesaka, who really helped and encouraged me a lot back when the forerunner to this book was being prepared in Toyama, Japan, as well as my stateside friend Donald Hammang, who encouraged me during those times when I just didn't have any push left in me.

I would like to thank all of those people who worked together with me on the production of this book, staring with the editor, Keith Fancher, who really does a great job of keeping the flow of the book smooth and consistent and makes you comfortable in the process. Hopefully, we have made his editing life easier this time around. Thanks also go out to Milo Casagrande, the technical reviewer on this edition, who did his best to ensure that all of the details in the book were straight duck, and Alison Law, the production editor, who made sure that every *t* was crossed and every bit of orphaned text was found and dealt with. Thanks also to Riley Hoffman and Serena Yang, who made sure the jumble of text and images we submitted turned into a properly formatted book, and to Jessica Miller, who handles the marketing side of things. A very special set of thanks goes out to William Pollock, who took a chance on the completely unknown writer that I was when I first submitted my original manuscript, thus allowing things to evolve to where they are today. Finally, I am glad to once again express my thanks to my co-author, Phil Bull, who provided new inspiration and ideas for the book and again made working on this new edition a lot less lonely than it was in the past. As I've said before, it's always nice to have someone to bounce ideas around with. Thank you, Phil!

Finally, a special thanks to my sweet little black cat and dear feline friend, Muju, who, despite vociferously protesting as I spent *her* time writing this book, continues to listen to whatever I have to say and keeps me sane when I'm feeling down—though I admit to losing it a bit when she demands that I spin her around on my swivel chair at 4 AM or when she decides at 6 AM that it is time for me to get up for no apparent reason, as is her most recent custom. Such is life in service to one's cat. Meow.

With two authors you get two sets of acknowledgments, so I'd like to take this opportunity to thank all of the people who've helped me (Phil) throughout the writing of this book.

First and foremost, I want to thank my parents, Julie and Jeff, for all of the love they've provided over the years. Their support gives me the confidence to go out there and do things, and I respect and admire them both more than they can ever imagine. I'm also grateful to my sister, Ellen, for keeping life interesting and for making me a proud big brother; to my grandparents, for their unwavering affection; and to my auntie and uncle, Pam and Roy, for nurturing my geeky tendencies.

I'm also fortunate to have a bunch of friends who've kept me in good humor (and relative sanity!) for all these years. They include Leo "Tweed" Huckvale, Will "Dirty Hipster" Whyles, and Kiran "Hype Man" Joshi, my partners in nerd-crime; Emily Johnstone, Mikey Wood, Myriam Yagoubi, Laura MacPhee, Asia Lindsay, and Alix Huk, who never fail to put a smile on my face; the impossibly excellent Adam Blundred, Jamie Poole, and Matt Glover; Mike, Sarah, Christina, Pete, Stephen, Gabe, and Kate, who never fail to bring fun times with them; and all of my other lovely friends, whom I'd be lost without. I also owe my friends and colleagues in astrophysics a debt of gratitude, especially Rich, Will, Tessa, Amy, Adam, Graeme, Phil, Pedro, Tim, Chris, and Alan for inspiring me, guiding me, or just plain indulging me.

Being involved in the open source community is an absolute privilege. It's filled with such wonderful people as Jim Campbell, Shaun McCance, and Tiffany Antopolski, whose dedication is awe-inspiring. It's always good to see them, and all the others (Kat, Dave, Mike, Ryan, Johannes, Julita, Natalia . . .) who make every conference and hackfest a super fun time. The fact that it's possible to write a book like this at all is a testament to their hard work.

I also want to thank all of the folks at No Starch for bringing the awesome. It's been a real pleasure to work with them again, and Rickford and I couldn't have asked for a better team to help us through. Rickford already named names, but I want to thank everyone again: Keith, Bill, Milo, Alison, Paula, Riley, Leigh, and Jessica, you've all been amazing, and I'm really grateful for everything you've put into this book.

Finally, my sincere thanks go to Rickford, for not only getting the ball rolling on this book all those editions ago, but also for being an absolutely splendid writing partner—as always. Cheers!

INTRODUCTION

If you're standing in the aisle of your local bookstore reading this right now, you may well be wondering who this book is for. *Ubuntu Made Easy*, as you might imagine, is for readers who are interested in Linux but who feel the need for a jumping-off point to get started.

If you're familiar with computers but unfamiliar with Linux, or if you are somewhat familiar with Linux but not with Ubuntu, this book is for you. This is not primarily a book for seasoned geeks or power users; it's an introductory guide that will provide you with some hands-on experience to get up, running, and comfortable with the Ubuntu Linux distribution without pain. Think of this book as a map, a compass, and a comfy pair of hiking boots rather than a harness, a rope, and a set of crampons.

Version Compatibility

Ubuntu Made Easy is based on Ubuntu 12.04 (Precise Pangolin) Desktop edition. The CD bundled with this book is the Ubuntu Desktop CD, which lets you both try Ubuntu without installing it and install Ubuntu to your hard drive once you're ready. It's called a *live CD*. You can boot your computer from the CD and run Ubuntu directly off the CD without touching your hard disk to see if you like Ubuntu and to make sure that Ubuntu will work with your hardware. If, after running the live CD, you like what you see and everything seems to work, you can install Ubuntu on your computer using the same disc. (There are instructions for doing so in Chapter 2.)

Concept and Approach

This book is intended as both a handy reference and a dynamic learning experience: You'll get some hands-on experience as you work through it. The text is organized by increasing skills, so that, as much as possible, you won't be asked to do something that you haven't already learned. In addition, you can put the various morsels of knowledge you acquire into practice through several exercises, or *projects*.

The projects in this book serve another purpose as well: By working through them, you will learn to configure and customize your Ubuntu system. By the time you finish this book, you should have a pretty good mastery of Ubuntu.

These chapter descriptions should give you a better idea of what is in store:

Chapter 1: Becoming a Penguinista—Welcome to the World of Linux
What's Linux? What's Ubuntu? What's a distribution? Can I . . . ? Will my . . . ? Chapter 1 holds the answers to these and many other questions you might have as it introduces you to the world of Linux and what it takes to get it up and running on your machine.

Chapter 2: Wading and Diving—Running and (If You Like) Installing Ubuntu
The CD that comes with this book works as both a live CD and an install CD. Chapter 2 tells you how to run a live Ubuntu session from the CD and, assuming you catch the Linux bug after doing so, how to install Ubuntu on your hard disk. You can install Ubuntu either as your sole operating system or together with Windows, and you get directions for both.

Chapter 3: A New Place to Call Home—Getting to Know the Desktop
You're probably already familiar with the concept of a desktop. Chapter 3 points out the differences between Ubuntu's Unity desktop and the one on your previous operating system, and it teaches you a number of cool tricks you can use to customize the look and feel of things.

Chapter 4: More Than Webbed Feet—Connecting to the Internet
"Have computer, will cybertravel," could well be the mantra of the Internet age, and that being the case, Chapter 4 is an indispensable part of your Ubuntu experience. In this chapter, you will learn how to connect to the Internet and set up wireless and mobile broadband connections. You'll also find tips for using a modem and some handy troubleshooting advice just in case you struggle to get connected.

Chapter 5: Slipping and Sliding—Exploring the Internet, Linux Style

With Chapter 4 behind you, it's time to get serious about all this Internet business and start putting it to good use. Chapter 5 takes you on a tour of Ubuntu's suite of Internet applications, in particular the Firefox web browser. You're introduced to Ubuntu's email and instant messaging tools before embarking on a crash course in social networking with Twitter and Gwibber.

Chapter 6: Rounding Out the Bird—Downloading, Installing, and Updating Programs the Easy Way

The default Ubuntu installation includes most of the software you need, but there's still much more available out there, free and waiting on the Internet. Chapter 6 teaches you how to easily download and install applications using the Ubuntu Software Center. You'll learn about system and application updating and how to broaden your software horizons using third-party repositories.

Chapter 7: A Tidy Nest—File and Disc Handling in Ubuntu

From creating folders to copying files to browsing your system and network, Chapter 7 covers all things file management. You'll learn how to work with USB storage devices, transfer files via Bluetooth, burn data CDs and DVDs, deal with CD-RW disks and multisession CDs, and create space-saving compressed archives of files and folders.

Chapter 8: Simple Kitten Ways—Getting to Know the Linux Terminal and Command Line . . . and the Cool Things It Can Do

Many people shy away from Linux because they perceive it as a system in which everything still needs to be done by entering commands. That perception is a load of squashed avocados, as the saying goes. Still, a lot of cool stuff can be done via the command line–based Terminal, and Chapter 8 will tell you all about it as it tames your fears and piques your interest in commands. Really.

Chapter 9: Dressing Up the Bird—Customizing the Look and Feel of Your System

Tired of looking at the same old desktop? Feeling nostalgic for the desktop in your previous operating system? Chapter 8 tells you how to beat the déjà vu blues by changing the look and feel of your system and how to take some control of Ubuntu's visual effects engine, Compiz.

Chapter 10: Gutenbird—Setting Up and Using Your Printer and Scanner

Just about everyone with a computer has or needs a printer. Chapter 10 tells you exactly how to get your printer (or scanner) working with Ubuntu.

Chapter 11: Polyglot Penguins—Linux Speaks Your Language

Need to jot off a note in Urdu? Write a book in Korean? Send a letter in Chinese to your friend in Chengdu? Chapter 11 gives you what you need to read and write in just about any language in the world.

Chapter 12: Penguins at Work—Getting Down to Business in Linux

Work can be a drag, especially when there are so many other things you could be doing. Still, wearing the ol' fingers to the bone is part of life for just about everyone outside of a Jane Austen novel, and you'll be glad to know that Linux has lots to offer in this regard. Chapter 12 introduces you to the various productivity applications available.

Chapter 13: Right-Brain Penguins—Linux Does Art

Those with an artistic bent will find Chapter 13 especially useful. Here you'll learn how to work with your digital camera by downloading images, modifying them, and then tagging and organizing them. You will also learn how to work with RAW image files and read a bit about other graphics programs.

Chapter 14: Tux Rocks—Music à la Linux

Chapter 14 is the music lover's treasure trove. You'll learn how to rip CDs, encode MP3 or Ogg Vorbis audio files, and create your own mix-and-match audio CDs. You'll also learn how to make music of your own, from creating or modifying guitar amp presets to putting it all together with your own digital audio studio.

Chapter 15: Pluggin' In the Penguin—Working with Your iPod, iPhone, and Other Digital Media Devices

Do you have an iPad? An iPhone? A Droid? A $10 MP3 player from the flea market? Want to use it in Ubuntu? Chapter 15 tells you how.

Chapter 16: Couch Penguins—Video and DVD Playback in Ubuntu

Sitting in your dorm room trying to figure out how to play your DVD copy of *The Baxter* on your Ubuntu-ized computer? Just finished filming a video of your sibling talking while asleep and want to do some creative editing of the evidence? Chapter 16 covers these and other video-related topics.

Chapter 17: Feathered Flippers—Linux Gaming

If music and art don't keep your mind off things enough, Chapter 17 presents you with more diversions: games. In addition to learning what games your system comes with, you will also learn how to add more, including commercial ones, and even how to run Java-based games.

Chapter 18: Sweet Home Antarctica—Linux Around the House

As if to drive home the point yet again, Ubuntu is not just for use in the office or home library by those with business, art, or geeky things in mind. It can also be used in a variety of ways related to home and family. In Chapter 18, you'll learn a number of ways to put Ubuntu to work at home, doing everything from finding recipes and keeping track of your weight to creating a family tree.

Chapter 19: Penguins at the Gates—Working with Ubuntu in a Windows World

Like it or not, Microsoft Windows is probably here to stay (for the foreseeable future, at least). Chapter 19 shows you how to share files between Windows and Ubuntu over a network, install Windows fonts, and even install Windows programs to run under Ubuntu. Dual-booters take note: You'll learn how to access your Windows files from Ubuntu and change the boot menu.

Chapter 20: Defending the Nest—Security

Although Linux is about as safe and secure an operating system as you are likely to use, Chapter 20 tells you how to add a few additional lines of defense to your system.

Chapter 21: A Colony of Penguins—The Ubuntu Community

If there's one thing that sets Ubuntu apart from most Linux distributions, it's the friendly, ever-growing Ubuntu community that surrounds it. In Chapter 21 you'll learn how to participate in the Ubuntu community by reporting bugs, discussing problems, and talking to other users.

Chapter 22: Wounded Wings—Fixing Common Problems

Don't panic! If a computer problem is spoiling your fun, flip to Chapter 22 and take heed of the many troubleshooting tips within. You'll find fixes for the most common issues and some general advice on diagnosing and treating your poor PC.

Appendix A: Installing Ubuntu from a USB Flash Drive

What with the proliferation of netbooks in recent years, installing Ubuntu from CD is beginning to seem a little *passé*. Appendix A shows you how to install Ubuntu from a USB memory stick, which will be particularly useful if your computer lacks a CD drive or if you found the disc included with this book far too attractive not to use as a coaster.

Appendix B: Ubuntu Desktop 64-Bit Discs

The CD bundled with this book is designed to work with i386 processors. It will also work with most 64-bit processors, although not in 64-bit mode. If you've got what it takes to run Ubuntu in 64-bit mode, Appendix B shows you how to get what you need to do it.

Appendix C: Manually Partitioning Your Hard Disk

If the basic partitioning advice in Chapter 2 wasn't enough for you, Appendix C shows you how to carve up your hard disk as you desire, free from the constraints of the Ubuntu installer's sensible, but ultimately simple, suggestions. If you're a dual-booter and want an easy way to share files between Windows and Ubuntu, this appendix is for you.

Appendix D: Resources

Are you crazy for Ubuntu and want to say so? Check out a forum. Do you have a hardware compatibility question? Some websites seem to have all the answers. Are you looking for free downloads, or do you want to read up on the other Linux distributions? Appendix D is a great place to start.

How to Use This Book

You can use this book simply as a reference, but that's not the main idea behind its design. Ideally, you should go through the book chapter by chapter, doing the projects along the way. This will give you a much broader understanding of how things are done (and of how you can get things done), and it will reduce the chance for anxiety, confusion, and, worse yet, mistakes.

It is best to read this book and complete its projects when you are relaxed and have time to spare. Nothing makes things go wrong more than working in a rush. And keep in mind that Linux and the projects in this book are fun, not just work exercises. Linux *is* fun, so enjoy it!

About the Conventions Used in This Book

There are a few points worth noting about the conventions used in this book. Items in **bold** type are ones that you need to click or manipulate in any way, such as buttons, tabs, and menus. Where words or phrases are defined, they have been set in *italics*. Text to input into a Terminal window is in a bold `monospace` font.

About the Projects in This Book

The projects and other information in this book are primarily geared toward readers who have installed Ubuntu using the CD that comes with this book. Most of the information also applies to Ubuntu live sessions run from the live CD. Note, however, that some projects and actions cannot be performed in live sessions because they require write access to your hard disk, which is not possible during live sessions. For more information on what it means to run Ubuntu from the live CD, check out Chapter 2.

1

BECOMING A PENGUINISTA

Welcome to the World of Linux

As the saying goes, there's no place to begin like the beginning, so in this chapter we'll do just that by introducing you to the world of Linux. We'll then get you up to snuff on what this Ubuntu thing is all about, why you might want to install and use it, and what you will need in order to do so. For those of you who already have joined the Linux world and have Ubuntu or another distribution installed on your machines, some of this may be old news, but a few bits of information may still be of interest to you. For those others who may be curious but are still unsure whether or not to take the plunge, or those of you who have no idea what Linux even is and have picked up this book to find out, this chapter will prove especially useful.

You will probably have lots of questions as you make your way through the book, and, like most people, you may also have a few doubts or worries. Hopefully by the time you finish, you will have your Linux system up and running; any doubts or worries you might have had will have been dispelled; and your questions, for the most part, will be answered. If you are reluctant to make a commitment by installing Ubuntu on your hard disk, remember that you can still follow along because the disc that comes with this book contains, in addition to the Ubuntu installer, a live Ubuntu environment—meaning that you can get a taste of the Ubuntu Linux experience without having to even touch your hard drive.

What Is Linux?

Your computer, despite being a collection of highly sophisticated parts, is really just . . . well, a collection of highly sophisticated parts. On its own, it can do nothing other than switch on and off and spin a disk or two. For it to do anything truly useful, it needs an operating system (OS) to guide it. The OS takes a well-endowed but completely uneducated hunk of a machine and educates it, at least enough so that it will understand what you want it to do.

You already know of and have probably used at least one of the many operating systems that exist today, or did in the past. Windows and Mac OS are such operating systems, as is Unix, the commercial-grade operating system behind many Internet sites and databases. And don't think that computers are the only place you run into operating systems. Those of you with smartphones, which are themselves miniature computers, are probably interacting daily with the Android operating system or iOS, the operating system on iPhones and iPads.

Linux is yet another operating system. It is, however, different from other operating systems in terms of both its capabilities and its heritage. Linux was not created by a corporation or by some corporate wannabe out to make money. The Linux core, referred to as the *kernel*, was created by computer enthusiast Linus Torvalds, a member of Finland's Swedish ethnic minority, who wanted to create a Unix-like system that would work on home computers—particularly his.

Rather than keeping his creation to himself, Torvalds opened it up to the world, so to speak, and compu-geeks around the globe worked to make it better and more powerful. It is this combination of applications built around the core of the Linux kernel that is the essence of all Linux distributions today.

Linux has acquired many fans and followers since its creation in 1991. Such devotees praise Linux for its many features, as well as for being robust, reliable, free, and open. Despite these positive characteristics, however, Linux is, on its own, just a text-based system. There is no pretty desktop, and there are no windows or charming little icons to make you feel safe and comfy once you are behind the keyboard. Powerful though it may be, Linux is still strictly a black-screen, command line–driven operating system. I guess you could think of it as DOS on steroids, though a Linux purist will surely cringe at the thought. Sorry.

Although you can use Linux by itself, accomplishing all your tasks by typing commands on a black screen (the most common way of doing things when Linux is used as a server), you don't have to do that. It is fair to say that with the advent in 1984 of the Macintosh and its easy-to-use graphical user interface (GUI, pronounced "goo-ee"), DOS users began suffering something akin to GUI envy. They began clamoring for a GUI to call their own. The final result was Windows, which gave DOS a GUI and eased many command-wary users into the Microsoft world.

Similarly, many members of the Linux world felt the need and desire to go graphical. The community at large developed various GUIs (called window managers and desktop environments) and a subsystem with which to handle them (somewhat confusingly referred to as the *Window System*). The graphical desktop environment that is included in your Ubuntu distribution—Unity—is one example of the fruit of that development.

About the Penguin

You may have been wondering about the penguin in the chapter title, so I might as well explain that now. The penguin was chosen by Linus Torvalds as the Linux mascot, and what has come to be thought of as *the* Linux penguin was designed by Larry Ewing and is named Tux (see Figure 1-1). This explains not only the ornithological references and graphics throughout the book but also why there are so many penguin icons in Linux distributions and so many programs that include *penguin* or *Tux* in their names, such as TuxRacer, Tux Paint, and Pingus. This, combined with the fact that Linux is a revolutionary OS, helps

Figure 1-1: Tux, the Linux mascot

explain why Linux users are sometimes referred to as Penguinistas. True, Ubuntu doesn't play up the penguin as much as other distributions, but Linux is Linux so the penguin lives in Ubuntu too . . . just a bit less conspicuously.

Should You Use Linux?

The goal of this book is not to twist your arm and make you dump your current OS for Linux. If you are happy with what you've got, then stick with it. However, many people have switched to Linux for one reason or another. For many, crass as it may sound, it is a matter of money.

Unlike life in the Windows and Mac worlds, all the software you could conceivably want usually comes bundled in a Linux distribution, and there are still thousands of additional applications that you can add for free. And unlike the freeware and shareware applications in the Windows and Mac worlds, which eventually ask you for $25 here and $35 there, you will not be hit up for money when you least expect it. You will also not have to worry about the applications installing, unbeknownst to you, *backdoors* or *keyloggers* or making your system a sudden garden of adware.

Although money is important to the average user, it is certainly not the only reason Linux users make the switch. For some, it is a matter of personal philosophy—the belief that software should be freely accessible to all. Others like it because it gives them total control over almost everything, from how things behave to how they look; in other words, Linux lets them geek around. Others like it because of the stability Linux is noted for. Try running your current system for a month without restarting and see what happens. Linux has been known to run without a reboot for more than a year without a hitch or decrease in performance. With its multilingual capabilities, Linux is also a perfect choice for language students or users in a multilingual environment.

Finally, with the advent of Microsoft's Windows 7 system and its more demanding hardware requirements (especially if the user is trying to take advantage of its most touted new features), some find their current machines on the fast track to obsolescence. Turning it into a Linux machine will give it several more years of working life. After all, it's a shame to put good hardware out to pasture so early.

What Is a Distribution?

An operating system consists of a lot of files that perform a lot of different functions. And because there is no Linux corporation to package and distribute the files that make up Linux, the task of getting Linux onto your computer in working order, along with the applications that you are likely to want, has fallen to a varied group of entities—companies, universities, user groups, and even private individuals. These entities create Linux system and application collections called *distributions*, or *distros*. You could bypass such distros and try to collect everything you'd need to set up a system all on your own, but you would undoubtedly lose your mind in the process. Most people, even the geekiest, opt for the distros.

Most of these distros, whatever their ultimate target audience, basically consist of the same main elements: the core operating system (that's the Linux kernel I mentioned earlier); some sort of installer program to get all the system parts and applications properly installed on your machine; the X Window System to provide graphical interface support; one or more graphical desktop environments; and a series of applications, such as word processors, audio players, and games; as well as all the files needed to make these things work.

There are, of course, a large number of distros. Some are geared toward specific audiences, such as businesses, educators, gamers, students, programmers, system administrators, and specific language users. What makes each distro different is the software that is bundled with the Linux kernel, as well as other convenience features such as the package (or application) installation mechanism and the installer for the system itself. Some distros are especially appropriate for home users because of their ease of installation. Ubuntu, a relative newcomer to the Linux world, is one of these, joining other distros that have long been popular in the ease-of-use arena, such as openSUSE and Fedora.

What Is Ubuntu?

Ubuntu is a completely free, easy-to-use, and extremely popular Linux distribution that is geared toward the desktop user. It is one of the hottest Linux distros in the marketplace today. It is also one of the few Linux distros with what could be described as a social agenda behind it.

Ubuntu was the brainchild of South African millionaire entrepreneur Mark Shuttleworth, who is probably better known for being one of the first space tourists—the first African in space, to be exact. Shuttleworth invested more than $10 million in starting the Ubuntu Foundation based on his belief in free software and in order to fix what he describes as "bug #1"—Microsoft's dominance of the desktop PC marketplace (*https://bugs.launchpad.net/ubuntu/+bug/1/*).

As Shuttleworth states in his blog (available at *https://wiki.ubuntu.com/MarkShuttleworth*):

> I believe that free software brings us into a new era of technology, and holds the promise of universal access to the tools of the digital era. I drive Ubuntu because I would like to see that promise delivered as reality.

As you can see, it's a vision thing.

Befitting the nationality and goals of the man who brought it into being, the word *ubuntu* comes from the Zulu and Xhosa languages. *Ubuntu*, according to Wikipedia, is a concept meaning something along the lines of "humanity toward others" or "I am because we are." If you're interested, the 2005 film *In My Country*, although not one of the greatest films ever produced, is on many levels a 100-minute examination of the concept of *ubuntu*.

Why Ubuntu Then?

With so many distros out there, you may wonder why you should opt for Ubuntu. Well, as they say, numbers don't lie, and Ubuntu's popularity is not without good cause. Like most Linux distributions these days, Ubuntu is easy to install and quite robust and dependable in terms of everyday use. Unlike other distributions, however, Ubuntu is based on the *Debian* distribution, which means that it utilizes Debian's very convenient DEB package system for application handling and installation. The graphical package installer that comes with Ubuntu, Ubuntu Software Center, makes installing those applications even easier, and with so many applications available there, you are likely to find more software than you'll ever know what to do with.

More importantly, Ubuntu is designed to be user friendly—it tries to enable average people to do what they do most often as easily as possible. It is designed with the needs of real people in mind, not just compu-nerds and geeks. As such, it is designed primarily as a desktop system, and perhaps for that reason, Ubuntu's desktop environment, called Unity, is a very comfy place for the average desktop user.

Finally, while some distros are updated at a snail's pace and others strive to be so cutting edge that they are often plagued with bugs, Ubuntu has a reasonable six-month release cycle. In this time frame, it tries to stay as up-to-date as possible, while at the same time making sure that things are not released before they are ready for prime time. In this way, you are ensured of having an up-to-date yet less buggy distro at your disposal.

Hardware Compatibility

If you haven't installed Linux on your machine yet, you might be wondering whether or not Ubuntu will run on it. This used to be an important consideration when installing a Linux distribution, but these days it's less of an issue for a number of reasons. Of course, there are so many minor parts to your machine that it is difficult to say whether each part will cooperate with your installation. There are video cards, sound chips, LAN cards, monitors, and so on, and they all need to be considered. Nevertheless, chances are good that Ubuntu will run on your machine. The even better news is you can test whether your setup will work by using the disc that comes with this book. If, after starting up your machine from the live disc, everything seems to be going as it should . . . well, your worries are over, and you can install the system whenever you're ready and willing. That is a great and pretty much risk-free advantage.

When Research Is Required

If things don't work out for you with the live CD, you will have to do a bit of investigating. You can start by taking a look at Chapter 22. If you don't find the answer to your problem there, search the Web to see whether you can identify what part of your hardware puzzle is causing your problems. (Or if you are looking to buy a machine on which to install Ubuntu, you can search for hardware that is supported by Linux.) Of course, before you can do this, you need to know what models of hardware you have. You should know at least what motherboard, central processing unit (CPU), monitor, and video card you have if you want to be able to find out anything of value. Identifying your CPU and monitor should be easy enough, but the motherboard and video card may require a bit more searching.

If you have no documentation that clearly states the make and model of these devices, you can find out most things you need to know from within Windows by going to the Windows Control Panel, double-clicking **System**, and then clicking the **Hardware** tab in that window. Once on the Hardware tab, click the **Device Manager** button and see what you can find out about your system components. Sometimes the information there is limited, so you might instead want to try a shareware application such as HWiNFO (*http://www.hwinfo.com/*) or Sandra (*http://www.sisoftware.net/*) to get more useful details, such as the specifications of your motherboard or the supported video modes for your current setup.

Both HWiNFO and Sandra should give you the information you need about your motherboard, but if they don't (or if you don't feel like bothering with them), you can always just open the case of your computer and look at your board. Note that I wouldn't recommend doing this if you have a laptop. Once inside, you needn't worry about damaging anything because you don't need to touch anything—so don't. You may need a flashlight to find it, but the model name and number should be stamped on there somewhere, either in the middle of the board or around the edges. Mine, for example, says quite clearly in the middle of the board "AOpen MX46-533V." You should be looking for similar information.

Once you have all your information, you can do a variety of things to check out your hardware's compatibility with Ubuntu. You can simply do a Yahoo! or Google search by entering your motherboard's make and model plus the word *Linux*. This works for other hardware devices too.

You can also post a question at the Ubuntu User Forums (at *http://www.ubuntuforums.org/*) or one of the other various Linux forums or mailing lists on the Web. Chapter 21 might provide you with additional sources of information, and Appendix D lists still other sources. When posting a forum question, just write that you are a newbie and want to know whether anyone has had any experience using Ubuntu with the board (or other hardware) in question. You will probably get quite a few responses. Linux users are usually rather evangelical in terms of trying to draw in new Penguinistas.

Hardware Requirements

All worries about compatibility aside, you will need to meet some minimum hardware requirements:

- Any computer with a 1 GHz or higher i386-based processor or an Intel or AMD 64-bit processor

- About 5 gigabytes (GB) of hard disk space, though having at least 10GB would be a bit more comfy

- Sufficient memory (RAM)

NOTE   *The CD that comes with this book is designed to work on machines with i386-based processors (basically, all the Pentium chips, including Celeron, Xeon, and the new Core Duo, as well as processors from AMD). Though this CD will install Ubuntu on a computer with an AMD or Intel 64-bit processor, it will run in 32-bit mode only. To make full use of your 64-bit processor, you need to download the 64-bit version of Ubuntu. Additional information is provided in Appendix B.*

As for random access memory (RAM), the official specs tell you that you need a minimum of 512MB to run Ubuntu. Although you can no doubt get by with this, you'd get by much better with more. My basic rule of thumb, no matter what OS I am dealing with, is that you need the recommended (not the minimum) memory plus at least 256MB, preferably 512MB. Regardless of what the official specs say, put in more. You won't regret it.

Saying "The more memory you have, the better," may sound a bit simple, perhaps even cavalier, but trust me on this one. When you have too little memory, no matter what system you are running, weird things happen: Applications seem to take years to open or don't open at all, menus take forever to render their little icons, and freezes and general system meltdowns just happen much more often. In other words, running your machine on too little RAM is sort of like trying to do jumping jacks in a broom closet. Sure, you could do it, but you would be all contorted, and you'd be smashing your hands into the walls every 1.4 seconds.

Fortunately, it is pretty hard to find a machine with less than 512MB or less of RAM these days, but if you do happen to have such a machine, you can take solace in the fact that memory is relatively cheap, so go for it.

Good News for 64-Bit Machine Users

It is again important to mention that the CD that comes with this book is designed to work on machines with i386-based processors, which pretty much covers the vast majority of PCs out there. If your machine is 64-bit compatible, you will be glad to know that it will also work, albeit not in 64-bit mode. Sorry, but no go.

Fortunately, there is good news for those of you who were a bit disappointed by the content of that previous paragraph. Ubuntu is available in a native 64-bit version. Check Appendix B for information on how to get it. The information provided there will also be of use to i386 users who happen to lose or damage the disc that comes with this book.

Mixed News for Mac Users

Those of you with pre–Intel era PowerPC Macs (such as those with G3, G4, and G5 processors) may be aware that previous Ubuntu releases have been available in PowerPC versions. Unfortunately, as of the Ubuntu 7.04 Feisty Fawn release, this is no longer the case. This means that if you are a PowerPC Mac user, you will have to use an unofficial community release of Ubuntu for PowerPCs (*https://wiki.ubuntu.com/PowerPCDownloads/*). For more information, check out the FAQ at *https://wiki.ubuntu.com/PowerPCFAQ/*.

Of course, if you are using an Intel-based Mac, you're in luck: The disc that comes with this book will work on your Mac. After all, the *i* in *i386* stands for *Intel*.

Speaking Ubuntu

It's worth noting that you are bound to come across a lot of weird phrases when dealing with Ubuntu, especially when searching for information on the Internet. In particular, I'm referring to seemingly incongruous phrases, such as *Warty Warthog, Hoary Hedgehog, Breezy Badger, Dapper Drake, Edgy Eft, Feisty Fawn, Gutsy Gibbon, Hardy Heron, Intrepid Ibex, Jaunty Jackalope, Karmic Koala, Lucid Lynx, Maverick Meerkat, Natty Narwhal,* and *Oneiric Ocelot.* These are the unlikely code names of each of the releases of Ubuntu since its first appearance in 2004. The important one for you to remember is that of the current release, which is the one on the book's disc: version 12.04, known as *Precise Pangolin.*

You are also likely to come across a few other variations of the Ubuntu theme. These are Kubuntu, a KDE-based version of Ubuntu; Edubuntu, a special version of Ubuntu designed for use in the classroom; Xubuntu, a lightweight version of Ubuntu based on the XFCE desktop; Lubuntu, another lightweight version of Ubuntu based on the LXDE desktop environment; and Ubuntu Studio, a new flavor of Ubuntu, aimed at "creative people," which contains a strong suite of graphics, video, and music applications. There are also two other specialized versions: Mythbuntu, specifically designed for creating a home theater PC with MythTV, and UbuntuTV, designed to create a TV-based online streaming and viewing environment.

Where Do I Go from Here?

Now that you know more about the world of Linux and Ubuntu and you have your disc in hand, it's time to get down to it. If you have already installed Ubuntu on your machine, just flip ahead to Chapter 3. If your machine is still Linuxless, though, it's time to take it out for a spin and see how you like it. So for now, saddle up, clip on your spurs, and go straight to the next chapter. It's time to become a Penguinista!

2

WADING AND DIVING

Running and (If You Like) Installing Ubuntu

As I have already mentioned, one of the great things about Ubuntu is that it comes on a live CD, which means that you can try it before you install it . . . or never install it at all, if that's what you prefer. Better yet is the fact that, unlike earlier editions of Ubuntu, you don't need an additional installation CD if you do choose to install it—the Ubuntu CD functions as both a live CD and an installation disc. And in the good-better-best swing of things, the best point of all is that installation from the live CD is actually much, much easier than any other installation process you've ever dealt with, and it even gives you more than one way to go about it.

In this chapter, I will cover the basics of starting up and running Ubuntu from the live CD and then, assuming you've caught the Linux bug, the painless steps of installing Ubuntu on your hard disk as your operating system, either in its own partition on your hard disk in a traditional dual-boot setup (with Windows in its own partition) or, for the slightly less adventurous, from within your Windows system.

If your computer doesn't have a CD drive, don't worry, you can still join in. Take a look at Appendix A to see how you can run or install Ubuntu from a USB flash drive instead. Whatever way you end up going about things, let's put this book to use and get Ubuntu up and running.

Going for a Dip

To get a taste of what Ubuntu is all about (and to check out your hardware to see whether it's all comfy-cozy with Ubuntu), there is probably no better way than to run Ubuntu directly from the live CD. To do this, just place the Ubuntu CD in your disc drive and restart your machine. When the machine starts up, it should boot up from the CD, and after a second or two, you should see a purple Ubuntu startup screen with a couple of icons at the bottom of it. If the screen does not appear and your machine instead boots up into your usual operating system, then very likely your machine's BIOS settings need to be changed to allow you to boot from a CD. Worry not: Although the procedure might sound rather technical, altering the BIOS settings isn't much of a hassle.

You can access your machine's BIOS by restarting and then pressing whatever key the onscreen startup instructions assign to accessing the BIOS setup. This is usually DELETE or F1, but F2, F10, F12, and ESC are also common—not all machines are the same. If the onscreen information passes by so fast that you miss it, you can check your user's manual to see what the correct key is.

Once you get into the BIOS setup, change the boot sequence so that your CD drive is first. To do this, you'll probably have to use the arrow keys on your keyboard to navigate between different options and the ENTER key to select them. Basic instructions on how to do this are normally displayed onscreen. When you're finished, make sure you save your changes and then restart the computer.

Once your machine boots from the live CD and you see the purple Ubuntu startup screen, either you can wait for a few seconds for Ubuntu to start booting into the live CD proper, or you can press a key (any key) to display a menu where you can choose your language and other settings. The default settings should suffice for our purposes, so leave the keyboard untouched for a few seconds, and the purple screen will give way to a loading screen (also purple).

NOTE *If you decide to explore this menu, you'll find that you have to make a choice as to how you proceed once you've chosen a language and so forth. Select* Try without installing *to get back on the right track.*

After a couple of minutes or so, the loading screen will disappear, and in its place will come an Install window with a swooshy purple desktop background behind it (Figure 2-1). Click Try Ubuntu, and the Install window will give way to a pristine Ubuntu desktop with a row of colorful icons down the left side and the same purple background. You should now be able to use your mouse as well as the keyboard, so feel free to explore. And remember, your hard disk will go untouched, so rest easy—you're not going to change, let alone hurt, anything. When you get to this point, you're ready to take Ubuntu for a spin—but I'll hold off on talking about that until Chapter 3.

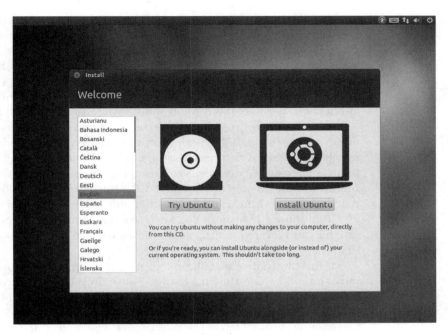

Figure 2-1: The Ubuntu live CD's Install window

NOTE   *Special input mechanisms that are required for typing certain languages (that is, Chinese, Japanese, and Korean) are not supported in live CD sessions.*

If you'd like to get out of the CD and return your computer to normal, click the power button at the very top right of the screen (it looks like a cross between a regular power icon and a gear), choose **Shut Down**, and then choose **Restart** again from the window that appears. After a little while, you'll be asked to remove the CD from the drive and press ENTER. The computer will restart and return you to your normal Windows desktop soon after. If you have no luck with the Restart button for some reason, it should be safe to turn your computer off and then on again just by using the power button on the front of the machine.

Choices, Choices, Choices—Installation Options

If you have already installed Ubuntu on your machine, are satisfied running it from the live CD, or still haven't made up your mind what to do, you can skip the rest of this chapter and continue to the next one to start working with the Ubuntu desktop. If, however, you haven't installed Ubuntu yet and are ready and rarin' to do so, then keep reading.

Going for a Swim—Installing Ubuntu Inside Windows (the Wubi Installer)

It used to be that if you enjoyed Ubuntu enough to want to run it off your hard disk but were afraid to do it for fear of damaging the delicate state of your Windows setup, you were . . . well, out of luck. Things have changed, however, because there is now an installation option called Wubi that lets you install Ubuntu directly on your Windows C: drive as if it were any other Windows program. Once it's installed, every time you start up your machine, you'll be able to choose between starting up into Windows or into Ubuntu from the Windows bootloader screen. Your Windows system stays as it is; you don't have to partition your hard disk, and if you want to get rid of Ubuntu later for whatever reason, you can do so as you would any other Windows application. It's a great way to go about things for the faint of heart.

Admittedly, this approach could be described as a half measure, in that it doesn't give you the full experience you would get from a dedicated Ubuntu installation. It's not as robust as a full Ubuntu installation, and it takes longer to install because Wubi needs to download the installation files from the Internet (the right ones aren't on the CD). But it is a pretty good compromise—it definitely runs quicker and is much, much more usable and enjoyable than an Ubuntu live CD session. You also have the added benefit of being able to save files and settings to disk, which means you can follow along with anything described in this book. Pretty cool.

If this alternative installation approach doesn't seem appealing to you, move on to "Taking the Full Plunge—Installing Ubuntu Outside of Windows" on page 17. If you haven't made up your mind yet and would like to know a bit more about this Wubi installer, point your browser to *http://wubi.sourceforge.net/*. If, on the other hand, you've decided that the Wubi installer is the answer to your prayers, here's what you need to do:

1. Insert the Ubuntu live CD that comes with this book into your computer's disc drive while Windows is up and running. A window like the one in Figure 2-2 will automatically appear.

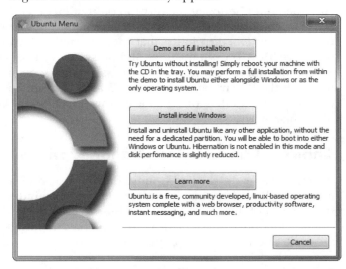

Figure 2-2: An Ubuntu live CD automatically launched in Windows

2. In that window, click the **Install inside Windows** button. The Ubuntu Installer window will appear (Figure 2-3).

Figure 2-3: Choosing to install Ubuntu inside Windows

3. Use the **Installation drive** option to specify where you want the Ubuntu files to be put. Make sure you have enough space on that drive!

4. Windows and Linux can't share the same disk space, so you need to set some aside for use by Ubuntu only (you can easily reclaim the space by uninstalling Ubuntu, discussed in a moment). Choose how much disk space you'd like to have available in Ubuntu by selecting a size from the Installation size drop-down list. Anything less than 10GB will probably be rather restrictive.

5. Leave the Desktop environment set to its default value (Ubuntu) and then choose a username and a password. Click the **Install** button once you're happy with your choices.

6. If your machine is not already connected to the Internet at this point, you will be told to get it connected. Do so if you need to and click the **Retry** button if the warning window appears.

    At this point, Wubi will begin downloading the files it needs in order to create a bootable Ubuntu installation within your Windows environment. Depending on your connection speed, this could take quite some time; about 1GB (around 1000MB) of data will need to be downloaded.

    After all is done, you will see a window like the one in Figure 2-4 asking you to reboot.

7. Select **Reboot now** and click the **Finish** button in that window, after which your machine will reboot. Don't forget to remove the Ubuntu disc from the CD drive before it restarts; otherwise, the computer will try to boot from that instead.

8. When the machine restarts, you will see the Windows bootloader, a black screen with white text, which allows you to decide whether to boot up in Windows or in Ubuntu. Use your down arrow key to select **Ubuntu**, and then press ENTER.

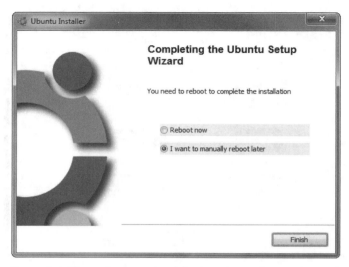

Figure 2-4: Ubuntu has completed the first phase of its inside-Windows installation.

Your machine will then begin the Ubuntu startup process, which should be new territory for you. Once the Ubuntu desktop appears, Ubuntu will get to work setting things up for you; this might take a bit of time, depending on the speed of your machine. When it's done, you will be delivered to the login screen (Figure 2-5); you can now flip to Chapter 3, because you are done here.

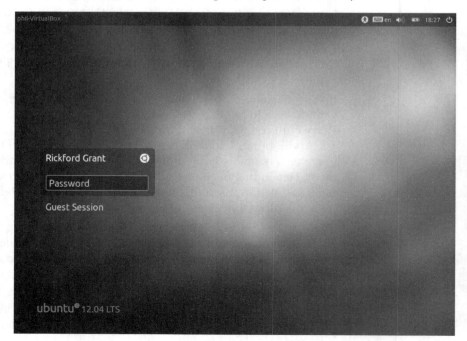

Figure 2-5: The Ubuntu login screen

If you decide that you do not want to keep Ubuntu on your machine, you can remove it from within Windows by going to the Windows Control Panel, selecting **Add or Remove Programs**, and then choosing removal.

Taking the Full Plunge—Installing Ubuntu Outside of Windows

If you don't already have Windows installed on your machine, you can skip this section. If you do, then you're going to have to decide whether you want to keep it.

It is possible to have both Windows and Linux installed on the same machine and for them to happily coexist. This is known as a *dual-boot* setup. It has become incredibly easy to set up such a system. I started out with a dual-boot setup, though I eventually found that I used the Linux side of things exclusively. Having so much disk space being taken up by a Windows system I didn't use seemed a waste of prime real estate, so eventually I just dumped the whole thing and went for a straight Linux-only setup.

My feeling is that you should try the Wubi route of installing Ubuntu inside Windows first and then, when you're ready, go for a Linux-only setup and ditch Windows completely. Most people find that Ubuntu can do everything they need, so there's no need to dual-boot unless you require some specific application that has no equivalent on Linux.

If you do opt for a dual-boot setup, starting up in either system is easy. When you start up your machine, you will be greeted by the GRand Unified Bootloader (better known as GRUB) screen, from which you can choose to continue booting up Linux or to boot up in Windows instead. After that, bootup proceeds as normal for the system you selected.

So whichever way you decide to go, you really can't go wrong. Just be sure to back up your important files before starting the installation. Proceed with common sense, patience, and a positive attitude, and you'll be fine. In short, don't worry.

Getting Ready for Action

You need to do less to prepare for an Ubuntu installation than for many other Linux distributions. Once you've decided whether you want to go the dual-boot route, all you really need to have on hand is your single Ubuntu CD and, for guidance and security, this book. The only mental energy you'll probably expend is in coming up with a username and user password, just as you do for most other operating systems.

Usernames and User Passwords

Your username is something that you will be seeing quite a bit. It will be on permanent display in the top right-hand corner of the screen, among other things, so be sure it is something you can live with. It can be just your first name or your initials or whatever you want it to be. It must, however, begin with a lowercase letter, followed by numbers and/or other lowercase letters. Mine, for example, is simply *rg*, but you could use something like *hope4u2pal*, though that would get rather tiring to look at. You also need to come up with a user password, which you will need to type every time you log in. You will need to use it when you install new software or change certain system settings, as well. It should be a minimum of eight characters in length and consist of numbers, letters (upper- and lowercase), and symbols for improved security. The harder it is for someone to guess, the better. You can, of course, get by with fewer characters and only letters if you prefer. The installer will advise you if the password you enter is unacceptable, so don't worry about this. Be sure to write it down and keep the paper you've written it on in a safe place, at least for a little while, so you don't accidentally lock yourself out of your system.

NOTE   *If you have experience working with other Linux distributions, you may be surprised to learn that the root account is disabled by default in Ubuntu. There is, therefore, no installation step for inputting a root password. You can check the forums (http://www.ubuntuforums.org/) to learn ways of getting around this setup. You can also set up a root password at any time after the system is installed, so if having a root account is important to you, don't worry.*

Doing the Deed

Well, now that I've covered all that preliminary stuff, let's get down to the actual Linux installation. Set this book on your lap so you can follow along, and then get ready for action. It's time to do the deed!

Fortunately for you, the installation process is extremely easy, because there are very few steps in which you actually have to do anything. Most of what you will be doing is clicking buttons on your screen. Nothing hard about that, eh?

Of course, when you look at the directions and descriptions listed here, the process may look like a long and cumbersome one. It's not. It will be over more quickly than you can imagine. As a beginner frequently referring to this text, you might take a bit longer, of course, but all in all the process is faster and easier than that for Windows or Mac OS X. And keep in mind that with Windows and OS X, you are installing the operating system with just a few bundled applications. In an Ubuntu installation, on the other hand, you are installing not only the operating system itself but also most of the applications you will ever want or need to use. You will thus be getting a lot done in one fell swoop.

One more thing before we start. Some people approach installing a system with a good deal of trepidation. The process makes them nervous, as if the house is going to go up in smoke if they click the wrong thing. Needless to say, there is no need for such concern. As long as you have backed up your data, ideally to an external hard disk or similar, you will be okay. If you screw up the installation the first time out, so what? Just start over. No harm done, because you have nothing to harm—all your files are safe and secure in your backup copy. Just make sure that you give yourself more time than you need for the process. Don't start installing an hour before you have to be at work or before you have to meet your friend downtown. Rushing makes people do weird things. Make things easy on yourself by giving yourself plenty of time and, as I mentioned before, by backing up any data you would mourn the loss of.

If you're ready—and why wouldn't you be?—here are the steps:

1. **Start 'er up.** If you haven't already done so, boot up your machine from the Ubuntu CD.

2. **Start the installation.** Once the live CD has loaded, you should be looking at the Install window. This is the first page of the installation wizard, Welcome (see Figure 2-1).

3. **Choose your language.** Select your language from the list to the left of the window and click **Install Ubuntu**.

4. **Prepare for installation.** The installer will now perform a few checks to make sure that everything is hunky-dory. The results of its checks will be shown at the top of the Preparing to install Ubuntu page of the wizard (shown in Figure 2-6). A green checkmark means that everything is okay, and a gray cross means that something was found wanting. The main thing is to make sure the installer has found enough drive space to make it happy; if not, the installation can't proceed. Other checks, like whether you are connected to the Internet or not, aren't necessary for installation, so it's generally safe to ignore them.

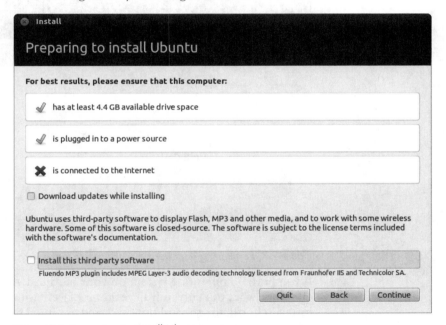

Figure 2-6: Preparing to install Ubuntu

5. If you are connected to the Internet (a topic that we'll cover in Chapter 4), you might like to check Download updates while installing. This will fetch any system updates that are available while the installation proceeds, saving you a bit of time later on (you'll learn about system updates in Chapter 6).

6. The final checkbox on the Preparing to install Ubuntu page asks if you'd like to install some software. This refers to a plug-in for playing MP3 audio files, which, unfortunately, has some license terms that mean Ubuntu can't just install it without asking you. Check the box and click **Continue**; we'll return to the topic of MP3 support in Chapter 14.

7. **Choose the installation type.** The Installation type page will now be shown. What you do at this point depends on what you have on your machine. Assuming you have an operating system on the disk already, such as Windows, accept the uppermost option (Install Ubuntu alongside Windows) and click **Continue**. When the installation starts, this option will reduce the size of your Windows (or other OS) installation to allow for installation of Ubuntu in a new partition. By default, the partitioner will use the minimum amount of space necessary to install Ubuntu, but you will no doubt want a bit more so as to give yourself room to grow and store files. To create a bigger partition for Ubuntu, drag the divider between the two partitions on the white and gray bar in the center of the window until you come up with a combination that you think will work for you (see Figure 2-7).

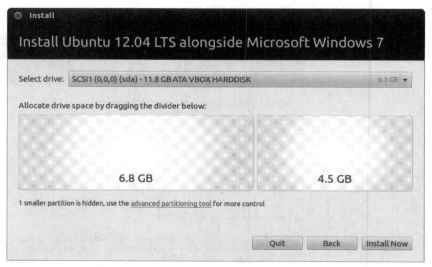

Figure 2-7: Partitioning your hard disk (or not) to make way for Ubuntu

8. If you have no operating system on your hard disk or if you intend to eliminate what you currently have and replace it with Ubuntu, you should instead choose the second option, listed as either *Replace Windows with Ubuntu*, or *Erase disk and install Ubuntu*. Click **Continue** and, if given a choice, select the main drive onto which you want to install the system.

   If you'd like to do something more elaborate with your disk space, such as having separate partitions for your data and system files (convenient if you ever need to reinstall or want to easily share files between Windows and Ubuntu), you'll need to specify the partitions manually using the last option, the whimsically named *Something else*. (This is more advanced—check out Appendix C for some guidance.) Once you're happy with your choices, get ready: The next step will start the installation.

WHAT IS A HARD DRIVE PARTITION?

I've mentioned *partitions* several times so far, but I haven't explained what they are. A partition is an area of your hard disk that is "cordoned off" from other areas of the disk. It's a useful way of keeping things such as operating systems separate. Because they are isolated from each other, different partitions are treated as if they are different hard disks attached to your computer, even though they're actually on the same physical hard disk.

Most computers have just one partition that fills up the entire hard disk. This is like having a house with a completely open floor plan—the whole house is just one big room. If you want to completely remove Windows and install Ubuntu instead, Ubuntu can happily take over the entire partition (and thus the entire disk) and kick out the former resident, Windows.

If you want to install two operating systems on the same computer, you have to give each one its own partition (after all, they need their privacy). Back with the house analogy, it's like erecting a partition wall to carve up the house into two rooms. If you choose to dual-boot Windows and Ubuntu, the installer will automatically do this partitioning for you. Of course, you can choose how big each partition is: The bigger you make the Ubuntu partition, the more disk space will be available to you in Ubuntu (and the less in Windows). After all, the house is the same size; it's just the position of the dividing wall that you're changing.

You can find some information on manually partitioning your hard disk in Appendix C, if you fancy taking control of the process yourself. There should be no need to, however, since the Ubuntu installer will be happy to handle the task for you.

9. Keeping in mind that this is the point of no return, click the **Install Now** button. A progress bar will appear at the bottom of the window, and the installation process will begin.

10. **Specify your location and keyboard type.** It will take a while to install everything, so in the meantime, the installer will ask a few questions that it will use to set up your user account. The first question asks you to specify your location; do this by clicking on the world map to select a nearby city.

11. Click **Continue** and choose your keyboard layout from the list. The installer should automatically select the right one, or you can try clicking **Detect Keyboard Layout**. You can test that it works as expected by typing into the box provided; pay special attention to quotation marks, the pound and @ symbols, and similar keys, since these are the ones you're most likely to have trouble with. When you're happy, click **Continue** again.

12. **Enter user account details.** The Who are you? screen will appear (shown in Figure 2-8). This is probably the most fun one—you get to choose the name of your computer, your username, and a password. Enter your name first, at the top. The installer will make suggestions for some of the other fields, but you don't have to take them. For the computer name, choose something short and simple with no spaces. Ditto for the username—as I mentioned in "Usernames and User Passwords" on page 17, it'll be a constant presence on your computer screen, so best not to choose anything

that might eventually become irritating. As I also mentioned above, you should choose a secure password containing a mixture of letters, numbers, and symbols.

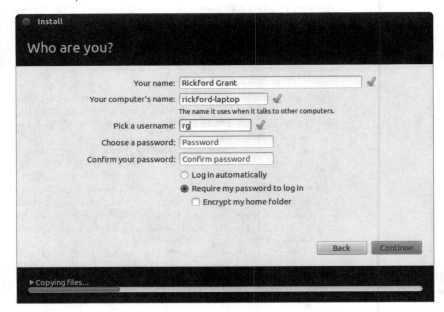

Figure 2-8: Providing your username, password, and computer name in the installation wizard screen

13. It's best to select **Require my password to log in** from the options at the bottom of the screen. Although this will necessarily increase the time between switching on the computer and the Ubuntu desktop's appearance, putting a password entry box in the way makes it much more difficult for anyone to gain access to your computer and all of the precious (and potentially confidential) files stored on it.

When you're done, click **Continue** to move on to the next step.

NOTE *The security-conscious among you might consider selecting the **Encrypt my home folder** option. This will scramble the contents of your Home folder (where all your documents are stored) so that no one can see any of the files in it without your password. It won't affect how you access your files, however, as they are descrambled for you when you log in. This is nice to have if you work with confidential information, since the data will be pretty safe even if your computer is stolen.*

14. **Migrate documents and settings.** If your machine already has another operating system on it and you are setting up a dual-boot system, the installer will scan your hard disk to try to find certain settings, folders, and documents that it can automatically transfer to your new Ubuntu system environment. This step shouldn't really matter, because you (hopefully!) made backup copies of all your important documents and settings before you started the installation. Still, it's more convenient than copying every-

thing from that backup onto your new Ubuntu system manually after the installation has finished. If a migration window appears, just check the boxes next to the items you want to transfer and then click **Continue**.

15. **Wait for installation to finish.** Now, with all of your details having been entered, the installer will continue to do its thing. Sit back and watch the Ubuntu slideshow. The progress of the installation will be indicated in the progress bar below it so that you don't have to fret (and so you'll know how much more time you have left to veg out in front of the TV).

16. **The installation is complete.** You'll be notified of this fact in a new window. You will be given the option of either continuing to use the live CD or restarting the machine and running Ubuntu directly from your hard disk. Well, you didn't go through all of this just to keep using the live CD, so let's go for the second option by clicking the **Restart Now** button, removing the live CD from your drive when it's automatically ejected, and pressing ENTER when prompted to do so. Your machine will then restart.

After that . . . well, that's basically it. You now have Ubuntu installed on your machine. Congratulations!

How Can I Get Back into Windows?

If you installed your system in a dual-boot configuration, with Ubuntu alongside Windows, you should see a new boot menu appear when the computer starts up. After 10 seconds, Ubuntu will boot up automatically, but you can just hit ENTER to speed up the process.

If you want to start Windows instead, use your keyboard's arrow keys to select the **Windows** option in the boot menu and then hit ENTER. Windows should start as normal. Take a look at Chapter 19 if you want to make Windows the default or change the boot time delay.

Oh No, My Computer Won't Boot!

If the installation process fails, you may not be able to boot your computer. Thankfully this is very rare—but if it happens to you, don't panic! There's plenty you can do to get up and running again, so flip your way to Chapter 22 for some troubleshooting advice.

3

A NEW PLACE TO CALL HOME

Getting to Know the Desktop

So here we are at the gateway of your new world. You've got Ubuntu installed, it is up and running, and you are ready and rarin' to go. If you are running Ubuntu from your hard disk, the first thing you may see, depending on how you set things up, is the login screen that will appear each and every time you boot up (Figure 3-1). If so, type in your password and press ENTER, and you'll be face to face with the Ubuntu desktop. If you set up your system during installation to bypass the login phase, or if you are still running Ubuntu from the live disc, you're already there. Either way, let's get down to getting to know your new home.

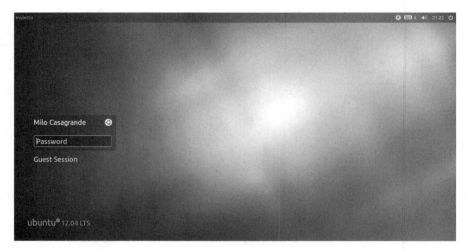

Figure 3-1: The Ubuntu login screen

Welcome to the Desktop

As you can see at first glance, the Ubuntu desktop (Figure 3-2) is a pretty familiar looking place. In fact, it looks a lot like what you might be used to in Windows, Mac OS, or even another Linux distribution. Look a bit closer, however, and you start to notice that things are not quite the same. There is no task bar or Start button at the bottom of the screen, there are no desktop icons, there seems to be only one menu in the top panel, and there is something that looks like the Mac OS X Dock on the left side of the screen. Yup, things are a bit different.

Figure 3-2: The Unity desktop in Ubuntu

Welcome to the Unity desktop environment, which Ubuntu has been using since its 11.04 release. Unity is designed to be usable on any number of devices, not just on PCs, meaning that someday you could conceivably be using the exact same operating system on your PC, your phone, your tablet computer, and who knows what else. Although Unity is a bit different from what you might be used to in terms of operation, it isn't completely alien, and working in Unity quickly becomes second nature. To get you started, I'll try to familiarize you with the elements of the desktop and how they all work.

Parts of the Unity Desktop Environment

Ubuntu's Unity desktop has three readily observable parts: the top panel, the desktop itself, and, on the left side of the screen, the Launcher. I'll discuss each of these parts, starting with the top panel, which is very useful.

The Panel

At the top of the screen is the panel (Figure 3-3), which looks a lot like the Mac OS menu bar at first glance. And like the Mac OS menu bar, the panel contains the *global menu*, which displays the menus for the currently focused application (unlike in Windows or other Linux distributions, where the menus are connected to the application window itself). To show the global menu, hover your mouse over the top left portion of the panel, and the menu will appear to the right of the window title (Figure 3-4). If you don't have any windows open, the Desktop menu will appear here instead.

NOTE   *Not every application works with Unity's global menu. The menus in LibreOffice, for example, will display within their own windows.*

Figure 3-3: The top panel in Unity

> **Ubuntu**   File   Edit   View   Go   Help

Figure 3-4: The top panel does double-duty as the menu bar for the system itself and most applications

Also similar to the Mac OS menu bar is the cluster of icons at the right side of the panel. Some of these are indicators, while others are menus that, like applets, allow you to perform certain functions. Here is what the stock set does (from left to right):

Messaging   Lets you know when you receive email or chat messages and allows you to easily send email messages and check your address book. It also lets you check and send messages to social networking sites such as Facebook, Twitter, and Flickr via an application called Empathy (which you'll learn more about in Chapter 5).

Network   Lets you see your network status and configure your network devices. When used with a wireless network connection, this icon indicates the wireless signal's strength and allows you to switch between wireless networks easily.

Audio   Lets you adjust the volume of your system and control music playback (Figure 3-5) via Ubuntu's bundled music player, Rhythmbox (which you will learn about in Chapter 14).

Clock   Shows date and/or time.

User   Shows the name of the current user and allows you to switch user accounts.

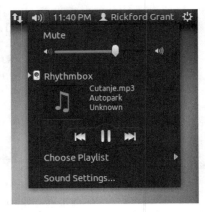

Figure 3-5: The top panel Audio menu allows you to control music playback through Rhythmbox.

System   Allows you to lock your screen, log out, shut down, or restart. It also provides access to a number of system settings.

Other indicators, such as the battery indicator or Bluetooth manager, will appear depending on your hardware configuration or system status. Certain applications, such as the sticky-note system Tomboy, may also place indicators or applets here.

To wrap up our discussion of the top panel, it is worth noting one rather unusual characteristic: When you maximize a window, by either clicking the maximize button or double-clicking its title bar, the top panel becomes both the menu bar and the title bar of that window, as you can see in Figure 3-6. (The *title bar* is the bar that runs across the top of a window, where the title of the window and its controls are located.) This shouldn't be a problem, of course, but it is something to bear in mind so you don't panic when you can't find the top of your window under the top panel. It's not under the panel—it *is* the panel! Fortunately this seemingly mysterious metamorphosis is easily altered. To get your window back to its earlier, normal size, just double-click the top panel or click the maximize button again on the left end of the panel.

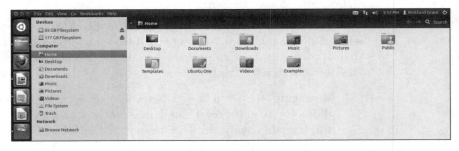

Figure 3-6: The top panel becomes the menu and title bar of a maximized window.

The Desktop

The biggest part of the Unity desktop environment is the desktop itself. This is completely empty out of the box, so to speak, and it is not as thoroughly utilized as it is in Windows and Mac OS systems or even in other Linux desktop environments. This is not to say that you can't use the desktop in some of the ways you might be familiar with, but as is, there are basically just two things you can put there as is: documents and folders. To create a folder on the desktop, just right-click anywhere on the desktop and then select **Create New Folder**. You can then drag, or copy and paste, anything you want to that folder. Of course, if you want to drag your documents or folders to the desktop, you can do that too.

The Launcher

The most unfamiliar part of the Unity desktop environment will likely be the Launcher. The *Launcher*, as I mentioned earlier, is that strip of icons that appears on the left side of the desktop. In some ways the Launcher functions very much like the Mac OS Dock. Out of the box, it comes with *Launcher icons* for some of the most commonly used applications, folders, and utilities. Also, just as in the Mac Dock, when you run any other application, a Launcher icon for that application also appears.

Working with the Launcher

Now that you're familiar with the parts of the Unity desktop environment, it is time to look at them in more detail. Since the Launcher is such a conspicuous (and important!) part of the desktop, I'll start there. By default, the Launcher contains a smattering of icons, which are essentially shortcut buttons that help you get to the most important tools and applications in your system. Starting from the top, here's what you'll find:

> **The Dash**   Probably the most important part of your system, the Dash is the place from where you more or less do it all: finding and running documents, applications, and other files on your system.
>
> **Home folder**   Here's where all your files are stored and drives and devices shown.
>
> **Firefox**   This is the default web browser in Ubuntu.
>
> **LibreOffice Writer**   This is Ubuntu's bundled word processor.
>
> **LibreOffice Calc**   And this is the spreadsheet application that comes with Ubuntu.
>
> **LibreOffice Impress**   Here you find Ubuntu's PowerPoint alternative.
>
> **Ubuntu Software Center**   All the applications and other support files available for Ubuntu are accessed here.

Ubuntu One   This helps you to install, set up, and connect to Ubuntu's Ubuntu One service, which provides you with your own "personal cloud." From here you can share files among your various devices.

System Settings   Opens the System Settings window, which is an access point to commonly used system settings such as keyboards, monitors, sound, network, and more.

Workplace Switcher   Reveals and allows you to switch among the various usually unseen portions of your desktop workspace. This is discussed in greater detail in "Workspace Switcher—Virtual Desktops" on page 37.

Trash   I believe no introduction is necessary. It is just what it looks like.

Using the Launcher is pretty intuitive. To run an application or open a file or folder, just click its icon. If you right-click any icon in the Launcher, a menu will appear with choices that vary by the item and whether or not it is already running or open. At the very least, you will be given the choice to lock the icon to the Launcher or to unlock it from the Launcher. The only exceptions to the lock/unlock option are the Dash, Trash, and System Switcher. Those stay where they are, like it or not. For many other Launcher icons, there are other options, as you can see in Figure 3-7, which shows those for LibreOffice Writer.

Figure 3-7: Right-clicking Launcher icons reveals available submenu options.

As I just mentioned, you can easily lock additional icons to the Launcher or remove those you don't really need or want to be there. To add an icon, run the app you want to add, right-click its icon in the Launcher, and select **Lock to Launcher**. To remove a Launcher icon, just right-click it and select **Unlock from Launcher**. As for emptying the Trash, since it's in the neighborhood, let's talk about it: Just right-click the Trash icon and then select **Empty Trash**.

If you end up placing a lot of icons on the Launcher, or if you happen to have a lot of applications open at the same time, you will find that the icons at the bottom of the Launcher get scrunched, as in Figure 3-8. If you just move your mouse down to the bottom of the Launcher, however, the contents will start moving up, with each button unscrunching in turn. You can then click the Launcher icon you are looking for without any difficulty. Once you're done, the icons will return to their previous space-saving state.

Figure 3-8: The Launcher scrunches up your icons when things get too crowded.

The Dash

The uppermost icon in the Launcher is often called the Ubuntu button because it has the Ubuntu logo on it (Figure 3-9), though it's also called the Dash button because it opens—you guessed it—the Dash. The Dash helps you find applications and files on your computer, and it can even help you find things on the Internet.

Figure 3-9: The Ubuntu button, aka the Dash button

You may be thinking that the Dash sounds like Ubuntu's answer to the Windows Start button, and in some ways you would be right, though working with is it is pretty different and its abilities are greater.

Click the Dash button to get your first view of the Dash. You can also bring up the Dash by pressing the Windows key, also referred to as the *super* or *meta* key, on your keyboard. The first time out, the Dash will be, in all its nearly transparent glory, empty (Figure 3-10). After you've used your system a bit more, the Dash will show your most recently used applications and files when it opens, but for now the only things you will see are the search bar at the top and a series of white icons at the bottom. Clicking these icons takes you to the Dash's different lenses.

Figure 3-10: The Dash

Lenses

You can think of *lenses* (Figure 3-11) as a kind of navigation tool—a category label by which your system helps you to narrow down what you are looking for, not only on your computer but on the Inter-

Figure 3-11: Lenses in the Dash

net via the Ubuntu Software Center or from other sites as well. By default, there are five of these lenses in Ubuntu—*Dash Home, Applications, Files & Folders, Music,* and *Videos.*

If you click one of these lenses, the Dash will fill with the first five items you currently have installed on your computer in that general category. If you have more items in that category installed, you can see them by clicking the **See *x* more results** link that appears next to each section heading. In the case of applications, it will also suggest other applications in that category that you might like to download from the Ubuntu Software Center, as you can see in Figure 3-12. (Check out Chapter 7 to see what to expect for some of the other lenses.)

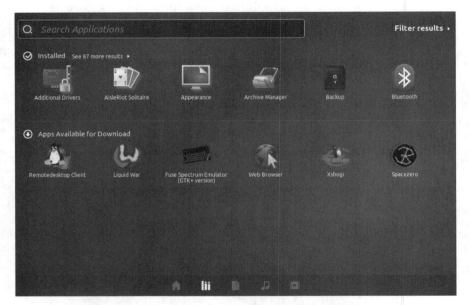

Figure 3-12: Results of clicking the Applications lens in the Dash for the first time

If you know which lens you want to go to before you click the Dash button, it's worth knowing that you can open the Dash directly to the lens of your choice by right-clicking the Dash button and selecting the lens you wish to use in the pop-up menu (Figure 3-13).

One of the most interesting things about lenses is the fact that developers are creating more of them. You can download and install these new lenses, and they will provide you with a quick way to search for more specialized results, particularly on the Web. If you're

Figure 3-13: Right-clicking the Dash button reveals a menu of the currently installed Dash lenses.

interested, in Chapter 18 you'll learn how to install a cooking lens that searches the Web for recipes. If you would like to find out what other kinds of lenses are available and how to install them, check out AskUbuntu (*http://askubuntu .com/questions/38772/what-lenses-for-unity-are-available/*) and OMG!Ubuntu! (*http://www.omgubuntu.co.uk/tag/lenses/*), both of which have a lot of information on the subject.

Filters

Working hand in hand with lenses are *filters*. You can think of filters as fine-tuning devices—a spoon to a lens's shovel, so to speak. When you click a lens, you will see the words *Filter results* at the top right corner of the Dash. If you click that, you will see a list of filters that can be applied to further narrow your search. For example, if you click the Applications lens and then click the Games filter, you will see just the games installed on your system and suggestions for games available from the Ubuntu Software Center (Figure 3-14).

Figure 3-14: Results of the Applications lens with the Games filter in the Dash

As you can begin to see, filters are not restricted to categories of applications but, depending on what the lens is, may select results by a number of other categories, such as Rating and Sources in the Applications lens. A look at the filters available for the Music lens reveals a number of different filter types (Figure 3-15), while those for the Videos lens consist entirely of online video sources.

Another interesting thing about filters is that you are not limited to using just one. You can select a number of different filters at the same time to narrow down your results even more.

Figure 3-15: Filter options for the Music lens

Finding and Running Apps with the Keyboard

Using lenses and filters is one way to find the apps that you want to run; however, if you know the name of the application you want to run, or even the name of a document you want to open, you can just start typing into the search box at the top of the Dash. As you type, results will start to appear. The more you type, the more the results will be narrowed down. If the app you want to run (or document you want to open) is the first in the list, you can simply press ENTER to open it. Otherwise, you can use your arrow keys to navigate to the target app and then press ENTER to open it.

Head-up Display

A feature similar to the Dash is Ubuntu's new Head-up Display (HUD). The idea of a head-up display is to allow users to do what they need to do without having to take their eyes away from their area of focus—allowing them to keep their eye on the ball, so to speak. To that end, the HUD allows you to do many normally mouse-driven tasks by keyboard. Whatever application is in focus—whether it be the desktop, the file manager, Firefox, or the Terminal—pressing the ALT key will bring up a command box for that application at the top left of the screen. (Figure 3-16 shows an example using Firefox.) In that box, you can tell the application what you want to do, where you want to go, or what you are looking for by typing commands or keywords and then pressing ENTER. Basically, if it can be done in the application's menus, it can also be done in the HUD.

Figure 3-16: Bookmarking a page in Firefox via the HUD

The HUD allows you to do all kinds of things you might not have imagined doing by keyboard. You can save a file, for example, by typing **save**, navigate from one folder to another in the file manager by typing the name of the folder you want to move to, or print a document by typing **print**. You can even play a song in Rhythmbox by typing the song's name. The more you play around with HUD and try to use it, the easier and thus more useful it will become.

The best thing is that you don't have to learn key combinations or know the exact command in order to get things done. Just type in a word, and the HUD will work with you, showing you all the options it can think of that relate to what you've just typed. Pretty handy, I must say.

Navigating a Sea of Open Windows

Once you get down to really using your system rather than just learning about it, there will likely be times when you have a few apps and a lot of windows open at the same time. When it's only a couple of windows you want to arrange more neatly, you can just drag one window to either side of the screen, and it will then automatically resize itself to fit into that area. You can do the same for the other window, making it easy to work with both items side by side.

However, when you're using several different applications and several different windows all at once, it can get confusing to figure out what's running or even where a certain window is, buried among what seems like a hundred others. In this case, the Launcher can come in handy—it's not only useful for starting up frequently used apps but also great for switching between applications or windows.

To help with this, the Launcher has a system of indicators that let you know what you've got open and running. When any Launcher item is running and its window is the one currently with *focus* (meaning it is the application window currently in active use), a small arrow will appear to the right of the Launcher icon for that item (as you see for the home launcher in Figure 3-17). When the window for an open or running Launcher item is not focused, an arrow will appear to the left of its Launcher icon (as you see for the LibreOffice Writer icon in Figure 3-17). If more than one application window is open, with focus or not, white dash marks will appear to the left of the shortcut button instead of an arrow—two marks if two windows are open and three if three or

more windows are open (also shown in Figure 3-17).
Of course, if a Launcher item is not running or
open, no marks will appear on either side of that
Launcher icon.

Switching between different running applications is easy enough to do by clicking the icons
for the application you want to switch to. You can
also do this from your keyboard by repeatedly
pressing ALT-TAB until you get to the application
you want to use.

Yet another way to switch applications (or start
an application that isn't currently running) is to
hold down the Windows key. After a second or
so, the icons on the Launcher will become num-
bered, as you can see in Figure 3-18. You can then
switch to the application you want by pressing the
number on your keyboard that corresponds to it. If
more than one window of that application is open,
the most recently used window will gain focus.

Figure 3-17: The Launcher shows you which apps are running and which have multiple windows open.

Even when you've gotten to the application
you want, you might still not be in the right place—
the window with focus may not be the one you
want to deal with at that moment. For example,
let's say you have six file manager windows open
and they're all piled on top of one another. The
one with focus is Documents, but you are looking
for the one with your photos of your trip to Cyprus
last summer. You could wade around with your
mouse, dragging windows out of the way until
you find the one you're looking for.

Figure 3-18: Switching between applications and windows on the Launcher by numbers

A slightly easier way of going about this is to click any one of the open
windows to give it focus, and then repeatedly press ALT and the key immediately above TAB (on most US keyboards, this is the key with the *accent grave*
and tilde symbols it) until you reach the window you want. Alternatively, you
can find the window in a more direct manner by clicking the Launcher icon
for your application (in this case the home button) once more, after which
all the open windows related to the application for that Launcher icon will
appear at once (Figure 3-19). You then just click the window you want to go to.

It is also possible to see all of the windows currently open, not just those
for a particular application, at the same time. To do this, press the Windows
and W keys. If you want to hide all of the windows so you can see the desktop
itself, press CTRL-ALT-D.

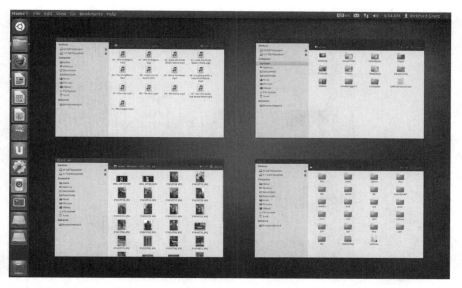

Figure 3-19: Seeing all the open windows for a single application via the Launcher

Workspace Switcher—Virtual Desktops

Figure 3-20: The Workplace Switcher button in the Launcher

Since we're on the topic of navigating through desktop space, this is a good time to discuss *virtual desktops*. Although the virtual desktop feature has only recently made its way into other operating systems, it has been a Linux feature for years (yes, it started here, folks). An easy way to think of virtual desktops is to think of your desktop as the top left quadrant of a four-times-bigger desktop. Most of the time you are using only that one piece of your total working space. But if you click the Workspace Switcher button on the Launcher (Figure 3-20), you can see the rest of your desktop kingdom.

Although you can see here what I mean about your desktop being four times bigger than it seems, you have to see it in action to get a good feel for it. If you click the Workspace Switcher button again, you will be back to your original, familiar piece of desktop. Now open a few windows. For example, click the buttons for the Home folder, LibreOffice Writer, LibreOffice Calc, and System Settings (or whatever apps you prefer). Once you have an open window for each of them, start by dragging the System Settings window toward the bottom of the desktop until you can only see about half of it. Drag the LibreOffice Calc window to the right of the screen until you see only half of it and then drag the LibreOffice Writer window to the bottom-right corner of the screen until you can see only about one-quarter of it. When you click the Desktop Switcher button this time, your screen should look something like Figure 3-21.

Figure 3-21: Viewing your virtual desktops

As you can see, your four virtual desktops look like one giant desktop, and you can move the windows to any quarter of that considerable area. Give it a try now. Drag those windows around until you have one window in each quarter of your desktop. Now, if you want to work with one of those windows, just double-click that portion of the screen. Your screen will now show only that portion of the desktop.

Want to go to another window in another portion of the desktop? Click the Workplace Switcher button and then double-click the quadrant where the window is located. It is all really easy once you get the hang of it. It's very handy too. You can separate your desktop into work areas, for example, with one part for writing a letter, another for all the budget items you are dealing with, and another for games when you need a little break.

Why Doesn't My Desktop Look Like That?

If your desktop doesn't look exactly like what you see in the screenshots in this chapter, it most likely means that Ubuntu automatically started you up in what is called *fallback mode*. Fallback mode is an environment that is simpler in appearance and less demanding of video hardware. It is also referred to as *2D mode*. In case you're wondering which mode you are in, the clearest give-away is the Dash button. If the Dash button is a dark charcoal-gray with a white Ubuntu logo, then you are in 2D fallback mode. If it is a pleasant plum color with a white logo, then you are in the standard 3D mode.

Ubuntu defaults to fallback mode when your hardware, particularly your video card, does not have what Ubuntu needs in order to run Unity, which is fairly demanding of graphics hardware. Possibly your card is too old or too new or just too underpowered, or the drivers your system needs to use the card to its full potential may not be installed. You can check if drivers are available for your machine by clicking the **System Settings** button in the Launcher. When the System Settings window appears, click **Additional Drivers**. The Additional Drivers window (Figure 3-22) will appear and let you know if there are any drivers available for you to install. If there are, then make any selection you are recommended to make and click **Activate**.

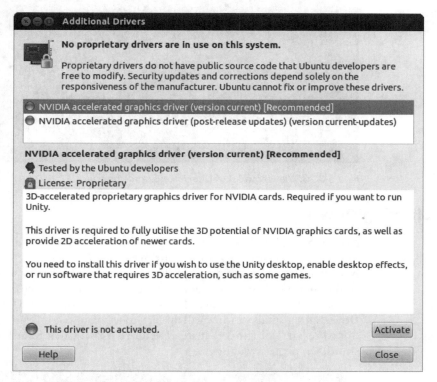

Figure 3-22: Installing video drivers

Keyboard Shortcuts

Throughout this chapter, and elsewhere in the book, I've given keyboard shortcuts for common system actions. Keyboard shortcuts are not unique to Ubuntu, but many will be different from those you know in your current operating system. Fortunately, it's easy to see a list of the Ubuntu keyboard shortcuts. Just press and hold down the Windows key. In addition to making numbers appear over the icons in the Launcher, this will show a chart that lists all of Unity's keyboard shortcuts (Figure 3-23). A very handy reference! You can even choose this as your default desktop wallpaper, if you want, but more on that in Chapter 9.

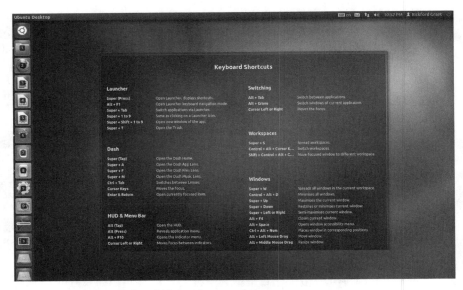

Figure 3-23: Viewing a list of Ubuntu keyboard shortcuts

Shutting Down

Now that you know your desktop environment so well, you may feel like calling it a day and shutting down your machine. To do so, just click the **Quit** button at the far-right corner of the top panel (it looks like a power button). In the menu that appears, there will be a number of choices in the lower half to choose from: Lock Screen, Log Out, Suspend, and Shut Down. Select **Shut Down**, and a small window will appear to ask you to confirm your decision or opt to restart (or cancel) instead (Figure 3-24). Click **Shut Down**, and the shutdown process will begin.

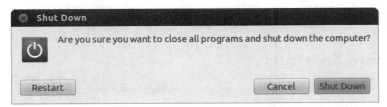

Figure 3-24: Shutting down or restarting Ubuntu

The actual shutdown will take a few seconds as the system closes its various services. When it is all done, the system should power down your computer as well, in which case you are done. On a few machines, however, the system might not be able power down the computer. You will know whether this is so in your case because all screen activity will come to an end. If you get to that point and nothing else happens for 15 seconds or so, then just power down the machine manually by pressing the power button. It is completely safe to do so at that point.

4

MORE THAN WEBBED FEET

Connecting to the Internet

These days, the average home computer user spends more time surfing the Web and writing email messages than doing just about anything else. Even if you're not much of a surfer, numerous applications that aren't really Internet applications per se still use the Internet in some way, such as by gathering song and album information when you rip audio CDs to create MP3 files. Having a computer that isn't hooked up to the Internet is like buying a new Maserati and then refusing to take it out of the garage.

Of course, how you connect to the Internet depends on your hardware and provider. There are a number of possibilities, including high-speed local area networks (LANs), cable modems, mobile (3G/4G) broadband, and ADSL connections from phone companies. Some computers still have an internal 56 Kbps modem or can be connected to external dial-up modems for slower connections over regular phone lines. Depending on what you have, setting things up on your system should prove a cinch in the case of LAN connections and any other types of connections that use your Ethernet port (such as cable modems), possibly a tad more work in the case of wireless and mobile connections, and sometimes a bit of a challenge when it comes to dial-up connections. In this chapter, you will learn how to set up these connections, and in the next chapter, you will learn a bit about what Linux has to offer in terms of the most commonly used Internet applications.

How Do You Connect?

The way you go about setting up your connection really depends on how you're trying to connect to the Internet.

- If you connect your computer to a wall socket, a router, or a cable modem by using an Ethernet cable, go to "Setting Up a Wired Connection" on page 43.
- If you connect to a wireless network or your own wireless router, head to "Setting Up a Wireless Connection" on page 45.
- If you have an ADSL or DSL modem that is built in to your computer or connects to a USB port, try "Connecting with a DSL or ADSL Modem" on page 49.
- If you connect using a dial-up modem connected to your phone line, "Setting Up a Dial-up Connection" on page 50 is the one for you.
- If you connect using a mobile (3G/4G) broadband connection that plugs in to your computer, go to "Mobile Broadband Connections" on page 52.

Whichever method applies to you, one thing is almost certain—you'll be using an application called Network Manager to help set up and manage the network connection. The easiest way of getting to Network Manager is through the Network icon on the top panel (mentioned in Chapter 3). It changes its appearance depending on what type of network you are connected to, but finding it isn't hard. Look at the row of icons on the right-hand side of the top panel, and you should find the Network icon sandwiched somewhere between the Messaging menu (which has an envelope icon) on the left, and the Sound menu (which has a speaker icon) on the right. You'll know you've got the correct icon if, when you click it, the item at the very bottom of the pop-up menu that appears says **Edit Connections** (as in Figure 4-1).

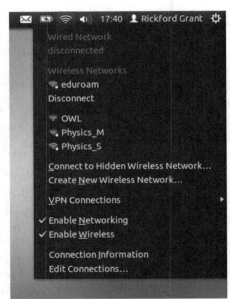

Figure 4-1: The Network menu

With that knowledge in hand, skip to the section that applies to your type of Internet connection and get connecting!

Setting Up a Wired Connection

If you have a high-speed Internet connection from your cable television company or ISP or if you are connected to the Internet by a LAN at your office, you are really in luck, because these setups are probably the easiest to deal with. I'm going to assume that you've already set up your router or modem according to your Internet provider's instructions so all that remains is to connect an Ethernet cable between the modem/router (or LAN wall socket) and your computer's network socket. After you've done that, you should be ready to go without any further settings to fool with.

Checking Your Connection

If the wired network has been detected and a connection has been established, the Network icon will change to look like two arrows. If you like, you can check whether you've connected successfully by opening Firefox (click the Firefox icon in the Launcher) and then, once it starts up, trying to navigate to a common site, such as *http://www.yahoo.com/*. If the site comes up, you know you're all set.

If you have a problem getting online and you are trying to connect via a LAN or cable modem, you could try to refresh your connection by clicking the Network icon on the top panel, unchecking the **Enable Networking** item in the pop-up menu, waiting a few seconds, and then checking the **Enable Networking** item in the pop-up menu again. If that doesn't work, try restarting your machine while physically connected to your Internet source with the Ethernet cable.

If the problem persists, it could be that your network or service provider does not automatically assign addresses via Dynamic Host Configuration Protocol (DHCP). *DHCP* is a means by which your Internet provider can automatically provide your system with the configuration information it needs in order to connect to the Internet. If your provider does not use DHCP, you will have to get the necessary information about settings from the network administrator or service provider and enter the settings yourself.

Setting Up a Cable or Ethernet Connection for Providers Not Using DHCP

To input your cable or Ethernet settings yourself, first get the settings you need from your network administrator or Internet provider and then perform the following steps:

1. Click the Network icon and select **Edit Connections** from the pop-up menu that appears.
2. Choose the **Wired** tab (shown in Figure 4-2), and select the network connection from the list by clicking it once (it should have a name like *Wired connection 1*). If there are no entries in the list, then your network card hasn't been properly recognized. Take a look at "Installing Drivers for Your Network/Wireless Card" on page 388 to see how to fix this.

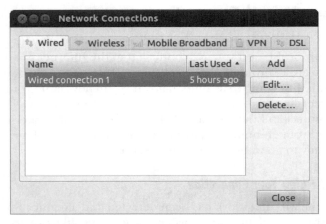

Figure 4-2: The Network Connections window

3. Click **Edit**, and you'll be presented with a settings window. Choose the **IPv4 Settings** tab and change the Method setting from Automatic (DHCP) to **Manual**.

4. Click the **Add** button to enter the IP address information for your computer. This should have been provided by your ISP or network administrator and will consist of an IP address, default gateway, and netmask (see Figure 4-3 for an example). Enter the DNS server address that you were given too.

Figure 4-3: Manually inputting network IP settings

5. Make sure that the **Available to all users** option is checked if other users of your computer will be using the connection.

6. Click **Save** to save the settings. You'll be asked to enter the password for your user account, so do that and then click **Authenticate**.

7. Network Manager will try to establish the connection using the details you just provided. If it's successful, a message will pop up saying that the network was connected.

8. If that doesn't happen, click the Network icon on the top panel and choose **Disconnect** from the Wired Network section at the top of the pop-up menu that appears. Then click the Network icon again and select your network underneath where it says *Wired Network*.

NOTE   *If you are wondering what Internet Protocol (IP) and Domain Name Service (DNS) are all about, you can simply think of them in this way: DNS translates the easy-to-remember URLs that you have come to know, such as* http://www.google.com/, *into numerical, or IP, addresses that the Internet can understand. The address* http://www .google.com/ *thus becomes* http://209.85.229.104. *You can type the numerical version into your browser later to see for yourself.*

Setting Up a Wireless Connection

With the right wireless hardware, you can now surf the Web just about anywhere you can catch a (radio) wave. Whether you happen to be at your breakfast table, in a public library, or at your local coffee shop, you can now go online without having to physically hook up your computer to anything.

Fortunately, the process of setting up wireless networking in Ubuntu is easy; it's not very different from the procedure for wired networks, described in the previous section.

Hardware

If you have led a solely wired existence or are just inexperienced in this area, there are a few things worth knowing. To get started, you need to have the right hardware. If you just want to go wireless, then all you need is a wireless network card (sometimes referred to as an *802.11a/b/g/n card* or *Wi-Fi card*). These are built in to almost all modern laptops, while for older models they are usually add-ons in the form of cards that pop into the PCMCIA slot on the side of your computer (as shown on the right of Figure 4-4).

Some wireless cards plug in to one of your machine's USB ports or, in the case of desktop models, one of its internal PCI slots. Although support for cards of this type has improved in the past couple of years, there are still gaps, and some cards can be tricky to deal with. You'll find some tips on how to deal with awkward cards in Chapter 22, but if you're looking for a sure thing, cards listed as having a Ralink 2500/RT2400, Realtek RTL8180, or Atheros AR9170 "chipset" are definitely supported by Ubuntu.

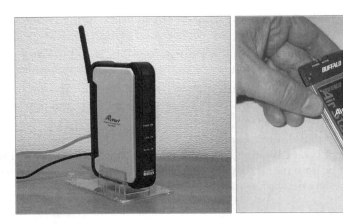

Figure 4-4: All you need for a Wi-Fi setup—an access point and a network interface card

As for cards of the built-in or PC card variety, you will find support much better, but even then you have to make sure, or at least hope, that the card you are using is Linux compatible. No matter what wireless card you are wondering about, the easiest way to find out whether it will work is just to try it. The Linux kernel now comes with many wireless drivers built in, and Ubuntu updates often provide new ones, so if you use a card that is compatible with one of those drivers, things will be smooth sailing. If things don't seem to work, check Ubuntu's list of supported cards (*https://help.ubuntu.com/community/ WifiDocs/WirelessCardsSupported/*) or check the Ubuntu forums to find a driver that is compatible or to see whether anyone has experience with your particular card. If you want to set up a wireless system in your home or office, then you will also need to get a *wireless access point (WAP)*, shown on the left of Figure 4-4. Fortunately, Linux compatibility is not much of an issue in this department, because the access point doesn't physically interface with your computer and the settings are handled via your web browser.

NOTE *Access points come in several types. The most common type is a wireless router, which many ISPs provide for free.*

You should be aware, however, that a small minority of access points require you to use Internet Explorer to handle their setup chores. Although it is possible to get Internet Explorer up and running in Linux via Wine (which you'll learn more about in Chapter 19), you can't be 100 percent sure that it will work. Unless you have a Windows machine somewhere in your house or office to handle such chores, it is probably a good idea to steer clear of access points of this kind.

Activating Your Wireless Card

Setting up a Linux-compatible wireless card is relatively simple. First connect your access point to your Internet source and then turn on the access point. Once it is up and running, plug your wireless card in to the PCMCIA slot or

USB port on your laptop (unless your wireless connection is built in, in which case you can forgo this step). Any LEDs on the external card will most likely light up at this time.

If your access point was on when you booted up your computer and your wireless card was in place during bootup, you probably don't need to do much else to access the Internet. Just follow these steps:

1. Click the Network icon on the top bar to reveal a drop-down menu showing the wireless signals that are present in your vicinity and the strength of each signal (Figure 4-5).

2. From that menu, select the signal for your access point (or any other wave you are entitled to latch onto) by clicking it.

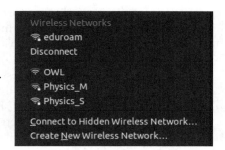

3. The Network icon will start to pulse, showing that your system is trying to connect to the Internet. Once a connection is made, the icon will morph into a small signal-strength indicator. Pretty handy.

Figure 4-5: The Network menu shows you available wireless networks and their signal strengths.

4. If your network has a WEP or WPA password, you'll be prompted to enter it. It can be useful to check **Show password** before you type the password so you can check for any mistakes. Click **Connect** when you're finished.

NOTE   *Most access points employ an added level of security in the form of a* Wired Equivalent Privacy (WEP) *or a* Wi-Fi Protected Access (WPA) *key. If you didn't choose your own password when you set up the access point, try looking for a sticker on the base or side of the access point to see whether a default password is used. If you're trying to connect to a network for which you don't happen to know the key, then chances are you are not supposed to be making the connection in the first place. Naughty, naughty.*

If you were not successful in making your wireless connection (the system will tell you whether that's the case), you have a few possibilities beyond the annoying incompatible card scenario. First, double-check to make sure your card is physically turned on. I know that sounds dumb, but I have been guilty of this oversight myself on numerous occasions. Many laptops have a key you can press to enable or disable the wireless card; on mine, you have to press the function key (FN) and F2 at the same time (there's a little wireless antenna icon on the F2 key to denote this).

Another possibility is that you are not entering the correct WEP or WPA password. The first thing to check is case sensitivity: It sometimes matters whether the letters you type are upper- or lowercase, so make sure you type them exactly as written. Additionally, some wireless access points require you to type the "wireless key" rather than a passphrase or password. A wireless key normally consists of a seemingly random string of numbers and letters that is 10, 26, or even 58 characters long and looks something like this: `af564ecb31ce4a678b23fe5981`. Try typing your own wireless key (not the one that I just used as an example!) instead of the passphrase and see if that works. If you don't have the wireless key written down anywhere, look through the access point's manual to see how to find it.

If you are trying to connect to a wireless network in a public place (for example, at a conference center, university, or airport or on a train), you may need to perform some additional steps to finish setting up the connection. These might include visiting a specific website in your web browser to register for the service or providing your *MAC address* to the network administrator. For the first of these, open Firefox and type the address that the provider of the wireless connection should have given you. Hopefully, a page will load, and you'll be asked to enter some details. If you're asked for your MAC address, you should instead click the Network icon and select *Connection information* from the menu that appears. Then find the Hardware Address (which will look similar to the one in Figure 4-6) and copy it down and give it to whoever needs it. This is your MAC address.

Figure 4-6: Connection information, including the MAC address

A rather less common possibility is that your network does not use DHCP, in which case you will have to manually input your connection settings as provided by your network administrator or service provider. Armed with that information, simply follow the steps listed in "Setting Up a Cable or Ethernet Connection for Providers Not Using DHCP" on page 43. Just be sure to use the Wireless tab instead of the Wired one.

If you still have no luck connecting wirelessly, the drivers may not be installed for your card, or Ubuntu may not support the card. You can try plenty of tricks to get things working, so head over to Chapter 22 and look for "Installing Drivers for Your Network/Wireless Card" on page 388.

Switching Off or Refreshing Your Wireless Connection

Sometimes you will want to disconnect from a wireless network, such as when you use your laptop on an airplane or when you just want to connect to a different network, as you might when moving your laptop from one wireless hotspot to another.

To do this, click the Network icon to reveal the list of available wireless networks (that is, signals). In that list, click the **Disconnect** option below the name of the wireless network to which you are connected. Within a second or two, you will be disconnected.

If you want to turn off your wireless card (as you should do if you're boarding an airplane) and you don't have a physical way to do it, like a switch or a button, just click the Network icon and then deselect **Enable Wireless**. And if you want to turn that card back on again, just get back to that menu and select **Enable Wireless** again.

Sometimes, your wireless card might lose its connection for no apparent reason, so you'll want to refresh the connection (that is, turn it off and on again) to try to get it back. The quickest way to do this is to click the Network icon and then click the name of the wireless network you're currently connected to. You'll be disconnected and automatically reconnected.

If that doesn't work, try disabling and then enabling the wireless connection using the Enable Wireless option, as described earlier. If you still have no luck, try turning the wireless card off and on again using a switch or button, if you have one, or unplug it and plug it back in again. Finally, if nothing seems to be working, try restarting the computer.

Connecting with a DSL or ADSL Modem

How easy it is to set up your DSL or ADSL modem depends on the connector that it has. If it can be connected using an Ethernet cable, use that and follow the instructions in "Setting Up a Wired Connection" on page 43; it'll be much easier than trying to use a USB cable! If you have a USB or internal modem, try the instructions in this section and hope for the best.

The first step is to check whether Ubuntu recognized your modem. Assuming the modem is already plugged in, click the Network icon on the top bar, select **Edit Connections** from the menu that appears, and select the **DSL** tab. If a connection is listed in that window, your modem was recognized, and you can begin setting it up. If the list is empty, refer to *https://help.ubuntu.com/community/UsbAdslModem/* to see whether there are any steps you can follow to get your modem working. Alternatively, flip to Chapter 21 to see how you can ask for help with setting up your modem from members of the Ubuntu community.

Select the connection by clicking it once and then click **Edit**. Click the **DSL** tab of the Editing window that appears and enter your username and password into the appropriate fields. Then enter your connection information (usually a phone number) into the Service box and click **Save**. Now click the Network icon on the top panel and choose your DSL connection from the list. Network Manager will try to connect using your modem—if it's not successful, go back and try changing some of the settings to see whether you can get it to cooperate.

Setting Up a Dial-up Connection

Although much of the world is moving to high-speed Internet connections, you may still be using a dial-up Internet connection, which means you need to have a traditional dial-up modem to reach beyond your box to the outside world. In case you broadband surf-gods have forgotten, modems are those wonderful machines that whistle, chime, screech, and spit whenever you dial up your Internet provider. I suppose you could think of them as noisy telephones in need of a good burp.

Now here comes the bad news—in the world of Linux, very few internal modems are supported, and for those that are, the setup process can be frustrating. The main reason behind this compatibility problem is that most built-in modems are software dependent and the software they depend on is part of, or designed for, Windows. Such modems are thus called *Winmodems.*

Of course, the Linux community has been working on ways to deal with these Winmodem beasts so that they will work with Linux systems. Though support for the wide variety of Winmodem models out there is still spotty, things are better than before, so you might luck out. My advice is to hold off on the wondering and worrying and just give your modem a try to see whether it works. If it does, then you're all set. If it doesn't, well, you do have some options, and at least you haven't done any damage to your system.

With all that intro-babble out of the way, let's get down to the steps for setting up your dial-up connection. First, get the settings information you need from your Internet provider. Most providers aim their operations at Windows and, often, Mac users, and very few offer Linux support. Still, there is no technical reason for your Linux system not to work via their setups, so just nag and push them until they give you the information you want. After that, make sure your modem is connected to a live telephone connection—for example, the phone jack in your wall.

Now it's time to set up the connection. I'll use the GNOME PPP program to do all of the setting up here, but there's a caveat: It's not installed by default, and you need an Internet connection to install it! If you have access to some other Internet connection that you can use temporarily, connect to that and use the Ubuntu Software Center to download and install GNOME PPP (see Chapter 6 to learn how to install software). The alternative is to use the pppconfig command, which is installed by default but is difficult to use. Find another computer and check out *https://help.ubuntu.com/community/DialupModemHowto/SetUpDialer/* for instructions if you have no alternative but to use pppconfig.

Assuming that you got GNOME PPP installed using a borrowed Internet connection, you can follow these steps to set up your modem:

1. Open the Dash, search for GNOME PPP, and click to open it.

2. Click **Setup** and make sure you're looking at the **Modem** tab.

3. Click the **Detect** button to identify your modem. If you get a message saying that no modem was found on your system, then you're out of luck—the best you can do is ask for advice on the Ubuntu forums (*http://www.ubuntuforums.org/*) or try selecting items from the Device drop-down list by trial and error.

4. How you change the rest of the settings depends on how your modem and ISP are set up, so select the defaults for now. If these don't work, trial and error is a potential way forward again.

5. Click **Close** to get back to the GNOME PPP window. Type your user-name and password and enter the phone number provided by your ISP.

6. Click **Connect**. You should hear your modem begin its dialing, spitting, and churning sequence as it makes the connection with your provider.

7. If you manage to get connected, you can start your browsing, emailing, or whatever else you do online. If you get an error message, there's little you can do but take a deep breath and click the **Setup** button to try tweaking your settings.

What to Do If Your Modem Isn't Compatible

Though it may not sound that way, what I've just described is pretty much a best-case scenario. What happens, however, if your modem and Ubuntu do not see eye to eye? Well, there are a few options. My first, more radical suggestion is to dump your dial-up ISP and find a broadband provider that covers your local area. If that is not an option, then you have two ways to go. One is to try to geek around with your modem to see whether you can get it to work. This is a slightly complicated process, but there are instructions at *https://help.ubuntu.com/community/DialupModemHowto/*. If you are faint of heart or a novice user, you may find the process to entail a bit more than what you're willing to deal with.

The simpler, although costlier, way to get your modem to work is to purchase a true hardware modem. *Hardware modems* are not software dependent, so they work with any operating system. You can think of them as telephones without a handset.

Such modems come in two forms: internal and external. As for the internals, the USRobotics models 56K V.92 Performance Pro Modem (internal slot) and 56 PC Card Modem (PC card slot, for laptops) are true hardware modems that are easily available and are said to work. You can check out the USRobotics site (*http://www.usr.com/*) for more information on these models, though checking the Ubuntu forums for suggestions is always a good idea as well. Perhaps the safest of all solutions is to buy an external dial-up modem.

They come with either serial or USB connectors and sit in a box outside your computer. They bring the advantage of not requiring you to open up the computer to install them.

Linux support for USB modems can be patchy, so do your research before buying one. Serial modems are a safer bet since most of them should work with your system . . . if you have a serial port, that is. Modern computers rarely have them anymore, so check to see whether you have one by looking at the back of your computer for a connector with little prongs in it (see Figure 4-7). If you are worried and are looking for a sure thing, USRobotics makes an external serial modem that is compatible with Linux, and the company says so right on its website.

If you find another model that you think will do the trick, before you commit to it by slapping down the cash, do a Yahoo! or Google search on that modem's make and model number, along with the word *linux*, and see what results you get. Of course, you can also try one of the Linux forums and ask about the modem make and model there. A lot of people are in the same boat, so you are sure to get plenty of opinions and advice.

Figure 4-7: Serial port and connector

Mobile Broadband Connections

Wireless networks, for all the convenience and freedom that they offer, have quite a limited range. This won't be an issue if your computer never strays from the general vicinity of your house or office, but it can get mighty inconvenient if you're on the road, miles from the nearest wireless-enabled coffee shop. This being the 21st century, there are, of course, ways around this limitation.

If you're a computer-equipped traveler, you've probably already come across mobile broadband technology, also known as *3G* (which has been upgraded to 4G in some places). All you need to get a high-speed connection on the go is a 3G or 4G card (also inexplicably called a *dongle*), which plugs into your computer and connects you to the Net via a cell phone network (Figure 4-8).

Figure 4-8: A 3G mobile broadband card

Ubuntu has pretty good support for most 3G cards right from the get-go, and the setup process is a snap (the process is the same for 4G cards):

1. Plug your 3G card or dongle into the computer; the New Mobile Broadband Connection wizard should open automatically. If it doesn't, click the Network icon on the top panel, select **Edit Connections** from the menu that appears, open the **Mobile Broadband** tab, and click **Add**.

2. The first page of the wizard has a drop-down list that should have the make and model of your 3G card displayed in it. If it says *Any Device* instead, your card may not have been recognized, so take a look at *https://wiki.ubuntu.com/NetworkManager/Hardware/3G/* to see whether there are any steps you can take to get Ubuntu to recognize the card.

3. Click **Continue**, select your country from the list, and then click **Continue** again.

4. Pick your mobile broadband provider from the list and then hit **Continue**.

5. Now you need to select your broadband billing plan from the drop-down list (Figure 4-9). It's important that you choose the right plan to avoid being wrongly charged. If you don't see a plan that looks appropriate, choose *My plan is not listed* and call up your broadband provider to ask what to put in the Access Point Name (APN) box.

6. Click **Continue**, check that all of the details look okay, and click **Apply**. You'll be taken to an Editing window where you can enter details such as your account PIN and password if needed.

7. Click **Save** and then close the Network Connections window to finish up.

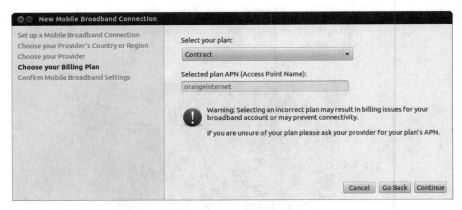

Figure 4-9: Choosing a broadband billing plan

To connect to mobile broadband, click the Network icon on the top panel and choose your broadband service from the list. Network Manager will spend a few seconds establishing the connection, after which you'll be notified that you're connected (or not, as the case may be). Disconnecting happens in just about the same way: Click the Network icon again but this time click **Disconnect** just below the name of your broadband service when the list pops up.

I'm Connected . . . So Now What?

Ideally you're now cabled in, wired up, or otherwise happily connected to the Internet. (If not, take a look at Chapter 22 for some connection-troubleshooting tips.) That's great news, because now you can put Ubuntu through its paces by trying some of the interesting web-related software that comes preinstalled. Prime your clicking finger for action and flip the page to see what life online is like for a new Linux user.

5

SLIPPING AND SLIDING

Exploring the Internet, Linux Style

Now that you have a working Internet connection, what can you do with it? The good news is that Linux can match anything that your previous operating system could do online, and in many cases it can do it faster or more easily. Ubuntu was born on the Web, so it should be no surprise that it comes with a very healthy suite of Internet-ready applications right out of the box.

In this chapter, you'll take a tour of Ubuntu's Internet software so you can get a feel for what this Linux stuff is capable of. You'll begin with old stalwarts like the web browser and email client, briefly tour instant messaging, and then head off in the more modish direction of Twitter and microblogging.

Firefox: Your Internet Browser

The default web browser in your Ubuntu system is Firefox, which is enjoying increasing popularity in not only the Linux world but also the Windows and Mac worlds. Chances are you are already a Firefox user, but if you're not, no worries. Things work more or less the same in all browsers, so you should be able to use Firefox's basic features without any instruction. Of course, some of its features do distinguish Firefox from its competition, so I will mention those.

Controlling Browser Window Clutter with Tabs

Usually when you click a link on a web page, the new page opens in the same window. On some pages, links are coded so that the new page opens in a new, separate window, or maybe you occasionally opt for opening a link in a new window by right-clicking the link and then selecting the Open Link in New Window option. This can be very useful; however, once you have more than a few browser windows open, it gets sort of hard to find what you're looking for. It can also slow things down a bit.

This is where Firefox's tab feature comes in handy (so handy, in fact, that almost every other browser out there has copied it). To see how it works, try it yourself right here and now. Open your Firefox browser by clicking its icon in the Launcher (shown in Figure 5-1) or by searching for Firefox in the Dash.

Firefox icon —

Then, search for the word *nyckelharpa* using Firefox's handy search box, which is at the top-right corner of the browser window (see Figure 5-2). By default, Firefox will perform searches for keywords entered in the search box using Google. You can, if you like, select other search engines or search particular websites by clicking the colored *g* icon in the search box and then making your selection. Amazon.com, eBay, and Yahoo! are available, to name a few, and you can even add others. For now,

Figure 5-1: The Firefox icon in the Launcher

however, let's stick to Google by typing **nyckelharpa** in that search box. Once you've finished typing, press ENTER. A page of search results should appear in the main pane of the Firefox window.

Figure 5-2: Performing a Google search from the Firefox search box

One of the top results should be the American Nyckelharpa Association, and you are now going to open that page in a new tab, rather than in the same or a new window. To do that, right-click the link and, in the pop-up menu that appears, select **Open Link in New Tab**. You can, if you prefer, make things a tad easier and dispense with the pop-up menu selection step by simply clicking the link with the middle mouse button (or with both mouse buttons simultaneously) or by holding down the CTRL key as you click the link.

Either way, the new page will appear in a new tab (see Figure 5-3), while your original page of search results remains, ready and waiting, in the other tab. I am pretty confident in saying that, once you get used to this feature, you will wonder how you ever got along without it.

Figure 5-3: A link opened in a new tab in Firefox

Save It for Later: Using History and Bookmarks

Chances are, you have a few favorite websites that you return to again and again, perhaps even checking some of them a few times a day. Typing the entire web address every time you want to check Facebook can get tedious, and putting the same search terms into Google five times a day feels clunky too. Surely there's a better way? In fact, Firefox is crammed with better ways! Let's take a look at some of them.

Bookmarks

First up is Firefox's Bookmarks feature. To save a web page for perusal at your convenience, all you need to do is click the empty star icon in the right-hand corner of the address bar. When you do that, the star will turn yellow, indicating that the page has been saved. But saved where, you ask? Go to the Bookmarks menu and look at the **Recently Bookmarked** menu item. A list will expand that contains your most recent bookmarks, including the one you just added. All it takes to revisit the page is to click the appropriate item in that menu.

There are other ways of getting at your bookmarks besides the Bookmarks menu, some of which you may find more convenient. One is the *Bookmarks sidebar*: Click **View ▸ Sidebar** and select **Bookmarks** to bring it up (or press CTRL-B if you're more keyboard shortcut inclined). A new pane will appear down the left-hand side of the window with an expandable list of bookmarks, as well as a search box (shown in Figure 5-4). Click through the lists or start typing in the search box to find the web page you're after. When you're finished, you can hide the sidebar by clicking the *X* in its top right-hand corner or by deselecting it in the **View ▸ Sidebar** menu.

Figure 5-4: The Bookmarks sidebar in Firefox

Another nifty way of accessing bookmarks is through the *Bookmarks toolbar*. By default, this is hidden away so you can't use it. To wake the toolbar from its slumber, click **View ▸ Toolbars** and select **Bookmarks Toolbar**. A new strip will appear immediately below the address bar, containing only two links (Figure 5-5). One of these, Most Visited, contains a list of the websites that you visit most frequently. Simply click **Most Visited**, choose one of the sites from the list that pops up, and you'll be taken directly to one of your favorite sites. The second item is a link to some instructions on "Getting Started," which you may wish to peruse later. For now, let's concentrate on populating the Bookmarks toolbar with regular bookmarks.

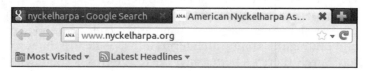

Figure 5-5: The Bookmarks toolbar

Adding bookmarks to the toolbar is quite straightforward. When you first bookmark a page by clicking the star in the address bar, click the (now yellow) star again. An *Edit This Bookmark* box will appear, like the one in Figure 5-6, giving you a number of options. To save the page in the Bookmarks toolbar, simply change the *Folder* option appropriately and then click **Done**. A new bookmark will appear on the toolbar, which you can access with a single click.

If you're a particularly intrepid web adventurer, you might soon find that you have an unwieldy number of bookmarks building up. Rather than curtailing your adventures, you might try a bit of spring-cleaning instead. Click **Bookmarks ▸ Show All Bookmarks**, and a Library window will open up. From this window, you can organize all of your bookmarks, renaming, deleting, and filing them away as you see fit. To see how this works, select **Bookmarks Menu** from the list on the left-hand side of the window and click

Organize ▸ New Folder. A new folder will appear, which you can rename as you like. With that done, try dragging some of the bookmarks into the folder. Repeat this procedure a few times, and you'll soon have your bookmark collection neatly categorized.

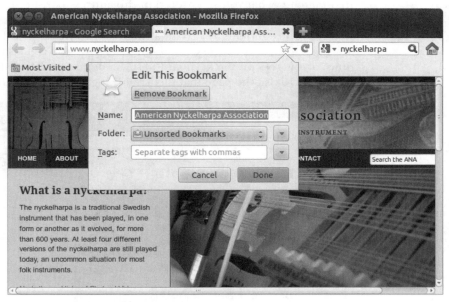

Figure 5-6: Editing a bookmark

History

The problem with bookmarks is that you have to remember to bookmark a page in the first place. That's all well and good if a website strikes you as worth keeping for later when you first visit it, but what if you found something a few days ago that seems important only in retrospect? For just such eventualities, Firefox keeps a detailed history of all of the websites you've visited over the last few months, or even longer. To view your web-browsing history, click **View ▸ Sidebar** and select **History** or press CTRL-H. This will bring up the *History sidebar*, which has a full list of websites you've visited, sorted by date. You can browse or search through these, just as you could with the Bookmarks toolbar. Clicking any of the pages in the list will bring it up in the main Firefox window again.

To find a page, it's also possible to sort the list by something other than date. Click the **View** button immediately to the right of the search box in the History sidebar and select one of the options from the menu that pops up to re-sort the list. For example, to view your browsing history grouped by website, rather than by date visited, select **By Site**.

Of course, trawling through your entire web history every time you want to find a previously viewed website isn't everyone's idea of fun. To this end, Firefox has what I think you'll agree is a rather awesome feature: the Awesome Bar. This is actually just another name for the address bar, which might leave you with the impression that there's perhaps more to the dull old text box than meets the eye. Indeed, there is: Open a new tab and start typing. As the letters appear in the address bar, a list will appear immediately below it, containing links to websites that you've previously visited (shown in Figure 5-7). Firefox is directly searching your web history as you type, finding anything that matches what you've entered in the address bar. Refine the search by typing a few more letters or scroll down through the list until you find the website you're looking for. With a single click, the page will load, negating any need to type its address out in full. Slick, no? You can also use the up and down arrow keys on the keyboard to select items from the list and use the ENTER key to visit the page that is currently highlighted—no clicking required.

Figure 5-7: The Awesome Bar, showing items from the web-browsing history

As well as web addresses, you can also type search terms into the address bar. For example, type **cat pictures** into the address bar and press ENTER. Firefox recognizes that *cat pictures* wasn't meant to be a web address and will perform a search instead, just as if you had typed those words into the search box to the right. While it might take a little time to get used to how the Awesome Bar works, it's a pretty nifty feature that can save you a lot of clicking around.

When I said that Firefox remembers everything you've looked at recently, I really did mean everything. If you don't want Firefox to remember the pages you visit, at least for a time, then you can try *Private Browsing mode*. This is handy if you want to look at something confidential, such as a banking website. Click **Tools ▸ Start Private Browsing** and start surfing—Firefox will instantly forget any and all of the pages that you visit while private browsing is enabled, and they won't appear in your web history or otherwise. When you want to return Firefox to its normal operation, simply go back to the Tools menu and click **Stop Private Browsing**. The window will return to whatever state it was in before you started private browsing, without any trace to be seen of the websites you just visited.

Keeping Up-to-Date with Live Bookmarks

The Web is awash in all sorts of news and information, and it can be hard to keep tabs on it all. Personally, I hate missing my daily dose of offbeat stories from Boing Boing, the aptly subtitled "directory of wonderful things" (*http://www.boingboing.net/*). Fortunately, Firefox has a neat way of dealing with your information overload called *live bookmarks* (also known as *RSS feeds*). These provide you with an automatically updated list of articles from any website that supports them (Figure 5-8).

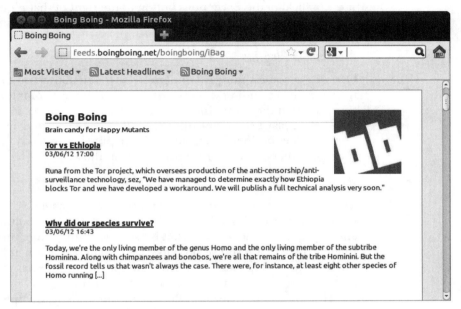

Figure 5-8: A live bookmark in action

You can check whether a website has an RSS feed by going to the Bookmarks menu and checking whether the *Subscribe to This Page* menu item is enabled. If it's grayed out, then bad luck—there's no RSS feed. If it's white, not gray, then you're in business! Let's use Boing Boing as an example: Load *http://www.boingboing.net/* in Firefox and go to the Bookmarks menu. The Subscribe to This Page item will be white, which means it's clickable. Click it, and you'll get a list of the most recent articles along with an invitation to subscribe to the feed in the box at the top of the page. Click **Subscribe Now**, and in the window that appears, click **Subscribe** to add the live bookmark to the same toolbar as the Latest Headlines link.

Some websites provide links to their RSS feeds rather than showing them in the address bar. If you find one of these links (it's normally called *ATOM* or *RSS/XML*), click it, and you should be taken to a list of articles with a box at the top, as in the previous example. From there, the steps for adding the feed to your bookmarks are the same.

Pop-up Manager

Firefox has a number of other useful features. One is its Pop-up Manager, which suppresses those annoying pop-up windows that too often appear when you access a new web page. You can enable or disable this feature from the Preferences window (**Edit ▸ Preferences**); click the **Content** icon in the top pane of that window and then check or uncheck the **Block pop-up windows** box. You can also permit certain sites to provide pop-up windows (some pop-ups are not only useful but also necessary for the correct functioning of a site) by clicking the **Exceptions** button to the right of that Block pop-up windows entry and inputting the web address for the site in question.

Multimedia Plug-ins

One of the coolest things about Firefox is that it allows you to expand its functionality by adding various extensions. The most commonly used extensions come in the form of *plug-ins*. These allow web pages to do much more than just display text and pictures—you'll often need a plug-in to watch videos or play games online, for example. Three plug-ins are used far more widely than any others, so I'll concentrate here on those.

Flash

The most frequently used browser plug-in for any system is Adobe's Flash Player. Flash provides websites with all sorts of exciting multimedia effects and capabilities, and as a result, it is used by a rather large number of sites. In fact, chances are you've probably seen numerous Flash-enhanced pages without even being aware of it. For example, if you've ever watched a video on YouTube, you've enjoyed the wonders of Flash.

How do you get the Flash Player plug-in? Well, if you opted to install third-party software when you first installed your system, you already have it. If not, all it takes is a few clicks and a working Internet connection:

1. Open the Software Center by clicking its icon on the Launcher or by searching for it in the Dash. (You'll learn more about the Software Center in Chapter 6; skip ahead if you need to.)

2. Type `adobe flash` in the search box at the top right of the window.

3. In the list that appears, double-click the **Adobe Flash plug-in** item. An information window will appear, hopefully with an Install button (Figure 5-9). If, instead, you get a button that says **Use This Source**, click the button and wait as the Software Center enables an extra *software repository* that it needs (more on this in Chapter 6). The Install button should appear once it's finished.

4. Click **Install**; then, if prompted, type your password and click **Authenticate**. The plug-in will be downloaded and installed.

5. When the plug-in has finished installing, a green checkmark will appear next to its icon in the list. Close the Ubuntu Software Center and open Firefox (if it was already open, close it and start it up again).

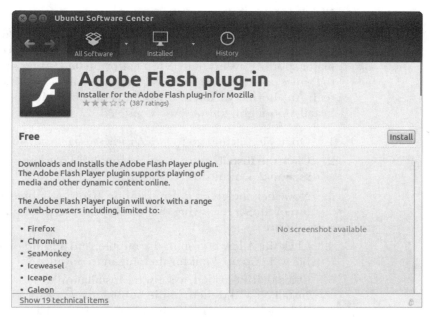

Figure 5-9: Installing the Flash plug-in with the Ubuntu Software Center

6. To check that the plug-in is working, find a site that uses Flash. If you don't know of one offhand, try YouTube (*http://www.youtube.com/*). Once you have arrived at YouTube, click any video link you see. If Flash was installed successfully, a video should appear and start playing (Figure 5-10).

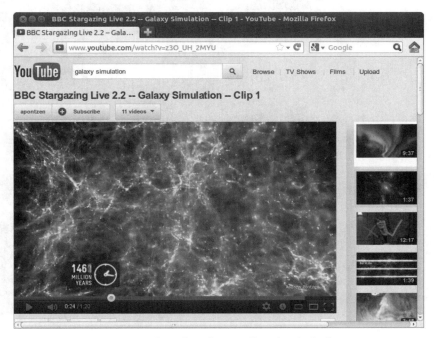

Figure 5-10: Playing a YouTube video after installing the Flash plug-in

Silverlight/Moonlight

A relative newcomer to the plug-in scene is Microsoft's Silverlight. It's less common than Flash but seems to be used on the websites of TV channels and major sporting events quite a lot. Unfortunately, Microsoft is a little behind the times, and it hasn't made Silverlight available for Linux yet. But never fear: An alternative, open source plug-in called Moonlight is available. To install Moonlight, follow these steps:

1. Open Firefox and go to *http://www.go-mono.com/moonlight/*.

2. Click the **Install** button on the Moonlight page and scroll down to section 2, Download the plug-in.

3. Now click the green down-pointing arrow. A bubble will appear at the top of the screen saying that the website was prevented from installing software.

4. Click the **Allow** button in the bubble, and an Add-on downloading bubble will pop up. Wait for the plug-in to download.

5. Once that's finished, a Software Installation window will appear. Click **Install Now** and then, in the bubble that appears, click **Restart Now** to finish installing the plug-in (all of the pages that you have open will reappear when Firefox opens again).

6. Head over to *http://www.farseergames.com/waterdemo/*. If Moonlight was installed properly, you should now see a little boat bobbing around on the waves (Figure 5-11).

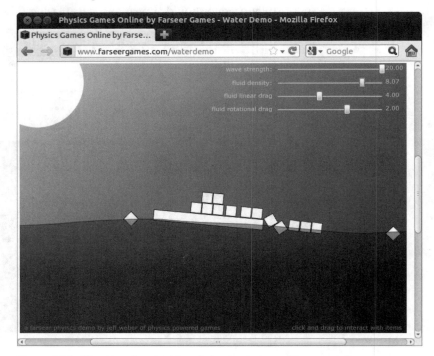

Figure 5-11: Checking that the Moonlight plug-in is working properly

Some Silverlight/Moonlight-enabled websites might require you to install extra plug-ins, especially if they are trying to display videos. If this is the case, yet another bar will appear at the top of the page, telling you that plug-ins are missing. Click the **Install Missing Plugins** button and follow the onscreen instructions to install everything that you need.

Java

One last plug-in that you're likely to encounter is Java, which is used to run *Java applets*. Java applets are little applications that you can run in your web browser, and they're commonly used for games and demonstrations. Installing Java is quite similar to installing Flash. Just open the Software Center, but this time search for *IcedTea Java Plugin* and install that. After installation has finished, it's a good idea to take a look at Java in action, so head over to *http://www.turbotanks.com/*. An arcade "tanks" game should load if Java is working properly (Figure 5-12).

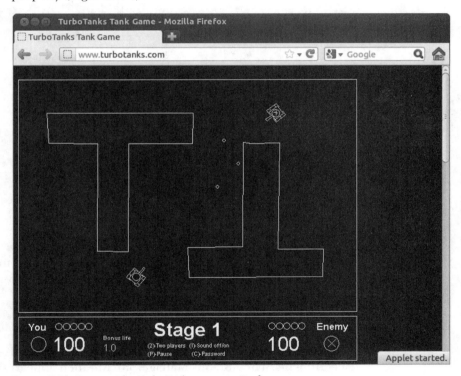

Figure 5-12: Running the TurboTanks game in Firefox

Project 5: Installing Firefox Extensions

The plug-ins I just covered are near-essentials that pretty much everyone has installed, but hundreds of other, less vital extensions are available for Firefox too. These come in the form of *add-ons* and include all sort of things; many are quite functional, while others are just plain fun and goofy. They range from blog-writing tools and to-do lists to image viewers and travel guides. For this project, you will install a blog editor called ScribeFire (Figure 5-13) that allows you to write entries, log in to your blog, and upload your new entry. All of this is available at the click of a button from an icon in the bottom-right corner of the window.

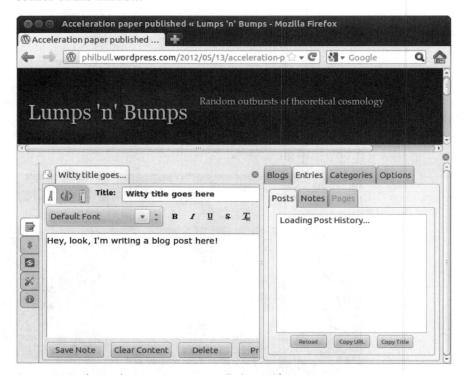

Figure 5-13: The ScribeFire extension installed in Firefox

NOTE *If you don't have a blog but you'd like to give blogging a try, you can sign up for an account on a free hosting website, such as* http://www.blogger.com/, http://wordpress.com/, http://www.tumblr.com/, *or* http://www.livejournal.com/.

5-1: Downloading and Installing the ScribeFire Extension

To get started with the process of installing any Firefox extension, you have to first find and download one. To do this, go to the Firefox **Tools** menu, and select **Add-ons**. The Add-ons Manager tab will then appear, showing you the extensions, themes, and plug-ins you already have installed. To add the ScribeFire extension, make sure that the **Get Add-ons** tab is selected from the list on the left side of the window. Firefox will display some Featured Add-ons and other recommendations that you can check out or ignore as you please.

ScribeFire isn't one of Firefox's recommendations as I write this, and chances are that it won't be when you open the Add-ons tab either. This being the case, just do a search for *scribefire* in the search box (Figure 5-14). Once you find it (listed as *ScribeFire Next*), click the **Install** button. A download indicator will then appear.

Figure 5-14: Adding extensions in Firefox

Once the installation process is complete, a message will appear in the Add-ons Manager tab prompting you to restart Firefox. To do this, click the **Restart now** link at the top of the ScribeFire item (Figure 5-15).

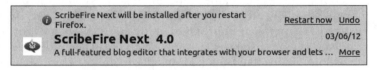

Figure 5-15: A message appears telling you to restart Firefox after the installation is complete.

5-2: Setting Up the ScribeFire Extension

When Firefox first starts up after you've installed the ScribeFire extension, click **Tools ▶ ScribeFire,** and ScribeFire will appear as a resizable pane in the lower half of your current Firefox window. A message will also pop up in a white bubble with instructions on how to add a blog. Follow the instructions to get it working with your blog.

Email with Thunderbird

Thunderbird (Figure 5-16) is Ubuntu's default email application. It is very straightforward to use, and it includes most of the most important email functions you've come to expect, such as junk mail filters. In fact, it's somewhat similar to Windows Mail in terms of appearance and handling. The fact that Thunderbird is also available in both Mac and Windows versions means that you may already be familiar with it.

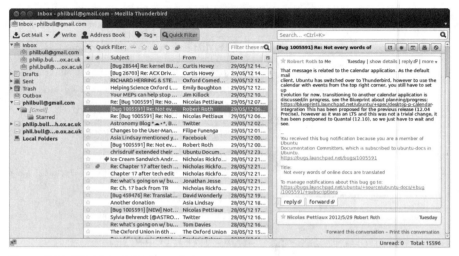

Figure 5-16: The Thunderbird email client

To open Thunderbird, bring up the Dash and search for it. When it starts up, you'll see a blue bird icon appear in the Launcher. If you'd like to keep it there so you have easy access to your email, right-click the icon and choose Lock to Launcher from the menu that pops up.

When Thunderbird starts for the first time, you'll be greeted with a Mail Account Setup window, which asks for a few basic details about your email account. Enter your name, your email address, and the password for your email account and click **Continue** to proceed. Now, exactly what happens when you enter your information in this window will be quite specific to your individual circumstances. If you have an email account with one of the big email providers, like Gmail, Hotmail, or Yahoo!, Thunderbird will automatically set up your email account with the minimum of fuss, updating the Mail Account Setup screen with only a couple of additional questions. If you use a lesser-known provider, such as your workplace's Exchange email server, however, you'll have to enter a few more details to get things up and running. Fortunately, Thunderbird is one of the most popular email applications out there, so most email providers will have detailed instructions on how to get it working posted somewhere on their website.

Once you've entered the details demanded of you, or followed the instructions of your email service provider, click **Create Account**. Thunderbird will start updating, checking your email account for new messages, and so forth. You'll notice that a few email-related folders appear in the bar on the left side of the screen, such as an Inbox and Sent Mail and Drafts folders. From here on, it's pretty much business as usual; you can do the same things that you'd do with any other email client. From the toolbar at the top of the Thunderbird window, you can click **Get Mail** to retrieve any unread messages from your email provider or click **Write** to start composing a new message. There's also an Address Book for managing your contacts and a handy search feature that you can use to find messages. As I mentioned, Thunderbird has a lot of other features; going into them all here would be somewhat time-consuming, so I'll leave it to you to explore for yourself. You might like to check out Thunderbird's excellent help and support website, which can be found at *http://support.mozillamessaging.com/*. In addition to troubleshooting advice, it has a number of guides to help you get started and information about everything that Thunderbird is capable of.

The Messaging Menu

Before we move on to look at some of the other Internet apps that come with Ubuntu, it's worth showing off a cute little feature that ties together a number of communication-related apps into one neat interface. See the envelope icon toward the right end of the panel at the top of the screen? This is the Messaging Menu (Figure 5-17). Click it, and you'll find entries for email, chat, and "broadcast," which refers to social media and microblogging services like Twitter and Facebook. You can use the Messaging Menu to do all sorts of things—compose a new email, start a chat, update your Twitter status. In short, use it for anything to do with communicating with the outside world. You'll find out more about the chat and broadcast options shortly, but for now, let's take a look at how the Messaging Menu handles email.

If Thunderbird is closed, you can start it up by opening the Messaging Menu and clicking Mail. As long as

Figure 5-17: The Messaging Menu, accessed by clicking the envelope icon

Thunderbird is running, the Messaging Menu will keep tabs on the current state of your email account. When you receive a new email, the envelope icon on the top panel will change color from white to blue. When this happens, click the envelope to display the Messaging Menu, and you'll find a summary of how many new emails you have at the bottom of the menu. This is especially handy if you have multiple email accounts; a breakdown of how many new emails you have in each account will be shown, and clicking the menu item for an account will bring up the new emails in Thunderbird. The Messaging Menu also has shortcuts so that you can quickly access your list of contacts or compose a new email. All in all, very convenient, as I'm sure you'll agree.

Chatting with Your Friends via Empathy

Email is an extremely useful tool, but there's often quite a delay between sending a message and getting a response. What if you just fancy a quick chat? That's where *instant messaging (IM)* comes in. If you're not familiar with the concept, all you do is find your friend on an IM network and type a short message to him. Your message will show up on his screen in the blink of an eye. He can then reply to it, and you receive the reply just as quickly. So it continues, until you say goodbye and disconnect from the network.

There are lots of different IM networks out there, such as AIM, Google Chat, MSN/Windows Live, and Yahoo! Messenger. You can usually talk only to those people who are using the same network as you, and you'll need an *IM client* application to connect to any of them. Ubuntu comes preinstalled with a fully featured IM client called Empathy, which has the ability to connect to multiple networks at once.

Starting a Chat

For this section, I'm going to assume that you already have a user account on an instant messaging network. If you don't, you'll need to go to the network's website and sign up (most of them are free). With your account details ready, let's get Empathy connected to your chosen network.

1. Open the Messaging Menu by clicking the envelope icon on the top panel and then click **Chat**. The Empathy Accounts window will open.
2. Change your name and nickname if you like and then click **Connect**.
3. You'll be taken to the Messaging and VoIP Accounts window, which will tell you that it's searching for people nearby. Ignore this for now, and click the + button underneath the list on the left side of the window.
4. Select your IM network from the drop-down list at the top of the window that opens and then enter your account details (Figure 5-18). You'll normally need to enter at least your username and password.

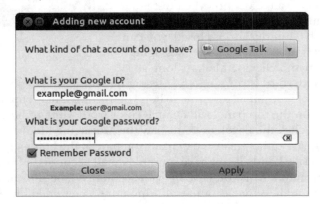

Figure 5-18: Entering your instant messaging account details

5. Click **Apply** to finish up.

6. Empathy will attempt to connect to your IM network. If it's successful, your contacts will appear in the Contact List window, and a few other options will appear in the Messaging and VoIP Accounts window. You don't have to do anything further from here—you're now fully connected. If Empathy is not successful in making a connection, it will tell you so by displaying a message in a colored bar at the top of the window. A number of things could have gone wrong, but the most common issue is an incorrectly entered username or password, so click **Edit Connection Parameters** and try entering your details again.

Your account should now be set up and ready to go, so let's take it for a test run. If someone is online and available to chat, she'll have a green speech bubble icon next to her name. Double-click her name to start up a conversation. A new window will appear—type a message into the box at the bottom of the window and then press ENTER to send it (see Figure 5-19 for an example). Your messages, and those of your friend, will be displayed in the main part of the conversation screen. Ending a conversation is easy too—just close the conversation window.

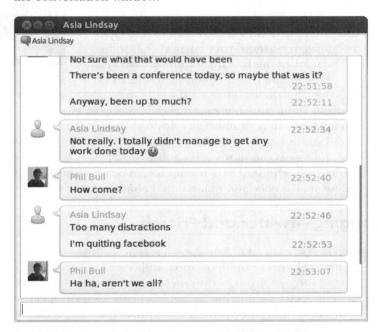

Figure 5-19: Chatting with friends using the Empathy IM client

It's okay to close the Contact List window at any point; you'll remain logged in to the IM service, so you'll still be able to send and receive chat messages. If you want to start a new chat with someone, however, you'll need to have the Contact List in front of you before you can do anything. To bring it up again, open the Messaging Menu and click **Chat**. The Contact List will reappear, and you can start a new chat by double-clicking a contact's name, as before. This is also how to open up Empathy when you first log in to Ubuntu. Unlike some chat applications, Empathy does not start automatically when you log in, so you need to start it manually by selecting **Chat** from the Messaging Menu.

I've only scratched the surface here. Empathy has lots of other features that you might want to try: You can send pictures and files to people, make phone and video calls, broadcast your location using *geotagging*, and even display your desktop on someone else's computer screen. Explaining all of this would probably take a whole chapter on its own, so instead I'm going to point you toward Empathy's user guide, which should give you the lowdown on what else you can do and how you can do it. In any Empathy window, select **Help ▸ Contents**, wait a few seconds for the help window to pop up, and then look through the list of topics until you find something relevant.

Telling People When You Don't Want to Chat

Chatting is great, but very few people have the stamina (or the spare time) to do it all day long. It can be annoying if people try to start conversations with you while you're busy. Fortunately, there's an easy way to let everyone know that you don't want to be disturbed. Open the Messaging Menu. Your current chat status will be marked out by a small white circle at the top of the menu. If you're connected to an IM network, the circle will be next to the green Available status, which means that other people

Figure 5-20: Changing your instant messaging status

can tell that you're online. Click any one of the other items to choose a different status (Away or Busy, for example) from the menu (Figure 5-20). Depending on the status you choose, other people either will be told that you're busy when they try to start a chat or won't be able to see that you're online at all. Peace and quiet, only a couple of clicks away.

Microblogging—Twitter and Friends

Blogging (writing an online diary/journal) is now a well-established Internet pastime. There are millions upon millions of blogs out there covering all sorts of subjects, from astronomy to economics to fluffy kittens. The quality of content varies wildly, but for the most part, blog entries are typical newspaper-opinion-column types of pieces. So, what if you had a blog where you were forced to write everything you wanted to say in less than 140 characters? That's the idea behind microblogging: making frequent, very short, bulletin-like posts.

Twitter is the most well-known microblogging website (*http://www.twitter .com/*). People find all sorts of uses for Twitter: You can let your friends know what you're up to at the moment, receive breaking news, discuss popular topics with other users, write posts using your mobile phone . . . the list goes on. I recently followed a Twitter conversation among a few of my friends who were watching a live football game. They sent messages every time something exciting happened, so I was able to follow the action textually, within seconds of it happening. News travels fast on Twitter.

Perhaps it's the sort of thing you need to try to appreciate, so if you don't have an account already, follow the instructions on the Twitter home page to sign up for one. Once you've done that, take a look around the website to see how things work. The basic idea is that you post messages (*tweets*) for your *followers* to see. People can choose to follow you by clicking a button when they view your user profile. You can choose to follow other people too— when you do this, all of their tweets will be displayed on your Twitter home page for you to read. Most people follow a few people and typically have a handful of followers themselves, but there are no restrictions on how many of each you can have.

Ubuntu's portal to the world of microblogging is called Gwibber. Let's get it set up so you can see what it can do:

1. Open the Messaging Menu by clicking the envelope icon on the top panel and, since this is the first time you've done this, select Setup Broadcast Account. The Broadcast Accounts window will come up, asking what sort of account you'd like to add.

2. Several types of accounts are available, but I'll use Twitter in this example. Select **Twitter** from the drop-down list and click the **Add** button just below it.

3. A Twitter account screen, like the one in Figure 5-21, will appear. Click **Authorize** and then enter your Twitter username and password in the window that appears.

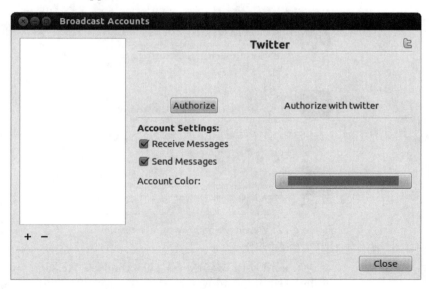

Figure 5-21: Entering your Twitter account details

4. Click **Authorize App** in that same window, and, assuming you entered your details correctly, you will be returned to the Broadcast Accounts window. There a brief message will tell you that your account has been authorized.

5. A new account will be displayed in the list on the left side of the Gwibber Accounts window. Click **Close** to finish adding accounts.

Now it's time to get microblogging! Click the indicator applet (the envelope icon) and select **Broadcast** from the list that pops up. The Gwibber window will appear and should look something like the one in Figure 5-22. Tweets from other users are shown in the main pane. If there's nothing in there, you probably need to go to the Twitter site and start "following" some people—just click the **Follow** button on their profile page, and any posts they make will turn up for you to read in Gwibber.

Figure 5-22: Viewing recent tweets in the main Gwibber window

To send your own tweets, click the New Message button in the top right of the Gwibber window (shown in Figure 5-23) and type something into the message box at the bottom of the window: `Ubuntu is awesome`, for example.

You're allowed a maximum of 140 characters per tweet, and the number of characters you have remaining is displayed in the bottom right of the box. When you're happy with what you've written, click **Send** to post the message for everyone to see. You can also send tweets using the Messaging Menu by clicking the Update Status item. Do this as often as you like; you can tweet away all day!

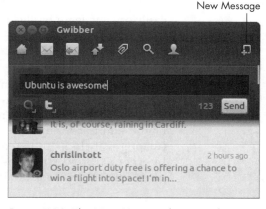

Figure 5-23: The New Message button in the Gwibber window

Twitter isn't solely a broadcast medium, and you can converse with other users in several ways. Move the mouse over a message in the main pane, and a colored icon (a *t* for Twitter) will appear inside it, at the top right of the message. Click it and select **Reply** from the menu that pops up, and the message box will appear containing that person's username with an @ sign in front of it (Figure 5-24). This is how you reply to someone else's tweet (sometimes called an "at-reply" because the @ symbol is used). Just type your message as normal, but after the other person's username.

There are a few other options to choose from in the menu that appears when you click the colored icon (Figure 5-25). *Retweet* is an interesting one—click it, and you'll post a copy of the message for all your friends/followers to see. This is how Twitter users share links and spread news throughout the network. It's often the case that you hear about something cool from the friend of a friend of a friend, all thanks to these retweets.

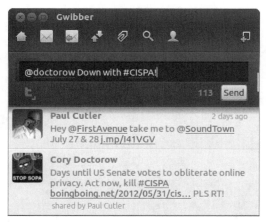

Figure 5-24: Replying to a tweet

Figure 5-25: Spreading interesting tweets using the Retweet option

If you're finished with Gwibber for now, just close the window. You can easily open it again by clicking the envelope icon, as you did earlier.

Other Internet Applications

What I've covered thus far in terms of Internet applications is just the tip of the iceberg (might as well use that worn-out phrase before there aren't any icebergs left, right?). There are still more Internet applications that you might want to consider downloading and installing after you've completed Chapter 6, including Liferea (a stand-alone RSS feed reader) and Miro (an Internet TV browser). If this sounds enticing, get those fingers of yours flipping—the mother lode awaits!

6

ROUNDING OUT THE BIRD

Downloading, Installing, and Updating Programs the Easy Way

Ubuntu has a lot of useful apps installed right from the get-go—"out of the box," as it were. You've got a web browser, an email client, a full office suite, a music player, solitaire. . . . What more could you want? Well, no matter how much is crammed into the default install, it's always good to have options. And Ubuntu is all about options.

Software installation works differently on Ubuntu than what you're probably used to. On Windows, you might have to root around on a website to find an *.exe* file to download or go to a store and buy a CD with the software on it. You'd then run the installer and click through a seemingly endless procession of options and questions before it decides to start installing your new application. On Mac OS, you might have to do something similar, although perhaps with a little less hassle.

Ubuntu, on the other hand, has the *Software Center*, a veritable one-stop shop for all of your software needs. No need to hunt around online for a download or wait for an install CD to arrive in the mail. No need to tell some snooty installer your shoe size and favorite color either. No, the Software

Center does it all for you, with a minimum of fuss. In many ways, it's like the "app store" on a smartphone, where you can get the latest and greatest apps with little more than a click.

The engine behind this, called *Advanced Package Tool (APT)*, allows you to easily download, install, update, and remove software packaged in DEB archives, or *packages*.

APT is a pretty foolproof way of installing programs; nothing will go missing, since APT automatically downloads and installs any files that the main application you are installing requires to run. Tracking down such files, called *dependencies*, used to be a significant headache for most Linux users. The painful quest of finding and then installing this file or that, as well as any dependencies that those files themselves might have, has led to the missing dependency problem being referred to as "dependency hell." APT makes that pretty much a thing of the past.

So, where does APT find all these files and applications? Well, the packages that APT searches for, downloads, and installs are located in a set of specific repositories. These *repositories* are online servers on which a great number of applications, support files, and more are stored for use with your system. All of the files that originally came bundled with your system, including the system (kernel) itself and updates, when available, are stored there too.

The one thing about APT that some people, especially beginners, might consider a problem is that it is a command-driven application. This means you control it by typing commands in a command Terminal. That's where the Software Center comes in—it's a *frontend* to APT. Broadly, this means that the Software Center controls APT, running all of the commands needed to install software in the background, without you needing to worry about them. Neat, huh? In this chapter, you'll be learning all about the Software Center, as well as a couple of other frontends that you might come across from time to time.

Project 6A: Installing Applications via the Ubuntu Software Center

Being the most graphically satisfying of the frontends, the Software Center is especially useful when it comes to browsing for cool or handy applications. To get a feel for it, click the Launcher icon, which looks like an orange bag with stuff exploding out the top (if you hover your mouse over it, the words *Ubuntu Software Center* will pop up). The window that opens will look similar to Figure 6-1.

It may not be the first thing to catch your eye, but the number at the very bottom of the window tells you just how much stuff there is available to download from the Software Center. As this book went to press, there were 41,091 items—enough to keep anyone busy for quite some time. Thanks to Ubuntu's open source origins, most of those items are completely free to download. That's a lot of software to choose from, at a price you can't argue with. There's also an increasing amount of commercial software available (more on that later).

Figure 6-1: The Ubuntu Software Center

But for now, how on earth are you supposed to wade through the gigantic mound of software that's just been dumped on your doorstep? Fortunately, the Software Center has a few routes open to you. On the left side of the window is a list of categories. If you click any of them, you will jump to a list of all the items available for that category, possibly with more subcategories for you to explore, as in Figure 6-2. Applications that are already installed are marked with a green checkmark over their icons, while those that are not installed display just the plain icon. Each application also has a star rating, telling you how good other users think it is. All in all, it looks and acts very much like an online store—think of it as an Amazon.com for all your Ubuntu software needs.

To see a list of all your installed programs, click the **Installed** button on the toolbar at the top of the window. A list of categories will appear; click any of them to see a list of what's already installed. You will already have seen many of the listed applications before, in the Dash or on the Launcher. Now, take a look at the very bottom of the list of categories. There, you'll find a small button asking if you'd like to show a rather large number of "technical items." Click the button if you like; the screen will update, and, when you open up some of the categories, you'll find a lot more items in the list, most of them unfamiliar. What you're looking at are some of the hundreds of other applications and tools that are installed by default in Ubuntu, ones that you'll likely never use yourself. You see, the Software Center isn't just a way of getting your hands on new, exciting apps. It also keeps track of important system software that is necessary for Ubuntu to work—the "technical items" that the button refers to.

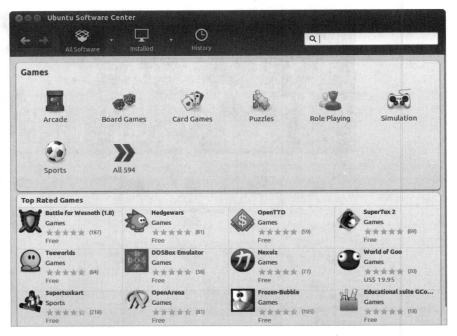

Figure 6-2: Browsing the selection of games available from the Software Center

For most people, there's no need to even think about these technical items, so you can happily hide them away again by clicking the **Hide** button at the bottom of the window. But if you're inclined to tinker with this sort of thing, you need to be aware of a few things before you dive in. Many of these items are actually quite important for the day-to-day running of your system, and removing them might have some negative side effects. There's a program that's responsible for managing your Internet connection, for example; it's probably best to leave that one alone. Also, many of the technical items are needed to make some of the more familiar applications work, like the web browser and email client. Because of the way APT handles these dependencies, removing the technical item will cause everything that depends on in to be removed too. Again, this is probably not what you want. In general, if it's hidden away in the "technical items" list, you probably don't want to uninstall it.

That's quite enough on the inner workings of Ubuntu for now. It's time for something practical. It's time to take the Software Center out for a spin.

6A-1: Selecting Applications for Installation

The Ubuntu Software Center can install multiple applications simultaneously, so to give it a whirl, you can try installing a few interesting applications. Let's start by selecting the very cool and decidedly useful diary/journal application RedNotebook (shown in Figure 6-3). If you're not already there, click the **All Software** button on the toolbar to go back to the Software Center's start screen. To select RedNotebook, click the **Office** category in the list to the left. A rather long list of available applications will appear, sorted by popularity. Hmm . . . RedNotebook doesn't seem to be at the top of the list. Hunting through the whole list for it could get tedious, so let's try sorting it in a different way: From the drop-down box in the top right of the window, choose the **By Name** option. This will put the list into alphabetical order. Scroll down the list of available applications until you start getting to the *R*s and double-click the **RedNotebook** item. A page containing information about RedNotebook will be displayed. You'll see that it comes highly recommended by other users—four and a half stars out of five—and that it's completely free to download. There's also a picture of it in action on the right that you can click to zoom in on. If you scroll farther down the page, you'll find a few more bits of information, followed by a bunch of reviews. "The best diary notebook out there at the moment," says Scott. Sounds good to me. Assuming you too are convinced by the glowing reviews, all you need to do is click **Install** and type your password if prompted. This will start the installation.

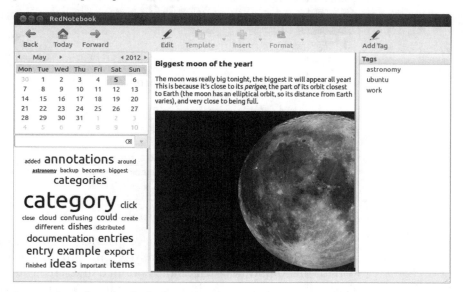

Figure 6-3: RedNotebook, the best journal app out there

A progress indicator will appear on the page while RedNotebook is being downloaded and installed. Once the installation has completed, the page will reload with a green check icon next to the word *Installed* to show that it was added to your computer successfully. If you like, you can add RedNotebook to the Launcher by clicking **Add to Launcher** on the bar that has appeared at the bottom of the window. Otherwise, go to the Dash and search for RedNotebook to start the program. That's all there is to it!

6A-2: Searching for Applications

Next up is Sound Converter (I'll talk more about using this application in Chapter 14). Scrolling through the list of programs can be tedious, so this time, try using the search feature. Click the **All Software** button in the toolbar to go back to the main Software Center screen and then start typing Sound Converter into the search box at the top right. The search results will start to roll in immediately. Sound Converter should appear at the top of the list of results before you've even finished typing, so click it once to select it and then click **Install**. The installation will start as before—but this time, try clicking **All Software** while the program is still installing.

All the installation magic will continue in the background, and you can still browse for other programs. No need to wait!

Finally, let's add a useful utility by the name of Sysinfo (Figure 6-4), a system profiler that can tell you all sorts of things about your computer. Just type `sysinfo` in the search box, click the **Sysinfo** search result that appears, and then click **Install** to add it to the installation queue. It'll be installed as soon as the Software Center has finished dealing with Sound Converter.

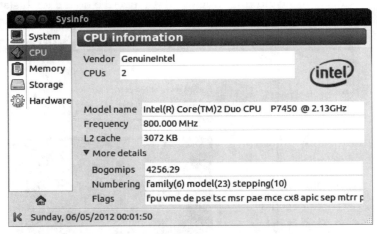

Figure 6-4: Keeping tabs on your system information with Sysinfo

You can run the applications you've installed by going to the Dash and searching for them, as usual. Alternatively, open up the Dash and click the icon for the Applications lens at the bottom of the screen (the one that looks like a ruler and some pencils, shown in Figure 6-5). Then, click **Filter results** and select the category that your chosen application was in from the list on the right. That would be Office for RedNotebook, Media for Sound Converter, and Accessories for Sysinfo. You'll find the application you're looking for in the main part of the window.

Figure 6-5: The icon for the Applications lens

6A-3: Uninstalling Applications

As you can see, installing applications via the Ubuntu Software Center is quite simple. And fortunately, it's just as easy to uninstall them. Navigate to (or search for) the program you want to remove, click it once in the list, and click the **Remove** button that appears. Enter your password again if asked and watch as the program is uninstalled. If you want to uninstall a few programs in one go, you might find it faster to click the **Installed** button on the toolbar and browse through the list of installed applications. For each one that you want to uninstall, select it with a click, and you'll see the Remove button appear again.

6A-4: Commercial vs. Free Software

A relatively recent addition to Ubuntu is the availability of commercial software. Back in the early days, Linux distributions like Ubuntu would include only free software—free as in "no charge for it" but also free as in "freedom." That was the open source way—lots of people sharing the programs that they wrote, usually just for the fun of it, without any hint of a desire to charge for them. For the most part, this is still how it works: The vast majority of the software developers writing programs for Linux have continued to share their apps openly. But more recently, a few distros have started to let in commercial software developers, people who charge for their products. Ubuntu is one of them. The idea is that most people are used to paying for software and aren't so bothered about the open source aspect that they don't like having more apps to choose from. The free apps will always be there, and they'll always be in the majority. But all the same, you can now buy software for Ubuntu.

To see what commercial software is available, click the arrow immediately to the right of the All Software button on the toolbar and select **For Purchase** from the menu that pops up (Figure 6-6). A pretty lengthy list will appear—there are lots of games, a number of ebooks and magazines, and the odd system utility here and there. The list is growing all the time as more and more software developers sign up to distribute their apps through the Software Center. To see what's been added recently, click **All Software** to go back to the main Software Center view and check out the What's New pane in the middle of the window. There's a More button at the top right of the pane that you can click to see a more complete list. You'll find that not all of the software listed is commercial, but a lot of it seems to be.

NOTE   *It might seem a little strange that books and magazines are available through the Software Center, but that's just the way it's been set up. Many of the books that are available are about Linux and computers in general, so the Software Center isn't such a strange place to display them.*

Installing commercial software isn't too different from installing the free stuff. The only difference is the payment step, which is quite similar to what you're used to if you shop online. If you find a commercial app that you like in the list, double-click it to go to its information page. The price will be displayed at the top left of the page in US dollars. Now, click the **Buy** button to the right. You'll be taken to a page asking you to enter your *Ubuntu single sign-on account* details. If you don't have an account already, click the **New Account** button farther down the page and follow the instructions it gives you. Once you have an account, log in and follow the instructions to give your payment details. Once everything has gone through, the download will start, and you'll be the proud owner of a brand new app.

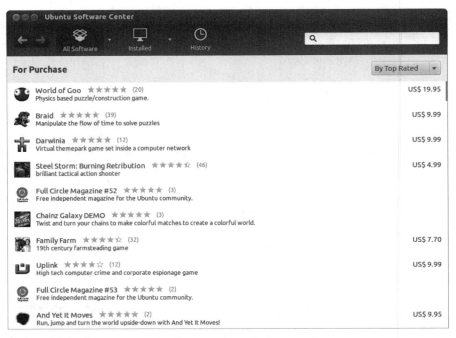

Figure 6-6: Finding commercial software in the Software Center

When you buy a commercial application through the Software Center, the purchase is recorded and kept with the details of your Ubuntu single sign-on account. If you ever need to reinstall Ubuntu, or accidentally uninstall an app that you bought, this means that all is not lost—you can easily reinstall any of your purchased applications. With the Software Center open, move your mouse to the very top of the screen to display the menu bar and click **File ▸ Reinstall Previous Purchases**. If prompted for your single sign-on account details, enter them in the window provided and follow the instructions onscreen. You'll have your paid-for apps back in no time.

Performing System Updates via Update Manager

Another graphical frontend for APT that I'll cover in this chapter is Update Manager, which is used for updating your system. Updates are made available quite regularly and consist of newer versions of packages you already have installed. Most of the time, a newer version will have been released because it fixes some security issue, but updates may also fix problems with software and introduce new features.

The Update Manager will pop up of its own accord when updates are available, so it's probably best just to forget about it until it decides to appear. But just this once, let's be a little more proactive. First of all, make sure that the Software Center isn't currently installing or removing anything; although it doesn't become an issue very often, be aware that you can't use two APT frontends at the same time. Now, open the Dash and search for Update Manager. Once the Update Manager window appears (Figure 6-7), click the **Check** button to make sure the package information is as up-to-date as possible. Strictly, you don't *need* to do this—it automatically checks for updates every day all by itself. But hey, you never know. A small window will pop up detailing its progress, and after a short while, a list of all the available updates will appear in the Update Manager window.

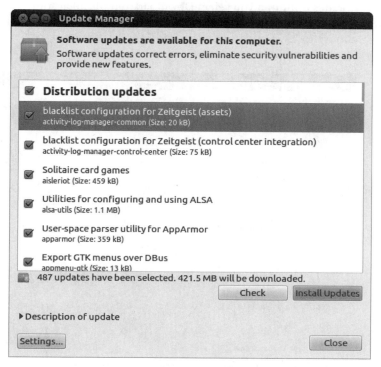

Figure 6-7: Upgrading packages en masse via Update Manager

If you've only recently installed Ubuntu, there might be quite a few updates in the list. You'll see just how many, and how long they will all take to download, just below the list. If there are any applications you don't want to upgrade, you can go through the list and uncheck the box next to their names. But for now, it's safest just to leave all the boxes checked. Either way, once you're ready, click the **Install Updates** button. The selected updates will then be downloaded and installed. Once the installation is complete, the Update Manager window will refresh itself, leaving you with a (hopefully) empty list. And there you have it—a thoroughly up-to-date system. Depending on what you installed, another notification may appear telling you that you will have to restart your system in order for the changes to take effect. If so, it's best to be obedient and reboot (but not before saving all of your work, of course).

How Often Should You Install Updates?

As I already mentioned, Ubuntu will check for updates every day, and the Update Manager window will appear on your desktop if it finds any. If this is happening too often and you find yourself feeling pestered, open the Ubuntu

Software Center and click **Edit ▸ Software Sources**. When the Software Sources window appears, select the **Updates** tab (Figure 6-8) and change the Automatically check for updates option to something else. Weekly updates should be fine if you're finding daily updates a bit too stressful. You'll find a couple of other interesting options there too. Under the When there are security updates option, if you select Download and install automatically, updates will happen silently, without any intervention from you. Alternatively, you can choose to have updates download in the background so they'll be ready to install immediately when the Update Manager pops up.

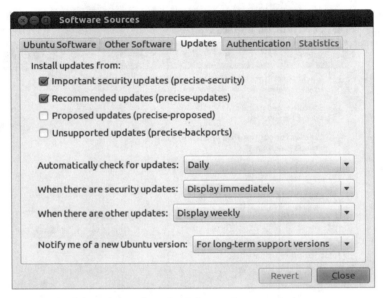

Figure 6-8: The Updates tab in the Software Sources window

If an Update Ruins Your Day . . . or System

Now, I don't want to worry you too much, but one thing about the massive system updates that come around every so often is that afterwards, things sometimes just go all screwy, leaving you with all sorts of regrets and a mouthful of expletives just waiting to be uttered. This happens quite rarely nowadays, but it's still a possibility no matter what operating system you are using. It can happen in Windows, it can happen in Mac OS, and it can happen in Linux. Therefore, it is always a good idea to wait a bit before installing a seemingly major update and to check the user forums first for any disaster stories about a particular update. Leaving a week between noticing an update and installing it should protect you from most mishaps (which again are rare), but there are no guarantees.

NOTE *To decide whether an update is "major," look for updates with* linux- *in their name (linux-generic, for example, as seen in Figure 6-9). These are important system packages and are the ones most likely to cause problems.*

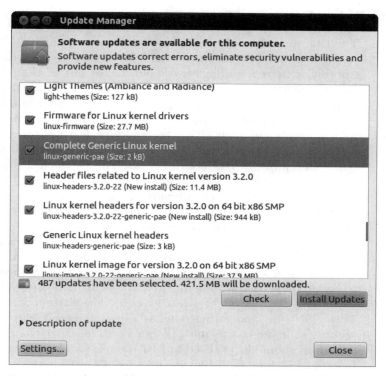

Figure 6-9: Updates with linux- *in their name are usually important system packages.*

If you install an update only to find that your system won't start up again, don't worry. All is not lost. In fact, nothing is lost . . . most likely. Just start up your machine again. If you have a dual-boot system, you will arrive at the GRUB boot menu, just like always. If you're not a dual-booter, you'll have to get to this menu by holding down SHIFT as soon as you start the computer. Don't let go of the SHIFT key until the GRUB menu appears (or Ubuntu starts, in which case you missed your cue, and you'll have to restart the computer and try again). In the GRUB menu, you will see that you seem to have more than one Ubuntu system installed on your hard disk, which is true to some extent. For a short-term fix, you can take advantage of this by traveling back in time to the core system (the Linux kernel) that you had in place before your ill-fated upgrade. Just use your arrow keys to select a kernel that ends in a number lower than the highest (3.2.0-22 rather than 3.2.0-24, for example), press ENTER, and voilá! You are back to the system you have come to know and love. You'll have to do this each time you start up your machine, but at least you will have the chance to back up your valuable files before doing some research on the problem and trying again later.

With all this disaster and recovery talk, I hope I haven't scared you away from the idea of updating your system. After all, chances are great that nothing like this will ever happen to you. Still, it is good to know that if things do go awry, there is no need for panic. You've got backup.

Adding Extra Software Repositories

The Ubuntu software repositories contain more than 40,000 packages—enough to last a lifetime, or so you might think. But as it turns out, a whole world of software is waiting for you outside the official Ubuntu repositories, and it's not much more difficult to reach. Various individuals and companies compile small numbers of packages that are not available in Ubuntu into their own *third-party repositories*. These are typically free to access, if you can find them. All you need to do is tell APT to search for packages in one of these repositories as well as Ubuntu's, and you'll be able to get at the extra software.

Each repository has its own *APT line*. This is similar to a web address but contains extra information about the repository, which APT uses to figure out what sort of packages it contains. You'll need to get the correct APT line from the website of the repository you're trying to add, so let's pick an example to see how it works. Open Firefox and head over to *http://www.getdeb.net/ updates/Ubuntu/all#how_to_install*. GetDeb specializes in making packages for software that hasn't officially made it into Ubuntu yet. There should be some instructions on installing packages from GetDeb in a box at the top of the page, so skip to the second item in the list and find the APT line, which should look something like this: deb http://archive.getdeb.net/ubuntu precise-getdeb apps. This follows the same format as all APT lines: the word deb, followed by a web address, followed by a couple of other words that specify which part of the repository should be checked by APT when it's looking for programs. Highlight the APT line, right-click it, and select **Copy** from the pop-up menu.

While you're in Firefox, you'll also need to grab the repository's *GPG key* (which I'll explain more at the end of this section). It should be linked to from the same website you got the APT line from; in the case of GetDeb, go to *http://archive.getdeb.net/getdeb-archive.key*; when the Opening getdeb-archive.key window appears, select **Save File** and click **OK** to save the key file.

Now that you're in possession of these vital bits of information, adding the repository to your system is pretty straightforward:

1. In the Software Center, click **Edit ▸ Software Sources** and then click the **Other Software** tab in the Software Sources window that appears.

2. Click **Add**. You'll be prompted to enter the APT line, so paste it into the box, and then click **Add Source** (Figure 6-10). When asked for authentication, enter your password and click **Authenticate**. A new entry should appear in the Other Software list.

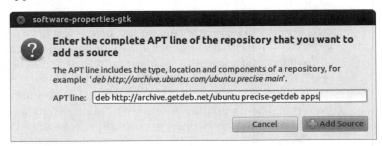

Figure 6-10: Entering the APT line for the GetDeb repository

3. Select the **Authentication** tab and click **Import Key File**. Use the window that appears to find the *.key* file you downloaded earlier. (It's probably in your Downloads folder.)

4. Select the *.key* file by clicking it once and then click **OK**. Check the list of trusted software providers to make sure that the GetDeb Archive Automatic Signing Key is now present, as it is in Figure 6-11.

Figure 6-11: Checking the list of trusted software providers to see whether the GetDeb key is there

5. Close the Software Sources window. APT will start working away in the background, updating its list of packages and so on. This can take a little while, and APT won't tell you when it's finished, so it's probably best to do something else for a while. You can use your computer normally while this is going on. Open the Software Center and click the down arrow immediately to the right of the All Software button. If APT has finished updating, you should find GetDeb in the menu that appears. If it's not there yet, wait a little longer and check again.

6. Now you can search for the program you wanted from the new repository. For instance, try searching for BookWrite, a fun little program to help you write your own novel. It should appear in the search results just like any other application, so you can install it in the usual way.

That was quite a few steps to go through, but it beats driving to your local computer store to buy a new program, eh?

One final note: Remember all that business about authentication and GPG keys? It was related to a security measure that checks whether the packages are from where you think they're from. (In theory, it's possible that someone could hijack a repository and put harmful fake packages in there.) If you don't add the GPG key, the Software Center will refuse to display any of the packages from the repository since it won't trust it. Having the GPG key isn't enough to keep you completely safe from nasty surprises, though. You should always exercise caution when using a third-party (that is, non-Ubuntu) repository; make sure it's trustworthy before you add it.

APT-URL: Installing from Websites

Now that you've added GetDeb to the list of available software repositories, you can take advantage of yet another APT frontend. Go to *http://www.getdeb.net/* and click the **Apps** tab. Peruse the list of programs until you find something agreeable—I chose a time management application called *hamster-applet*—and click **Install this now**, just below its picture. Now you can click a link on a website to install software, without needing to visit the Software Center!

A Launch Application screen will appear with the Ubuntu Software Center option selected—click **OK** and enter your password if prompted. The Software Center will open (if it wasn't open already), and you'll be taken to an information page for the app you selected. From then on, it's business as usual: Click **Install** and wait as the familiar downloading and installing activity carries on. When it's all over, close the Software Center and go find your new application in the Dash. Quick and easy.

Plenty of websites support APT links, but you won't be able to download software from them unless you've added their repository to your computer, as you did with GetDeb. If the link is for a program that is already available in the Ubuntu repositories, however, the software can be installed as normal, without any further messing around in Software Sources.

Project 6B: Installing Software from a PPA—Turtle Arena

Many Ubuntu enthusiasts catch the programming bug and decide to develop their own software. There are all sorts of little programs out there that someone has written to scratch an itch of theirs, and plenty of them are available to you, for free, if you know where to get them. Luckily, most of them can now be found in *personal package archives (PPAs)* on Ubuntu's project website, Launchpad. PPAs are miniature software repositories that are an easy way for people to share their home-brewed software with others (emphasis on the home-brewed—sometimes software from PPAs doesn't work very well). Increasingly, PPAs are also being used by the developers of important software like Firefox to get their latest and greatest out to users. Whether it's official updates or homebrew apps that you're looking for, you can find software in PPAs by visiting *https://launchpad.net/ubuntu/+ppas/* and searching for what you want.

In this example, you'll see how to install Turtle Arena, a ninja battle game that involves a strangely familiar cast of turtles(see Figure 6-12):

1. Type **games** into the search box at *https://launchpad.net/ubuntu/+ppas/* and click **Search** to get underway.

2. Look through the results to find Turtle Arena, and then click that link. You might need to click the Next button once or twice before you see it.

3. Copy the bit that says `ppa:zturtleman/turtlearena-stable`—it's a shortcut that you can use to add this repository, instead of having to use the more cumbersome APT line. (You can still see the APT line by clicking the Technical details about this PPA link, if you're curious.)

4. Open the Software Center, click **Edit ▸ Software Sources**, and then click the **Other Software** tab in the Software Sources window that pops up.

5. Click **Add** and paste the PPA shortcut into the box provided. Enter your password when prompted, and the PPA will be added to the Other Software list.

6. This time, the GPG key will be added automatically, so you can close the Software Sources window now.

7. On returning to the main Software Center window, wait for APT to update its list of packages, just as it did when you added the GetDeb repository. This may take a little while, and it will happen in the background, without telling you when it's finished. To see if APT has finished updating, click the down arrow to the right of the All Software button and see if Turtle Arena is listed.

8. Once the PPA has appeared in the list, you can install Turtle Arena just as you would any other package.

NOTE *If the PPA does not appear in the list, try closing the Software Center and then opening it again. This should give it chance to update the package list and make sure the GPG key has been automatically installed. Alternatively, take a look at "A Software Repository/ PPA That I Added Doesn't Show Up in the Software Center" on page 398 for more advice.*

Figure 6-12: Playing Turtle Arena

This is just an example—PPAs aren't used only by enthusiasts to distribute nostalgic games. Some Ubuntu developers use PPAs to make the latest versions of software available, if they are released before the next version of Ubuntu is due out. Some of these PPAs are provided in an unofficial and untested manner, so you have to watch out when using them—things might not work as expected. Increasingly, however, major software developers are starting to provide their own *official* PPAs from which you can obtain the very latest release of their programs. If a new version of LibreOffice or Firefox comes out, for example, keep your ear to the Ubuntu forums (*http://www.ubuntuforums.org/*) to see whether the developers have made the latest and greatest available through a PPA.

Project 6C: Installing DEB Packages Not Available via the Ubuntu Repositories—Google Earth

As you may recall, the applications you install from the various repositories via the Software Center are in the form of DEB packages. And although it might seem that these repositories contain just about every piece of software imaginable, certain packages, for one reason or another, will never find their way into a repository. Google Earth is one of these packages.

Google Earth, shown in Figure 6-13, is an advanced map/atlas program that lets you explore every place in the world through detailed satellite images, maps, and even 3D renderings of cities. There's a whole cottage industry of people who digitally scour the planet, compiling lists of interesting places that you can visit in Google Earth. They normally bundle these lists into *.kmz* files so that you can download them and explore for yourself. For example, if you visit *http://www.gecoolplaces.com/ancient-constructions.php*, you'll find a list of various ancient landmarks that you can tour, all from the comfort of your armchair.

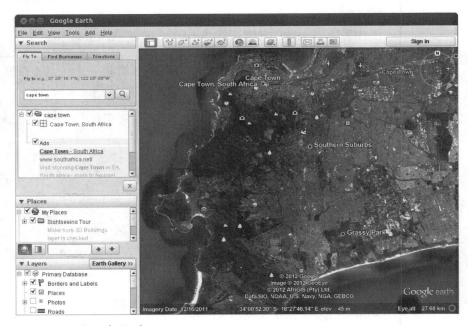

Figure 6-13: Google Earth

Google Earth can do lots more besides, like mapping out local businesses and services, tracking flights, and providing information on public transport. Other, similar applications and websites exist, such as Bing Maps (*http://www .bing.com/maps/*), but Google Earth is by far the most fully featured out there.

Because Google Earth is not available from the Ubuntu repositories, you will need to get it yourself from its website (*http://www.google.com/earth/*). Once there, click the **Download Google Earth** button, which will automatically take you to the download page for Linux versions of Google Earth. On that page, select **32 bit .deb (For Debian/Ubuntu)**, click **Agree and Download**, and then click the **Save File** button in the window that appears.

Once the download is complete, you will find the Google Earth DEB package on your hard disk, probably in your *Downloads* folder. Double-click that package, and the Software Center will open to an information page for Google Earth. Click **Install**, enter your password if prompted, and watch as the installation proceeds as usual. Once Google Earth has been installed, you can run it by bringing up the Dash and searching for it. After a brief wait while the app downloads a few maps, you'll be free to glide around the world with the click of a mouse.

Some computers seem to struggle with Google Earth because of the way it displays 3D graphics. Check out *http://support.google.com/earth/* and search for `ubuntu` if you're having problems—you'll find a few tips there on how to get things up and running smoothly.

7

A TIDY NEST

File and Disc Handling in Ubuntu

No matter which operating system you are using, you have to deal with files. Some people are very organized, placing every file in a logically named folder as soon as that file is saved for the first time. Then there are people like me, who save everything to the desktop until it is so full of junk that they can no longer make out the wallpaper, and only at that point do they start organizing in earnest (if placing all of those files in a single folder called *March17Cleanup* can be called organizing).

Of course, not only do files get stored on your hard disk, but they are also copied to and from CDs, DVDs, external hard disks, flash drives, and other storage media and devices. They are also often saved in archives, which are then compressed to reduce their size, making them easier to send via email or to fit onto removable storage media.

With that introduction, you may have already guessed that in this chapter I will be dealing with file handling in Ubuntu, particularly in relation to the file search in the Dash and the Nautilus file manager, which is at the heart of Ubuntu's file-handling capabilities.

Find It Fast—Searching for Files with the Dash

If you're anything like me, you've been collecting computer files for quite some time now. My laptop is packed full of files, from vacation photos, letters, financial documents and spreadsheets to my music collection, home videos, ebooks, and work documents. It even hosts a bunch of files from my Windows days—bad computer artwork, unfinished poems, and old desktop background pictures. There is a *lot* of stuff—too much stuff, in fact. There's a point at which even the most competent organizational mind has to throw his hands in the air and admit defeat: It's practically impossible to keep so many files organized while at the same time having easy access to them. And that's where the Dash comes in.

As you've already seen in Chapter 3, the Dash has a rather powerful search feature. All you need to do is open the Dash and start typing. Then, within a second or two, search results from the four corners of your computer will start to flood in. After that, you can use lenses and filters to narrow your search results until you find whatever you're looking for. Nothing more to it, right?

Well. . . not *quite*. In addition to the basic search and filtering features I mentioned in Chapter 3, the Dash also has some nifty extras to help you find your files. In this section, I'll take you on a whistle-stop tour of what's on offer, accompanied by a neat trick or two that just might help you find it faster (whatever "it" is). Read on!

Recent Files and Downloads

As you've probably already established, searching is the quickest way to find files. But when you first open the Dash, you'll see that three bands of results are displayed before you've even typed a thing. At the top is a list of applications that you've recently used; forget that for now. In the middle, you'll see a band called *Recent Files*, and you'll see *Downloads* below that. The Recent Files band is, unsurprisingly, a short list of the files you've been working with recently. If you're looking for that letter you wrote yesterday, there's no need to search for it—it'll probably be right there in this list.

The Downloads band is also pretty handy if, like me, you spend quite a bit of time on the Web. It's a list of all of the files that you recently downloaded with your web browser, as explained in Chapter 5. Everything you save off the Web is stored in a special *Downloads* folder for future reference, so there's no need to sit around scratching your head, wondering which website you found that tax form on last week—it's probably somewhere in the *Downloads* folder.

Finding More Elusive Files

What if you can't find the file that you were looking for? There are a number of things to try. The first is to double-check what you are searching for. The search in the Dash isn't case sensitive (you can use uppercase and lowercase letters, and it doesn't care), but it does care about spelling. If the search term you use doesn't appear somewhere in the name of the file, exactly as you typed it, then it won't show up in the search results. Also, be aware that the search doesn't look inside the files—only at the name of the file. Say, for example, that you wrote a word-processed document with the title "Clouds Are Fluffy" and saved it with the filename *clouds.doc*. Searching for *clouds* would find the file, but searching for *fluffy* would not. Where you saved the file also matters: In general, most of the places where you might save files are fine (they should be in your *Home folder*, which you'll learn more about shortly), but if you put it on a removable USB memory stick, it won't show up in the results.

A Closer Look at Lenses and Filters

Sometimes, there are just too many files. No matter what you type into that search box, however specific, you still end up with tens, or even hundreds, of search results. As you've already seen, the Dash comes equipped with a few handy tools to help you wade through the deluge in the form of lenses and filters. In this section, I'll show you how to get the most out of the three file-based lenses—*Files & Folders*, *Music*, and *Videos*.

Files & Folders

To bring up the Files & Folders lens, click the icon that looks like a folded-over sheet of paper at the bottom of the Dash. Click **Filter results**, and a host of new options will appear down the right-hand side of the screen (Figure 7-1). You can filter the search results by *Last modified* (the last time the file was changed), *Type* (what sort of file it is), and *Size* (how much disk space it takes up). Click on any of the options under those headings to narrow the search; you can select several at once, if you like. To deselect an option, just click on it again, or, if you want to remove all of the filters, click the **All** button next to each of the headings.

Figure 7-1: Filtering search results in the Files & Folders lens

For concreteness, let's consider an example of how you might use filters to find a file. Your Uncle Garfield is coming over in a couple of hours, and he absolutely loves lasagna. As luck would have it, you remember writing up a delicious lasagna recipe a couple of months ago, seasoned to perfection following a particularly successful session of experimentation with your herb collection. But where'd that pesky recipe go? You open the Dash, type **recipe**, and, unsurprisingly for a culinary whiz such as yourself, 112 results appear. A quick scan of the first few files reveals pictures of your marvelous creations, a few word-processed documents containing recipes, and a song or two off the Ray Charles album *Ingredients in a Recipe for Soul*. Hmm, not so helpful. So what do you do?

Wading through the results one by one seems like a chore, so click through to the Files & Folders lens and click **Filter results**. You usually write up recipes using a word processor (more on that in Chapter 12), so you know that the recipe must be in a regular document—it's not an audio or video file, at least. The thing to do here is to select Documents from under the Type filter. The search is narrowed, and the photos and songs vanish from the results. There are still 40 results left, though. Since you only came up with the recipe a couple of months back, you click **Last year** under the Last modified filter (meaning that files modified in the last year will be shown). *Et voilá*, there's the lasagna recipe, peeking out at you from a rather more manageable list of only 12 search results. *Bon appetit!*

Music

What with iPods and other audio devices attaining ever higher capacities and online music stores gaining in popularity, large digital music collections have now become the norm. A quick perusal of my own collection reveals 3,206 songs by 202 artists. That's the equivalent of some nine nonstop days of music! No matter how your audiophilia compares to mine, you have to admit that finding that one favorite Christmas song in among the rest of it would be a daunting task without some trusty computerized assistance. You'll learn more about managing your music collection in Chapter 14, using a handy app called Rhythmbox, but in the meantime, the Dash has plenty to offer the music maestro in you.

Click the musical note symbol at the bottom of the Dash, and your music collection will be spread out before you, assuming that you've already transferred it onto the computer (if not, see Chapter 14 to learn how to do this). In exactly the same manner as you work with other parts of the Dash, you can start typing to search. Unlike searching for other types of file, however, the Music search is capable of matching more than just a song's filename—it also looks as the song title, artist name, and album title. What's more, the search results will come back with the album artwork displayed for each song—a nice touch that makes the experience that little bit closer to rooting through physical stacks of records.

When you search for something, the results will be displayed in three bands this time—Songs, Albums, and Available for purchase. The last one has to do with the music store that's built into Ubuntu—more on that in Chapter 14. The first two show only those songs and albums that are currently saved on your computer. From here on, it's pretty similar to what you had with the Files & Folders lens—you can click **Show more results** to see a full list of everything that matches your search terms, and you can click **Filter results** to narrow your search. The only difference is that, this time, you can filter by *Decade* and *Genre* rather than by *Size* and *File* type. Neat, huh?

Videos

It's not just music that gets a lens all to itself in the Dash. There's also a Video lens, with an icon that looks like a film strip with an arrow on it. I'll spare you the details—it works in a very similar manner to the other lenses—except to pick out one rather fun feature. Open up the Dash, bring up the Video lens by clicking its icon, and search for *cat*. If you're connected to the Internet, you'll see a band of results called Online with a number of pictures of some feline or another. What's happening here is that the Dash is searching through a bunch of popular video websites, like YouTube and Vimeo, and bringing the results directly to your screen. If you click **Filter results** and expand the section called *Sources*, you can see a full list of the websites that are being searched. Click one of the videos, and it'll pop up in your web browser, ready to view. Ubuntu Dash: the perfect procrastination tool. Who would have thought?

Nautilus: The Fully Featured File Manager

The Dash is a handy tool for finding your files in a hurry, as you've just seen. It's not so useful if you need to move, collect, or otherwise organize your files, though. It's also light on more advanced features, like accessing files over the network and transferring documents to USB memory sticks and other devices. Fortunately, Ubuntu has something a bit more substantial to handle that sort of thing in the form of Nautilus. Nautilus is the program that creates the file-viewing and organizing interface on your system. You may not have thought of an operating system's file manager as a program before, but in fact, that is what it is. (The Windows file manager is called Windows Explorer.) To take a look at Nautilus, click the **Home folder** icon in the Launcher, as marked out in Figure 7-2.

Home folder ——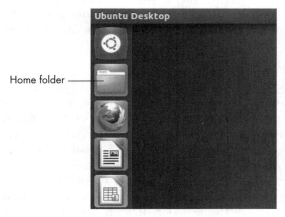

Figure 7-2: The Home folder icon in the Launcher

When Nautilus opens to your Home folder (shown in Figure 7-3), you will find that you can store your files thematically: *Documents*, *Downloads*, *Music*, *Pictures*, *Public*, *Templates*, and *Videos*. Another folder, titled *Desktop*, will show everything you have stored on your desktop (a lot in my case; most likely nothing in yours), if double-clicked. Yet another folder, called *Examples*, contains sample files that give you an idea of what Ubuntu has in store for you.

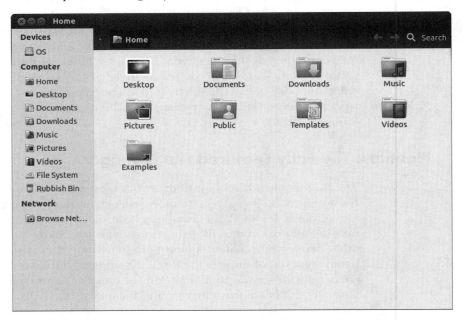

Figure 7-3: The contents of your Home folder as viewed in a Nautilus window

You can create additional folders and files to your heart's content, so this preconfigured state of affairs is sure to change once you get down to really using your system. In fact, you will be making some changes in Chapter 9 that will make everything look a bit more lived in.

The Sidebar

Nautilus has a lot of interesting features that deserve mention, and the most obvious of these is the sidebar, which appears at the left side of the window. The sidebar allows you to view a variety of information via a couple of selectable views. You can make your choices by going to **View ▶ Sidebar** in the menu and choosing either Places or Tree.

The default view in Ubuntu is Places, which is a sort of quick navigation tool. In Places, you will find icons representing various data-storage locations available to your system, such as your Home folder, desktop, full filesystem, any network shares you are connected to (more on that in a moment), and any removable storage media or devices you have in or connected to your system. Clicking any of these icons will show the contents of that location in the right panel of the Nautilus window. The other view is Tree, which provides you with an expandable hierarchical view of your filesystem.

Now You See It; Now You Don't

The sidebar is a handy feature, but sometimes you may prefer to have more space to view the contents of your window and thus want to get rid of the bar temporarily. You can do this easily by going to **View ▸ Sidebar** in the Nautilus menu and then deselecting **Sidebar**. The checkmark next to that entry will disappear, as will the sidebar. (Alternatively, press the F9 key on the keyboard to do the same.) To get the sidebar back, just return to the **View ▸ Sidebar** menu and select **Sidebar** again. The checkmark will reappear, as will the sidebar itself.

If you'd prefer not to hide the sidebar but would still appreciate a little more space, you can change its width instead. Move your mouse over the narrow gray line that marks the boundary between the sidebar and the rest of the window (note that there's also a subtle change in the shade of the background color on either side of the line). When it's hovering exactly over the line, the mouse pointer will change from its usual appearance, a single arrow, to a horizontal pair of arrows pointing in opposite directions. This tells you that the border of the sidebar, the thin gray line, can be dragged in order to resize the sidebar. Getting the pointer directly over the line can be a little frustrating, in that it might take a few goes to get the double arrow to appear, but once it does, click and drag to resize the sidebar.

File Handling in Nautilus

Since Nautilus is primarily a file manager, it only makes sense to get down to the business of using it at that level. Of course, most folks who use computers today are already familiar with the basics of drag-and-drop and a few other means of creating folders and copying, cutting, and moving files. But if you're unfamiliar with one way or another of performing these essential procedures, no worries—I'll spell it all out.

Creating, Naming, and Renaming Folders

Creating a folder is a simple enough task, and there are two ways of going about it. The easiest (in my opinion) is to right-click any empty space within a Nautilus window and select **Create Folder** in the pop-up menu that appears. If you prefer using menus over right-clicking empty space, you can instead start things rolling by selecting **File ▸ Create New Folder**.

Regardless of where you made your Create Folder selection, a new folder with the name *Untitled Folder* will appear in the Nautilus window. The name box of the folder will be highlighted and surrounded with a black box, which means you can immediately give that folder a name by simply typing one—nothing to click or do other than that. Press ENTER or click any open space in the Nautilus window to complete the job.

If you later decide that the name you gave your folder needs some tweaking or even a complete revision, you can rename it by right-clicking it and selecting **Rename** in the pop-up menu. Alternatively, you can click the folder once to highlight it and then select **Edit ▸ Rename**. After that, you can type the new name for the folder and then press ENTER, or you can click any open space in the Nautilus window to seal the deal.

Moving Files and Folders

Perhaps the easiest of all file manipulations you can perform in Nautilus is moving a file by means of drag-and-drop. There is another way of moving files and folders, however: cut-and-paste.

The easiest way to cut and paste is to right-click the file (or folder) you want to move and then select **Cut** from the pop-up menu (**Edit ▸ Cut** will also do the trick). At this point, it will seem as if nothing has happened because the file will still be there, but don't worry.

After that, right-click any open space in the folder to which you want to move the file and then select **Paste** in the pop-up menu. The file will disappear from its original location and appear in its new one.

Can you use key combinations to do this? Sure. Follow the directions I just gave, but press CTRL-X to cut and CTRL-V to paste.

Copying Files and Folders

Based on the instructions you just read, you can pretty well imagine how you'll copy files and folders, because copying is essentially a variation on the same theme. Just right-click the file you want to copy, select **Copy** from the pop-up menu, right-click any open space within the target location, and then select **Paste**. Keystroke-wise, that would be CTRL-C to copy and, as before, CTRL-V to paste.

It is also possible to copy folders and files via the wonders of drag-and-drop, though this involves more hands than required for a drag-and-drop move; fortunately, the two you have will do nicely. Just press and hold the CTRL key while you drag the file or folder you want to copy to the target location. Be sure to release the mouse button first and then the CTRL key (releasing in the opposite order will not work), and you will find a copy of the file in its new location and the original still safely where it was.

Navigating in Nautilus

Navigating through your various folders and subfolders in Nautilus is quite straightforward. In fact, all is conceptually pretty much the same as what you are accustomed to in Windows and Mac OS. You can simply move into and out of folders through a combination of double-clicking folders and clicking the Back and Forward buttons.

Browsing with Breadcrumbs in Nautilus

In addition to the hierarchical view option provided in the side pane, another handy feature can make your navigation chores even easier: Nautilus's breadcrumb bar feature. As you wander ever deeper into your forest of folders, Nautilus will leave a trail of breadcrumbs (they look like buttons, actually) in the navigation bar for each folder you opened on the way to the one you are currently viewing.

Say, for example, that you have a folder called *gooseberries* inside a folder called *Dalarna* inside a folder called *SwedeStuff* inside a folder called *NordicStuff*, which itself is in your Home folder. As you click your way to that *gooseberries* folder, starting by double-clicking the *NordicStuff* folder, Nautilus will display a button for that folder . . . and any folder opened before it. Take a look at Figure 7-4 to see what I mean.

Figure 7-4: Breadcrumb navigation in Nautilus

As you can see, there is a button for each of the folders within the path from your Home folder to your target: *gooseberries*. So what, right? Well, say you want to go back to the *NordicStuff* folder to open a file to grab some text and copy it into a document in the *gooseberries* folder. That sounds like a minor pain, right?

Well, rather than goof around with the Back button, just follow the breadcrumbs! Simply click the **NordicStuff** breadcrumb button, and the contents of that folder will be there before you. Need to go back to *gooseberries*? Just click the **gooseberries** button. Back to *SwedeStuff*, you say? Just click the **SwedeStuff** button. All quite *fantastisk*!

Spelling It Out—Typing File Paths in Nautilus

If you prefer typing to clicking, you will be happy to know that you can navigate to a folder by typing its path. Just click the **Go** menu and select **Location** (keyboard shortcut lovers can press CTRL-L instead). A box will appear in the location bar (Figure 7-5) showing the current location, which, in the case of my berried example, would be /home/rg/NordicStuff/SwedeStuff/Dalarna/gooseberries. You can type the path to your target folder in that box and then press ENTER, after which the contents of the target folder will appear below in the main pane of the Nautilus window.

Figure 7-5: Typing the path to your target folder

Bookmarks Within Nautilus

With all this clicking away to deeply buried subfolders, it is worth mentioning another very handy feature of Nautilus: bookmarks. Yes, Nautilus lets you bookmark folders to which you have navigated. Although you are probably familiar with creating bookmarks for web pages that you frequent, you may be wondering why on Earth you would want to create bookmarks within your filesystem.

Well, imagine that you have a folder you need to use often, but it is even more buried than my *gooseberries* folder in the previous section. Getting there would take an excessive number of mouse clicks, and all that clicking is bound to eventually give you a bad case of carpal tunnel syndrome. Although that is great for your doctor, it is most decidedly not good for you. Instead of maiming yourself, you could click your way to that folder once and then, in the Nautilus window, select **Bookmarks ▸ Add Bookmark**. After that, whenever you want to get back to that buried folder, you can just click the **Bookmarks** menu, and the folder will be right there waiting for you in the drop-down list.

Another handy thing about Nautilus bookmarks is that they also appear in Save As dialogs, such as when you save a LibreOffice document or download a file via Firefox. To use them in any such Save As dialog, just find your bookmark in the list on the left-hand side.

Understanding the Linux Filesystem

With all that path typing, navigating, and bookmarking you've just learned, you should pretty much be able to figure out how to get from here to there in your Home folder. Still, it's probably a good idea to know where your Home folder actually is in the scheme of things, just in case you manage to get yourself really lost someday. To understand this, you should have a basic understanding of the Linux filesystem, which, as you will find, is a bit different from what you were accustomed to in your previous operating system.

Unlike Windows, the Linux filesystem all stems from a single point called *root* and is represented by a solitary forward slash (/). Your own user account folder is located within a subfolder of root called *home*. This is represented as */home* or, to put it into words, the Home folder within root. If your user account were to have the same name as mine, *rg*, the path to that folder would be */home/rg*, or the *rg* folder within *home* within root. Whatever the name of your user account or the names of any other accounts you have on your machine happen to be, just remember that when you are lost, your folder and those of all the other folks with user accounts on your machine are located within the Home folder. If you're a more graphically oriented person, the map in Figure 7-6 should help you.

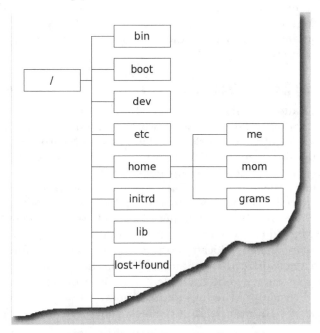

Figure 7-6: The location of your users' folders within the Linux filesystem

What's in All Those Other Folders?

Needless to say, there is more to the Linux filesystem than the root, Home, and user account folders. Several other directories appear at the same level as Home, though for the most part, you shouldn't be mucking around with them unless you know what you're doing. Fortunately, most of these folders are write protected, so you should be fairly well protected from yourself. Still, it is natural to be curious about what those other folders are there for, since . . . well, they're there. So, to satisfy your curiosity a bit, I'll do a little explaining.

In Ubuntu, four folders contain most of the applications on your system. The essential elements of your system are located in */sbin*. Other elements that need to be there such as commands and the like, though they may not be used, are located in */bin*. Most of the applications that you actually think of as applications and use in a hands-on way are located in */usr*. Finally, some add-on applications, such as RealPlayer, install themselves into */opt*.

Three other top-level folders that might be of interest to you are */etc*, */lib*, and */media*. The first of these, */etc*, is the location of all the configuration files on your system. The second, */lib*, is the home of all of the libraries that are required by your system or applications installed on it. These libraries are the Linux equivalent of a Windows *.dll* file. Finally, */media* is where the contents of your various attached external media (such as USB drives and CDs) appear when present.

There are other top-level folders, but their purposes are a bit less straightforward for the average Linux newbie and, to be honest, probably not all that interesting to you at this stage. Anyway, as I mentioned, there is no reason for you to be mucking around with any of these folders for the time being, because you can access the items located within them in different, and much safer, ways.

Using Nautilus as a Network Browser

Another handy Nautilus feature is its ability to function as a network browser. You can, for example, see what networks and shares are available to you on your home or office network by clicking **Browse Network** in the Network section in the sidebar of the Nautilus window or by going to the Go menu and selecting **Network**. Icons for any networks or computers on that network would then appear in the Nautilus window, as in Figure 7-7. From that window, you can double-click your way to a share that you have permission to access, such as the *Shared Documents* folder of a Windows machine or the public folders of a Mac. In case you are wondering what a share is, I'll clear that up for you: A *network share* is a location on a computer, such as a folder, where other users on a network can access and save files. The *Shared Documents* folder on a Windows system is a good example. Other users on a network can copy files from and (usually) write files to the *Shared Documents* folder, whereas they cannot access any other part of the filesystem on that host computer.

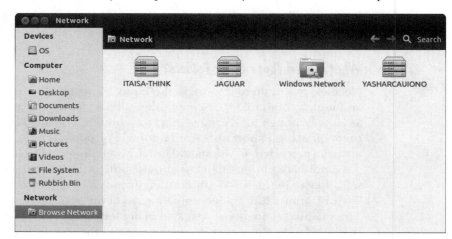

Figure 7-7: Viewing the computers on your network

If the share you are trying to open requires a username and password, you will be asked for those in a new window. Note that, in this case, the username and password you need to enter are those for the computer to which you are trying to connect—not the ones you're using in Ubuntu (unless the usernames and/or passwords happen to be the same, of course). You can then copy files to and from that share as if it were a folder on your own hard disk.

In some cases, especially when trying to access shares on a Mac running OS X, the double-click method may not work. You will not be able to access any share on a particular machine, even if an icon for that machine appears in the Nautilus window. In such cases, double-click the icon for the machine you are trying to access and then, once it's open (to an empty window), select **Go ▸ Location**. A text box will appear in the location bar (just as in Figure 7-5) with the location of the machine you are trying to access already listed.

To that location, add a forward slash (/) followed by the username used on the target machine. For example, if the target machine is called *cowboycats* and the username is *mewtoyou*, the location would be smb://cowboycats/mewtoyou. You can also narrow things down to a particular folder on the machine, as long as you know the path to that folder, by adding to the path you've already typed—smb://cowboycats/mewtoyou/Documents, for example. If you prefer, you can type smb:// and your Mac's IP address, which consists of a set of four numbers separated by dots. In the case of one of my machines, I would type smb://192.168.0.100. (You can find a Mac's IP address by going to the Mac's System Preferences, clicking **Sharing**, and then clicking **Windows Sharing**. The address should appear immediately below the service selection pane.)

NOTE *In case you are wondering, the* smb *at the head of that path stands for* server message block, *but to make things easier (and perhaps more useful in terms of your memory), you can just think of it as being short for* Samba, *which is software used by Unix-based systems (such as Linux and Mac OS X) in order to interact with Windows networks.*

Once you've made your way to the folder you want to browse on the networked machine you've connected to, it might be a good idea to use the bookmark function in Nautilus to bookmark that open share window. You can then easily access that share in the future by choosing the share's name in the Nautilus Bookmarks menu. Pretty cool, no?

Using Nautilus as an FTP Client

Not only does Nautilus allow you to browse and mount shares on local networks, but it can also act as a File Transfer Protocol (FTP) client. FTP is used, for example, when you want to change the files for your website on a remote server. To do this, go to the Connect to Server window (**File ▸ Connect to Server**) and then select **FTP (with login)** for the service type. Type the information provided by your website host and click the **Connect** button. An FTP Network Share icon will appear in the sidebar. Click that icon, type your password (for that account—not the one for your Ubuntu system, unless it happens to be the same) when prompted to do so, and you will be able to view and add to the files you have there.

File and Folder Permissions Within Nautilus

As you make your way in the world of Ubuntu, you will find that occasionally you'll come across files or folders that are in some way locked in terms of your being able to read them, alter them, or both. These readability and alterability states are referred to as *permissions*.

Now, you may be wondering what the point of this permissions business is, so I will give you some examples of how it can be useful. Let's say you have some files that you don't want your spouse or kids to see—some bad poetry or a Christmas shopping list, for example. By denying read permission to those files or to a folder containing those files, you keep anyone else from sneaking a peek unless that person is savvy at changing permissions and has the permissions necessary to change permissions for those files or folders.

As another example, imagine you have a file that you have worked many hours on and have finally completed. To alleviate fears that you might accidentally ruin that file in some way, you could deny yourself write permission. By doing this, you wouldn't be able to save any changes you make to that file. You would be given the Save As option so that you could save a new copy of the file, but if you wanted to change the original file, you would have to change the permissions. When you place such restrictions on a file or folder, a lock emblem appears on the icon for it, as shown in Figure 7-8.

Figure 7-8: Nautilus tells you when permissions restrict your freedom of movement.

Changing File and Folder Permissions in Nautilus

To change file or folder permissions in Nautilus, right-click the file or folder in question and then select **Properties** from the pop-up menu. Once the Properties window opens, click the **Permissions** tab, and you will see who the owner of the file or folder is and what you and others are allowed or not allowed to do with it. As you can see in Figure 7-9, the options for folders and files are slightly different.

You might find this permissions business a bit confusing, but it is really quite simple. Permissions can be granted or denied to the *owner* of the file or folder (you), to a specified *group*, or to *others* (everybody else). Traditionally, these permissions are referred to as follows:

Read   Permission to view the contents of a file or folder

Write   Permission to alter the contents of a file or folder

Execute   Permission to run a program or script (or, for folders, permission to browse the files in the folder)

Nautilus has tried to spell things out a bit more, as you can see in Figure 7-9. In general, however, you needn't worry all that much about setting permissions for your own files, because you are really the only one who has access to your user account. One possible exception you might run into is when you transfer files from CD to your hard disk. In this case, the files might be write protected, meaning you cannot alter the files until you change the permissions for them. You can change the permissions of such files in order to allow yourself to alter them by going to the **Owner** section of the Properties window and selecting **Read and write** in the menu next to the word *Access* (for files) or **Create and delete files** in the menu next to the words *File access* (for folders). Once you are done, click the **Close** button, and you'll be on your way.

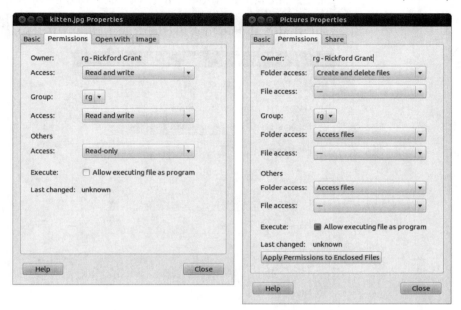

Figure 7-9: Changing permissions in a Nautilus Properties window for files (left) and folders (right)

Keeping Your Home Folder Private

Another exception to my you-don't-need-to-worry-about-permissions claim, and a potentially important one at that, is the state of permissions for your Home folder, particularly when other people have user accounts on your machine. In Ubuntu, when someone logs in to his own account on your computer, he can click his way to your user folder and view its contents.

To remedy this situation—and thus protect the sanctity of your Home folder, the privacy of its contents, and the peace of mind of its owner (you)—you can change the permissions of your Home folder. Here's what you need to do:

1. Open a Nautilus window and then click **File System** in the sidebar. The contents of your entire hard disk will appear in the right pane of the Nautilus window.

2. Look for and then double-click the folder named **home**. When the contents of the Home folder you just clicked appear in the right pane, there should be only one folder there—your own folder, which will have the same name as your own username. For example, mine, as I mentioned earlier, is named *rg*.

3. Right-click your folder and then select **Properties** in the pop-up menu.

4. In the *username* Properties window (mine says *rg Properties*), click the **Permissions** tab.

5. In the Permissions tab, go down to the Group and Others sections and select **None** in the drop-down menus next to the words *Folder access*. Be sure to do this in both the Group and Others sections. When you're done, your window should look like mine in Figure 7-10. If so, click **Close**.

Figure 7-10: Changing the permissions of a Home folder for privacy

Reading Data CDs and DVDs

Dealing with data CDs and DVDs in Ubuntu is quite simple, because everything is automatic. To read a CD or DVD with data on it, rather than music or video, place the disc in your drive, and a CD or DVD icon (they look the same) will automatically appear at the bottom of the Launcher and in the Nautilus sidebar. You can click once on the icon, after which the disc's contents will appear in Nautilus. Then you can copy files from the CD or DVD to your hard disk using standard drag-and-drop or copy-and-paste procedures.

When you want to remove the CD or DVD, just right-click the icon for that disc in the sidebar and then select **Eject** in the pop-up menu. The disc will be ejected automatically.

Burning Data CDs and DVDs

Burning data CDs and DVDs in Ubuntu is extremely easy, as long as you have a CD or DVD burner hooked up to your computer! All you have to do is place a blank CD-Recordable (CD-R) or DVD (DVD-RW, DVD-R, and DVD+RW are all supported) in your drive, making sure to select a media format supported by your drive, and a Blank Disc window will appear asking what you want to do. Click **OK** to open Nautilus's CD/DVD Creator window, which as you no doubt notice looks pretty similar to other Nautilus windows, save for the options and buttons at the top of the window (Figure 7-11).

Once the CD/DVD Creator window is open, copying the files you want to burn to disc is pretty much a simple drag-and-drop. Just open a new Nautilus window and drag the files you want to burn to disc from that window to the CD/DVD Creator window.

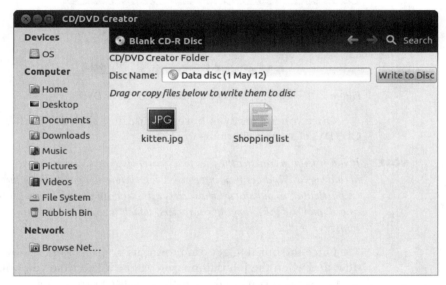

Figure 7-11: A Nautilus CD/DVD Creator window with files ready to be burned to disc

If you prefer to do things in a decidedly Windows-esque fashion, you can select the files you want to transfer to disc by clicking each file once while holding down the CTRL key for multiple selections. If you want to select multiple consecutive files, you can click the first file in the group, press and hold SHIFT, and then click the last file in the group, automatically selecting all the files in between. Once you've made your selections, release the CTRL or SHIFT key, right-click any of the highlighted files, and select **Copy** in the pop-up menu. After that, go back to the CD/DVD Creator window, right-click any open space, and then select **Paste** in the pop-up menu.

It is worth mentioning that the files you copy to the CD/DVD Creator window are not actually copied. Instead, what you see in the CD/DVD Creator window are essentially links pointing to the original files in their original locations. Thus, if you move one of the files from its original location before burning the contents of the CD/DVD Creator window to disc, the link won't work anymore, and the file won't be copied onto the disc. This isn't too much of a problem, since all of the other files will be put onto the disc correctly, but it is something to be aware of.

Once you have copied all the files you want to burn to disc, click the **Write to Disc** button, after which a window (shown in Figure 7-12) will appear. It tells you, among other things, how many megabytes of files you can still add to the disc (click **Cancel** to go back and add more files if you want). Most people are happy to accept the default options (which are pretty sensible), so all that remains is to choose a more interesting name for the disc. However, if you'd rather not leave anything to chance, you can adjust the speed at which your disc will be burned (a slower speed means fewer chances for errors) by clicking **Properties** and picking a slower speed.

Figure 7-12: Setting options before burning a CD or DVD

Once you are ready to burn the disc, just click the **Burn** button, and the CD/DVD Creator will do its work.

NOTE   *If you intend to transfer the files to a Windows system, make sure you rename your files according to Windows naming conventions before you get down to the actual burning. In particular, avoid special characters and diacritics (such as umlauts and accents), and do not use the following characters, which are reserved for Windows system functions: / : ? * ' < > | .*

Once the burning gets underway, its progress will be shown in a new window, and when the job is done, you will be asked what you would like to do next. Assuming you are done with your disc burning for the day, click **Eject** and then **Close**.

In case you are wondering, the discs you burn in Linux *will* be readable in other operating systems.

Dealing with CD-RWs

CD-RWs are pretty much like CD-Rs except that they can be erased and then written to again. They are also quite a bit more expensive than CD-Rs and, generally, cannot handle faster burning speeds.

Using CD-RWs is much like working with CD-Rs. If the disc is blank, there is no difference in the process at all. And, even if the CD-RW already has data on it that you want to replace with something else, the process is only slightly different.

One of these differences is that Nautilus will treat your CD-RW as a regular data disc rather than as a blank one. This means that when you pop your disc into the drive, a regular Nautilus window, rather than a CD/DVD Creator window, will automatically open.

To write to the disc, you will need to manually switch from the Nautilus window to a CD/DVD Creator window, which is easily done by clicking **Go ▸ Location** and typing `burn:///` into the location bar (followed by ENTER). Once you've done this, the window will become a CD/DVD Creator window. Now drag the files you want to burn to CD to that window; once you are ready to burn, click the **Write to Disc** button.

As is the case with regular CD-Rs or DVDs, a CD/DVD Creator window will appear. When you click the **Burn** button in that window with a used CD-RW in the drive, however, something slightly different happens. At this point, a new window will appear telling you that the disc seems to have files already written on it. Click the **Blank Disc** button in that window, and the CD/DVD Creator will erase the files already on the CD-RW and replace them with the new ones that you dragged to the CD/DVD Creator window. Not bad at all, eh?

Burning ISO Images to Disc

When you download Ubuntu or other Linux distributions from the Internet, you usually download them in the form of one or more disc images, which are commonly referred to as *ISOs* because such files end in the *.iso* extension. An ISO is an image of a CD's file contents, which means that it is the CD minus the media itself. To put it another way, if CDs had souls, the ISO would be the soul of a CD; take away the CD's metal and plastic, and the remaining data would be an ISO.

It is of course impossible to download a physical CD over the Internet, but the bodiless ISOs are the next best thing. For example, to get a working copy of Ubuntu from the Web, you usually need to download an ISO, which you then burn onto a blank CD in order to give the images their bodies back, so to speak. In the process, you create the working installation disc that you need to install Ubuntu.

Fortunately, burning an ISO to disc is a pretty simple chore. Just open a Nautilus window and locate the icon for the ISO file you want to burn to disc. Right-click the icon, and in the pop-up menu that appears, select **Write to Disc**. Once you do this, the CD/DVD Creator window will appear; just click the **Burn** button, and you'll be on your way.

Creating Your Own ISO Images

While on the topic of ISOs, it is good to know that you can create ISOs of your own. While you're probably not going around creating your own Linux distros, you might come up with a set of files that you need to repeatedly burn to disc now or in the future, for example. To create your own ISO, follow the normal process for creating a data CD, but when the CD/DVD Creator window (Figure 7-12) appears, select **Image File** from the drop-down menu and then click **Properties**. This will open a new window asking for a filename for your new disc image. Give it a name, click **Close**, and hit the **Create Image** button. In a very short time, you will have an ISO of your own creation.

Burning Multisession CDs

If you are coming from the Windows environment, you may be familiar with multisession CDs. These are CDs on which data is added one session at a time. For example, you burn a few files to disc today and add a few more to the disc tomorrow and a few more files the day after that. Each time you burn additional files to the same disc, you are adding a session, which explains the name *multisession*. You can basically think of the CDs as working like floppy disks (albeit with a lot more storage capacity).

Nautilus has basic support for multisession discs, but let's try something a little more specialized this time: Brasero, which is a more fully featured application that you can use for all of your disc-burning chores.

You can run Brasero by searching for Brasero Disc Burner in the Dash. In the main Brasero window that then opens, click the **Data project** button.

To burn the first session to a CD, drag the files you want to burn from Nautilus into the empty Brasero window (Figure 7-13) or click the **Add** button (which looks like a plus sign) on the Brasero toolbar to browse for files manually.

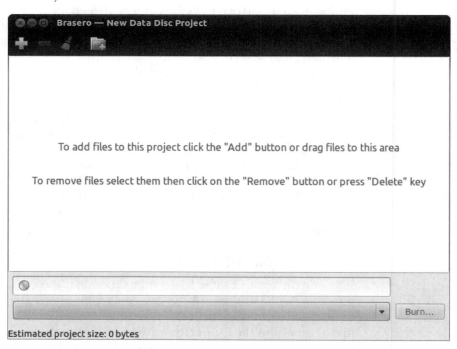

Figure 7-13: Using Brasero to create multisession discs

When you have all the files in place that you want to burn, put a blank disc into the drive, choose a name for the disc using the box at the bottom of the screen, and click the **Burn** button. A Properties window will appear. In that window, check the **Leave the disc open to add other files later** box. (This is the step that sets up a multisession disc.) Once you've done that, click **Burn** to start the burning process. Brasero will eject the disc when the burn is complete.

Burning Subsequent Sessions

Adding a new session to a multisession disc in Brasero is similar to the process used for creating the initial session. Here's what you do:

1. Run Brasero and click the **Data project** button.
2. Insert your multisession disc into the drive, and when the drive stops spinning and you've gotten any Nautilus windows for that disc out of the way, click the **Import** button, after which the contents of your previous session will appear in the Brasero window.
3. Add files to the previous session, using either of the methods you used when creating the original session (via drag-and-drop or by selecting and clicking **Add**).
4. When you've added the files you want, click **Burn**. The process from then on out is exactly the same as it was for the first session. To add files in subsequent sessions, just follow the process outlined earlier yet again.

Duplicating CDs and DVDs

Now that you are familiar with Brasero, I'll introduce another of its features: CD/DVD duplication. To duplicate a disc, place it in the drive, start Brasero, and then click the **Disc copy** button. In the window that appears (Figure 7-14), click the **Copy** button.

Brasero will begin copying your disc. When it's done, it will eject the disc and ask you to insert a blank one. A few seconds after you insert the blank disc, Brasero will automatically start writing to it. When the process is complete, the disc will be ejected. Nothing to it.

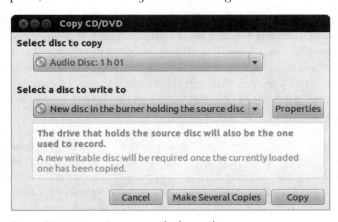

Figure 7-14: Using Brasero to duplicate discs

USB Storage Devices

You may well be familiar with USB devices. Your printer is very likely a USB device, as is your scanner. And although your digital camera is not a USB device in the traditional sense, chances are that every time you connect it to your computer in order to transfer photos, you are doing so via a USB connector. Among the most popular USB devices out there are those used for file storage. These include external hard disks; flash memory card readers; and the tiny, finger-sized devices known as *flash drives* (Figure 7-15). Flash drives are especially popular today and deservedly so: They are inexpensive, handy when you need to transfer large amounts of data, and pretty safe in terms of cross-platform (including Linux) compatibility.

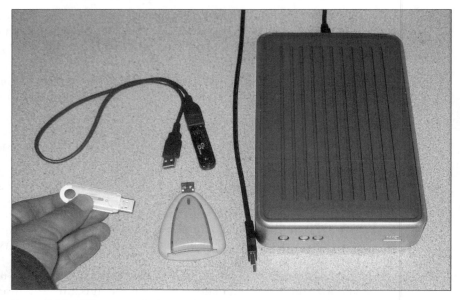

Figure 7-15: USB storage devices

Working with USB storage devices is easy. Just plug the device into one of the USB ports on your computer. The LED on the device will do a bit of blinking while the system reads what's on it, and a few moments later, a Nautilus window will open, revealing the contents of the device. An icon for the USB device will also appear in the sidebar of the Nautilus window and at the bottom of the Launcher. You can then copy files to and from the device using the drag-and-drop or copy-and-paste procedures I mentioned earlier in this chapter.

Once you are done and want to remove the device, right-click its icon in the Launcher or in the Nautilus sidebar and select **Safely Remove Drive** in the pop-up menu. If there is any data that needs to be written to the device, the system will start writing. Once it's complete, the icon for the device will disappear from Nautilus. Make sure that you always safely remove USB drives like this, rather than by simply disconnecting them—otherwise, you risk losing data.

Working with Bluetooth Devices

While we're on the topic of file handling, it is probably a good time to learn how to work with Bluetooth devices. As I mentioned in Chapter 3, if you have a Bluetooth adapter in your machine, either built in or plugged into a USB port, a Bluetooth icon will appear in the right half of the top panel.

Pairing Devices

Before you can transfer files between your Bluetooth devices, you need to pair them. This is how you do it:

1. Before you start, make sure that Bluetooth is turned on for both the computer and the device you want to pair with. For the computer at least, you can do this by clicking the Bluetooth icon on the top panel and checking that *Bluetooth: On* is displayed at the top of the menu that pops up.

2. You should also make sure that the device you want to pair with is set to be *discoverable* or *visible*. This makes it possible for Ubuntu to find it when it scans for nearby Bluetooth devices.

3. Click the Bluetooth icon on the top panel again and select **Set-up New Device**.

4. In the Bluetooth setup wizard that appears, click **Continue**.

5. Ubuntu will then search for Bluetooth devices in the vicinity of your computer. Once it discovers a device, that device will appear in the center pane of the window, as in Figure 7-16. Once the device you want to pair to appears, click it and then click the **Continue** button.

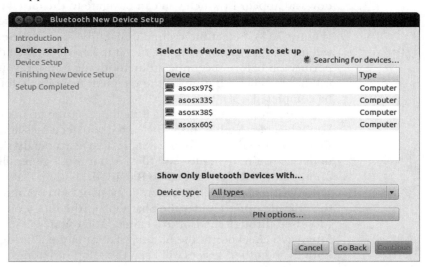

Figure 7-16: Searching and selecting nearby Bluetooth devices in Ubuntu

6. In the next page of the wizard, a personal identification number (PIN) will appear (Figure 7-17). An input window should also appear in the Bluetooth device you're trying to connect to. Input the PIN into that input box.

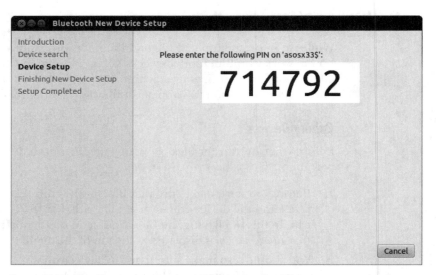

Figure 7-17: The Bluetooth wizard provides you with a PIN to input into the device you're pairing to.

7. Assuming the pairing is successful, the final page of the wizard will then appear. Click **Close** to complete the pairing process.

Sending Files by Bluetooth

To send a file by Bluetooth from your computer to another Bluetooth-capable device, click the Bluetooth panel icon and select **Send Files to Device**. A window will appear in which you can navigate to the target file. Once you have made your selection, click **Select**. The Select Device window will then appear (Figure 7-18). Select the recipient machine and click **Send**. Your machine will then begin transferring the file. If the recipient machine is set up to seek permission before accepting a Bluetooth file transfer, you or the recipient will have to click a button on the recipient machine before the transfer can be completed.

Some devices might need a little more setting up in order to receive files. You'll be able to tell if this is the case if you get a message that says *Unable to find service record* after you press Send. The exact details depend on the type of device you're trying to send files to, but you'll generally be looking for an option on the device to "enable Bluetooth sharing," "allow other devices to send files," or something similar. On a Windows computer, you should find the relevant option under the Share tab of the Bluetooth Settings window (accessed through the Control Panel), and on Mac OS X, the option can be found as a checkbox at the bottom of a list in the Sharing settings window. Phones and other devices will keep the relevant settings in still different locations, so you might need to refer to the manual to find where the correct option is hiding. Once you've enabled Bluetooth file sharing, go back to the File Transfer window on Ubuntu and click **Retry** to try sending the file again.

Figure 7-18: Selecting a Bluetooth device to send files to

Receiving Files by Bluetooth

To receive files via Bluetooth from another Bluetooth-capable device, you have to first set up your computer to allow such transfers. To do this, bring up the Dash and open Personal File Sharing. In the Personal File Sharing Preferences window that appears, check the **Receive files in Downloads folder over Bluetooth** box. For your safety (so that no one can send files to you without your permission), select **Only for set up devices** in the **Accept files** drop-down menu. Your window should then look like that in Figure 7-19. If so, click **Close**. Your machine will automatically receive files sent to it via Bluetooth and save them to the Downloads folder.

Only devices that you have already paired with will be able to send files successfully. To make things a little easier for

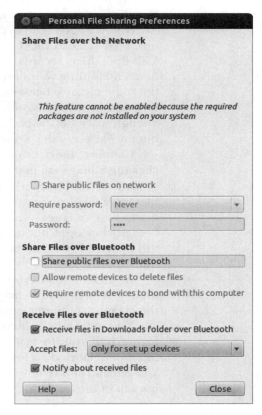

Figure 7-19: Setting up your system to receive files sent from other Bluetooth devices

when you come across new devices, you can allow the other device to do all the hard work of pairing with your computer, rather than having to do it yourself (as described above). Enabling this feature is a simple matter of clicking the Bluetooth icon on the top panel and making sure that the Visible option is checked in the menu that appears. As long as Visible is checked and Bluetooth is turned on, other devices will then be able to pair with your computer without you having to initiate the pairing process. A message will pop up asking for confirmation when this happens and, once paired, the other device will be able to send you files—as simple as that.

Backing Up Your Files

You've worked hard to accumulate all of your files. Hours of typing, hundreds of photos, piles of music CDs—they're all there on the hard disk. So, what happens to them if something goes wrong with your computer? In many cases the answer is, unfortunately, that all of the data is lost forever. To avoid the pain of this experience, you'll want to make regular backups.

Plenty of backup utilities are available, but Ubuntu comes with one installed by default called, simply, Backup. Open the Dash and search for Backup to open it. Since you haven't created any backups yet, you can click **Just show my backup settings** in the window that appears.

Now is a good time to decide what you're going to use to store your backups. I have an external USB hard disk that does the trick, but you can use a USB flash drive, recordable CD or DVD, or even a web server. I wouldn't recommend putting your backups on the same computer. The best policy is to put some distance between the original files and the backups so if there's a fire or some other disaster, you'll have an intact copy. Make sure you have enough space for the backup too; regular recordable CDs are only 700MB, but my *Pictures* folder alone weighs in at a whopping 5.8GB!

Connect, insert, or otherwise prepare your chosen backup device and click the **Storage** tab in the Backup window. You'll see a window like the one in Figure 7-20. Choose the location in which you'd like to save the backup files from the drop-down box. Depending on which option you choose, you might have to enter some more details; for example, if you choose Local Folder, click the Choose Folder button to select where exactly the backups will be stored (this can be an external disk like a USB flash drive or something similar).

If you want to put your backup files on a CD or DVD, you'll have to save them to a folder somewhere first and then copy that folder onto a disc using the burning software mentioned earlier in this chapter.

Now, select the Folders tab and you'll be presented with the screen in Figure 7-21. Your first task is to decide what you want to back up, so check out the list labeled *Folders to back up*, which should be empty at the moment. You can add and remove items as you please using the plus and minus at the bottom of the list.

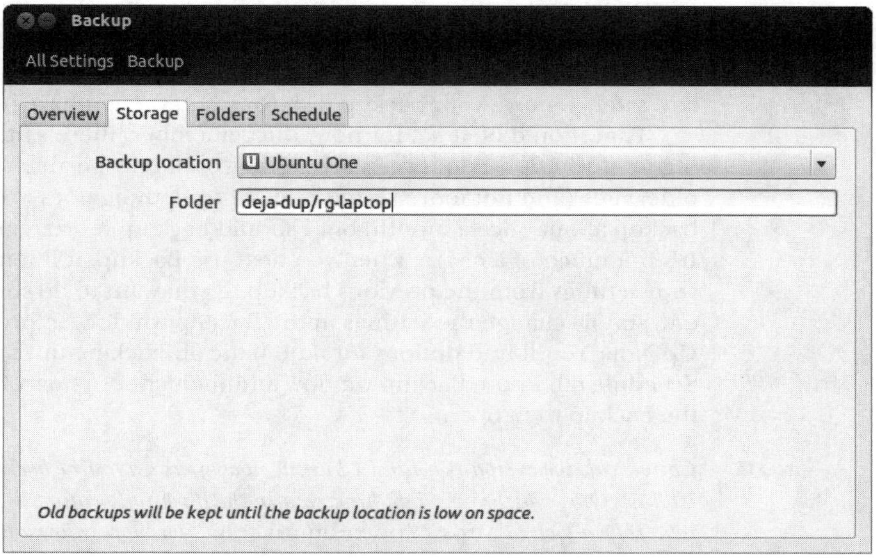

Figure 7-20: Choosing where to save the backup files in the Backup application

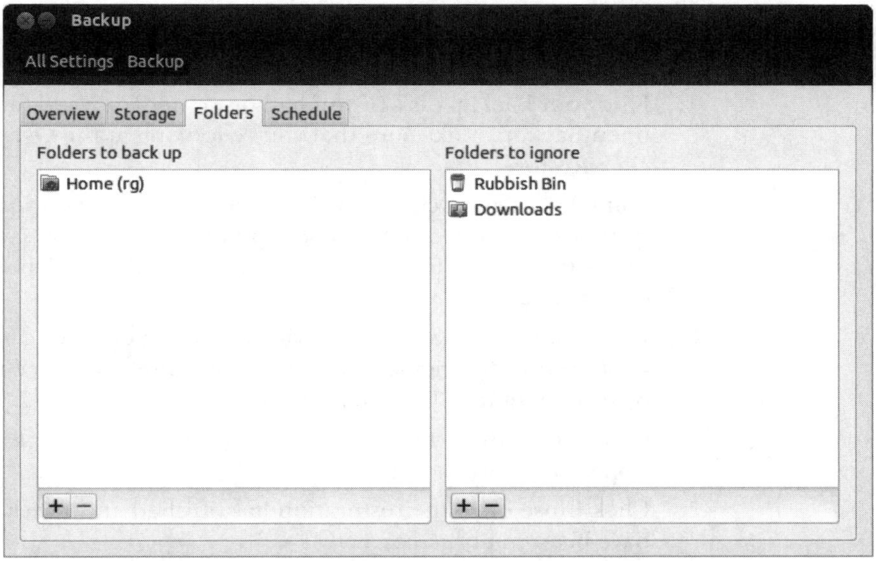

Figure 7-21: Selecting which files you want to back up

There's another list on that screen, labeled *Folders to ignore*. You can use this to define any files or folders that you *don't* want to back up. Say, for example, that you want to back up everything in your Home folder except for your pictures—maybe you don't have space on your backup disk for all of them. All you need to do is to make sure that your Home folder is in the *Folders to back up* list and your *Pictures* folder is in the *Folders to ignore* list.

When you've chosen what to keep and what to ignore, go to the Overview tab to see a summary page. Check that everything looks hunky-dory, and click **Back Up Now** to start the backup. Once that's finished, close the window and safely remove your backup disk (or whatever you have instead).

That should be it . . . for now. But remember, there's little point in backing up if you don't do it regularly, since you'll only be able to recover your older files (and not more recent ones) if something goes wrong. I make a backup about once a month, but I should back up more regularly than that. It's not much of a chore; when you next use Backup, it'll remember all of your settings from the previous backup. If you want to do something different, simply change the settings in the Backup window before clicking Back Up Now. You'll find options for automatically backing up as well; check the **Schedule** tab in the Backup window and then choose how often you'd like the backup to happen.

NOTE   *Canonical, the company behind Ubuntu, now offers an online backup service called Ubuntu One, which you might have seen in the Backup Location list under the Storage tab. Take a look at* https://one.ubuntu.com/ *for more information on that.*

Recovering from a Backup

Ideally you'll never have to recover your backup, but if you do, here's a quick guide:

1. Find your backup disk (if you had one), hook it up to the computer, and open Backup. Make sure that you're looking at the Overview tab and click **Restore**.

2. You'll be asked to choose which backup location you want to restore from. Choose the one that corresponds to where you saved the backup in the first place (for example, a removable disk or Ubuntu One) and click **Forward**.

3. If you want the files to be put back exactly where they came from, choose **Restore files to original locations**. Otherwise, you can choose a folder to restore them to. Click **Forward** again.

4. Glance over the summary to make sure everything looks okay and click **Apply** to restore your files.

5. Click **Close** once the restoration has finished and check that the files have been put back correctly.

Everything should be back to normal now. Phew!

Removing Unwanted Files

Remember all that talk of keeping a tidy nest at the start of the chapter? Well, now it's time to dust off your spring-cleaning gear and give your Home folder the once over.

The first stop is the Trash. Sometimes I'm surprised by just how much stuff accumulates here; I can go for weeks on end without emptying it. Luckily, this trash lacks the unpleasant odor of its real-world counterpart, so all that stands in your way is a quick check to make sure you didn't accidentally throw away anything important. Click the Trash icon at the bottom of the Launcher, and when the window opens, click **Empty Trash** to delete all the files in there. They will be deleted permanently, with no way of getting them back.

Next up is something a little more sophisticated. If you're running low on hard disk space and want to know why (or just want to snoop around your files a little), open the Dash and search for **Disk Usage Analyzer**. Open it and, when the window appears, click **Scan Home**. Wait a while as your folders are sized up. A colorful ring chart will appear, accompanied by a list showing where all your hard disk space is being eaten up. Hover the mouse over one of the colored segments on the chart to see what's taking up the most room or double-click one of the segments to zoom in on a particular folder. After that, it's up to you to weed out the hard disk hogs: Click a folder in the left-hand list and choose **Move to Trash** to delete it.

Project 7: Creating and Extracting Compressed Files

Since I have been talking about file storage, it seems only fitting to wrap up this chapter by teaching you how to create and extract compressed files. In the Windows world, these are generally referred to as *Zip files*, while in the Linux world, *tarball* is the operative name. The Linux name, in case you're wondering, comes from the application that is used to create the archive for such files, Tar. Compressed archives are great for two reasons: They let you bundle a load of files into one handy package, and they squeeze all the files down so that they take up less space on your hard disk. If you've ever tried to email a bunch of files to someone, you know how useful this can be.

To get some of the hands-on stuff down, you'll be creating a Windows/Linux/Mac–friendly Zip file and then extracting it. You can get down to business by opening a Nautilus window and creating a couple of dummy files to work with. Do this by going to the Nautilus **File** menu and selecting **Create New Document ▸ Empty Document**. A new file will appear in the Nautilus window, with its name highlighted. You can type a name for the file; I'm using *dogwood*. Now repeat the process to create a second file; I'll be calling that one *violet*. Use something equally evocative for yours.

Now that you have two files to work with, you can create the compressed archive by following these steps:

1. Select the two files either by clicking your mouse to the side of the files and then dragging the cursor (with the mouse button still pressed) over both files until they are highlighted or by holding down the CTRL key and clicking each file individually.

2. Once both files are highlighted, right-click either one and select **Compress** from the pop-up menu.

3. In the Compress window that appears, type **blossoms** in the Filename text box and then select **.zip** from the drop-down menu button to the right of that. Once everything looks like what I've set up in Figure 7-22, click the **Create** button, after which a compressed archive of your two files (*blossoms.zip*) will appear in your Home folder.

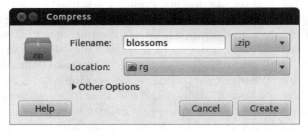

Figure 7-22: Creating a compressed archive

Now that you know how to put things together, let's learn the equally simple task of ripping it all apart—well, okay, *extracting* your files:

1. Drag the original *dogwood* and *violet* files to the Trash to get them out of the way.

2. Double-click the *blossoms.zip* file you've just created. A window showing the contents of the file will appear (Figure 7-23).

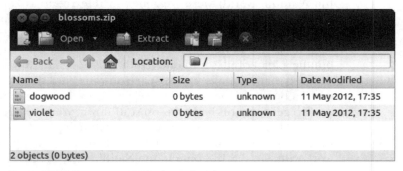

Figure 7-23: Extracting a compressed archive

3. In that window, click the **Extract** button, after which another window, Extract, will appear.

4. Click the **Extract** button in that window, and within a second (two at the most), you will find two new copies of *dogwood* and *violet* in your Home folder.

Now you've created and extracted a compressed archive, which is in this case a Zip file. You can also create a compressed tarball in the future by following the same procedure (probably with real rather than dummy files), but when it's time to select an archive type, select *.tar.gz* instead of *.zip*. Other than that single step, it is the same creation and extraction process.

8

SIMPLE KITTEN WAYS

*Getting to Know the Linux Terminal and Command Line . . .
and the Cool Things It Can Do*

Many people shy away from Linux because they envision it as a system for compu-geeks, an environment in which you do everything the hard way—by command line. In this era of graphical interfaces, the idea of typing commands to get things done seems like a dreadful throwback to the days of DOS, and that puts many people off, especially those who remember the "old days."

This reaction is fair enough, but it is not an accurate reflection of the reality of the Linux world. After all, most Linux users today utilize some sort of graphical interface. They can, and often do, achieve all that they hope to achieve through drop-down menus and mouse clicks alone. Many are able to survive quite happily without ever once opening their Terminal. The same could be true of you.

Be that as it may, there is still much to be said for the power and convenience of the command line. The fact that the command line can now be utilized within a graphical environment also makes it much less forbidding. The Terminal is just a tiny text-based island in a sea of graphical bodies (see Figure 8-1). Using the command line can be as pain-free as anything else you do on your system, and it can actually provide you with a little fun if you are willing to give it a try.

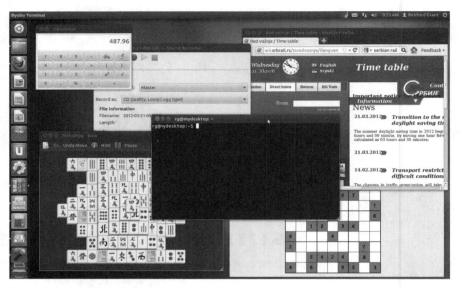

Figure 8-1: Putting the Terminal into perspective

Unfortunately, many guides to using the command line are written by hard-core command-line junkies, whose enthusiasm for what they see as a really good thing inadvertently makes what they write seem even more off-putting to the recent Linux immigrant or wannabe.

For your sake, I will try not to gush with enthusiasm so as not to scare you right back to Chapter 6 and the more comfortable world of the Ubuntu Software Center. I will also try to help you keep things in perspective by teaching you, whenever possible, to use the command line as a complement or alternative to the various graphical tools that you have at your disposal, rather than presenting it as the sole way of going about things. Of course, I am not going to cover every possible angle in this regard—just enough to give you some exposure and experience and, ideally, make you feel at least a little more at ease with the command line. Who knows? You might actually come to think of using the command line as . . . fun? Well, I won't get too carried away.

Meet the Terminal

You can run the Linux command-line Terminal application in your Ubuntu system by going to the Dash, typing **terminal**, and pressing ENTER. When the Terminal opens, it will, in all its simplicity, look much like Figure 8-2.

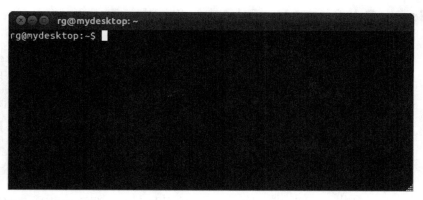

Figure 8-2: The Terminal application

As you can see, all it says is `rg@mydesktop:~$`. In this case, `rg` is my username, `mydesktop` is the name I gave my computer during installation, and the tilde (~) signifies that I am in my Home folder. If it were to say `~/Music`, for example, it would mean that I am currently in the *Music* folder within my Home folder. Of course, all this will be different in your case, because your username and computer name will be different. If your username is *frog* and your computer's name is *wetrock*, for example, the command line will say `frog@wetrock:~$`. If all this is sounding rather obtuse to you, just think of it this way: *username@computer_name*`:~$` in the Terminal is the equivalent of your Home folder in Nautilus.

Typing in the Terminal is straightforward enough; you just type as you usually do. You can also delete and insert letters or phrases by using the DELETE and BACKSPACE keys and the arrow keys. For practice, try the following:

1. Type **I like strawberries so very much**.
2. Change strawberries to cherries. (You've changed your mind!) Start by using your left arrow key to move the cursor in front of the first *s* in strawberries.
3. Tap your DELETE key as many times as necessary to erase the word strawberries (that would be 12 times, methinks).
4. Type **cherries** and then use your right arrow key to move the cursor back to the end of this meaningful sentence.

Now that you've completed this fascinating bit of typing practice, press the ENTER key. As you will almost immediately see, the Terminal's response to your efforts thus far is merely a dismissive `I: command not found`. Although you've typed a string of text that has meaning to you, it means absolutely nothing to your system. In fact, the system was so shortsighted that it could see nothing other than the first word you typed in the Terminal (`I`), and because `I` is not a valid command, the system had no idea what do to with it.

Some Goofy yet Useful Fun with the Command Terminal

A rather cool thing about typing in the command Terminal is that it has what you might call *short-term memory*. Try it by typing the word **cherry** and then pressing ENTER. Ignoring the command-not-found message, go on and type **vanilla** and press ENTER. Now type **gelato** and press ENTER. So far, so dumb, right? Well, not really. Let's type everything we've typed thus far again, but this time let's do it with only one key.

Huh?

Yes, just press the up arrow key once, and what do you see? That's right—the last command you typed appears, which in this case would be gelato. Press the up arrow key again, and the command that you typed before that will appear—vanilla. One more time? Yes, cherry. And one more time for the grand finale . . . I like cherries so very much.

Considering what we have thus far, this may all seem a bit silly, but imagine that you're not typing goofy little words and instead have to deal with considerably longer strings, such as a simple copy command (which you'll learn about later in this chapter) like this:

```
cp Photos/mypics/stpierre/coastal/onthebeach1_27.jpg /home/frog/photos_for_mom/stpierre
```

By typing that string, you are copying an image called *onthebeach1_27.jpg* from the *coastal* folder to another folder called *stpierre*. If you wanted to copy another photo in the *coastal* folder, *onthebeach1_16.jpg*, for instance, you could simply press the up arrow key once, use the left arrow key and DELETE key to move over to and delete the **27**, and replace it with **16**. All in all, it would be much simpler and much faster. It would also help you avoid mistakes in typing. Not so dumb anymore, eh?

Nontoxic Commands

As you now know, all of this typing is easy enough, but to actually do something useful with your Terminal, you need to type commands—and there are more of them than you could ever hope or need to know. To get you started, we will begin with some commands that are easy to understand, nontoxic, and completely kitten friendly.

$ whoami

There is no command as easy, safe, or even as seemingly useless as whoami. Rather than help those with multiple personality disorders discover who they are at any given moment, the whoami command simply tells you which user is currently logged in. Try it by typing **whoami** after the $ and then pressing the ENTER key. Remember that commands are case sensitive.

The Terminal will now tell you the username of the person currently logged in. If you are logged in as *frog*, you should get frog as the answer to your command.

$ pwd

If you know who you are but aren't exactly sure where you are, pwd (print working directory) should come in handy. The pwd command tells you exactly where the Terminal is in your directory tree.

Let's say, for example, that my Terminal is in my personal home directory (which is called *rg*) in the system's home directory (which is called *home* and which is where all the user account directories are located). When I use the pwd command, I would get /home/rg printed to my Terminal. You should get similar results if you try it.

NOTE   *The word* print, *in this case, has nothing to do with your printer; it merely means that the response will be printed to, or displayed in, the Terminal.*

$ df

Another safe and easy, but much more useful, command is df (disk filesystem). The df command tells you how much disk space you have used, as well as how much space you still have available, on each of the partitions on your various mounted disks. Try it by typing **df** and then pressing ENTER. Your output should look something like that shown in Figure 8-3 (depending, of course, on the size of your mounted disks and how they are set up.)

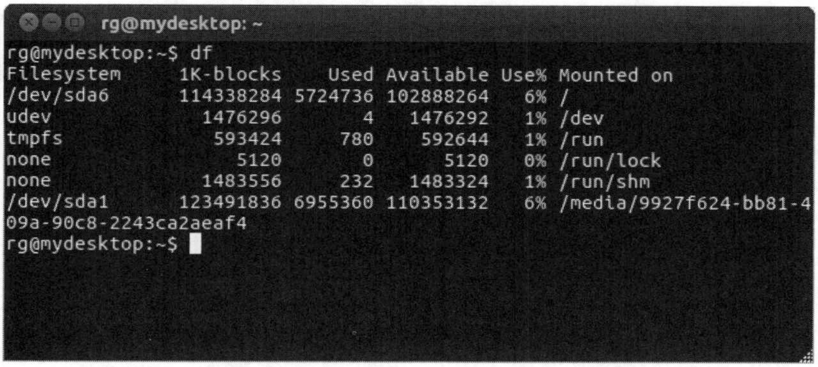

```
rg@mydesktop: ~
rg@mydesktop:~$ df
Filesystem      1K-blocks      Used Available Use% Mounted on
/dev/sda6      114338284   5724736 102888264   6% /
udev             1476296         4   1476292   1% /dev
tmpfs             593424       780    592644   1% /run
none                5120         0      5120   0% /run/lock
none             1483556       232   1483324   1% /run/shm
/dev/sda1      123491836   6955360 110353132   6% /media/9927f624-bb81-4
09a-90c8-2243ca2aeaf4
rg@mydesktop:~$ 
```

Figure 8-3: Output from the df command

As you will notice, the sizes are given in kilobytes (KB) rather than the gigabytes (GB) and megabytes (MB) you are probably more used to, but there is a way around this. Many commands accept a *flag*, or *option*, to further fine-tune how the command performs. You type flags directly after the main command and precede them with a space and a hyphen.

In this case, you can try using the -h (human readable) flag to have your figures come out in the way you are most familiar with. Try this by typing **df -h** on the command line and pressing ENTER. The output should now appear in a more familiar format (see Figure 8-4).

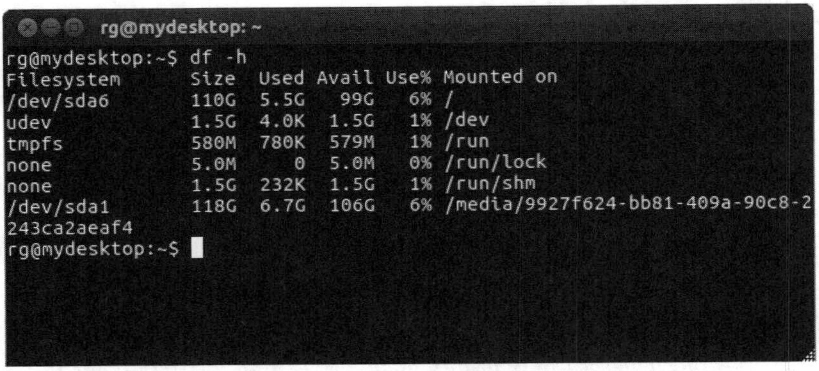

Figure 8-4: Output from the df command with the -h flag

$ ls

Another harmless but handy command is ls (list directory contents). The ls command shows you what is in your current directory. This is the nongraphical equivalent of double-clicking a folder in Nautilus to see what is inside. Try it by typing **ls** and then pressing the ENTER key.

If you've been following *my* commands so far, your results should list all of the folders in your home directory. You can also use the -R flag to show not only the list of files in the folder but also what is within the subfolders. Of course, you might not have created any subfolders yet, so you can hold off experimenting with this for a while. Instead, try typing **ls -a** to see your invisible, or *hidden*, files.

$ calendar

I'll let you experiment with this one on your own. Just type **calendar** and press ENTER to see the somewhat interesting results.

$ exit

The exit command is a simple one that allows you to exit the Terminal. Just type **exit** and press ENTER. The Terminal window will close.

Commands with Some Teeth

The simple commands you have tried so far are all of the safe-and-sane, fire marshal–approved variety; they merely print information to your Terminal. Now you are going to try to get some tangible results from commands. These commands are also essentially safe and sane if you follow my instructions.

$ mkdir

You have already learned how to create folders by means of menus and your mouse, but you can also do this using the command line. The command is mkdir (make directory), and it is easy as pie to use (though I've never been quite sure how pie is easy).

To see how this command works and to work with the commands that follow, use the mkdir command now to create a folder called *command_exp* (for command experiments). All you have to do is type **mkdir command_exp** in a new Terminal window and press ENTER. The new folder should appear in your Home folder, so go ahead and check to see whether it is there by clicking the home icon on your desktop.

Okay, good, *bra, bueno*! Now let's create another new folder within that new folder—a *subfolder*, if you will. We'll call this one *sub*. So, just type **mkdir command_exp/sub** and press ENTER. If you like, take a peek and see whether the *sub* folder has appeared within the *command_exp* folder.

$ mv

The next command is the mv (move) command, but before you experiment with it, you need to create a dummy file—you need something to move, after all. You can do this by using another command—touch. To make the file—let's call it *expfile.txt*—go to the Terminal, type **touch expfile.txt**, and press ENTER. The new file will appear in your Home folder.

To move the file that you've just created, you will use the mv command, of course. Just type **mv expfile.txt command_exp/sub** (this tells the system which file to move and where to move it to) and press ENTER. The file will now be in your *sub* folder.

$ cd

Until now, you have been using the command line from your Home folder. With the cd command, you can change your Terminal's location to another folder. You'll be using this very handy command quite a lot when doing the projects in this book. To take it out for a spin, let's get inside the *command_exp* folder by typing **cd command_exp** and pressing ENTER. If you've done this correctly, the prompt in your Terminal will now read *username@computer_name*:~/command_exp$. If so, you can pat yourself on the back.

While you are there, you might as well try the ls command with the R (recursive) flag to see how that works. Just type **ls -R** and press ENTER. Your Terminal should show that you have a subfolder here called *sub* and a file inside that subfolder called *expfile.txt*.

That is all you really want to do in there for now, so to get back to your home directory, just type **cd** and press ENTER, which will take you back home, so to speak.

For future reference, it is worth noting a couple of other cd command shortcuts. If you are within a subfolder of a subfolder and want to move back a step (from */home/rg/peas/pudding* to */home/rg/peas*, for example), you can do so by typing **cd ..** (with a space between cd and ..) and pressing ENTER. You can also type **cd -** (with a space between cd and -) in order to get back to the directory where you were previously (from */home/rg* to */home/rg/peas/ pudding*, for example).

$ cp

You might decide that not only do you want your *expfile.txt* file in the subfolder but you also want a copy in your home directory, where it was in the first place. To copy *expfile.txt*, you can use the cp (copy) command.

The command needs to know where the file you want to copy is, what it is called, and where you want to copy it, which in this case is to your Home folder. Normally you would type cp command_exp/sub/expfile.txt /home/*username* to do this, but if you recall, you can abbreviate the /home/*username* portion of the command string to ~/, which means the same thing. (This is an important tip to remember, because the tilde is frequently used in online instructions.) Because reducing wear and tear on the fingers is always a desirable goal, type the following command and then press ENTER:

```
cp command_exp/sub/expfile.txt ~/
```

Be sure to put a space between the name of the file you are copying and its destination (in this case, between expfile.txt and ~/).

Once you've done this, you should have two copies of *expfile.txt*, one in your Home folder and one in your *sub* folder. Go take a look to see the fruit of your endeavors.

$ rm

When you were a kid, you may well have experienced the joy of building a castle out of LEGO bricks and then the even greater joy of tearing the whole thing down (preferably by hurling D cell batteries at it). You will now embark on a similar move. The first tool in this nostalgic endeavor is the rm (remove) command, with which you can trash files.

The rm command, albeit very useful and easy to use, should be handled with caution. Once you remove a file with this command, there is no going back. The file will not be placed in the Trash—it is gone for good.

To play it safe, let's try the rm command by getting rid of that new copy of *expfile.txt* that we just created in the Home folder. The basic rm command structure consists of the command itself, rm, followed by the name of the file you want to remove. In this case, you want to remove the file called *expfile.txt* located in your Home folder. Assuming your Terminal shows you to be home, remove the file by typing **rm expfile.txt** followed by a tap on the ol' ENTER key. The file will then be gone, and gone for good.

Now, double your pleasure by getting rid of the version of *expfile.txt* that is located in the subfolder *sub*. In this case, you need to specify where the file is because it isn't in the folder that the Terminal is in. Just type **rm command_exp/sub/expfile.txt** and then press ENTER. Oooh, very cool. Brings ya back, doesn't it?

$ rmdir

You will now continue the fun with the rmdir (remove directory) command, which is a bigger and more powerful version of the rm command.

You should use the `rmdir` command, like the `rm` command, with caution. There are no do-overs with `rmdir`. Once you remove a directory or folder with this command, it is gone for good.

To try this command, you can get rid of that *sub* folder you created. Type `rmdir command_exp/sub` and press ENTER. The *sub* folder should now be gone. Finally, to round out the fun, use the `rmdir` command once more to get rid of the *command_exp* folder you created earlier. You know the drill: Type `rmdir command_exp` and press ENTER.

$ chmod

In Chapter 7, you learned how to change file permissions via the Nautilus interface. This is without a doubt an easy way to go about such things, but sometimes it may be easier to use the command-line approach.

The command for changing file permissions is `chmod` (change mode). To use it, just type the command followed by the permissions you want to extend to a file and then the location of the file itself. For example, let's say you copied a JPEG file, *mybirthday.jpg*, from a CD to the *personal* subfolder within the *Photos* folder on your hard disk and the file is write protected. To change the file so that you have write permissions (meaning that you can alter the file), you would type the following and then press ENTER:

```
chmod 644 ~/photos/personal/mybirthday.jpg
```

To change the permissions of all the files and subfolders (and all the files within those subfolders) in one fell swoop, you can add the `-R` (recursive) flag to the `chmod` command. The command would thus be as follows:

```
chmod -R 744 ~/photos/personal
```

The number 744, by the way, extends read and write and execute (run) permissions to you, the owner, but gives read-only rights to everyone else. This is a pretty safe choice when in doubt. If you want to figure out permission numbers for yourself, it's pretty easy. You are basically dealing with three number positions, each of which has eight numerical possibilities (0–7). The left slot represents permissions for the owner, the center slot represents permissions for the group, and the third slot represents permissions for others. The meanings of the numbers themselves are as follows:

7   Read, write, and execute permissions

6   Read and write permissions

5   Read and execute permissions

4   Read-only permissions

3   Write and execute permissions

2   Write-only permissions

1   Execute-only permissions

0   No permissions

Figure 8-5 points out the meaning of each of these numbers and what each number slot represents. In fact, if you don't mind a bit of simple addition, things are even easier to understand. To start with, remember that 1 = execute, 2 = write, and 4 = read. Add any of those numbers together, and you get the other permission combos. For example, 1 (execute) + 4 (read) = 5 (read and execute). As you can see, permissions aren't all that complicated.

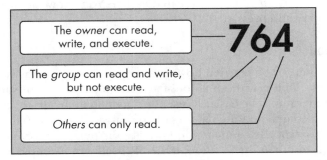

Figure 8-5: The meaning of permission numbers

Now if you're more of a letters than numbers sort of person, you'll be happy to know that there is another way to change permissions that is probably even easier. With this approach, you only have to deal with two groups of letters and the symbols + and -.

The first group consists of the following:

u   User (owner of the file)

g   Group (specified group of users)

o   Others (anyone who is not the user or a member of the group)

a   All (all of the above)

The second group consists of the following:

r   Read

w   Write

x   Execute

You might already be able to figure out how this is all going to work, but I'll spell it out just in case your intuition is worn out for the day. Let's say you want to change the permissions of a file (*butterhaters.txt*, for example) so that all users on your machine can read and write to it. After opening a Terminal window, you can make the change by typing `chmod a+rw butterhaters.txt` and pressing ENTER.

Oops! Just remembered that you don't want anyone changing the content of the file, eh? Well, to take back the write permissions for that file, you just need to type `chmod a-w butterhaters.txt` and press ENTER. As you can see, the + gives permissions, while the - taketh away.

That's much simpler, you've got to admit.

$ sudo

When you tried to install software from the Ubuntu Software Center in Chapter 6, you were asked to input your password. The reason for this, as I mentioned then, is that the Ubuntu Software Center installs the files it downloads in various folders throughout your system, almost all of which are write protected. By supplying your password, you are telling your system that you, as holder of the password, have the right to allow the Ubuntu Software Center to do that.

The command-line version of that same password-giving process is the sudo command. To perform an operation in a folder that is write protected, you would first type **sudo** and then the command you want to perform. For example, if you wanted to copy an icon image—let's call it *myicon.png*—to the globally located and write-protected *pixmaps* folder (*/usr/share/pixmaps*), you would type **sudo cp myicon.png /usr/share/pixmaps**.

After typing a command preceded by the sudo command and pressing ENTER, you will be prompted for your password. Once you type your password and press ENTER again, the command will be executed. I should mention that once you input your password, it will stay in memory for about five minutes, so you won't be prompted for your password again when using the sudo command within that time frame.

$ locate

Now that you are familiar with the sudo command, let's take it out for a spin by working with the locate command. The locate command is essentially a command-line alternative to the graphical Search tool found in the Places menu. Using the command is quite easy: Simply type the command followed by a space and the name of the file you want to find.

Before you can use this command, though, you should update the database of filenames that locate uses. This is where using the sudo command, along with yet another command, updatedb, comes into play. Just type **sudo updatedb** and press ENTER. Type your password when asked to do so—and then it will seem as though nothing is happening. But don't worry. As long as the cursor in your Terminal is blinking, progress is being made, and when your user prompt returns, you will have successfully created the database file. After that, you can use the locate command.

Oh, and in the future if you think that the process seems to be taking longer and longer, don't worry—it is. The more files and applications you add to your system, the longer it will take your system to catalog them all.

To take this new command for a test drive, let's look for the LibreOffice Writer icon, *libreoffice-writer.png*. Just type the following and press ENTER:

```
locate libreoffice-writer.png
```

Your results should look like those in Figure 8-6.

Figure 8-6: The results of a `locate` search

$ apt-get

Let's move on to a command that might seem a bit familiar: apt-get. Yes, this command is indeed a means of controlling the powerful package download and installation tool, APT, which I covered in Chapter 6. Although it might not be as pleasing to use APT via the command line as it is via the Ubuntu Software Center, doing so can come in handy. I'll cover the basics for you here.

Just for fun and to get a bit of nontoxic practice with apt-get, open a Terminal window, type **apt-get moo**, and press ENTER. The result of this endeavor, as you will see, is an example of an Easter egg (Figure 8-7), those little snippets of code that programmers seem to enjoy throwing into their work for just for fun. They're useless, yes, but they're also harmless, and this one is a safe first step in working with apt-get.

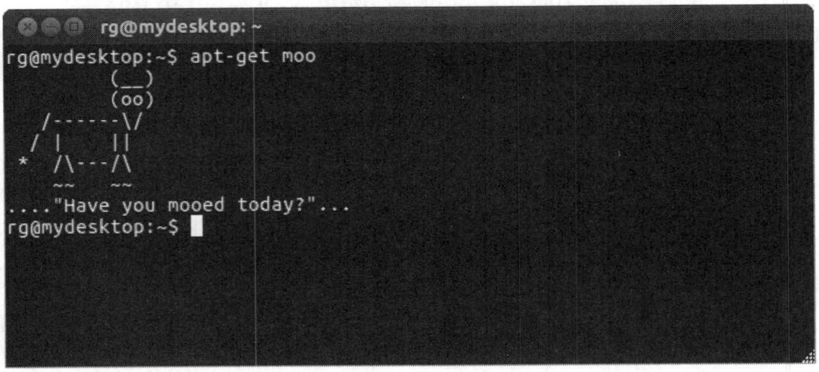

Figure 8-7: Discovering an Easter egg via apt-get

To actually put the apt-get command to use, start by making sure to close any APT frontends you might have open, such as the Ubuntu Software Center. As I mentioned in Chapter 6, you can run only one APT tool at a time. Once the coast is clear, you should always start out any operations involving apt-get with an update of the APT database so that you will be downloading the newest stuff. To do this, just type the command **sudo apt-get update**.

If you want to install a single package without heading over to the Ubuntu Software Center, you can do so by typing `sudo apt-get install` *package-name*. For example, if you want to download and install the Shufflepuck game clone, Tuxpuck, you would type `sudo apt-get install tuxpuck`. If you eventually get annoyed with Tuxpuck after having lost one too many times, you can uninstall it by typing `sudo apt-get remove tuxpuck`.

Finally, bearing in mind all the warnings offered in Chapter 6, if you want to upgrade your entire system via the command line, you can do so by typing `sudo apt-get dist-upgrade` (but only after doing a `sudo apt-get update` first).

$ finger

If you enjoyed discovering who you are with the `whoami` command earlier in this chapter, then you might enjoy finding out even more about yourself using the `finger` command. You can use the `finger` command in a number of ways, but a very simple one is finding out about a particular user. In order to try it out yourself, you have to install finger first, since it is no longer bundled with Ubuntu.

This is an excellent chance to get some more practice with the apt-get command you just learned. Open a Terminal window, type `sudo apt-get install finger`, and press ENTER. Once you've typed your password and the installation is complete, you will see your Terminal prompt again and be ready to try finger out. Just type **finger** and then your username. In my case, that would be `finger rg`. Once you've typed the command, press ENTER and see what you get. You can see my results in Figure 8-8.

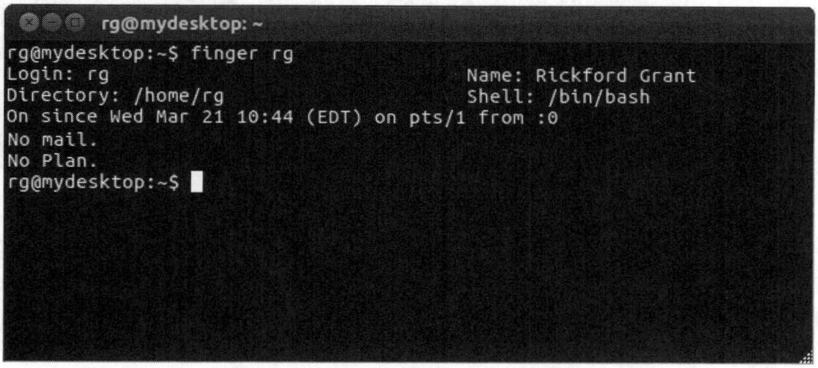

```
rg@mydesktop: ~
rg@mydesktop:~$ finger rg
Login: rg                              Name: Rickford Grant
Directory: /home/rg                    Shell: /bin/bash
On since Wed Mar 21 10:44 (EDT) on pts/1 from :0
No mail.
No Plan.
rg@mydesktop:~$
```

Figure 8-8: Output from the `finger` *command*

As you can see, my login name is *rg*, my real name is Rickford Grant, my home directory is */home/rg*, and I am using the Bash shell for typing my commands. I have been logged on since Wednesday, March 21, at 10:44 Eastern Daylight Time (EDT), and I have no mail or plan. It doesn't tell you my Social Security number or my mother's maiden name, but it is pretty cool, don't you think?

What Is a Shell?

As you noticed, I mentioned that the results of the finger command showed I was using the Bash shell, so you may well be wondering just what Bash is. Well, *Bash (Bourne Again Shell)* is one of the many shells that are used in Linux systems, and it's the one that happens to come with your Ubuntu distro (and most others, for that matter). A *shell* is a program that interprets the commands you type into the Terminal and delivers them, so to speak, to your system so that it can act upon them. I like to think of it as a command-handling subsystem, for which the Terminal acts as a graphical frontend.

What Is a Plan?

I also mentioned that the results said I had no plan, so you may also be wondering what that is all about. A *.plan* file is a small file kept in your Home folder that other users see when they use the finger command on you. Traditionally, a *.plan* file contained information about where you were going to be or what you were working on. These days, however, most people use them to leave odd little messages, quotations, or whatever, much as they do in email signatures. Take a look at Figure 8-9 to see what happens after I add a *.plan* file to my Home folder.

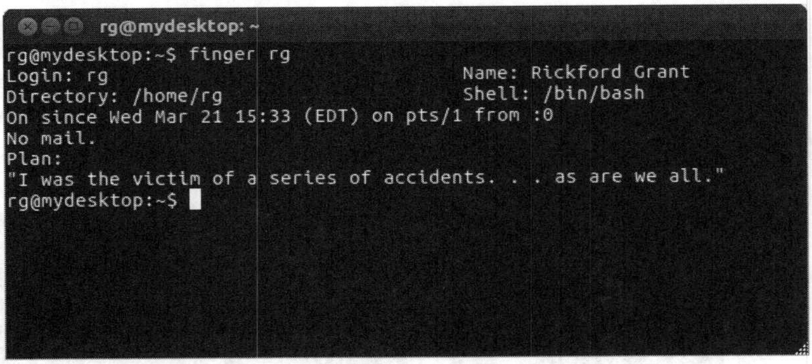

Figure 8-9: Output from the finger *command with a plan*

You can now see my plan, which is a quotation from Kurt Vonnegut's *The Sirens of Titan* (or Al Stewart's song by the same name, for that matter). Of course, you can put anything you want in your own. You will get the chance to create your own plan file in "Project 8A: Creating a Plan" on page 141, so if this seems fun to you, more fun is in store.

Other Uses of the finger Command

Before moving on, I should mention that you can also use the finger command to do a little domestic espionage of sorts. Let's say your child, Chris, has a user account on your machine. Chris, who wants your permission to go to the movies, claims to have been hard at work on the computer all day writing a report for school. Having your doubts, you could type **finger chris** to see what the facts actually are. It may be a bit underhanded and rotten, but it works. It also works both ways; others can check up on you as well. You can try it out if you create a new user account in Chapter 9. Just type **finger**, the name of the account you're not currently in, and then press ENTER.

You can even use the finger command to find out facts about people on other systems, providing their network's finger service is active and you know their email address. Typing something like **finger** *username@hostname.com* would do the trick. It's kind of cool but also kind of spooky, I suppose.

A Couple of Other Commands You'll Be Using Soon

This is as good a place as any to introduce two more commands that you will be called upon to use in this chapter and elsewhere in the book: ln and tar. You needn't practice with these yet, because you will be using them very soon, but you might as well know what they are all about.

$ ln

You use the ln (link) command to create a link file that launches or activates another file located in a separate folder. This is very useful when you want to activate a file that is buried deep in the subfolder of a subfolder of a sub-folder somewhere on your hard disk. The command is often used with the -s (symbolic) flag, which provides essentially the same thing as the shortcut you've come to know in Windows, or the alias on the Mac.

The easiest way to use the ln command is to first use the cd command to change the Terminal's location to the folder where you want to place the link. Then you can type the **ln** command on the command line, followed by the path of the file to which you want to link. For example, let's say you want to put a link in your Home folder for a LibreOffice Writer file of your auto-biography called *myLife.odt*.

The file is pretty well buried in a nest of subfolders deep within your Home folder: */home/<username>/Documents/personal/self/autobiography/ myLife.odt*. To create the link, you would open a new Terminal window, type the following command string, and then press ENTER:

```
ln -s Documents/personal/self/autobiography/myLife.odt
```

Once you are finished, the link will appear in your Home folder as an icon matching the original file in appearance, albeit sporting an arrow to signify that it is a link.

$ tar

In Chapter 7 you learned to create and extract archives, or *tarballs*, but did you know that you can also create and extract tarballs using the command line? The tar command is your key to doing this.

To create an archive, you would simply type **tar -cvf**, followed by the name the final tarball will be and then the name of the folder or file you are trying to archive. For example, let's say you want to create an archive of your photos folder and you want to call it *pics4pals*. In this case, you would type the following command and then press ENTER:

```
tar -cvf pics4pals.tar photos
```

As you no doubt noticed, there are some flags after the `tar` command in that string. The c tells the tar program to *create* a new archive. The v tells the program to be *verbose* or, in other words, to tell you what it is doing in the Terminal as it is doing it. Finally, the f tells the program that what follows is the *file information*.

If, after creating the archive, you suddenly remember that there is one more file you want to add to the mix, you can use the -r flag to append the archive.

For example, to add a file called *cranky.png* to the archive, you would type the following and then press ENTER:

```
tar -rvf pics4pals.tar cranky.png
```

Of course, chances are that you will be doing more tarball extracting than creating, so you no doubt want to know how to do that. Fortunately, the process is pretty similar to what you do when creating the tarball. The main difference is in the first flag. Rather than using the `tar` command with the -c flag, you would use it with the -x flag, which tells the tar program to *extract* the specified archive. So if you want to extract a tarball called *spicyfood.tar*, type the following command and press ENTER:

```
tar -xvf spicyfood.tar
```

What you have been doing thus far is creating and extracting archives, which are basically just collections of files. They are not, however, compressed. In fact, most tarballs you find will be compressed, and you can tell by the ending *tar.gz*. That *gz* means that the archive was compressed using the gzip program. Extracting a compressed tarball is just as easy as extracting a straight tar archive; all you have to do is add the -z flag, which tells your system to use the gzip program to decompress the archive. For example, if you want to extract a compressed tarball called *goosedown.tar.gz*, type the following command and press ENTER:

```
tar -xzvf goosedown.tar.gz
```

Well, now that you know how to decompress and extract a gzipped tarball, you probably want to know how to create one. This is, again, little different than creating the tar archive itself; you would just add the -z tag to tell the program to use gzip to compress the folder. For example, to create a compressed version of your *Pictures* folder, which we'll call *tightpics.tar.gz*, you would type the following and press ENTER:

```
tar -czvf tightpics.tar.gz Pictures
```

It's worth mentioning at this point that you may also come across some files compressed with the bzip program. Such files are recognizable by some variation on the *.bz* or *.bz2* file extension. Dealing with these files should pose no problem, because the commands are almost identical to those for gzip. Just substitute -j for -z in the command string.

Compressing and Extracting Compressed Single Files

If you want to compress or decompress a single file, you don't really need to use the tar program at all, since its purpose is to create archives consisting of several files. You can instead use the gzip and gunzip commands directly. For example, to compress a file called *matilda.jpg*, you would type **gzip matilda.jpg** and press ENTER. The *matilda.jpg* file would then become *matilda.jpg.gz*. To decompress the file, you would type **gunzip matilda.jpg.gz** and press ENTER, after which the *matilda.jpg* file would be back to normal.

So, can you compress an archive you've already created with the tar command? Sure. For example, to compress the *spicyfood.tar* archive mentioned earlier, you would type **gzip spicyfood.tar**, and *voilà*—you've got yourself a compressed *spicyfood.tar.gz* archive. Pretty cool, don't you think?

Project 8A: Creating a Plan

Now that you have a bit of command experience, it's time to get some practice and put all those commands to good use. In this project, you'll create a *.plan* file, like the one mentioned earlier in "$ finger" on page 137.

The actual *.plan* file is a hidden file (as you can see by the dot before its name) and contains the plan or message that you add to it. That message will appear in the output of someone's Terminal when he uses the finger command to find out more about you. You may not need such a *.plan* file, but it's an easy enough way to work a bit more with commands and the Terminal itself, so let's give it a try.

To start out, you will open the Terminal-based Nano editor to create the *.plan* file. To do this, open a Terminal window, type **nano .plan** (being sure to put a space between nano and .plan), and press ENTER. Your Terminal should now look a bit different, as shown in Figure 8-10.

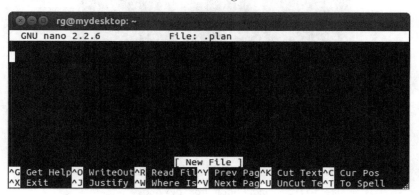

Figure 8-10: The GNU Nano editor

You will now be looking at your new, and totally empty, *.plan* file within the Nano editor. All you have to do is type your plan or message. Once you've done that, press CTRL-X to exit the Nano editor, and it will ask you whether you want to save your work. You do, so type **y**, after which you will be presented with a set of save options. You have already named the file *.plan*, as you can see near the bottom of the screen, so all you have to do is press ENTER. You will be back at your now-familiar user prompt in the Terminal window.

To wrap things up, change the permissions of the new *.plan* file by typing `chmod 644 .plan` in the Terminal window and then pressing ENTER. The *.plan* file should now be in your Home folder and readable (see note below) by all, so go on and test your work by typing `finger `*`username`* and pressing ENTER. The message you entered in your *.plan* file should now appear in the results in place of the No Plan you found there earlier. If you want to change the contents of your *.plan* file later, just follow the same steps and change the text when the *.plan* appears in the Nano editor.

NOTE   *The name of the* .plan *file is preceded by a dot, which means that it is a hidden file. Thus, if you take a look in your Home folder, you will not be able to see the file unless you have checked the Show hidden and backup files box in the File Management Preferences window.*

Project 8B: More Command Practice with pyWings

Now let's get some more experience with the Terminal by installing a simple, and admittedly kind of silly, oracle program called pyWings (see Figure 8-11). pyWings will give you cryptic guidance in response to whatever questions you may ask it.

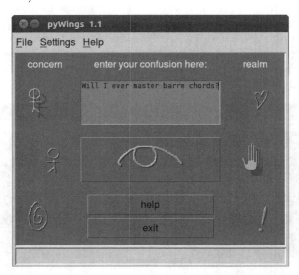

Figure 8-11: Seeking wisdom from pyWings

To use pyWings, type whatever your confusion or dilemma is in the input box, click one of the concern icons on the left (self, another, world), click one of the realm icons on the right (love, work, truth), and hit the big button that looks like half an eye. The oracle will then tell you what it has to say. As an example, I asked the oracle if I would ever master barre chords on the guitar, and I picked *self* as my concern and *work* as the realm. Figure 8-12 shows the wisdom that was bestowed upon me.

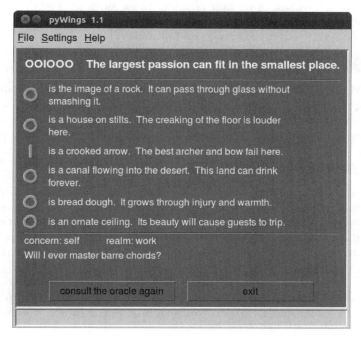

Figure 8-12: pyWings bestows its wisdom.

As you can see, the oracle told me, "The largest passion can fit in the smallest place," which I will interpret as . . . well, I'm not sure how to interpret it.

Hmm. I guess that's encouraging.

pyWings was written in a programming language called Python, which actually creates scripts rather than conventional programs. You will learn a little more about this distinction later in the chapter, but one of the differences I can mention right off the bat is that you don't actually have to install pyWings; you are simply going to put it on your hard drive in your Home folder and run it from there, more or less as is.

8B-1: Getting Ready for pyWings (Installing Tkinter)

As I mentioned, one difference between pyWings and most of the other applications you use is that pyWings is a Python script. To create a graphical interface for itself, pyWings uses a toolbox known as Tkinter, which is the de facto standard (though not the only) GUI toolbox for Python. Tkinter, however, no longer comes bundled with Ubuntu, so you will need to download and install it yourself. Fortunately, this is quite easily done.

Although it is possible to whip open the Ubuntu Software Center and install Tkinter by the simple means learned in Chapter 6, it seems more appropriate in this command line–oriented chapter to . . . yeah, you got it, use the command line. That said, open a Terminal window, type `sudo apt-get install python-tk`, and then press ENTER. When asked for your password, type it and then press ENTER. APT will search the online repositories and find your file, along with anything else it requires to function properly. Once it is ready, it will ask you whether you want to continue. You do, so type **y** and then press ENTER. When your username prompt reappears, you'll know the job is done, and you can go on to the next step.

8B-2: Getting pyWings

You are just about ready to "install" pyWings, but before you do, you need to get it from *http://sourceforge.net/projects/pywings/*. Once there, click the **Download** button, which will download the file *pywings-1.1.tar.gz*. When prompted, choose **Save File** and click **OK**. The file will be downloaded to your *Downloads* folder.

8B-3: Creating a LocalApps Folder for pyWings

As I mentioned earlier, you will be installing the pyWings program locally in your Home folder. Installing a program *locally* means that you are installing the program and all its support and data files in your Home folder. This makes things a bit easier, but it also means that the program will not be available to other users. It also means that if you're not careful, you might inadvertently delete it.

To make things a bit easier and safer, you are going to create a folder in your Home folder in which to place pyWings and all other applications that you may install locally on your machine in the future. You will, logically enough, call the folder *LocalApps*.

Let's make the folder using a command in order to get some more practice. Go to the Terminal, make sure you are in your Home folder, type the following command, and then press ENTER:

```
mkdir LocalApps
```

8B-4: Extracting the pyWings Tarball

Now it is time to extract the tarball. You could do this by the double-click method you learned in Chapter 7, but since you're working with the command line here, let's use that instead.

To start, you're going to place the tarball in the same folder into which you extract its files. Usually this isn't necessary because the contents of most tarballs are already packaged in a folder of their own. By double-clicking the tarball to open it in File Roller, you can see whether things are packed in a folder or simply as a group of files. In the case of pyWings, it is the latter, so follow these steps:

1. Create a *pywings* folder by typing `mkdir pywings` and pressing ENTER.

2. Move the pyWings tarball into that folder by typing `mv Downloads/pywings*.gz pywings` and pressing ENTER.

   You can see that in this step you used an asterisk (*) to save some wear and tear on your fingers. The asterisk is a wildcard character, which in this case told your system to move any file beginning with *pywings* and ending in *.gz*. Fortunately you had only one item matching those criteria.

3. Move to the new *pywings* folder by typing `cd pywings` and pressing ENTER.

4. Now you get down to extracting the tarball itself using the `tar` command. To do this, type `tar -xzvf pywings*.gz` and press ENTER.

   Again, notice that you used the asterisk to save yourself some keystrokes, though you could just as well have typed `-1.1.tar`.

5. Finally, type `cd` and press ENTER to bring the Terminal back to your Home folder.

8B-5: Moving the pyWings Folder to Your LocalApps Folder

The extraction process is now complete. Before going on to run pyWings, however, let's move it to the new *LocalApps* folder you created in "8B-3: Creating a LocalApps Folder for pyWings" on page 144. To do this, type the following command and press ENTER:

```
mv pywings LocalApps
```

8B-6: Running pyWings

Now that you have pyWings in place and ready for action, let's start up the great oracle right now so that you can get a better perspective on how to deal with the aspects of life that trouble you.

In the Terminal, make sure you are in your home directory, type the following command string, and then press ENTER:

```
python ~/LocalApps/pywings/pywings.py
```

Since *pywings.py* is a Python script, rather than an application, you are calling Python's attention to that fact so that Python will know it needs to deal with that script. If all has gone according to plan, pyWings will soon be making you a wiser person.

8B-7: Creating a Launchable Link for pyWings

The method of running pyWings that you've just used works well enough. However, it's a pain to open your Terminal and type that somewhat lengthy string every time you want to find out what fate has in store for you. Let's find a way to make things easier in the future.

To run an application from the Terminal, you generally type the name of that application or, to put it more precisely, the name of that program's executable file; the application's name thus acts as a sort of command. For your system to recognize that command, however, the command (the executable file or a link to it) must be in a location where the system can find it. Whenever you run a command of any sort, your system checks a series of locations (most of which are *bin folders*, where executable files are located) to find that command.

You can easily find out where these locations are by typing `echo $PATH` in a new Terminal window and then pressing ENTER. As you will see, on your Ubuntu system, these locations are as follows:

> */*
> */usr/lib/lightdm/lightdm*
> */usr/local/sbin*
> */usr/local/bin*
> */usr/sbin*
> */usr/bin*
> */sbin*
> */bin*
> */usr/games*

The results of the `echo $PATH` command will not appear as they do in the (easier to read) chart shown here but, rather, in a single line divided by colons. The actual output shown in the Terminal is `/usr/lib/lightdm/lightdm:/usr/local/sbin:/usr/local/bin:/usr/sbin:/usr/bin:/sbin:/bin:/usr/games`.

If the command you typed is in one of those locations, the program or script will run. As you no doubt know, however, pyWings is not in any of those locations. It is in */home/*username*/LocalApps/pyWings* and is thus, in a sense, out of your system's sight.

To remedy this situation, you could add the path of your pyWings script to the list of paths that the system checks for run commands so as to make the system aware of your new application's existence. However, let's try another method that I think is easier. What you will do is create a link to pyWings, a sort of launchable alias, in one of the locations your system does check for commands.

To create this link, you will use three commands: `cd` (to change directories), `sudo` (to give yourself write access to the destination folder), and `ln -s` (to create the link).

1. In the Terminal, type `cd /usr/games` and press ENTER. This puts you in one of the folders your system searches when you enter commands.

2. Type `sudo ln -s /home/`*username*`/LocalApps/pywings/pywings.py pywings` and press ENTER. (Note that there is a space between the terms `pywings.py` and `pywings` at the end of that command string.)

   The `pywings` at the end of that command string is the name that you are giving the link; the name of the link thus becomes the command you will use to run the application. If you type nothing, the link will be called *pywings.py,* which would mean three more keystrokes for you every time you wanted to start the program.

3. Type your password when prompted to do so and then press ENTER.

4. Now make your new launcher executable by changing its permissions: Type `sudo chmod +x pywings` and press ENTER.

5. Type `cd` and press ENTER to return the Terminal to your Home folder.

8B-8: Running pyWings Again

Now that you have created the link, you should be able to run the pyWings program much more easily. To try it out, quit pyWings (if it is still running), type `pywings` in the Terminal window, and press ENTER. Your personal pyWings oracle should appear again.

You've managed to cut down on the number of keystrokes required to run pyWings from the Terminal. However, if you are really into this pyWings thing and want to use it often, it will probably be handiest to add a launcher to your panel, a drawer, or the Applications menu.

Project 8C: Command Practice Review with Briscola

If you want to reinforce the skills you've put to use in the previous project, why not go a bit Continental and try Briscola? Briscola is a simple, yet very traditional, Italian card game (see Figure 8-13), which is also widely played in the Adriatic areas of Croatia and Herzegovina under the name briškula, as well as in Spain and Mexico, where it is known as briscas. Unlike pyWings, which is a Python script, Briscola is a script of a different flavor. It's written in a scripting language called Tcl, which uses Tk to create its graphical interface—the same Tk used for the pyWings interface.

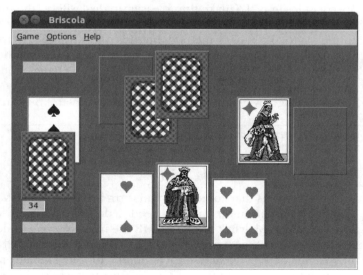

Figure 8-13: Briscola

8C-1: Getting Briscola

You are just about ready to begin "installing" Briscola, but before you do so, you must get it. You can get Briscola by going to the project's home page at *http://www.rigacci.org/wiki/doku.php/tecnica/download/local_software* and downloading it in the traditional manner, but since we're working with commands, let's instead get Briscola by using a new command: wget.

To do this, just open a Terminal window, type the following command string, and press ENTER:

```
wget http://www.rigacci.org/comp/software/briscola/briscola-4.1.tar.gz
```

In your Terminal window, you will see wget in action as it connects to the site where Briscola is stored and then downloads the file. When it's done, you will find the Briscola tarball in your Home folder.

8C-2: Extracting the Briscola Tarball and Renaming the Briscola Folder

Extracting the Briscola tarball is essentially the same process as that for pyWings. The only difference is that Briscola is already packaged within its own folder, so you won't have to create a special folder for it.

You know what to do: Just open a Terminal window, type the following command, and press ENTER:

```
tar -xzvf briscola*.gz
```

A new folder, *Briscola-4.1*, will appear in your Home folder with all the Briscola files in it. To make things easier to deal with in the future, let's shorten the name of the folder to simply *briscola*. You already know how to do this via the right-click method, but this time around let's to do it via the command line. You use, perhaps surprisingly, the mv command followed by the name of the file whose name you are going to change, followed by the new name of the file.

Give it a go by typing the following command and pressing ENTER:

```
mv briscola-4.1 briscola
```

8C-3: Preparing the Briscola Script

Most applications that come in tarball form include a README file, which includes information on what you need to do to install and use the application. If you double-click the **README** file in the *briscola* folder in the file manager, you will see that the "HOW TO START" section tells you to adjust the first line of the *briscola.tk* script to point it to your Tk shell and to adjust the second line of the script to point to the directory where the various Briscola files are located.

To perform the adjustments as instructed in the README file, just follow these steps:

1. Find the Tk shell, called *Wish*, by typing `locate wish` in the Terminal window and pressing ENTER. Note the location on a piece of paper. You may get a number of locations in your search results, but the one you want is /usr/bin/wish. If you don't see it, it's probably because you haven't updated the database since doing "Project 8B: More Command Practice with pyWings" on page 142, so type `sudo updatedb`, press ENTER, and then try locating Wish again.

2. Direct the Terminal to the *briscola* folder by typing `cd briscola` and pressing ENTER.

3. Use the GNU Nano editor, which we used in "Project 8A: Creating a Plan" on page 141, to edit the *briscola.tk* file by typing `nano briscola.tk` and pressing ENTER. The *briscola.tk* file will appear in the Nano editor in your Terminal window.

4. Change the very first line of the *briscola.tk* file from #!/usr/local/bin/wish to **#!/usr/bin/wish**.

5. In the second line, change /usr/local/games/briscola to **/usr/share/games/ briscola**, which is where you will place Briscola in just a bit. Your editor window should now look like Figure 8-14.

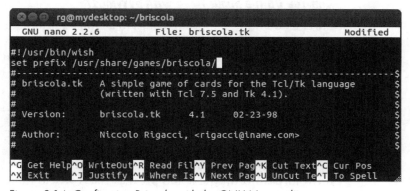

Figure 8-14: Configuring Briscola with the GNU Nano editor

6. Press CTRL-X on your keyboard.

7. Type **y** and press ENTER to save your changes.

8. Type **cd** and press ENTER to return the Terminal to your Home folder.

8C-4: Moving the Briscola Folder to a Global Location

You could move the *briscola* folder to the *LocalApps* folder and play the game from there, as you did with pyWings. But this time around, let's do things a bit differently by moving the whole thing to global territory. This not only keeps it safe from any obsessive housekeeping tendencies you might have but also allows all users on the same computer to play the game. You will need to use the `sudo` command to do this so that you can have write access in those protected folders.

Just type the following command in the Terminal window and press ENTER:

```
sudo mv briscola /usr/share/games/briscola
```

When you are prompted for your password, type it and press ENTER.

8C-5: Creating a Launchable Link for Briscola

Even though you've moved Briscola to a global location, you still can't run it with a simple one-word command because the *briscola.tk* file is not in the system's command search path. Just as you did for pyWings, you will now create a launchable link for Briscola to solve that problem. Here are the steps:

1. In the Terminal, type `cd /usr/games` and press ENTER.
2. Now create the link by typing `sudo ln -s /usr/share/games/briscola/briscola.tk briscola` and pressing ENTER.
3. Type `cd` and press ENTER to return the Terminal to your Home folder.

You can now easily run Briscola by typing `briscola` in the Terminal and pressing ENTER.

Can You Do the Same Thing with pyWings?

Sure. If you want to move pyWings to a global location, just follow the same procedure for moving the *pywings* folder and creating the link as you did for Briscola, making the necessary substitutions, of course. You will have to remove the previously created pyWings link, though, by typing the following command and pressing ENTER:

```
sudo rm /usr/games/pywings
```

After that, move the *pywings* folder to global territory by typing `sudo mv ~/LocalApps/pywings /usr/share/games/pywings` and pressing ENTER. When prompted for your password, type it and press ENTER. You can then create the launchable link by typing `cd /usr/games`, pressing ENTER, typing `sudo ln -s /usr/share/games/pywings/pywings.py pywings`, and pressing ENTER once more.

Playing Briscola

As I already mentioned, Briscola is easy—about as easy a card game as there is. It is a trick-taking game, which means that you put out a card and then your opponent puts out a card, and the one who puts out the higher point-value card wins the hand, or *trick*. Points are awarded on the basis of the cards involved in that trick. The winner of the trick then goes on to *lead* the next trick, meaning that the winner puts out his or her card first the next time around. When all the cards are played, the points for each player are tallied, and the player with the higher points wins. It's even much simpler to do than it is to describe.

If you would like a more detailed set of rules for playing Briscola (and just about any other card game in the world), check out *http://www.pagat.com/*. There are also great video guides out there on YouTube, including my favorite at *http://www.youtube.com/watch?v=jpXpMNBPN8c*.

Project 8D: Compiling and Installing Programs from Source—Xmahjongg

Though it was far more common in earlier days, *compiling programs from source* seems to be a phrase you still hear more in the Linux world than in any other. For the beginner, just the mention of compiling a program from source seems off-putting. The words *compile* and *source* seem to instill a sense of foreboding in the heart of the new user. That certainly was the case for me, anyway.

You can live long and prosper without ever bothering to compile anything on your system. You can move along quite happily with your system as is, or you can just install programs by means of the much more convenient Ubuntu Software Center. Still, once in the Linux world, you are likely to come across this installation method and may well become curious, especially if you move into the geekier side of the community.

What Is Source?

To get started, it is probably a good idea to understand what *source* is so as to understand a bit about how a program actually metamorphoses from its primitive state on the programmer's computer into an up-and-running application on your machine. First the programmer writes a program in a programming language. You have probably heard of programming languages such as BASIC or C, and there are many others. What the programmer actually writes with such a language is a set of instructions called the *source code*, or *source*. Your computer, however, cannot actually understand any of that source on its own. It is as if the computer speaks ancient Greek and the source code is all written in French.

The various languages that programmers use are called *high-level languages*—they are relatively easy for programmers to read. The computer, on the other hand, understands only *low-level languages*, which are quite difficult for most mere mortal programmers to deal with. To convert the high-level language instructions into a low-level language, the computer needs some other program to translate. To put it another way, the computer needs an interpreter.

If this translation process takes place while a program is running, the translator program is actually called an *interpreter*. Applications that run using an interpreter are usually called *scripts*. The pyWings and Briscola applications earlier in this chapter are examples of such script applications.

The problem with such scripts is that they can be slower than most of the applications you're familiar with—the computer must run an interpreter, interpret the source code, and run the application all at the same time. This is like having a French book translated into Greek by a live interpreter; it's very slow indeed.

As an alternative, most programs use a compiler instead of an interpreter. A *compiler* translates the high-level source code into low-level *machine code*, or *object code*, that the computer can understand before the application is run. Once this translation is done, the computer never has to bother with the high-level instructions again; it can merely read the translated version each time it runs the program. This is like having a translated version of a foreign book that you can read any time you want. Because computers can run compiled programs without simultaneously using an interpreter, compiled programs run faster than scripts. Most applications for all operating systems are, therefore, compiled.

The Basics

The process of compiling an application from source and then installing it is straightforward—a truly "one, two, three" bit of presto change-o. Basically, after extracting the source code from an archived file (usually in the form of a tarball), you would use the following commands to accomplish the task:

`./configure` To configure a *makefile*, which provides instructions for the make command

`make` To translate the source code into object code that the computer can understand

`sudo make install` To give yourself write privileges in protected folders and then install the application

`make clean` To tidy up the leftovers once the process is complete (to clean up the mess)

I know that sounds like a lot of commands, but as I always say, just doing it is easier than reading it on the page, so fear not.

8D-1: Installing the Tools You Need

Before doing anything else, you have to get your system ready to do what you're about to ask of it. Because Ubuntu is designed with the average computer user in mind, it does not come with the various applications and libraries you need to compile applications from source. Fortunately, however, everything you need to get the job done is available via the Ubuntu Software Center. To get ready for the work at hand in this chapter (and many other jobs you are likely to do on your own in the future), perform searches for and install the following packages:

- build-essential
- libgtk2.0-dev

8D-2: Downloading and Extracting the Xmahjongg File

To get some hands-on experience with compiling a program from source, you will be working with a game called Xmahjongg, which you can see in Figure 8-15. If you've tried the version of Mahjongg that comes with your Ubuntu distribution, you will notice that this one is much easier on your eyes and is a bit more colorful (check out the project site at *http://www.lcdf.org/xmahjongg/* to catch a glimpse of it in its full-color glory).

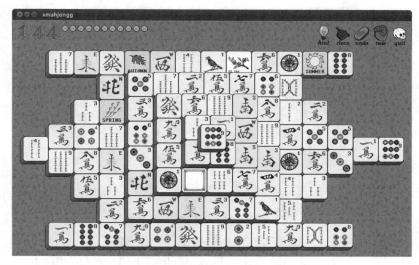

Figure 8-15: The Xmahjongg game

Xmahjongg is available via the Ubuntu Software Center, so it's not absolutely necessary to install it in the way you are about to, but doing so provides a perfect opportunity to learn how to compile a program from source. The amount of source code isn't all that great, so compiling won't take too much time, and it requires no tinkering.

To get started, you will have to download the Xmahjongg source code. You can get this from the Xmahjongg project page at *http://www.lcdf.org/xmahjongg/*. Download the tarball *xmahjongg-3.7.tar.gz* or a newer version if there is one. Do not download any of the other file types available on that page.

If you prefer, you can instead download the Xmahjongg tarball by using the wget command that you learned in "8C-1: Getting Briscola" on page 148. Just open a Terminal window, type the following command, and then press ENTER:

```
wget http://www.lcdf.org/xmahjongg/xmahjongg-3.7.tar.gz
```

Once you have the file on your hard disk, untar the *xmahjongg-3.7.tar.gz* file. You can do this either by using the command line, as you learned to do earlier in the chapter, or by double-clicking the file and dragging its contents into the appropriate folder. To make it easier for you to follow along with the directions I'll be giving you, be sure to place the untarred Xmahjongg folder in your Home folder. Then you will be ready to roll.

Normally at this point, you would look through the folder to find some instructions for dealing with the package, just as you did earlier in the chapter for Briscola. In most source code packages, this information is included in an INSTALL file, like the one in the *xmahjongg-3.7* folder (Figure 8-16). To read the INSTALL file, just double-click it, and it will open in Text Editor.

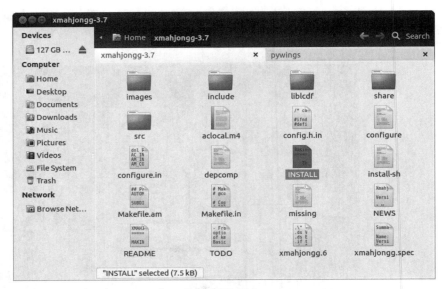

Figure 8-16: Identifying a package's INSTALL file

In this case, you can simply close the INSTALL file, because it prescribes the same steps I list next. However, in the future, when you install other programs from source, you will need to follow the instructions in the INSTALL files that come with the source files. Fortunately, the instructions in most INSTALL files will match the process I am about to describe.

Of course, it may well happen that you take a look at the contents of the INSTALL file and start wondering what alien tongue it is written in. In cases when you have no idea what the INSTALL file is going on about, just look for a *configure* file in the package folder. If you find one, you should be able to follow the instructions in this project.

8D-3: Running configure and make for Xmahjongg

Now that you have downloaded and untarred the Xmahjongg tarball, installation is pretty standard. Here's what you need to do:

1. Open a Terminal window and then move into the new folder by typing **cd xmahjongg*** and pressing ENTER.

    The next step is sort of a setup phase that runs the configure script in the *xmahjongg-3.7* folder. The configure script checks what files, compilers, and other things it needs, and then it searches your computer to see whether those things are there and, if so, where. Based on this information, it writes a file called a *makefile*, which is a set of instructions that will tell the make command in the subsequent step how to set things up specifically for your system configuration.

2. Configure the program by typing **./configure** and pressing ENTER.

    While you are running configure, you will see lots of odd and mysterious things flowing through your Terminal window; this is essentially a running account of what is going on, every step of the way. This can take a bit of time, but don't worry. As long as the mysterious text keeps flowing and you don't get an error message at the very end of the whole process, all will be well.

Once configure has done its thing, you will see your prompt again, and you can go on to the translation, or *compilation*, step. The make command reads the makefile created by configure to see how things need to be set up on your machine. Then it proceeds to call on the compiler to translate the high-level source code into low-level, machine-readable files that can be installed in the subsequent step.

3. To perform this translation, type **make** and press ENTER.

Again, you will be treated to even more mysterious text flowing through the window and a short wait, usually a tad longer than for the configure process. Once make has done its job and you see your prompt again, you are ready to install the program.

Up to this point, you have not changed your system in any way. All the changes thus far have taken place in the *xmahjongg-3.7* folder only—your system is still as pure as the day you started. Of course, all that is going to end right now when you perform the final installation step.

8D-4: Installing and Running Xmahjongg

Now you've come to the last step in this part of the process, make install. Here you are telling your system to install what you have created, or *compiled*, in the make step. Note that because installation takes place in permissions-protected parts of your system, you will need to add sudo to the command string to give yourself administrative privileges.

To perform the installation, type **sudo make install** and press ENTER. You will be prompted for your password. After you type it and press ENTER, the installation process will take place. Once your Terminal brings you back to your user prompt, Xmahjongg will be installed and ready to run from the Terminal. Just type **xmahjongg** and press ENTER.

8D-5: Cleaning Up and/or Uninstalling Xmahjongg

Once you are done and everything seems to be working as it should, you would normally tidy things up in the Xmahjongg folder by getting rid of any unnecessary files. You can do this via the Terminal by using the cd command to go back into the Xmahjongg folder, typing **make clean**, and then pressing ENTER.

If you want to uninstall Xmahjongg, open a Terminal window, go back to the Xmahjongg folder by using the cd command, type **sudo make uninstall**, and finally press ENTER. The routine is essentially the same for any applications installed in this way, though as you might imagine, uninstallation isn't always as smooth a process as what I've just described (and it's definitely not as easy as it is via the Ubuntu Software Center).

The main reason for the uninstallation process being less than cooperative is that the make uninstall routine requires you to have kept the original project folder, which means you have to keep a bit of clutter you normally wouldn't need to bother with. On top of this, some projects do not provide a make uninstall routine at all. This means that you have to keep track of where everything has been installed in your system and then remove each item using a series of sudo rm commands.

All that aside, go ahead, have some fun, and put your command-line skills to the test. You'll have something to tell your grandkids about in the future.

Customizing the Terminal

The Terminal is a very simple application in terms of looks, though you can spice things up a bit if you're so inclined. Not only can you change the background and text colors in the Terminal, but you can even display one of your favorite photos as a background (as shown in Figure 8-17) or make the background transparent.

Figure 8-17: A Terminal window with customized background and font colors

To change the Terminal background, right-click anywhere in the Terminal and select **Profiles ▸ Profile Preferences**. When the Editing Profile window appears, click the tab for the part of the profile you want to edit. For example, to add a background image, click the **Background** tab, select **Background image** (Figure 8-18), and then navigate to the photo you want to use as your background by clicking the **Menu** button next to the words *Image file* and finding the file in the Select Background Image window. Once you've found the photo of your choice, click **Open**. Depending on the image you use for your background, you may find it rather difficult to see text once your image appears in the Terminal. If so, try moving the slider under the words *Shade transparent or image background* in the Editing Profile window. If that still doesn't do the trick, click the **Colors** tab, deselect **Use colors from system theme**, and then try some of the preset Foreground and Background combinations from the menu button next to the words *Built-in schemes*.

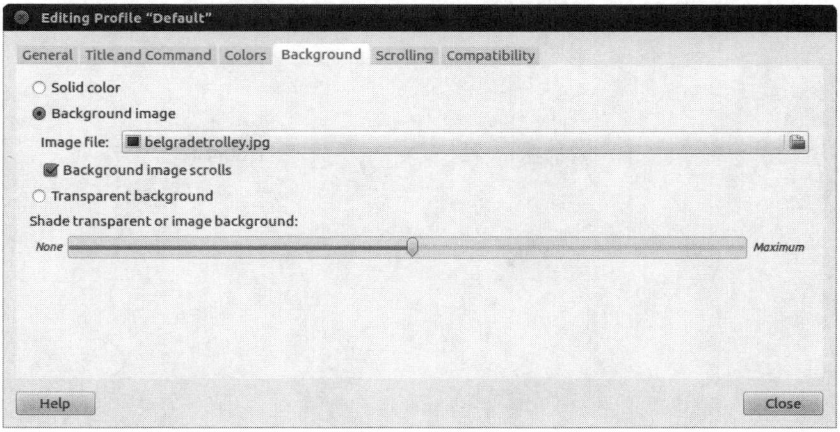

Figure 8-18: Customizing the Terminal window

If you just want to make the background transparent, go back to the **Background** tab, select **Transparent background**, and drag the slider to the right. You can also use the slider to adjust the shading of your background image if you choose to go that route.

Depending on the colors in your background image or in your desktop wallpaper (if you've gone the transparent route), you may also want to change the font color for your Terminal to make things easier to see. To do this, click the **Colors** tab, deselect **Use colors from system theme**, and then make the appropriate font color selection.

Tabbed Shell Sessions in the Terminal

To wrap things up in this chapter, I thought I'd mention one particularly convenient feature of the GNOME Terminal: tabs. Just as you can view multiple web pages in one Firefox web browser window through the use of tabs, tabs in the Terminal application allow you to have more than one shell session running at the same time without having more Terminal windows open (see Figure 8-19). This reduces the amount of desktop clutter and generally makes things easier to deal with. You can open a new Terminal tab by clicking anywhere in the Terminal and selecting **Open Tab** in the pop-up menu.

Figure 8-19: Running multiple shell sessions in tabs within the Terminal

9

DRESSING UP THE BIRD

Customizing the Look and Feel of Your System

One of the nice features of Linux has always been that you can change its appearance to varying degrees. I don't mean just desktop backgrounds and colors and display fonts but things like window borders too. You can even change the entire desktop environment if you're so inclined.

For customization fans, however, one thing that is slightly disappointing about the Unity environment in Ubuntu is that it is not as easily customizable as others. The main way to give yourself total customization freedom is to actually get rid of Unity, which is delving into pretty geeky territory, but there are some things you can do without getting all that drastic. So, let's just start off by discussing the easy tweaks you can do and then gradually work our way into a bit of minor geekdom for those of you who want to get down and a little (just a little) dirty.

If you're reluctant to alter the look of your current setup, you can create a new user account and experiment with making the changes in this chapter when logged in to the new account. If you opt to go this route, your regular home environment will remain untouched, because look-and-feel customizations that are performed in one user account do not affect other user accounts. When you're done with the project, you can then simply delete the new user account.

9A-1: Creating the Account

To set up a new user account, follow these steps:

1. Click the **System Settings** button in the Launcher.

2. When the System Settings window appears, scroll down to the end of the System section and click **User Accounts**.

3. In the User Accounts window, click the **Unlock** button. Provide your password when asked and then click **Authenticate**.

4. Now click the + in the bottom-left corner of the window.

5. In the new window that appears (Figure 9-1), type a name in the Full name box and a username in the Username box. To keep things simple, I am just going to use *graphika* for my example. For Account Type, choose **Administrator** so that you'll have permissions to do what you want.

6. Click **Create** to add the new user. Provide your password when asked and then click **Authenticate** in that window.

Figure 9-1: Creating a new user account

7. Now click the new account in the left pane of the User Accounts window and then click the words **Account disabled** next to the word *Password*.

8. In the window that appears (Figure 9-2), enter a new password for the new account (for this experiment, the same password as for your regular account is fine), type it again in the Confirm password box, and then click **Change**.

9. When done, click the **Lock** button in the top-right corner of the User Accounts window and then close the window itself.

NOTE *Normally, the privilege to install software and perform other system-wide changes (Administrator) is not selected by default on new user accounts, since you probably don't want your kids, workmates, or anyone else with his or her own user account on your computer installing all sorts of weird stuff and screwing up your system settings. We need it here, though, because we're going to be installing things.*

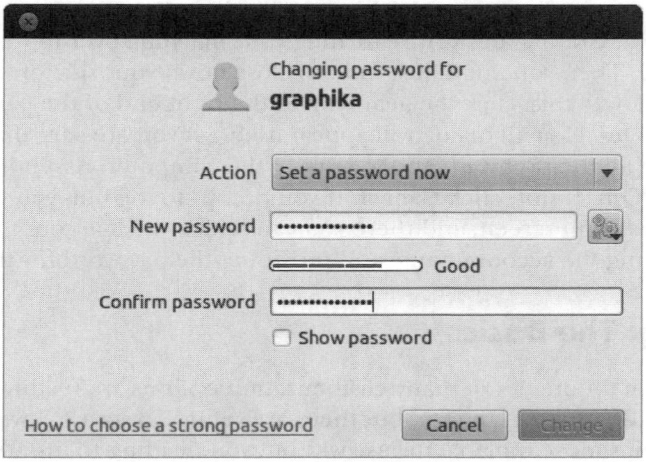

Figure 9-2: Inputting a password for the new user account

9A-2: Logging In to Your New Account

When you create a new user account, it will automatically appear in the User menu, which appears when you click your username in the right end of the panel. Click that account name, and after a few seconds, you will be at the login screen. The username for the new account should be highlighted, but if it is not, click it once, type the password for the account, and press ENTER. Within a few seconds, you will be at the new, untouched desktop of your just-created user. When you want to get back to your original user account, just follow the same procedure but instead select your original user account in the menu. Pretty cool.

When you *switch users*, as I just described, all the programs you have running and windows you have open are put on hold, waiting there for you to come back. In other words, you will return to your original account with everything as and where it was when you left—your browser still open to whatever it was open to, the same image being edited in the GIMP, and your résumé still open in Writer. This is very convenient when you are switching between accounts or when your child needs to log in to his account for a

moment to do a quick email check, burn a CD to play on the way to the beach, or print a file for school. When your child is done, you can quickly get back to what you were doing without having to reopen files, web pages, or whatever else you happened to be dealing with. You can even see which accounts are open when you click the User menu at the right end of the panel (Figure 9-3). All open accounts, dormant or active, will have checkmarks to the right of them, while the account that is open and currently active will also have a dot to the left of its menu entry.

Figure 9-3: Switching between user accounts

This is all very cool and handy, but let's say you're done with whatever you were doing and you're turning your machine over to your spouse or child. Then you might just want to close down your side of things by *logging out*. To do this, click the gear icon at the right end of the panel and select **Log Out**. A small dialog will appear asking if you are sure that you want to close all the programs and log out of the computer. Assuming you do, click **Log Out**. If not, click **Cancel**. If you do opt to log out, you will be returned to the login screen, and there you can select which account to log into by clicking the account name and providing the password for that account.

Customizing: The Basics

As I mentioned, not many customization options are readily available in the default setup of Ubuntu, but there are some. To start off, we'll discuss those options most available for use without you needing to install any software or resort to the command line.

Changing the Desktop Background

Changing your desktop background (often called *wallpaper*) is about the easiest customization you can do. Just right-click any open space on the desktop and select **Change Desktop Background** in the pop-up menu. This will open the Appearance window, in which you can see what wallpapers you have installed and select from among them (see Figure 9-4).

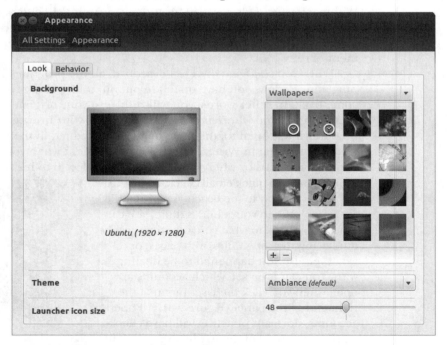

Figure 9-4: Changing your desktop wallpaper

Installing Additional Wallpapers

The default wallpaper in Ubuntu is called *Ambiance*. If the purple world of Ambiance is not your thing, click any of the other wallpapers to immediately make a change. There are quite a few to choose from, but maybe you'd prefer to use some images of your own. These could be photos from a digital camera, works of art you created on your computer, or just about anything else you want to put there.

If you are going to venture out onto the Web, a number of sites provide free desktop wallpaper. Two sites specifically geared toward Linux users are *http://www.gnome-look.org/* and *http://art.gnome.org/*, but you can get wallpaper from wherever you like. Astronomy Picture of the Day (*http://apod.nasa.gov/apod/astropix.html*) is a particular favorite of mine. Many company sites (cars, sodas, guitars, you name it!) have wallpapers available as well.

Once you've downloaded your wallpaper, move it from your *Downloads* folder into your *Pictures* folder. (You may want to create a *Wallpapers* subfolder to keep things better organized, but that's up to you.) After that, you can install the new image by clicking the + button right below the wallpapers pane in the Appearance window. In the window that appears, navigate to your new wallpaper, click it once to highlight it, and then click **Open**. The wallpaper will appear highlighted in the Appearance window and appear on the desktop within seconds.

Once the wallpaper shows up, you can adjust how it appears on the desktop with the little drop-down menu button just to the left of the + button in the Appearance window. Your choices are *Tile, Zoom, Center, Scale, Fill*, and *Span*. Try them all to see which works best for the image you've selected. Once done, click **Close** to complete the process.

Wallpaper from Internet to Desktop—Quick and Easy

It's also possible to almost automatically set an image from the Web as your desktop wallpaper by right-clicking that image within your web browser and then selecting **Set As Desktop Background**. A small window will appear in which you can preview what the download will look like onscreen (Figure 9-5).

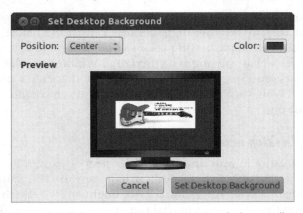

Figure 9-5: Selecting web page images as desktop wallpapers

You can also adjust the position (tiled or centered, for example) and background color for your desktop in this window. Once you're done making adjustments, click the **Set Desktop Background** button. The image will then appear on your desktop, while the image file will be saved to a download location (your Home folder, by default) with the title *Firefox_wallpaper.png*.

Changing Themes

Before leaving the Appearance window, it's worth mentioning a few more customizations you can perform from this window. The first can be accomplished from directly below the Wallpapers pane. There you will see a drop-down menu button that says Ambiance, which is the name of the default Ubuntu theme. If you click that button, you will see there are also three more themes: Radiance, High Contrast, and High Contrast Inverse. Slim pickings to be sure, but interesting enough. To see the effects, just try each of them out, and within a few seconds you will see how they look. If you like what you see, you can just close the window.

Changing Your Launcher Icon Size (Unity 3D Only)

Another customization you can perform has to do with the size of the icons in the Launcher. If you look at the bottom portion of the window, you can see a slider that allows you to change the size of these. The default size for the Launcher icons is 48×48, but you can shrink them to a very manageable 36×36 or puff them up to 60×60. Just move the slider, and the icons will change size. When you are satisfied, close the Appearance window.

Autohiding the Launcher

There is yet one more customization you can perform from the Appearance window—autohiding the Launcher and setting the desktop hotspot you will use to make it appear again when you want it. To do this, click the **Behavior** tab. In the Behavior tab (Figure 9-6), switch on the on/off switch in the top-right corner of the window, select where on the desktop you want the reveal hotspot to be, and then use the slider at the bottom to determine how sensitive you want that hotspot to be. I would recommend choosing Left side and making the sensitivity rather high, because getting the Launcher to pop out of hiding can take some getting used to; the process just doesn't have the same smooth feel as you might be used to in Windows or Mac. You kind of have to whack the cursor against the left side of the screen and then draw away gently. Well, you'll get the hang of it, and when you do, you'll find that it works just fine.

Stretching Desktop Icons

One more feature in your desktop environment is worth noting—stretchable icons. You can make individual desktop icons any size you want, which can be aesthetically pleasing. For example, you might stretch the thumbnail of a photo file so that it appears as desktop art or of a folder or file so that it is easy to find and open (see Figure 9-7).

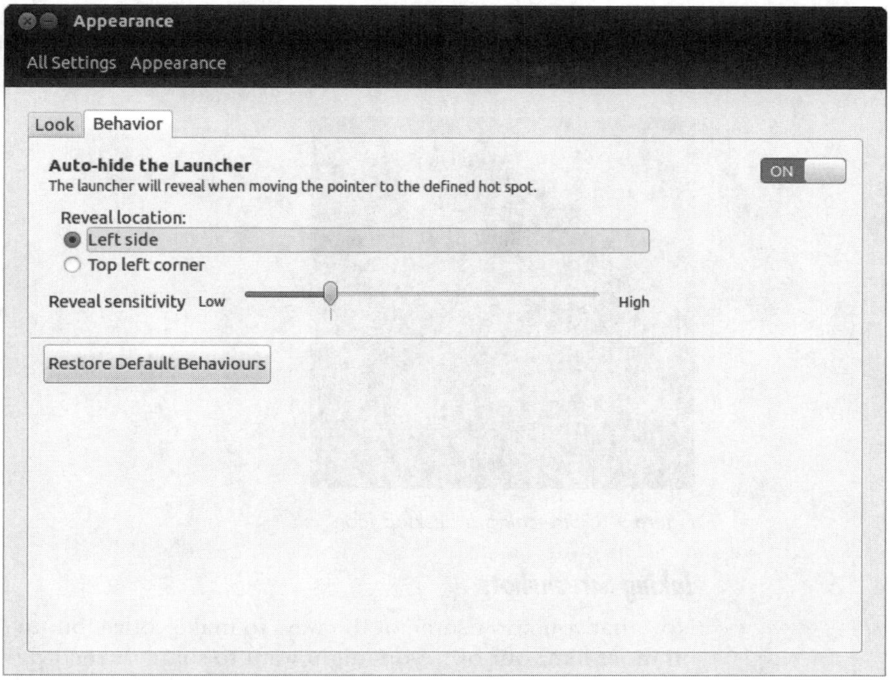

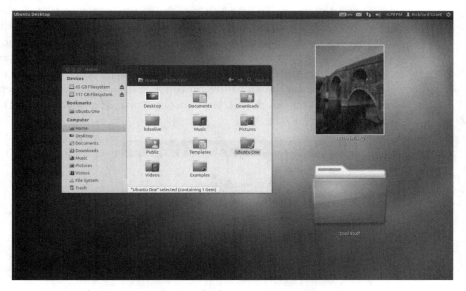

Figure 9-6: Autohiding the Launcher and setting a hotspot to make it reappear

Figure 9-7: Desktop icons can be stretched to any size you want.

To stretch a desktop icon, right-click the icon and select **Resize icon** in the pop-up menu. Four blue squares will appear at each of the corners surrounding the icon (as shown in Figure 9-8). Just click and drag any of those squares until the icon is the size you want. Once you are done stretching, click anywhere on the desktop, and the squares will disappear. If you have second thoughts and want to revert the icon to its original size, right-click it and choose **Restore Icon's Original Size** from the menu.

Figure 9-8: Stretching a desktop icon

Taking Screenshots

Now that you know some of the ways to make your Ubuntu desktop look a bit more like your own, you might want to share or record the results of your endeavors—either now or after going through the rest of the chapter. Taking screenshots lets you do just that. The easiest way to go about this is via key combinations. To take a shot of the entire screen, just press the PRINT SCREEN key. To take a shot of a single window, press ALT–PRINT SCREEN.

If you want to add a timed delay to your shots or to fine-tune other features, then you will want to use the Screenshot application, shown in Figure 9-9. You can run Screenshot from the Dash by clicking the application lens and then the **Accessories** filter button and then looking for Screenshot in the results. You can do the same just by typing **screenshot** in the Dash and then pressing ENTER.

Figure 9-9: The Screenshot application

Whether you take a screenshot via keystrokes or the Screenshot app, you will hear a shutter-like *kashya* sound when the shot is taken, after which a window like the one in Figure 9-10 will appear. In that window, you can name the image and decide where to save it.

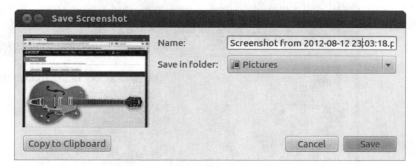

Figure 9-10: Saving a screenshot in Ubuntu

Customizing Your Desktop Environment: The Next Level

Now that you know what cosmetic tweaks you can do to your system without any outside assistance, it is time to move on to the next level so that you can tweak things a bit more. There are two applications that allow you to manipulate things you can't change with the tools that come bundled with your system. These are MyUnity and CompizConfig Settings Manager, both of which can be easily obtained from the Ubuntu Software Center. Both allow you to perform a variety of system tweaks without resorting to the command line.

NOTE *The features discussed in this section pertain to the Unity 3D environment. If you are running Unity 2D, you will find that many of the features discussed are not available.*

Customizations with MyUnity

MyUnity (Figure 9-11) focuses on appearances and behaviors of the Launcher, your windows, and other fixed graphical interface items. You can run it from the Dash by clicking the Applications lens and then clicking the Customization filter button. You can also just type `myunity` in the Dash and press ENTER.

Changing Launcher Properties

As you can see in the MyUnity's opening tab, launcher, MyUnity allows you to change the look and behavior of the Launcher. True, some of the tweaks you were already able to accomplish via the Appearance window, such as changing icon size and autohiding the Launcher, but MyUnity allows you do some other things as well. For example, you can have drives and disks be shown or not shown in the Launcher and adjust the Launcher's background transparency and icon backlighting. You can best understand the latter effects by playing around with options and seeing what happens (you can just set things back to what you see in the figure here if you want to get everything back the way it was).

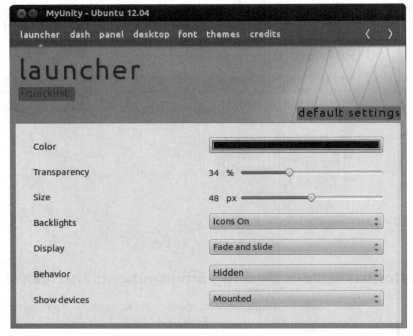

Figure 9-11: Changing Launcher settings with MyUnity

Changing Dash Properties

By clicking the dash tab, you can see the options available to you in MyUnity for customizing the Dash (Figure 9-12). These include being able to toggle on and off the displays of recently used apps and apps available for installation from the Ubuntu Software Center (they're both on by default). There is also a setting for Blur, which adjusts the background blur of the Dash to make items behind it less crisp. There's a Dash size option, which lets you switch between Desktop size, which covers only a portion of the screen, and Netbook size, a full-screen alternative.

Changing Panel Transparency

From MyUnity's panel tab, the only thing you can do is adjust the transparency of the top panel (Figure 9-13), but this cool feature is worth a look. Of course, the desktop background you are using will have an effect on how a more transparent panel will look, so bear that in mind as you experiment.

Changing Desktop Features

From MyUnity's desktop tab (Figure 9-14), you decide what items you want to show up automatically on your desktop (nothing is the default, as you know). These can include your home folder, drive, network, trash, and more. You can also toggle on and off window animations, if you are trying to speed up an old machine or if you don't much care for such things, and you can adjust the number of virtual desktops you have, both horizontally (H Desktop) and vertically (V Desktop).

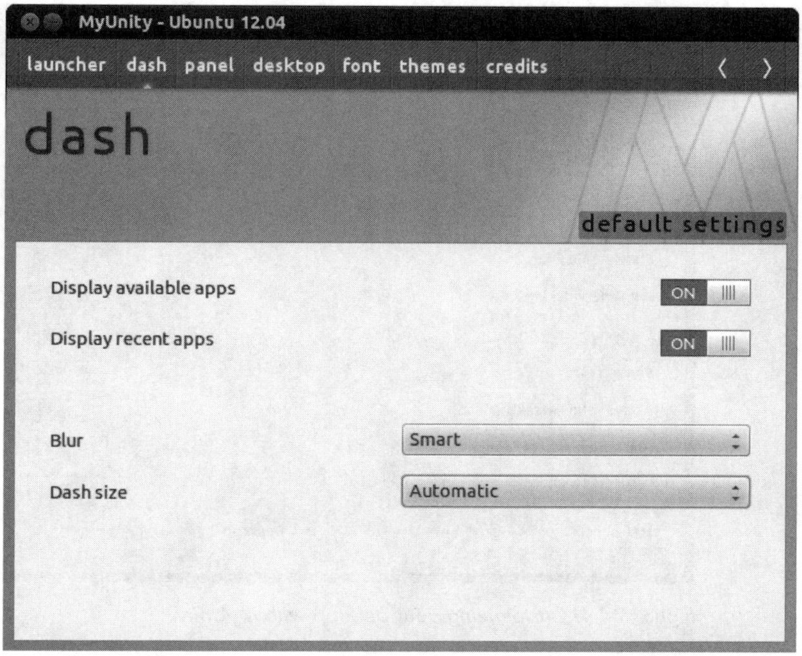

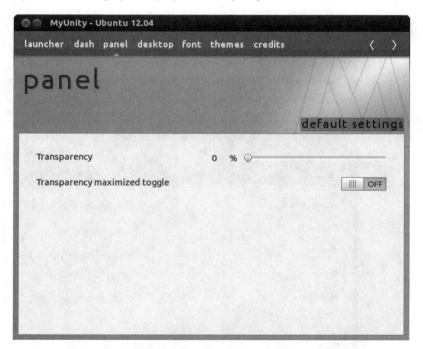

Figure 9-12: Changing Dash properties in MyUnity

Figure 9-13: Changing the transparency level of the top panel in MyUnity

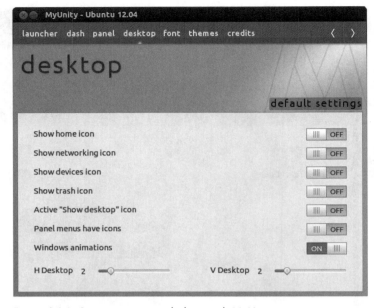

Figure 9-14: Customizing your desktop with MyUnity

Changing Display Fonts

The font tab (Figure 9-15) allows you to change the font face and size that appears in various part of your system interface. You can change the fonts for the panel, for the desktop, and for other parts of the system and even the default font for documents.

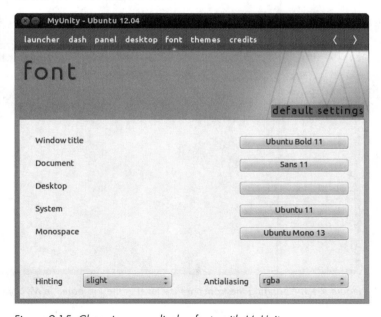

Figure 9-15: Changing your display fonts with MyUnity

Changing Themes

Finally, the themes tab (Figure 9-16) brings about the most dramatic visual effects. Selecting from the various themes and icon sets in the two columns allows you to change the overall look of your system by changing the window borders and icon sets in use. Just click the theme you want to try, and the changes will take place within seconds; see an example in Figure 9-17. The same is also true for the icon sets. Click a set and then take a look at a file manager window to see the effects. If you want to get back to the way things were, just remember that the default theme is called *Humanity* and the default icon set is called *Ubuntu-mono-dark*.

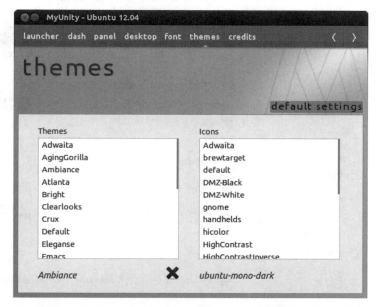

Figure 9-16: MyUnity allows you to change your window and icon themes.

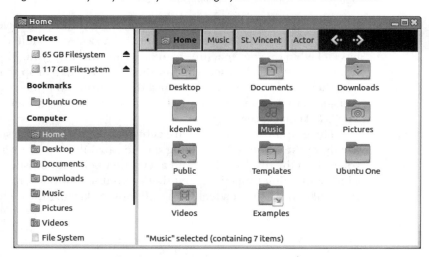

Figure 9-17: The results of a theme and icon change via MyUnity

Customizing Visual Effects with CompizConfig Settings Manager

Starting where MyUnity leaves off, CompizConfig Settings Manager, also known as CCSM (Figure 9-18), allows you to tweak more system elements and to configure effects. Compiz is the compositing engine at work in Ubuntu that provides it with its 3D effects, such as shadows and window animations. Its job is to bring together all the various elements at work in your system that create the graphical environment and then, in conjunction with your 3D–compatible video card, make everything seem to be working as one graphical unit. You might say it is the eye-candy engine for your system, and as such it is a busy bit of software indeed! CCSM is the graphical interface by which you can control Compiz's features.

Figure 9-18: CompizConfig Settings Manager

Compiz is automatically enabled at startup only if you have a graphics card that supports its basic set of features. An easy way to tell whether Compiz has kicked in on your machine is to open any window (your Home folder, for example) and check to see whether that window has a drop shadow. If it does not, then Compiz is not at work, and this section will not be of much use to you—skip to the next section. If it does have a shadow, however, Compiz is at work, so keep on reading.

The graphical effects that are active by default in your system are really the tip of the iceberg. Depending on the capabilities of your graphics card, you will get the drop shadows and a few other bells and whistles, such as cooler window-opening transitions, but that's about it—on the surface, at any rate. If you like, you can get a feel for it right now by kicking the effects up a notch.

First run CCSM by going to the Dash, clicking the Applications lens, and then clicking the **Customization** filter button and looking for it in the results shown. Or if you prefer, just type `compiz` in the Dash and press ENTER.

The very first thing you will see, along with the CCSM window, will be another window warning you that CCSM is an advanced tool and that you should proceed with caution. The warning is right, so if you're not sure what something in CCSM is or does, then perhaps you shouldn't fool with it. You should be safe trying out the things I mention here, however, starting out with *Wobbly Windows.*

To give Wobbly Windows a try (and thus get a hands-on feel for CCSM), click the **Effects** button on the left side of the CCSM window and then in the next screen check **Wobbly Windows**. In the screen after that, check the box next to the words **Enable Wobbly Windows**. In the small window that then appears, click the **Disable Snapping Windows** button. Now drag the window around. As you will see, the whole thing will start wiggling like jelly when you move it—freaky and totally distracting, but kind of cool. You can uncheck the Wobbly Windows box if the feature is getting on your nerves.

Another interesting tool is the Annotate tool, which can actually have some practical uses as it allows you to write on the screen (Figure 9-19). To activate the Annotate tool, click the **Extras** button in the left side of the screen, and then check the box next to **Annotate** in the new screen. Click the word **Annotate** itself to get to the preferences for that tool (this is the same way you access preferences for all tools and features), as shown in Figure 9-20, and thereby learn how to activate the tool's features.

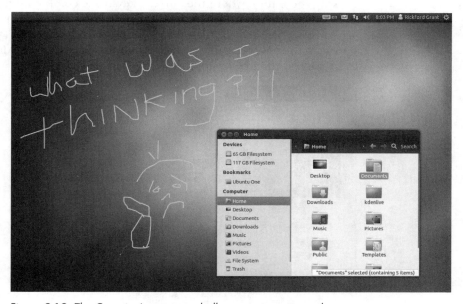

Figure 9-19: The Compiz Annotate tool allows you to write on the screen.

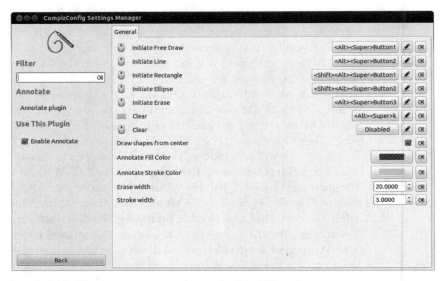

Figure 9-20: Almost every Compiz feature and tool has its own settings.

NOTE *Some of the keys used for the default Compiz shortcuts may seem unfamiliar; of these, the most commonly used ones are the* Super *key (typically the Windows key on your keyboard) and* Button1 *(usually your left mouse button).*

You can also edit the various keystroke combinations for certain tools by clicking the button where the current keystroke combination is shown and then making your new choices in the Edit window that appears (Figure 9-21). When you're done with the settings for an individual feature, click the **Back** button in the lower-left corner of the CompizConfig Settings Manager window to go back to the main screen.

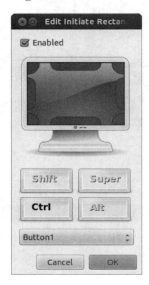

Figure 9-21: Changing the keystroke combination used to initiate or use a Compiz feature

Project 9B: Customizing Your Desktop Environment— There's No Place Like GNOME

We have now covered the major ways that you can alter the looks of your system using graphical frontends. However, you can also do some other things that are considerably more dramatic and that will give you the chance to put the command-line skills you acquired in Chapter 8 to good use. Now you'll have the chance, if you're so inclined, to journey to another world . . . well, another desktop environment anyway.

While Ubuntu is one of the most popular Linux distributions today, many folks are not too keen on the Unity desktop, and after giving it a shot, you may find yourself among the ranks of the disgruntled. If so, you need not despair for long—there are alternatives, and in this project you'll learn how to install perhaps the most well-known of them: GNOME. Not only will you install and learn to log in to the desktop environment that was there in the pre-Unity days, the *GNOME Classic desktop* (Figure 9-22), but you'll also install and learn how to switch to what GNOME has become—the *GNOME Shell* (Figure 9-23). Best of all, if you like the new GNOME Shell today and Unity tomorrow and GNOME Classic the day after that, it's no problem because all of those environments will be present in your system, waiting for you to call them to duty if and when you want or need them. Of course, since the interfaces of these environments are somewhat different from that of Unity, not all of the environment-specific information you've learned in this book will apply, but it should all be pretty easy to figure out.

Figure 9-22: The GNOME Classic desktop environment

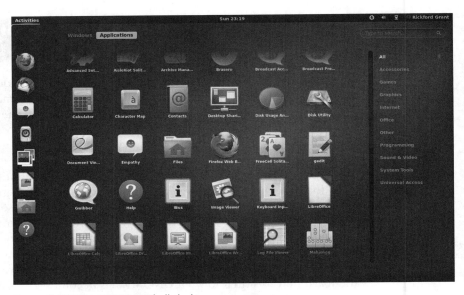

Figure 9-23: The GNOME Shell desktop environment

9B-1: Installing the GNOME Desktop Environments

For all the big changes that installing the GNOME desktop can bring about, it is surprising how simple it is to do. Here are the steps:

1. Open a Terminal window, type `sudo apt-get install gnome-session-fallback`, and press ENTER.

2. Type in your password when prompted and then press ENTER.

3. You will soon be asked if you wish to continue. Type **y** (for *yes*) and then press ENTER. The process will take up to a minute to complete.

4. When you are returned to the user prompt, type `sudo apt-get install indicator-applet-appmenu` and press ENTER. This process should take only a few seconds.

5. When you are back at the user prompt again, type `sudo apt-get install gnome-tweak-tool` and press ENTER.

6. When prompted, continue by typing **y** (for *yes*) and then pressing ENTER. This process should take the longest, probably over a minute.

7. When the process is complete and you are back at the user prompt, close the Terminal.

8. Log out.

9B-2: Switching to the GNOME Desktop Environments and Back Again

Once the installation process is complete and you've logged out, it is very easy to switch back and forth between desktop environments. At the login screen, click the Ubuntu logo next to your account name, as shown in

Figure 9-24. Another menu (Figure 9-25) will appear, showing you the available desktop environments. These should be *GNOME* (for GNOME Shell), *GNOME Classic* (for the good ol' GNOME of days past), *GNOME Classic (No effects)* (for graphically challenged systems), *Ubuntu* (the default Unity environment), and *Ubuntu 2D* (the default *fallback mode* mentioned in Chapter 3).

Just select the environment you want to use for the session you are about to log in to, after which you will be returned to the regular login screen. Type your password there, press ENTER, and voilá!

Figure 9-24: The Ubuntu logo in the login screen

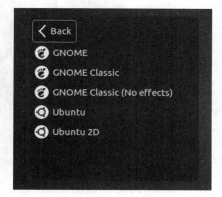

Figure 9-25: Selecting which desktop environment you want from the login screen

Project 9C: Switching from Unity to Cinnamon

Recently vying with Ubuntu in terms of popularity is another Linux distribution, itself based on Ubuntu, called Mint. Mint uses a desktop called Cinnamon, which might be described as a cross between GNOME Classic and MS Windows. It is a simple and clean yet very familiar-feeling environment, which might explain its popularity. Fortunately, you don't have to switch to Mint to get it; you can add it yourself. To install Cinnamon (shown in Figure 9-26), you have to add a repository to those already used by apt-get and the Ubuntu Software Manager, so you are branching out of the purer confines of the Ubuntu world, so to speak. But if you want to give it a try, here's what you do:

1. Type `sudo add-apt-repository ppa:gwendal-lebihan-dev/cinnamon-stable` in a Terminal window, and press ENTER. This adds the repository.

2. Type your password when prompted and then press ENTER.

3. You will be asked if you want to continue with the process of adding the PPA or cancel. Press ENTER to continue (or CTRL-C to cancel, just as it says in the Terminal).

4. Once you are back at your user prompt, update the database, as you learned to do in Chapter 8, by typing `sudo apt-get update` and pressing ENTER. This process will take a minute or so.

Figure 9-26: The Cinnamon desktop environment

5. Next, install Cinnamon by typing `sudo apt-get install cinnamon` and pressing ENTER.

6. You will be asked if you want to continue. Type **y** and press ENTER. The download and installation will take a couple of minutes or so.

7. Once the installation is complete, you will be back at your user prompt. You can then close the Terminal.

To see your new desktop environment, log out and then, once at the login screen, click the Ubuntu logo next to your username. At the top of the list that appears (which you saw earlier in the chapter when switching to the GNOME desktops), you will see a new entry in the list: *Cinnamon*. Click that and then proceed with the normal login procedures.

Once in the Cinnamon environment, you might want to make a few customizations so that the remnants of the Unity's Ambiance theme do not seem so out of place with that of Cinnamon's *Adwaita* theme. To make the changes, just follow these steps:

1. Click the **Menu** button in the bottom-left corner of the screen, hover your mouse over **Preferences**, and click **Cinnamon Settings**.

2. In the Cinnamon Settings window, click the **Other settings** tab. Then, from the drop-down menu button next to the words *GTK+ theme*, select **Adwaita**.

3. If you like, you can also change the icon theme by choosing from among the choices in the drop-down menu button next to *Icon theme*.

10

GUTENBIRD

Setting Up and Using Your Printer and Scanner

Two of the most common computer peripherals are printers and scanners. This only makes sense, because it is those two tools that turn a web-surfing, game-playing, music-churning, number-crunching box of chips into a meaningful production tool—a virtual publishing house, if you will. These devices help your computer convert digital information into hard copy (in the case of printers) and convert hard copy into digital information (in the case of scanners). It is not surprising, therefore, that these tools often come together these days in the form of multifunction printers.

In this chapter, you will learn how to connect these useful devices to your computer, how to set them up, and how to use them. You'll also learn how to find and install new fonts so you can make your printed documents look their best. If you're more into working with your digital camera than with a scanner, you might want to sneak a peek at Chapter 13; otherwise, put on your printer's smock and read on.

Printers

Unless the only thing you use your computer for is playing games, listening to MP3s, or stopping doors on hot, breezy days, you will no doubt want to hook up your machine to a printer. Despite the paperless-office era that the personal computer was supposedly going to usher in, it seems that the computer's strength as a desktop-publishing and general work tool has made producing high-quality printed documents an even more attractive proposition than ever before.

Confirming That Your Printer Is Supported

Setting up a printer to work with your new system is a pretty easy task, and it seems that printer support in the Linux world gets better with each release. In general, support for most printers is pretty good, with only very few makes and models struggling with compatibility.

If you really want to make sure your printer is supported, just try it by following the instructions in the next section. If you are thinking about buying a printer or are trying to decide whether to switch to Linux, go to *http:// www.openprinting.org/printers/*, where you can check out an online database to see whether your printer is currently supported and, if so, to what degree. Listings for supported printers also include information on which drivers are best for your purposes. If you're thinking of buying a printer for use with your Linux system, those manufactured by HP and Epson tend to be a pretty safe bet. You may also want to consult Ubuntu's list at *https://wiki.ubuntu.com/ HardwareSupportComponentsPrinters/*.

Getting Ubuntu to Automatically Recognize and Set Up Your Printer

Printer handling in Ubuntu is pretty much a no-brainer, because Ubuntu automatically detects most printers. If you have a USB printer, connect it to your computer and then power up the printer (vice versa should work just fine, too). If Ubuntu recognizes your printer—and chances are it will—it will be set up automatically in the background, without you needing to click a single button. The process only takes a couple of seconds, so you should be ready to print straightaway. To check that everything is hunky-dory, click the power button on the far right of the top panel and select **Printers** from the menu that appears (alternatively, search for *Printers* in the Dash). If your printer has been set up correctly, the Printing window will contain an icon with the make and model of your printer listed beneath it. There is nothing more for you to do in this case—your printer is set up and ready to roll.

It is also possible, however, that Ubuntu will recognize your printer but not find a driver that is an exact match for it. In this case, a window should pop up after you connect the printer, offering a substitute driver. If you find yourself in this situation, it wouldn't be a bad idea to print a test page to see whether the substituted driver works as it should. You can do this by selecting **Printers** from the top panel's power button menu and then double-clicking your printer in the Printing window that appears. A Printer Properties window will open. Make sure that *Settings* is selected from the list to the left of the window and then click the **Print Test Page** button (Figure 10-1). If the test page looks normal (something like Figure 10-2), everything should be fine, and you can close the Printer Properties and Printing windows.

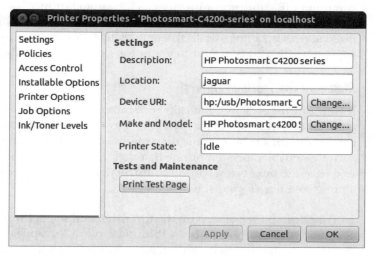

Figure 10-1: Printing a test page with your new printer via the Printer Properties window

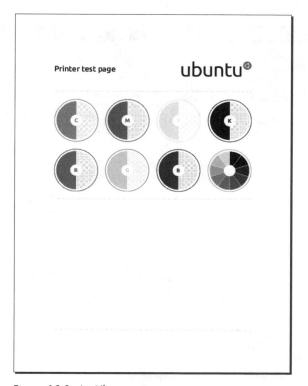

Figure 10-2: An Ubuntu printer test page

If you have a printer that plugs into your computer's parallel port, auto-detection and setup should also work if the printer was connected when you turned on the computer. If it was not, shut down your system and turn your computer off, connect your printer to the computer, turn on the printer, and then start your computer again. With luck, your printer should be recognized and set up automatically this time around. You can also try this same approach with a USB printer that was not recognized initially.

Manually Configuring Printers

If your printer isn't automatically recognized, you can still set things up manually. In this section, I'm assuming you have a printer that connects to your computer with a cable of some description, either USB or parallel. If you have a wireless-enabled printer, or one that's connected to your local network, skip to one of the next two sections for instructions. But for the cable-enabled among you, here's what you need to do:

1. Click the power button on the top panel and select **Printers** from the menu that appears. Either a Printing window will appear, showing the printers that have already been recognized, or a message will tell you that no printers have been configured yet.

2. Click the **Add** button, after which the system will show any new finds in a New Printer window (Figure 10-3).

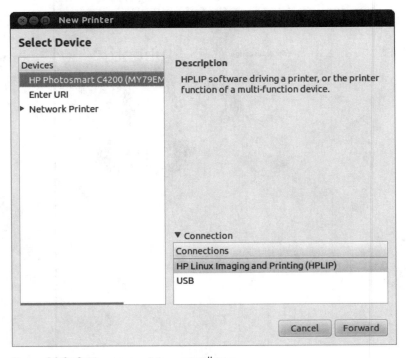

Figure 10-3: Setting up a printer manually

3. Click the entry for your printer in the left pane of that window and then click **Forward**. The system will begin searching for drivers for your printer.

4. If your printer is supported, the next page or two of the wizard will ask you to enter some basic details about the printer. These might include its make and model, for example. Fill in the blanks to suit your needs and then, when you get to the last page, click **Apply**.

5. The wizard will close, and you'll be asked whether you'd like to print a test page. To make sure that everything is hunky-dory, it is always a good idea to print a test page, so click **Yes**.

Your system will send a test document to your printer and let you know it has done so in a small window, which you can close. The printer should print the test page shortly.

NOTE *If your test page didn't come out the way it should or if your printer wasn't configured automatically or correctly by the system, check out* http://www.openprinting.org/ printers/ *to see whether there are any special requirements or caveats for your model.*

Setting Up Wireless-Enabled Printers

Printers with built-in wireless (Wi-Fi) adapters are becoming increasingly common. You normally have the choice of connecting them in the traditional way, using a USB cable, or by setting them up to connect to your wireless network. In the latter case, any computer that is also connected to the network can access the printer. Neat, huh? If you have such a printer and would like to make use of its wire-free capabilities from your Ubuntu machine, read on:

1. Make sure that the printer is turned on and connected to your wireless network. Exactly how you do this varies depending on the make and model of printer, so check out the printer's manual for instructions.

2. You'll need to get a couple of vital pieces of information about the printer's wireless network settings before you can continue. In particular, you're looking for its IP address. The printer will probably have a way of displaying this itself, either through a small built-in screen or by printing out an information page. Check the printer manual for details.

3. With the printer's IP address in hand, get back in front of the Ubuntu computer and click the power button on the far right of the top panel. Select **Printers** from the menu that appears, and a Printing window will appear.

4. Click the **Add** button, after which the New Printer window will appear.

5. Select **Network Printer ▸ Find Network Printer** in the left pane of that window by clicking that entry once. Now, enter the printer's IP address into the Host box, as shown in Figure 10-4. (Note that your printer's IP address will probably be different from the one shown here.)

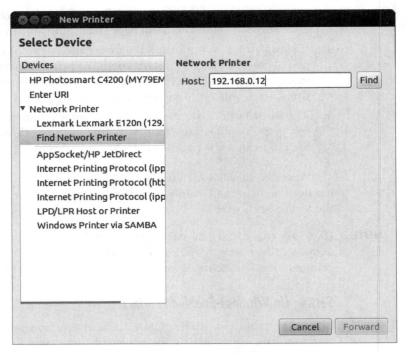

Figure 10-4: Connecting to a wireless-enabled printer

6. Click **Find**. After a little while, your computer should find the printer, and you will be taken to a page where you can specify information about its make, model, and so forth.

7. Now continue from Step 4 in "Manually Configuring Printers" on page 182.

Unfortunately, some wireless printers are a little fiddly to set up in Ubuntu, so the instructions above might not work. You may need to install extra software or try a slightly different type of "network printer" configuration than the one I discussed. If you suspect that your printer might be one of the awkward ones, try searching the Ubuntu Forums at *http://www.ubuntuforums.org/* to see if anyone else has figured out how to set it up. And of course, if nothing seems to work, you can always fall back on using a USB cable.

Setting Up Printers Connected over a Network

If you want to use a printer connected via a home or office network, just follow these steps:

1. Click the power button on the far right of the top panel and select **Printers** from the menu that appears. A Printing window will appear, showing the printers that have already been recognized and/or configured.

2. Click the **Add** button, after which the New Printer window will appear.

3. Select **Network Printer ▸ Windows Printer via SAMBA** in the left pane of that window by clicking that entry once and then click the **Browse** button in the top-right corner of the page.

4. In the SMB Browser window that appears (Figure 10-5), navigate your way to the printer you want to use. Sometimes it takes a little while for the information to load, so hang tight if things seem to have stalled. When you find the printer you're looking for, select it and then click **OK**. Once you're back in the New Printer window, click the **Forward** button.

5. Now continue from Step 4 in "Manually Configuring Printers" on page 182.

Figure 10-5: Browsing for printers connected over a Windows network

For the Driverless Among You

As I mentioned, Linux does not yet have built-in support for a few printers. If you find yourself with such a printer, you can take a few routes in order to get things working.

Checking the Connections

You'd be surprised how many times I have triumphantly solved someone's printer problems by simply turning on the printer or wiggling or replugging the USB or parallel connectors. Printers that are powered down and/or have loose connections are often to blame if the printer's model name fails to appear in the first page of the printer setup wizard.

If that approach fails, browse to *http://www.openprinting.org/printers/*, because sometimes Linux can support certain printers only if they are connected via the parallel port, even if they work via USB in other systems.

Trying Your Windows Drivers

If your printer came with an installation disc, you might want to see whether you can find a driver for it there. The driver on such a disc should end in *.ppd* (for "PostScript printer description"). To use one of these drivers, try adding your printer as described earlier, but when you get to the New Printer window where you select your printer's make, click the **Provide PPD file** option. Then try to locate the appropriate file by clicking the button that says **(None)** in the middle of the page. If you find your driver, click the **Forward** button and then continue the printer setup.

Using Third-Party Drivers

Recently, more Linux printer drivers are becoming available. If you don't find your printer on that second page of the printer setup wizard, just try searching the Web for the make and model of your printer plus the word *linux*. In the past, for example, I had a laser printer that did not appear at *http://www .openprinting.org/printers/*, so I searched for the printer, *samsung+SCX4100+linux*, which led me to *http://www.driverstock.com/*, a site that provides free printer drivers for most operating systems, including Linux. On that site, I found not only the driver for my printer but also the driver for its built-in scanner.

You might also want to check the website of the manufacturer of your printer, because many now provide Linux drivers for a number of their printers. Brother, Lexmark, Hewlett-Packard, Canon, and Samsung do, to name a few. There is also a German company (*http://www.turboprint.info/*; site in English) that provides Linux drivers, albeit for a fee, for machines that are really hard to deal with and for high-quality graphics solutions.

If you happen to find and download a driver for your printer that does not come with its own installer, just follow the directions given for trying Windows drivers. Finally, don't forget to give the Ubuntu forums (*http:// www.ubuntuforums.org/*) a try to see whether anyone there has any experience getting the printer in question to work on his system.

Trial and Error

Finally, there is always the old trial-and-error approach, which works on occasion. When setting up your printer via the wizard window, try choosing one of the other printer models and/or drivers available from your printer's manufacturer.

After you are done with the wizard, double-click the printer you added in the Printing window, click the **Settings** tab, and then click the **Print Test Page** button to see what happens. If nothing happens, click the **Change** button at the far right end of the Make and Model row on the Settings screen; select a different printer model and/or driver; and then, back on the Settings screen, click the **Print Test Page** button again. Repeat that process until something works. With any luck, something will . . . might . . . well, just give it a try if you're desperate.

Printing Details

Now that your printer is set up, you will no doubt want to start printing! This is an easy task, and it isn't very different from how it works in the Windows and Mac worlds, so you shouldn't need much explanation to proceed. In fact, printing in Ubuntu has become easier than ever, because all the settings you would normally want to toy with are all on their own tabs within the Print window that appears when you select Print in an application's File menu. I would even daresay that figuring out printing options in Ubuntu is now easier than it is in Windows or OS X.

You should be aware that the function of the tabs can vary depending on the application you happen to be printing from. For instance, the tabs you'll see when printing from the GIMP will be slightly different from those you will see when printing from Firefox. The General and Page Setup tabs will almost always be there, however. All that said, I'll give you an idea of some of the settings that are available within some of the Print window's tabs:

General   Printer selection, pages to print, number of copies, order of printing, collating

Page Setup   Pages per sheet, scaling, paper type, paper source, output tray

Options   Print frames, shrink to fit page, print background, headers and footers

Image Settings   Size, resolution, page positioning

Job   Print timing (now, later, at time), cover page

Image Quality/Advanced   Output resolution (DPI), printing speed and quality

Printing in LibreOffice

Occasionally, you will come across an application such as LibreOffice that has a slightly different way of handling printing. Fortunately, the differences may actually make printing in LibreOffice more Windows-like and thus easier for newbies from the Windows world to follow along with. As you can see in Figure 10-6, the main Print window for LibreOffice applications allows you to select the printer you want to use, the range of pages, and how many copies you want to print. You can access other options by clicking the Properties and/or Options buttons.

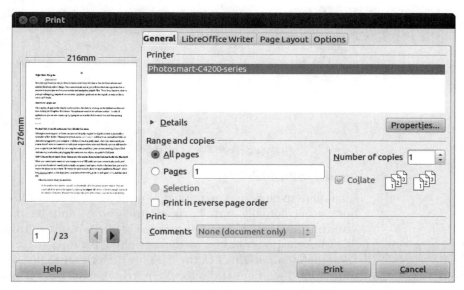

Figure 10-6: Print settings in LibreOffice

Printing to PDF

One of the nice features of Linux is that you can save most documents and web pages as PDF files. In some cases, such as in LibreOffice, you do this by exporting the document to PDF. In most other applications, however, you do it via the Print window, in which case you are said to be "printing to PDF." Whether you are *saving as* PDF, *exporting to* PDF, or *printing to* PDF, you are essentially doing the same thing: creating a PDF file of your document.

This is very handy, because it allows you to create documents that cannot be altered by others yet can easily be read regardless of the word processor program or operating system the reader is using. Best of all, this feature, which you would have to pay a pretty penny for in the Windows world, costs you nothing because it is built in to your system.

In most applications, you can print to PDF by going to the **File** menu of the application in question and selecting **Print**. When the Print window (Figure 10-7) appears, select **Print to File** in the list of printers and make sure **PDF** is selected as the output format. Choose a name for the PDF file and then click the **Print** button to save it.

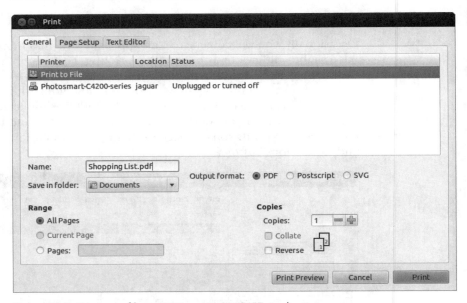

Figure 10-7: Printing a file to PDF in most GNOME applications

Canceling a Print Job

It happens to all of us. You wanted to print just 1 page of a 57-page document, but you accidentally started printing the whole thing. What can you do to save your ink and 56 sheets of paper? Fortunately, the solution is simple.

Click the power button on the far right of the top panel and select **Printers** from the menu. Right-click the icon for the printer that's overzealously handling your document and select **View Print Queue** from the pop-up menu. A window showing your current and queued print jobs will appear (as shown in

Figure 10-8). Your errant print job will be listed in that window, so right-click the name of the job to select it and then, in the pop-up menu, select **Cancel**. You'll be asked whether you really want to cancel the job; click **Yes**.

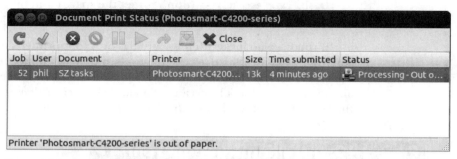

Figure 10-8: Canceling a print job via the Print Queue window

After you do this, the print job listed in the queue window will disappear, and your printer will stop printing. You can then close the print queue window. You may well find this easy process is more effective than what you've experienced in other operating systems.

In some cases, things will be even easier, particularly if you installed your printer driver yourself by means of the installer that came packaged with the driver. In such cases, the driver might provide its own progress window that will appear whenever you print a document. If so, you can simply click the **Cancel** button (or equivalent) in that window to cancel the printing job.

NOTE　*In some cases, you may have to clear your printer after canceling a print job. You can do this by turning your printer off, waiting a few seconds, and then turning it on again.*

Checking Ink Levels and Other Printer Maintenance Tasks

Printer ink or toner has a knack for vanishing like freshly baked cookies, so it's natural to want to check up on how your cartridges are doing. You might also run into problems with the printer, such as streaks on printouts or jagged lines that should really be straight, so it may be necessary to clean or align the print heads too. Unfortunately, there's no one simple method of doing this since every make of printer handles it differently. I'll just mention a few ways you can access these options for the most common brands:

HPLIP　This works only for Hewlett-Packard printers. Open the Ubuntu Software Center and install HPLIP Toolbox. Search for **HPLIP Toolbox** in the Dash to run it; use the Supplies tab to check ink levels and the Actions tab to align and clean your cartridges.

Mtink　This works for a number of Epson, Canon, and HP printers—check *http://xwtools.automatix.de/english/overview.htm#PRINTERS* to see whether your printer is supported. Open the Ubuntu Software Center, install Mtink, and then open it from the Dash to check your ink levels.

escputil   This works for some Epson printers and is worth a try if Mtink doesn't support your model. Open the Ubuntu Software Center and install *escputil*. Then open a Terminal by searching for Terminal in the Dash. Type `escputil -i` (don't forget the space) and hit ENTER to display the ink levels. To clean the print head, type `escputil -c`.

If you have no luck with these utilities or if your printer's make isn't listed, you might still be able to access ink levels and maintenance functions using the manufacturer's own Linux driver, if one exists. Also, some newer printers allow you to check ink levels and align and clean cartridges using controls on the printer. When in doubt, check your printer's manual.

Project 10: Installing TrueType Fonts

On some level, printing is all about presentation. If you're going to all the trouble of printing something out, it's more than likely that you want it to look *good*. And few things affect presentation more than your choice of font: Unless you're a children's entertainer, you probably won't get far using a wacky font like Comic Sans on your résumé. Likewise, a medieval-looking gothic font would probably be wasted on that letter to your bank manager. Fortunately, your Ubuntu system comes with a wide variety of very usable and, at least to my eyes, handsome TrueType fonts. However, these tend to be a bit on the conservative side of the aesthetic spectrum, and many users will want to add a few more distinctive fonts to the system repertoire.

Your bank manager may not appreciate that Gothic font, but you may want to print an award for an event using it. Or you might be preparing a newsletter for the local chapter of your snail-breeders society and want to use a font that is round, bubbly, and slimy. Whatever your penchant, purpose, or desire, you will probably reach a point when you want to install some other TrueType fonts on your system, so in this project I'll tell you how to do just that.

How you install fonts depends on who is going to use them. If you have only one user account on your machine, the easiest way is to install the fonts locally, as described in "10-2: Installing Fonts Locally" on page 191. Locally installed fonts are ones that only you or someone logged in to your user account will be able to use. On the other hand, if you have more than one user account and want the fonts to be available to all the users on your machine, you'll need to install them globally—in this case, see "10-3: Installing TrueType Fonts Globally" on page 192.

10-1: Getting the Font Files

The Internet is awash in free fonts. For this project, I will point you to the *http://www.fontfreak.com/* site, which has a very nice collection of fonts. Once you get to the FontFreak home page, click the **Fonts** link under the "FREE FONTS" heading on the left side of the page. The next page will ask you whether you want to download all the free fonts on the site in one single file; click **No thanks, I will download them one by one**. This will lead you to the main list of free fonts; browse through the various pages until you find one that is to your liking and then click it. Which font you download is completely up to you, but be sure to choose the PC version, not the Mac version. You can do this by clicking the small Windows icon immediately to the right of the font's name. When the download window pops up, choose **Save File** and click **OK** to save the font as a Zip file. To follow along with this project, download a couple of fonts—I chose Aajax Surreal Freak and Accidental Presidency.

When you've finished downloading, drag the font files from the *Downloads* folder (or wherever you saved them) to your Home folder so it's easy to follow along with my instructions. Also, be sure to unzip your font files before going on to the installation steps. (Right-click each Zip file and choose **Extract Here**.)

10-2: Installing Fonts Locally

If you're the sole user of your computer, installing fonts locally will do just fine. To get started, you need to set up your system by providing it with a location for your fonts. You will need to do this only the very first time. Here's what you must do:

1. Open your Home folder and, in that window, create an invisible fonts folder by selecting **File ▸ Create Folder**.
2. When the folder appears, name it *.fonts* (the period before the name means that it will be hidden).
3. Hide the new folder by selecting **Edit ▸ Reload**. Your *.fonts* folder should no longer be visible. If this is the case, you can close the window—your setup was successful.

Now that everything is set up, let's continue with this project using one of the fonts you downloaded. After you've decided which font to use, follow these steps:

1. Choose the unzipped font file (its name probably ends in *.ttf*), and copy it by right-clicking and selecting **Copy**.
2. Press CTRL-L or select **Go ▸ Location**. This will display the location bar in Nautilus.
3. In the location bar, type ~/.fonts and press ENTER. The ~ sign is a short-cut that means "my Home folder."
4. You should be taken to the empty *.fonts* folder you just created, like the one in Figure 10-9. Right-click anywhere in the folder and select **Paste** to copy the font into the folder.

Now that you have installed your font, you can give it a try in one of your applications, such as LibreOffice Writer. (Any running applications need to be restarted before the new font will appear in that application's font menu.)

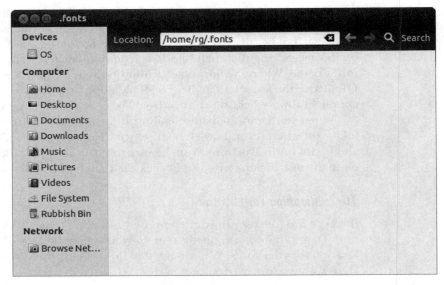

Figure 10-9: The empty .fonts folder

10-3: Installing TrueType Fonts Globally

As I mentioned earlier, the font you just installed locally can be used only when you log in under your usual username. If, however, you want to install fonts that can be used by you and anyone else who has an account on your computer, the process is slightly different and will require a little "superuser" action. You can use the other font you downloaded for this part of the project.

The folder for globally installed fonts is in root territory, so you will need to open the file browser as superuser in order to install the fonts. *Superuser* is another name for the root (administrative) user. It's possible to run a program as root without switching to a different user account by using a system called sudo (discussed in Chapter 8), but since root can modify important system files, you shouldn't run a program in sudo mode unless you absolutely must.

Here are the steps for getting your font file into the global font directory:

1. Press ALT-F2 and then type `gksudo nautilus /usr/share/fonts/truetype` into the box that appears. Press ENTER and type your password if prompted.

2. A file browser window will open. Select **File ▶ Create Folder** to create a new folder; call it *MyFonts*.

3. Open a normal file browser (Nautilus) window by right-clicking the **Nautilus** icon on the Launcher and selecting **Open a New Window**. Find the *.ttf* font file you want to install, and copy it (for example, by right-clicking it and selecting **Copy**).

4. Switch back to the TrueType file browser window, open your newly created *MyFonts* folder, and paste the font file into it.

5. Be sure to close the superuser file browser window—leaving it open is a recipe for disaster!

The gksudo command in Step 1 is the graphical environment version of the nongraphical sudo command that you saw how to use via the command Terminal in Chapter 8.

Now you can test things by opening LibreOffice and looking for the font in the font menu. Remember that you will need to restart LibreOffice if it was already open when you installed the font.

Scanners

Scanners are extremely useful and about as cheap a peripheral device as you can get. They allow you to put images or pages of text into digital form and input them into your computer—in much the same way as you would duplicate a document on a copy machine.

Even though scanners have been around for a relatively long time, support for them in Linux is still a bit spotty. Fortunately, this is changing for the better with every new Linux release. The backend—the hidden part of your system that handles scanner recognition and support in Linux—is called *Sane*. If you are wondering whether Linux will be able to recognize your scanner or if you are trying to figure out what type of scanner to buy, you can visit the Sane website at *http://www.sane-project.org/sane-mfgs.html*. There you will be able to see whether your scanner is supported or get tips about what scanner to buy. The page is pretty long, so you might want to use the Find function in your web browser (select **Edit ▸ Find** in Firefox) to search for your scanner model. As I have mentioned, you can also try the Ubuntu forums (*http://www.ubuntuforums.org/*) and ask for Ubuntu-specific recommendations there.

Scanning, No Questions Asked, with Simple Scan

Simple Scan is a relatively new addition to Ubuntu's lineup of default applications, and it certainly lives up to its name—it doesn't take many clicks to get a document from scanner bed to computer screen. To run Simple Scan, make sure that your scanner is connected and switched on and then open **Simple Scan** from the Dash. If you get a warning saying that no scanners were detected, skip to "Unrecognized Scanners" on page 196.

Assuming that your scanner has been recognized, you'll be presented with the screen in Figure 10-10.

It's pretty easy from here—select the type of document you're scanning (Text or Photo) from the drop-down menu next to the Scan button (the menu's icon is a small down arrow) and then click **Scan**. Your scanner will roar into action, and, after a short wait, you'll be presented with a preview of the picture or document you placed on the scanner. You can crop and rotate the image by using the options in the Page menu or by right-clicking the preview. When you're happy with your scan, select **Document ▸ Save** to finish up.

One little tip: To change the resolution of your scans, select **Document ▸ Preferences** and tweak the settings in the window that appears. Higher resolutions take longer to scan and take up more disk space, but lower resolutions can look terrible, so choose wisely!

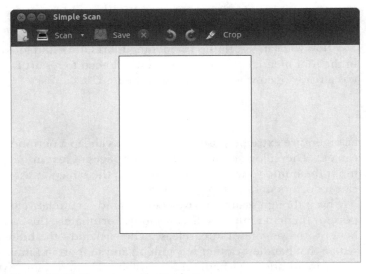

Figure 10-10: Scanning with Simple Scan

Not-So-Simple Scanning with XSane

Simple Scan will be able to handle most of your scanning needs, but if you have some particularly complex scanning that you need to do, you can use XSane. XSane is a real monster of a scanning program, packed full of professional features and fine-tuning options (see Figure 10-11). Search for and install XSane using the Ubuntu Software Center and then open **XSane Image scanning program** from the Dash. XSane will perform a search for an attached scanner. If it finds one, it will start up. If it doesn't, a window will appear that says "No devices available." If this happens, click the **Close** button and skip to "Unrecognized Scanners" on page 196.

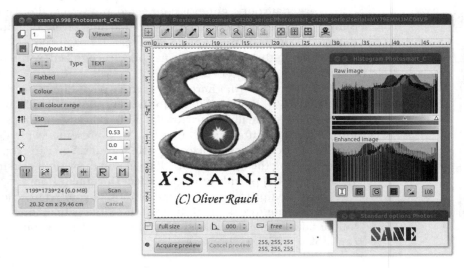

Figure 10-11: Scanning with XSane

To scan something, place your photo or document on the scanner bed and click the **Acquire preview** button in the bottom-left corner of the XSane Preview window. Once the preview appears, use the selection tools to define the exact area you want to scan. Then choose your resolution and color depth settings in the main XSane window. When everything is ready, click the **Scan** button. Your scanned image will appear in a viewer window (as shown in Figure 10-12).

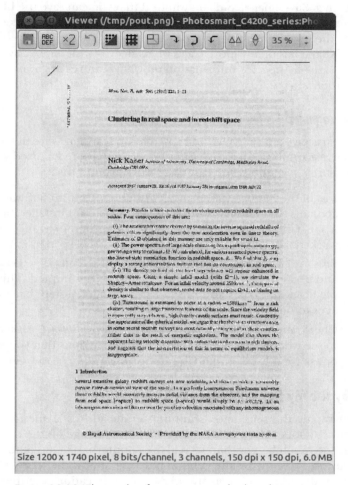

Figure 10-12: The results of your scan are displayed in a separate viewer window.

In that window, you can perform some minor tweaks of the scanned image using the buttons and menu items provided and then save the image by selecting **File ▸ Save image**.

If you want to convert a scanned document into a text file, you'll first have to install the *Gocr* package using the Ubuntu Software Center. Gocr performs a process called *optical character recognition*, which tries to figure out what text the image contains by recognizing the shapes of individual letters. (It only works for typed text, not handwriting.)

Once Gocr is installed, scan your document into XSane as before. This time, click the second button from the left (the one that says **ABCDEF**) before you click **Save image**, and you will find that you can save the file as a text document now as well. The text recognition isn't perfect, so make sure you go over the text file to look for typos afterward.

XSane has plenty more tricks up its sleeve—visit *http://www.xsane.org/doc/sane-xsane-doc.html* for information on what features are available and how to use them.

Unrecognized Scanners

If you receive a message telling you that no scanners were detected when you open a scanning program, Ubuntu may not have recognized your scanner. Here are a few things you can try to work around this:

- Install the *libsane-extras* package using the Ubuntu Software Center. This contains a handful of scanner drivers that aren't installed by default. Once it's installed, try opening your scanning program again to see whether it worked.

- Press ALT-F2 to open the Run a command screen. Type `gksudo simple-scan` and press ENTER, entering your password if prompted. This will start Simple Scan with root (administrator) privileges, a step that sometimes manages to raise the scanner from its slumber.

- Check out *https://wiki.ubuntu.com/HardwareSupportComponentsScanners/* to see whether there are any special instructions that you need to follow or ask for advice on the Ubuntu forums (*http://www.ubuntuforums.org/*).

Why Are My Scanned Images So Big?

To wrap up this section on scanning, let me address a question that seems to confuse a lot of people: Why does a scanned image on the computer screen seem so much bigger than its real-life counterpart? One of the first areas of confusion arises from the general blurring of how the terms *pixels per inch (ppi)* and *dots per inch (dpi)* are used. Most applications use these terms interchangeably, yet they aren't really the same thing. To make things simple, when you're talking about images on your screen, you are talking about *pixels* (the little squares that make up your screen image) per inch, and when you're talking about printer resolution, you are talking about *dots* (of printer ink) per inch.

Your computer screen generally has a resolution of 96ppi, while most modern inkjet and laser printers have a resolution range of 300 to 1200dpi or sometimes even more. This means that a photo scanned at 96ppi, which looks just fine on your screen, ends up looking pretty lame when you print it.

On the other hand, when you scan a picture at 300ppi, the image will look much better in your printout but will be gigantic if you display it "full size" on your screen. This is because there will be three times as many pixels per inch, so it looks three times bigger onscreen.

As an example, look at Figure 10-13, where you can see an identical image scanned at three different resolutions: 96ppi, 150ppi, and 300ppi. As you can see, the 96ppi image at the far left (measuring 5 by 6 inches—about the size of the hard copy itself) is the smallest, while the other two images are proportionally bigger (about 10 by 12 inches for the 150ppi image and about 22 by 25 inches for the 300ppi image).

Figure 10-13: The same image scanned at three different resolutions

Which Resolution Should I Use When Scanning?

Which resolution you use when scanning depends on a variety of factors, the most important of which is what you plan to do with the image when you're finished. When I look at Figure 10-13 on my computer screen, the smallest image looks best, the middle image looks okay, and the largest looks a bit odd, not as sharp as the other two. Basically, when scanning images for display on a computer—on web pages, for instance—it is probably best to stick with a ppi similar to typical screen resolutions or slightly larger: 96ppi to 150ppi.

When it comes to printing, a whole new set of considerations comes into play. First, there are the limitations of your scanner, since different models have different maximum resolutions. The resolution limits of your printer are also, naturally enough, a major consideration. For example, laser printers and inkjet printers have different characteristics; laser printers will generally produce better-quality images than inkjet printers, while inkjet output will be more greatly affected by the type of paper used than a laser printer will be. Of course, your printed output is not going to suffer if you scan your images at higher resolutions than those at which you plan to print them, but you will end up with a lot of files taking up too much disk space. Remember, *the higher the resolution of a scanned image, the greater the file size in terms of disk space.* If this is of concern to you, you can simply resize the images after you're done printing using an application such as the GIMP (more on that in Chapter 13), but if you would prefer not being so cavalier with your use of disk space from the get-go, you can follow these very general guidelines:

- If you are using a laser printer, scan at the same resolution at which you are going to print.
- If you are going to use an inkjet printer with photo-quality paper, scan at about 80 percent of your target printout resolution—about 240ppi for a 300dpi printout.
- If you are using an inkjet printer with regular paper, scan at about 65 percent of your target printout resolution—about 195ppi for a 300dpi printout.

Needless to say, these are just suggestions to get you started. What works best for you and your particular scanner/printer setup may be slightly different. Nothing works better than a bit of experimentation and trial and error. In this case, you can't really go wrong. Just give yourself some time, don't get frustrated, and, most importantly, don't wait until you desperately need to scan something before trying things—stay ahead of the game.

11

POLYGLOT PENGUINS

Linux Speaks Your Language

These days, almost all operating systems are multilingual, or at least capable of becoming so. This is true of Linux as well. Just open your web browser, and, without performing any special installations, you can read pages in any European language, including those with non-Roman alphabets such as Bulgarian, Greek, Russian, and Serbian. You can even view pages in Chinese, Japanese, Thai, Arabic, and Hebrew, to name but a few.

But the multilingual capabilities of Linux are much greater than this, and the way that it handles multilingual matters makes it easy to take advantage of these capabilities. As you will soon see, you can even set up your system to give you a totally foreign-language environment, allowing you to function completely in the language of your choice. Add to this the ever-expanding number of free programs available for language study, and you have a truly meaningful language-learning tool.

Read-Only Language Support

If all you want is to be able to read web pages or documents written in a foreign language, you don't need to install any additional language support, except in some rare cases. From the get-go, you will be able to view documents in just about any language you happen to throw at your system—it doesn't matter if it's Swedish, Italian, Chinese, Japanese, Arabic, Hebrew, Russian, Vietnamese, Armenian, or Thai. You will be able to read whatever you are linguistically capable of reading (see Figure 11-1 for an example).

Figure 11-1: A Japanese web page displayed in Firefox

Almost all web browsers these days can automatically recognize the language in which a web page is written and thus display the page correctly. Sometimes, however, the author of the page may neglect to include the character coding for that page in the HTML, in which case your web browser, not knowing that the page is prepared in another language, will often open it in the default language of your system. The result is a page on which you see nothing but odd combinations of symbols and letters that have no meaning. In such cases, try changing the character coding in your browser to the language encoding you believe the page is in. Some languages employ more than one encoding scheme, so if you're not sure which one the page is prepared in, give each possibility a try. In Firefox, you can make your choices by selecting **View ▸ Character Encoding**. From the submenu there, you can select the appropriate coding for the language of that page.

Typing Nonstandard Characters

Typing characters that are not standard in English, such as *é, ç, ß, ø, æ,* and *å,* can be done quite easily in Linux without any modifications. In most situations, you can do this by using the Character Map utility included in your system, which can be found by going to the Dash, typing `character map`, and pressing ENTER. Alternatively, from the Dash you can click the Applications lens and then the **Accessories** filter button. When you run Character Map, a window like the one shown in Figure 11-2 will appear.

Figure 11-2: Inputting characters with the Character Map utility

To input the character you want, just select the language or character set in the left pane of the window and then, in the right pane, double-click the character you want to input. The character will appear in the little input box next to the words *Text to copy* at the bottom of the window. Just click the **Copy** button and then paste the character into whatever application you want to place it in.

LibreOffice offers a method of its own, which you can also use. In the menu bar, select **Insert ▸ Special Character**. A selection window will open, and you can select the character you want there. Once you've done that, click the **OK** button, and the character will appear in your document, after which the selection window will close by itself. Double-clicking the character you want will accomplish the same thing.

Using the Compose Key Option

If you need to type an accent or umlaut only once in a while and don't feel particularly keen on opening an application or going to a special menu to do so, using the *compose key option* for your keyboard is a good way to go. Basically this means you use one of the lesser-used keys on your keyboard in conjunction with six symbols (` , ' ~ " ^) to help in the creation of accented characters.

Before you can use this feature, you have to select which key you want to use as your compose key. For this example, I'll use the right ALT key, since most people don't use it much. Here's what you need to do:

1. Go to the Dash, type `keyboard layout`, and press ENTER.
2. In the Keyboard Preferences window that appears, click the **Options** button.
3. The Keyboard Layout Options window will now appear. In that window, click **Compose key position**.
4. Check the box next to the key you want to use as your compose key (Figure 11-3). Then close the Keyboard Layout Options window and the Keyboard Preferences window.

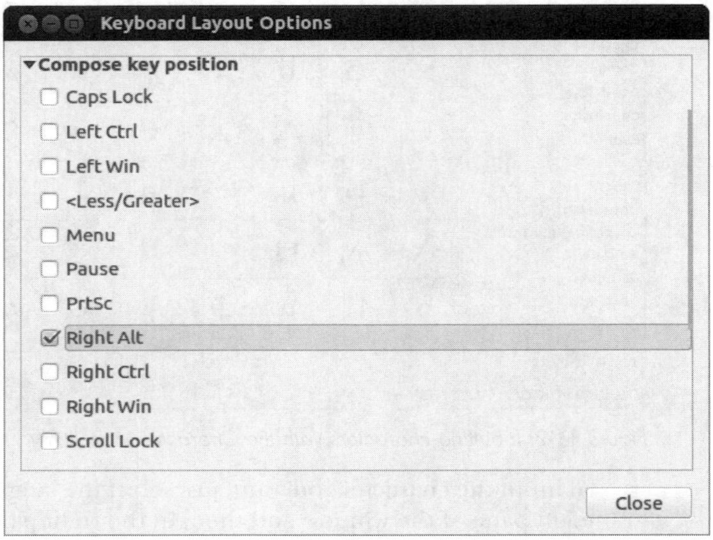

Figure 11-3: Selecting your compose key

Once you've done that, you can use your compose key to type those characters. Let's say, for example, that you want to type an umlauted *u* (that is, *ü*). While pressing the right ALT key (or whatever key you selected as your compose key), you'll press ". Then you'll release the right ALT key, type **u**, and voilà—you'll have yourself an *ü*! Here are some more examples:

á	right ALT-**'** then **a**
ç	right ALT-**,** then **c**
è	right ALT-**`** then **e**
ñ	right ALT-**~** then **n**
ô	right ALT-**^** then **o**

NOTE   *These sequences are based on US keyboard layouts. Combinations for other layouts may differ.*

Adding Keyboard Layouts

If you often type in a particular foreign language, it might be more convenient for you to add a whole new keyboard layout for the language or languages you use. For example, if you often type in Swedish and thus use the characters *å*, *ä*, and *ö* regularly, using the appropriate keyboard layout would be easier than repeatedly using the Character Map. This is even more true if you type in Greek, Russian, Serbian, Georgian, or any other language that uses a completely different alphabet. Of course, you will have to familiarize yourself with the keyboard layout, or *keymap*, for each language you choose, but this is a relatively easy task.

To add foreign-language keyboard layouts to your system's repertoire, here's all you need to do:

1. Go to the Dash, type **keyboard layout**, and then press ENTER.
2. In the Keyboard Layout window, click the + button at the bottom left of the window.
3. In the Choose a Layout window that then appears, select the keyboard layout you want to add, and when done, click **Add** (Figure 11-4).

Figure 11-4: Selecting foreign-language keymaps

4. Repeat Steps 2–3 to add other layouts (up to a maximum of four layouts).
5. When done, your window should look something like Figure 11-5, albeit with keyboard layout selections different from mine.
6. Close the window to complete the process.

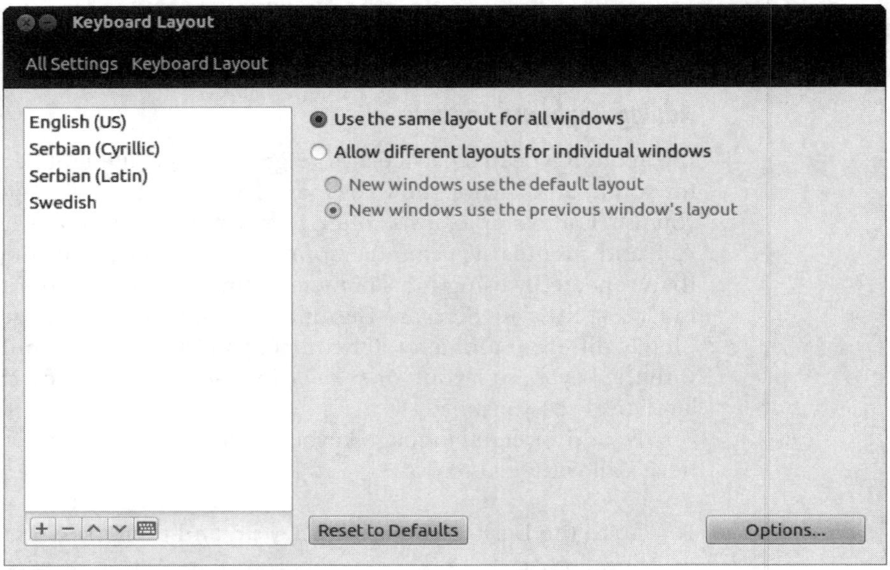

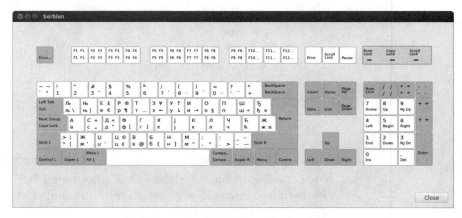

Figure 11-5: Selecting the active keyboard layouts on your system

After closing the Keyboard Preferences window, a keyboard layout indicator will appear in the upper-right corner of the top panel. The letters *en* will appear, indicating that you are currently using your English language keymap. If you click that indicator, you will toggle between any of the other layouts you've activated. If you are not sure where the keys are located in your current keymap, you can get some help by right-clicking the indicator and selecting **Show Current Layout** in the drop-down menu, after which a map of the new layout will appear in a separate window, such as that shown in Figure 11-6. The keymap shown in that window can be rather hard to make out, so you will probably need to expand the window by dragging it by one of its bottom corners.

Figure 11-6: Having a look at a map of your current keyboard layout

If you want to choose just a single keyboard layout to replace your current one (such as British English instead of American English or German instead of Spanish), you can do so from the Keyboard Preferences window. Simply add the keyboard layout you want to use and remove any additional layouts by clicking each one and then clicking the – (minus sign) button.

Chinese, Japanese, and Korean Input

For most European languages (and many other alphabet-based non-European languages), pressing a letter on the keyboard simply prints that letter to the screen. However, Chinese, Japanese, and Korean require a kind of conversion process, which is handled by a special application (actually a set of applications) called an *input method editor (IME)*. Each of these languages has its own IME, and each is quite different because of the basic differences in the three writing systems.

Chinese

Although most people (at least those in the linguistic know) would think that Chinese would be the most complicated system, because the writing system consists of thousands of characters, it is in fact the simplest. The Chinese IME simply takes the Romanized keyboard input, known as *pinyin*, and converts it into Chinese characters, or *hanzi*. For the IME, it is essentially a simple dictionary lookup task—big dictionary, simple IME. In the event that there is more than one character for the pinyin input, a list of possible candidates will appear, and the user simply selects the appropriate character from that list, as shown at the top of Figure 11-7. At the sentence level, the Chinese IME now also has predictive capabilities with which it can guess which character you intend to type based on the context of what you've typed so far, as shown at the bottom of Figure 11-7.

Figure 11-7: Chinese IMEs can predict what you're going to write . . . kind of.

Japanese

The Japanese IME has a considerably more complicated task to perform, because it has three writing systems to deal with: *kanji* (ideographic characters borrowed long ago from China), *hiragana* (the phono-alphabetic system used mainly for tense and case endings), and *katakana* (used mainly for words borrowed from other languages). Still, the standard input method for Japanese is primarily via the standard Roman keyboard layout, plus a few extra special-function keys. Thus, typing in Japanese is a two-step process whereby the IME first converts the romanized text into hiragana as it is typed and then converts it to appropriate kanji, katakana, or hiragana elements after the spacebar is pressed.

You can see an example of these steps in Figure 11-8. In the first line, the IME has already converted the Romanized input on the fly. It has converted *rinakkusudenihongonyuuryokugamodekimasu* (which means *You can input Japanese in Linux*) to hiragana. When a line of hiragana is highlighted, it means that the line has not yet been converted beyond that. In the second line, however, the user has subsequently pressed the spacebar, which caused the IME to convert the hiragana string into the appropriate kanji, hiragana, and katakana elements. The first word, *Linux*, has been converted to katakana text because it is a borrowed word, while *Japanese input* has been converted to kanji; the rest stays in hiragana.

りなっくすでにほんごにゅうりょくができます。

リナックスで日本語入力ができます。

Figure 11-8: IME conversions while typing in Japanese

Korean

The job of the Korean IME is again quite different from that of the Chinese and Japanese IMEs, because the language is written in a very different way. Korean is written either entirely in alphabetic letters, called *hangul*, or in a combination of hangul and ideographic characters borrowed from Chinese called *hanja*. While the hanja characters are essentially the same as their Chinese and Japanese counterparts, hanzi and kanji, the Korean phonetic alphabet, hangul, has it own unique appearance, as you can see in the Korean word for Korea, *Hangug(k)*, in Figure 11-9.

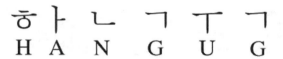

Figure 11-9: Korea (Hangug) written horizontally in hangul

This seems simple; however, the representation is not quite correct, because Korean is very distinctive in the way that its alphabetic characters are put on the page. Unlike the usual side-by-side positioning of hiragana, katakana, and most alphabets, hangul letters are grouped in pairs, triplets, or even quadruplets, which are written, as a general rule, clockwise. The IME, therefore, must take the input (usually based on a Korean alphabetical keyboard layout) while it is being typed, and it must adjust the size, spacing, and positioning of each of the letters as it puts them into appropriate clusters (see Figure 11-10).

Figure 11-10: An example of the clustering process in the Korean IME

Project 11: Setting Up Asian-Language Support

So what do you do if, for example, you want to be able to type Chinese, Japanese, Korean, Thai, or Vietnamese while still in your usual English environment? What if you want to be able to type all of those languages in the same document? Can you do it?

You bet.

There are actually several ways of going about this, but the default method in Ubuntu is the easy-to-use *Intelligent Input Bus (IBus)*. IBus supports most East Asian languages, including Chinese, Japanese, and Korean, and it provides a number of input methods for many of these.

11-1: Installing IBus Input Methods

IBus is very easy to use, but out of the box, so to speak, it comes with only two input methods, both for Chinese: pinyin, used for simplified character input (the standard in mainland China and Chinese language classes around the world), and bopomofo, used for traditional character input, as found in Taiwan, Hong Kong, and overseas Chinese communities. To input other languages, you will have to install the appropriate input methods yourself. Just go to the Ubuntu Software Center and search for *ibus japanese* (there will be a number of methods, so I suggest trying *Anthy* first), *ibus korean*, *ibus thai*, and/or *ibus vietnamese*.

11-2: Selecting Input Method Modules

Once you have installed the input method you need, you will need to start up IBus and then select the input methods you want to use. Here are the steps:

1. Go to the Dash, type **keyboard input**, and press ENTER.
2. A window will appear asking whether you would like to start the IBus daemon. Click **Yes**.

NOTE *A daemon is a program that runs in the background, unbeknownst to the average user, providing a system with added functionality. In the case of IBus, that added functionality is the ability to input complex character sets.*

3. Another window will appear, telling you what to do if you cannot get IBus to work. Click **OK** in that window.

4. The IBus Preferences window will then appear. Click the **Input Method** tab.

5. On that tab, check the box next to **Customize active input methods**.

6. Next, click the **Select an input method** drop-down menu button, select the input method you require, and then click **Add**. The input method you just added will appear in the main pane of the window.

7. Repeat the previous step for any other input methods you want to add. When done, your window should look similar to Figure 11-11, depending on which languages you selected.

8. When you are done making your selections, click the **Close** button.

Figure 11-11: Adding Asian character input methods in IBus

11-3: Typing Asian Languages with IBus

Once you have chosen your input methods and closed the IBus Preferences window, a small icon that looks like a mini keyboard will appear to the left of the mail notification icon on the panel. If you have enabled multiple keyboard layouts in the previous section of this chapter, the keyboard will appear to the left of the identical keyboard selector icon. When you click that new IBus icon, a menu showing all the available input methods will appear (as shown in Figure 11-12). To be able to actually select a method, however, you will need to be using an application that accepts text input, such as Text Editor, LibreOffice, or even a web browser search box. To try things out, open LibreOffice Writer.

Figure 11-12: Selecting language input methods from the IBus panel applet

Once Writer appears, click in the document area and then select the input method you want to use from the IBus panel menu. You can now start typing in Writer using the input method you've selected. If you do not see the characters you intended to type but instead see nonsense characters (boxes or seemingly random symbols), try using another font.

To switch from one input method to another, there are two options. First, you can go to the IBus Panel applet and change methods from the menu options. Second, you can switch between methods with hotkey combinations: CTRL-spacebar toggles IBus on and off, while ALT-SHIFT-L switches you from one input method to the next.

Setting Up IBus to Automatically Start Up When You Log In

As you probably recall from when you first opened the IBus Preferences window, you have to start up IBus each time you log in to your system. If you use IBus a lot and would thus prefer forgoing this extra step, you can easily set up your system to start it automatically when you log in.

To do this, open the Language Support window by going to the Dash, typing **language support**, and pressing ENTER. In the Language tab of that window, select **ibus** in the drop-down menu button next to the words *Keyboard input method system*, as shown in Figure 11-13. When done, close the window. The next time you log in, IBus will automatically start up and be ready for action when you need to use it.

If IBus still does not start up automatically the next time you log in, try adding it to your system's list of startup applications. To do this, go the Dash, type **startup applications**, and press ENTER. This will open the Startup Applications Preferences window. In that window, click the **Add** button. In the Name box of the window that appears, type **IBus**, and in the Command box, type **/usr/bin/ibus-daemon -d**. When done, click **Add** and then close the Startup Applications Preferences window.

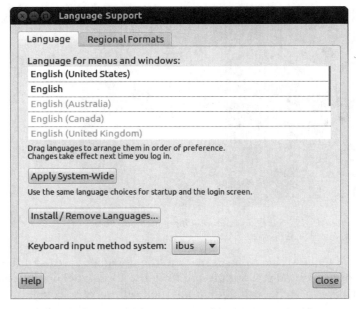

Figure 11-13: Setting up your system so that IBus automatically starts at login

Viewing Your System in Another Language

One of the many things that originally attracted me to the Linux world was being able to install language support for languages other than English and come up with a whole new system in a different language. I used to have one machine with support for Chinese, Japanese, Swedish, and my default, English, installed. After just a few clicks and simply logging out, I could log back in with an interface in a totally different language. I could have a Chinese, Japanese, or Swedish system whenever I wanted (or whenever a student visiting my office needed).

This is very useful if you're in an environment where not everyone shares the same native language. At my former university, for example, where my Japanese and Chinese students sometimes used my computer, the additional language support allowed them to log in using their own language. It's even pretty handy if you are studying a foreign language and want to give yourself as much exposure as possible to it. All in all, it is a very useful feature.

Taking advantage of this feature in Ubuntu is very easy. Basically all you have to do is install a group of support files for each language you want to add to your system. You can do this by running Language Support from the Dash and then clicking the **Install/Remove Languages** button in that window. When the Installed Languages window appears, choose from the various languages available by checking the appropriate boxes. (Figure 11-14).

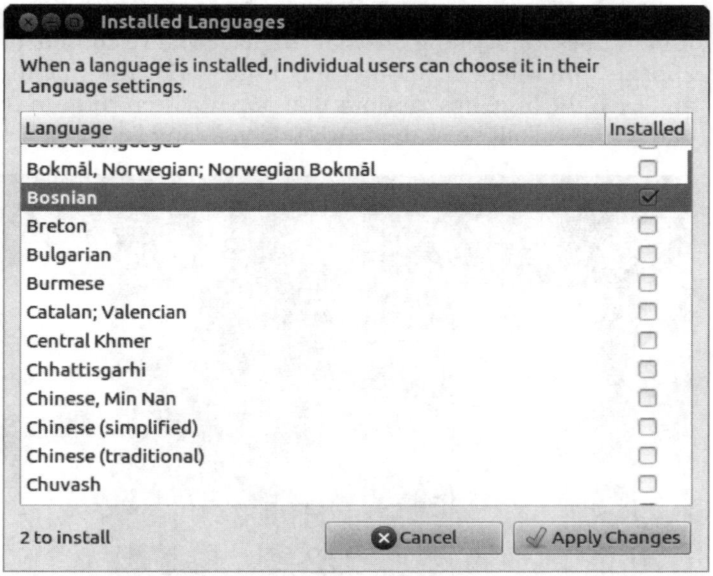

Figure 11-14: Selecting additional languages to install

Once you've made your selections, click the **Apply Changes** button. You will be prompted for your password at this point, so provide what is required, and the Language Support tool will begin downloading and then installing the support packages you specified. Once it is done, you will be notified and left with the Installed Languages window.

Once you have installed support for additional languages, you can choose to have your system open in a different language environment from the Language Support window by selecting the language you want to use when you next log in and dragging it to the top of the list (Figure 11-15). For languages with complex input systems, you can also select your input method of choice, such as IBus, in the menu button next to the words *Keyboard input method system*. You can then close the window, log out, and then log in again, after which your system will appear in the language you chose.

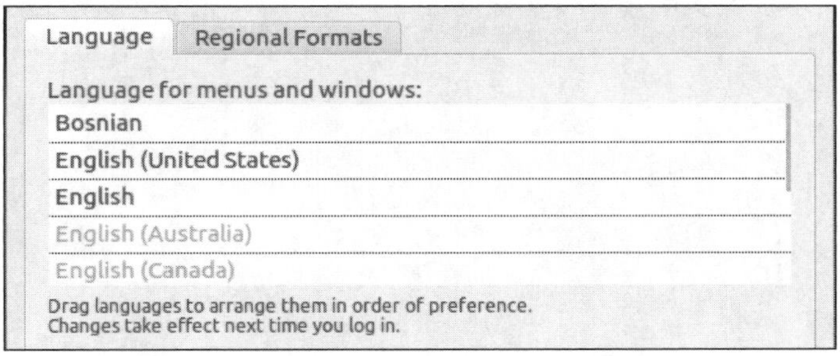

Figure 11-15: Selecting the language in which you want your system to appear when you next log in

Your startup process will then continue, and everything will progress as it usually does. Depending on what language you've chosen, once your desktop appears, you will be in another linguistic world. Your menus, applications, and even the little tips windows that pop up when you run your mouse over a panel icon will all be in the newly selected language (Figure 11-16).

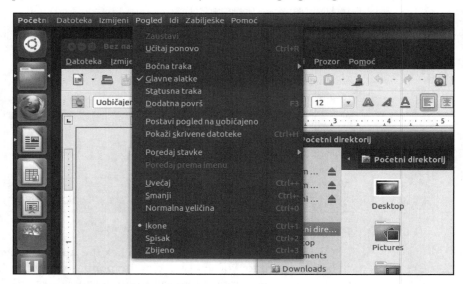

Figure 11-16: Portions of Ubuntu shown in Bosnian

12

PENGUINS AT WORK

Getting Down to Business in Linux

Although computers are used for such diverse (and fun!) activities as programming, making music, creating art, and playing games, at some point or another almost every one of us has to sit down in front of our machine and get some work done. That being the case, many users want to know what office-related applications are available for their system.

Fortunately, Linux can get down to business as well as the next OS. More importantly, since there are so many applications freely available for you to try, you might find that you actually end up using far more office-related productivity apps than you would if you had to pay for everything up front. In this chapter, I'll walk you through the offerings that come bundled with Ubuntu and then point you to yet others you might want to consider adding to your collection.

Where the Apps Are

The majority of apps in this chapter can be run from the Dash by clicking the Applications lens and then clicking the **Office** filter button. Exceptions are noted in the relevant sections. As with all applications, you can also run an app by typing its name in the Dash's search box and then pressing ENTER.

LibreOffice

When it comes to work, most people turn to office suites, which contain the apps they use most often—a word processor, spreadsheet, and presentation editor. The de facto standard among office suites is Microsoft Office, which is available in both the Windows and Macintosh worlds. Of course, because it is a Microsoft product, you can be relatively sure that no Linux version is (or ever will be) available.

Fortunately, Linux has an exceedingly capable office suite, and it comes bundled with Ubuntu. The suite is called LibreOffice, and it is the open source community-supported descendant of OpenOffice.org, the office suite originally bundled with most Linux distros until it was taken over and later jettisoned by Oracle (a bit of recent history there in case you wondered). LibreOffice is not some lightweight sour-grapes substitute for the Microsoft Office–less Linux world; it is a full-featured contender. LibreOffice, incidentally, is also freely available (as in *free*) in Windows and Mac OS X versions.

LibreOffice Applications

The entire LibreOffice office suite consists of a number of application modules, all but one of which come bundled with Ubuntu. These include a word processor (Writer), a spreadsheet (Calc), a presentation creator and player (Impress), and a very handy vector-drawing program (Draw). You can find all of these by going to the Dash, clicking the Applications lens, and then clicking the **Office** filter button. A database module (Base) is also available for LibreOffice as a separate download via Ubuntu Software Center (just search for *base*).

Since giving full and detailed instructions on how to use each of these applications would take up an entire book (and there are entire books on the subject), I will simply introduce each module to you. There is help, should you need it, in the LibreOffice Help system (**Help ▶ LibreOffice Help**) and online at *http://libreoffice.org/get-help/documentation/*. There are also numerous video tutorials available on YouTube.

Writer

As I mentioned earlier, the word processor is the office application that the majority of users turn to most often. Fortunately, LibreOffice Writer is a good one (see Figure 12-1). It is chock-full of features and can read and save Microsoft Word files. Like Word, it will even let you save your documents as HTML files so that you can easily change your documents into web pages. In terms of usage,

Writer is a very straightforward word processor, so I won't go into any more detail here. Again, check out LibreOffice Help or the online documentation mentioned in the previous section if you require more information.

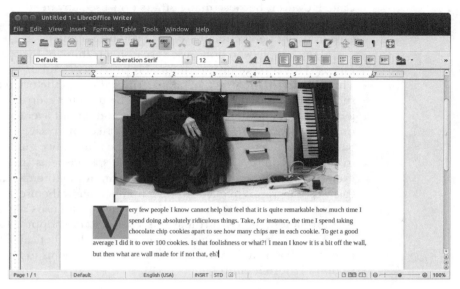

Figure 12-1: LibreOffice Writer

Calc

Calc is the LibreOffice spreadsheet application, and it is similar to Excel in terms of capabilities and general layout (see Figure 12-2). It can also, quite importantly, read and save Microsoft Excel files.

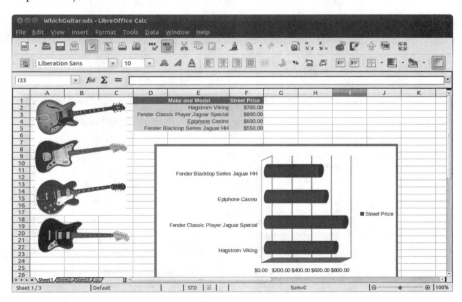

Figure 12-2: A graph created in LibreOffice Calc

Since most people who use spreadsheets generally understand what they are all about and, after a bit of poking around, can figure out how to use them, I won't take up your time here with any sort of primer about using Calc. However, because many others don't see any need to even try using spreadsheets, I will mention a few of the simpler tasks that can be done with Calc in the hope of enticing some of you into trying it.

Many people who don't use spreadsheets think of them as giant calculators used for computing uncomfortably large sets of numbers, such as payrolls. That view is not incorrect, of course, since that was the original purpose of such applications, but spreadsheets can be used for everyday tasks too. Projecting household budgets, calculating grade point averages (by teachers or students), figuring out how long it will take you to save up for your trip to San Marino, or even tracking prices for the four or five guitars you are trying to choose among . . . these are all tasks that spreadsheets are made for. What's even nicer is that when doing any of these minor mathematical tasks, you can easily create graphs to make abstract numbers show themselves to you visually.

If numbers are just not your thing, you can still use Calc for creating lists of information, such as birthday lists, class rosters, shopping lists, and address lists. You can even have Calc put the lists into alphabetical order, sort them by date of birth, and so on. Everyone eventually seems to find a use for Calc, so don't ignore it entirely.

Impress

Impress (Figure 12-3) is LibreOffice's answer to Microsoft's PowerPoint, with which it is compatible. It allows you to create attractive slides for use in presentations and allows you to create notes or handouts to accompany the slides. Although these features make Impress quite handy in business and education settings, you may not find as much value in it as a home user.

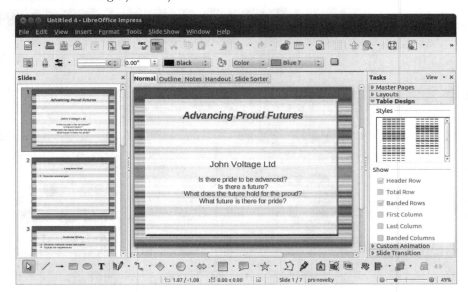

Figure 12-3: LibreOffice Impress

Draw

More useful to the home user is LibreOffice Draw, which just happens to be my favorite and, next to Writer, most frequently utilized LibreOffice module. Although Draw isn't great for creating true graphics in the artistic sense, it is very useful for creating flowcharts; organizational diagrams (such as seating arrangements for wedding receptions or conferences); or any other document in which you want a bit more control over the placement of text and graphics (especially when the two are combined), such as fliers, awards, diagrams, and newsletters. In this sense, Draw can be used quite effectively as a simple page layout program, as you can see in Figure 12-4.

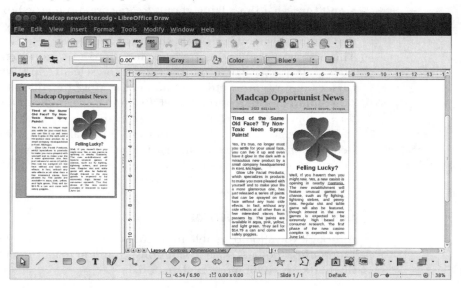

Figure 12-4: A newsletter created (and displayed) in LibreOffice Draw

Microsoft Office and LibreOffice File Compatibility

Although I mention the point throughout this section, it is worthwhile to reemphasize that LibreOffice can read and write Microsoft Office files. This compatibility is quite good, though tables sometimes prove slightly problematic.

To read Microsoft Office files, all you need to do is double-click the file in question, and it will open in the appropriate LibreOffice module. When saving files within LibreOffice for use in earlier versions of Microsoft Office, however, you must save them into the appropriate format. Otherwise, LibreOffice will by default save files into its native format (*.odt* for Writer documents, *.ods* for Calc documents, and *.odp* for Impress documents), and only the most recent versions of Microsoft Office can deal with these files.

To save a file in the format you will need, click the words **File type** near the bottom left of the Save window and select the appropriate Microsoft Office format from the list of available file formats that appears below—choose **Microsoft Word 97/2000/XP/2003** for a Writer document, for example.

LibreOffice Features

The three main applications in LibreOffice (Writer, Calc, and Impress) are quite similar to their pre–Office 2007 equivalents in Microsoft Office (Word, Excel, and PowerPoint), so switching to the LibreOffice applications should be relatively easy if you grew up with those versions of Microsoft Office.

If you don't have any experience with Microsoft Office, you should still find using LibreOffice applications straightforward because the basic layout is pretty intuitive. And if you are lacking in the intuition department, the built-in Help files are pretty good, too. To further help you along, the Tips system works just like tool tips in the Windows and Mac worlds. (In case you aren't sure what I'm talking about, *tool tips* are those little boxes that pop up to tell you what a button or menu item does when you place your mouse over that button or menu item.) Another cool and useful help feature is What's This, which works like the Tips system but provides more detailed explanations of what a particular button does. If you select **Help ▸ What's This**, your cursor will turn into a little question mark. Move that question mark cursor over almost any item in the LibreOffice interface, and you'll find out what it does rather than just what the item is called.

Despite all the straightforwardness I am speaking of, a few interface items will most likely be unfamiliar to you, so I will briefly discuss them. I'll be using the word processor, Writer, as I describe these things, so you can run Writer while following along to make things easier.

Getting to Know the Buttons

Although you should be able to figure out what most of the buttons on the LibreOffice toolbars do, a few buttons, common to all LibreOffice modules, might deserve a bit more explanation.

Export to PDF

The Export to PDF button is situated to the left of the two printer buttons (Print and Page Preview). You can use this button to *export*, or save, your document as a PDF file.

Hyperlink

Clicking the Hyperlink button, the button to the left of the Table button, opens the Hyperlink window, from which you can assign links to specified documents—not only to web pages but also to documents on an individual computer and even targets within that document. Although a hyperlink on a web page is something we have all come to take for granted, the idea of hyperlinking between text documents sounds a little radical. It has, in fact, been around since before you or I even heard of the Internet.

Navigator

The fourth to the last button in the top row (the one that looks like a starburst) is the Navigator button. Clicking this button (or just pressing the F5 key) opens the Navigator window (see Figure 12-5), a pretty cool navigational feature that comes in handy when you are working with lengthy or otherwise complex documents.

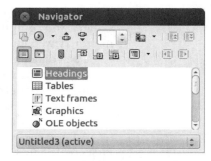

Figure 12-5: The Navigator window

The Navigator allows you to bounce back and forth easily between pages in a document or even between elements therein, such as sections, links, and so on. Let's say you have a document with lots of illustrations in it (like this chapter), and you want to jump directly from graphic to graphic. In this case, you would double-click the word *Graphics* in the main pane of the Navigator window and then click the jump buttons (the odd little buttons to the left of the page number selector) to begin jumping.

If you are dealing with a document containing various heading levels, such as all of the chapters in this book, you can also use Navigator to switch among those levels. Say you've decided to add a new main heading at the last minute to a document you've been writing. You thus need to drop all of the headings you had before down a notch, with the former main heading becoming a subheading and so on. When you double-click the word *Headings*, the text of all the headings you have listed in the document appears. You can then select a heading in that list and click the Demote Level button (that's the one at the far right of the second row of buttons) to move it down a level.

Gallery

To the right of the Navigator button is the Gallery button. By clicking this button, you cause the Gallery, a library of graphical elements for use in your documents or web pages, to appear in a separate pane at the top of your document window (see Figure 12-6). The elements within the Gallery range from various types of lines to buttons to colored three-dimensional doughnuts, and you can add items of your own.

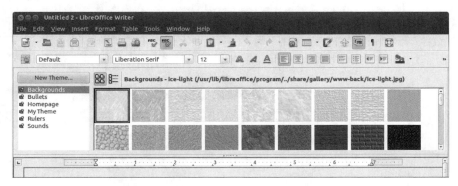

Figure 12-6: The Gallery

Inserting a graphic into your document is a simple enough task even when not using the Gallery. Just select **Insert ▸ Picture ▸ From File** and then locate the image file you want to insert. It can be handier to use the Gallery, however, when you intend to use certain graphics frequently. Once in the Gallery, your graphics are always only a click or two away and can be conveniently viewed in the Gallery browser window.

The collection of artwork that comes with LibreOffice is mostly geared toward building web pages, but other clip art is available elsewhere. For example, you can find a great collection online at *http://www.openclipart.org/*. Everything there is in the public domain, so it is all free to use. Be sure to check out the "Game baddie" collection—it's one of my favorites.

Adding these (or any other) graphic files to the Gallery is relatively easy. First create a new category (called a *theme*) for each group of images you want to add. To create a Gallery theme of your own, click the **New Theme** button in the Gallery window. This will open the Properties of New Theme window, where you should give your theme a name. Once you've done that, click the **Files** tab and then the **Find Files** button, which will open the Select Path window. From there, you can navigate to the folder in which you are storing your clip art, photos, or other graphics. Once you have found the folder, click the **OK** button, after which a list of all the files in that folder will appear in the Properties of New Theme window.

From this window, you can easily add images to your new Gallery theme by clicking the name of each image you want to add and then clicking the **Add** button. (You might want to make sure that the box next to the word *Preview* is checked to make things a bit easier.) Once you have done that, a copy of the image will immediately appear in the Gallery browser in your theme, where it will remain for future use (Figure 12-7). When you are done adding images to your new theme, click **OK**. The Properties of New Theme window will close, revealing your new theme and its contents. To use one of the images in the Gallery, just right-click the image you want to insert into your document, choose **Insert**, and then select **Copy** or **Link** in the pop-up menu.

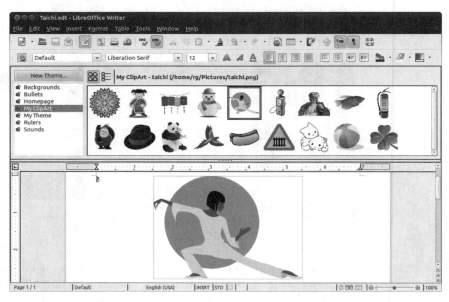

Figure 12-7: Viewing clip art and your own collections in the Gallery

Styles and Formatting

The final stop on our tour through LibreOffice's unfamiliar buttons is the Styles and Formatting button, which is located at the far left side of the second row of buttons. This button acts as a toggle for the Styles and Formatting window (Figure 12-8), from which you can select and then apply styles to any of the various elements within your document. Oh, and if you just can't take your hands off the keyboard for a moment to fiddle with the mouse, you can also open the window by pressing the F11 key.

Figure 12-8: The Styles and Formatting window

To give you an example of how convenient using styles can be, imagine that you are typing a bibliography page for a report you've prepared. You typed each entry as you might any paragraph, as in the following:

> Smythe, W. (2004). Reconsidering the need for speech between non-human interlocutors beyond the age of seven. *The Journal of the Society of Elves, Faeries, and Garden Gnomes,* 20(2), 125–147.

As are most paragraphs you type, the entry is formatted with a first-line indent, which is fine and dandy—except that you want a hanging indent, which is the norm for bibliography entries. Rather than messing around with tabs or margins to get things the way you want, all you have to do is click your mouse anywhere within the paragraph and then double-click the **Hanging indent** entry in the Styles and Formatting window. After that, as if by magic (though you know better), the transformation is made:

> Smythe, W. (2004). Reconsidering the need for speech between non-human interlocutors beyond the age of seven. *The Journal of the Society of Elves, Faeries, and Garden Gnomes,* 20(2), 125–147.

You could follow the same procedure for each of your other entries or, with Hanging indent selected, click the **paint can** button in the Styles and Formatting window. Now your mouse cursor, when placed over the document, will appear as a paint can. Click in any other paragraph in your bibliography, and that entry, too, will be formatted in the new style. The process is essentially the same when applying different styles to any other document elements.

Word Processing Done Lightly with AbiWord

If LibreOffice's Writer is a bit more powerful than what you need for your everyday word processing chores and you would prefer something that pops up as soon as you click the Launcher icon, then you might want to consider another word processor, AbiWord (Figure 12-9). If you're curious, install it from the Ubuntu Software Center.

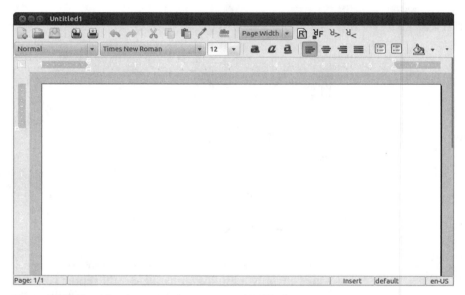

Figure 12-9: The other Linux word processor—AbiWord

AbiWord has a straightforward and easy-to-use interface, which you should be able to figure out without much, if any, help. It also has a couple of interesting features, such as its autoresize function, which magnifies the onscreen document size (fonts, images, and everything) or shrinks it as you increase or decrease the size of the program window. And in case you're wondering, AbiWord can save and read Microsoft Word *.doc* files and save documents as PDF files.

FocusWriter

While discussing alternative word processing applications, it's worth mentioning an unusual new entry available from the Ubuntu Software Center called FocusWriter. FocusWriter developers refer to it as a distraction-free writing environment, and you'll see exactly what they mean when you run it for the first time. To spoil the suspense for you, what you will see is nothing but a gray screen. No menu bars, no buttons, no menus . . . nothing. It is designed to give you the feeling of typing on a blank sheet of paper.

True, the idea seems a bit gimmicky, but the environment does provide a different atmosphere that might well be what you want or need when doing something creative. With the selection of a nice font or the addition of a pleasing background image (Figure 12-10), the imaginative side of you might well be drawn out of hiding. FocusWriter could be your digital muse.

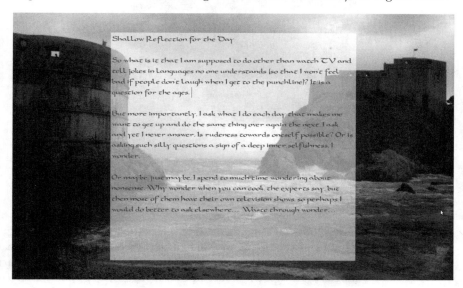

Figure 12-10: Distraction-free word processing with FocusWriter

Some Other Cool Productivity Apps

In addition to the more traditional office applications already discussed, a number of other applications are available from the Ubuntu Software Center that can be grouped together under the "productivity" label. I will introduce a few of those to you here.

Dlume

Let's start off with perhaps the simplest of the applications in this arena, Dlume (Figure 12-11). Dlume is a simple standalone address book application that feels light and easy to use. It allows you to easily search for names in your address book and to export all your information in CSV or HTML formats. You can run Dlume from the Dash by clicking the Applications lens and then clicking the **Accessories** filter button, or just type the name in the search box and press ENTER.

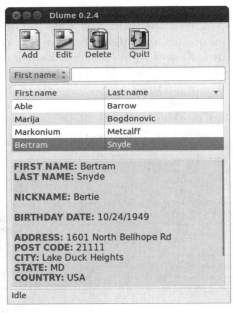

Figure 12-11: Dlume address book application

gLabels

One of my personal favorite office-esque apps is gLabels (Figure 12-12), which I've used from my very earliest days as a Linux user. As the name suggests, gLabels is an application for laying out and printing various types of labels; although the name does not suggest it, gLabels is also great for making business cards. It includes templates for most, if not all, of the label and card stock out there from Avery and a few other manufacturers. While it's true that you can do most of what gLabels does in LibreOffice or Scribus (which I will mention later in this chapter), I'm sure you will find gLabels to be the easiest and most intuitive way to get the job done, especially when it comes to setting up cards or labels with graphics or special layouts.

Tomboy

One of the downsides of the new Unity desktop environment is that you can't run most GNOME panel applets anymore . . . well, not easily anyway. Sticky Notes, the app that allowed you to post little yellow Post-it–like notes on the desktop, is one such app. Fortunately, the more full-featured answer to Sticky Notes, called Tomboy (Figure 12-13), does work in Unity. Once installed and launched, Tomboy works as a panel applet, positioning itself with the other status indicator icons at the right side of the Unity top panel. From that Tomboy menu, you can add and edit notes and control other Tomboy functions.

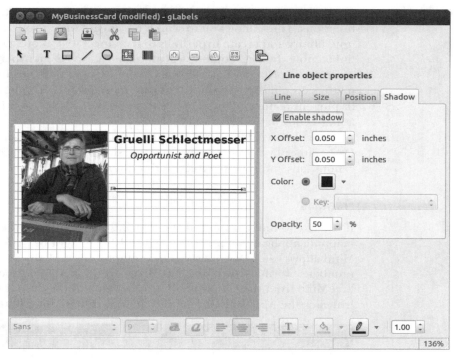

Figure 12-12: gLabels

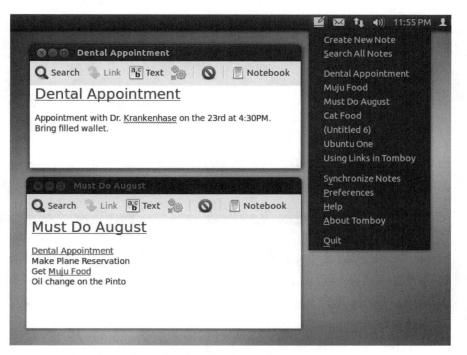

Figure 12-13: Desktop notes with some oomph—Tomboy

One of the most touted of Tomboy's features is its search and hyperlink functions. These allow you to search for entries within your entire Tomboy note library and create hyperlinks that connect text in one note to another linked note. In fact, Tomboy will automatically create a hyperlink whenever you type a word that matches one of your existing note headings. To make matters even more exciting (or at least more useful), Tomboy, by means of its plug-ins feature, allows you to export notes to HTML or print them, either as hard copy or as PDFs.

Once you've downloaded and installed Tomboy, you can run it from the Dash, either by typing its name and pressing ENTER or by clicking the Applications lens and then the **Accessories** filter button.

FreeMind

If you like to think graphically by charting out your ideas, then the mind-mapping application FreeMind (Figure 12-14) might be perfect for you. Free-Mind allows you to lay out your ideas graphically and save your results in a number of formats, including PDF, PNG, JPEG, and SVG. You can download FreeMind from the Ubuntu Software Center and then run it from the Dash. Just click the Applications lens and then the **Office** filter button.

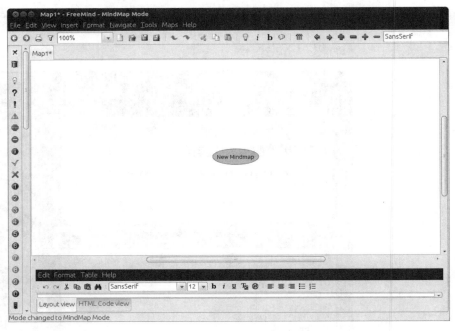

Figure 12-14: Freemind

Scribus

To round things out, we come to an open source desktop publishing application, Scribus (Figure 12-15) for those times when LibreOffice Writer and Draw just don't cut it. Scribus is designed to produce commercial-grade output, and it supports professional publishing features, such as CMYK colors, PostScript handling, and creation of color separations, to name but a few. There is a fairly good support network out there for Scribus and an online tutorial too (*http://wiki.scribus.net/canvas/Get_Started_with_Scribus*), so you won't be alone if you find yourself getting into this application.

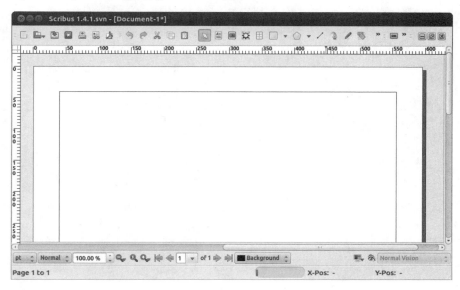

Figure 12-15: Scribus

13

RIGHT-BRAIN PENGUINS

Linux Does Art

Now that you know you can get down to business in Linux, it is time to don that beret of yours and address the artistic side of things. Yes, Linux does art, and as you will soon find out, a good number of programs on your system allow you to create and manipulate graphic files. These days, however, there is perhaps nothing so important to most users' graphical repertoires as their digital cameras, so that is where we'll begin.

Where the Apps Are

The majority of apps in this chapter can be run from the Dash by clicking the Applications lens and then clicking the **Graphics** filter button. Exceptions are noted in the relevant sections. As with all applications, you can also run an app by typing its name in the Dash's search box and then pressing ENTER.

Project 13A: Importing Images from Digital Cameras

Although scanner support for Linux can prove a bit spotty, support for digital cameras is practically a worry-free affair. In fact, Ubuntu pretty much treats your camera as if it were an external hard drive or flash drive plugged into your computer's USB port (which is pretty much what it is). And even if your camera doesn't seem to communicate with your computer when connected directly, you can still transfer your images to your hard disk by removing the memory card from your camera, inserting it into a USB flash memory card reader, and plugging that reader into one of your computer's USB ports.

13A-1: Importing Images from Camera to Computer Somewhat Automatically via Shotwell

When you connect your camera to your computer via a USB cable, put your camera in play mode, and power it on, Ubuntu will usually automatically recognize it and open a window that asks how you want to import the photos on the camera. To import the photos via the photo manager application Shotwell, select the **Shotwell** option in the drop-down menu button, as shown in Figure 13-1, and then click **OK**.

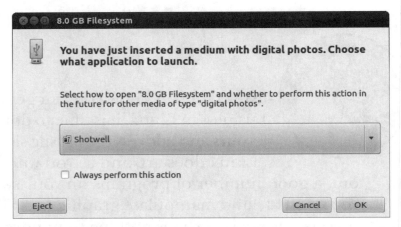

Figure 13-1: Ubuntu recognizes your camera and asks you how to proceed.

After that, here's what you need to do:

1. In the window that appears, you will see thumbnails of all the photos on your camera. You can import all of the photos that appear by clicking the **Import All** button in the bottom right corner of the window. However, if you prefer to copy only some of the images, you can do so by holding down the CTRL key and then clicking the images you want to import, as shown in Figure 13-2. Once you've made your selections, click the **Import Selected** button.

Figure 13-2: Selecting which photos to import from your digital camera via Shotwell photo manager

2. Shotwell will save your photos to a dated subfolder in your *Pictures* folder. Once it is done importing the images from your camera, it will tell you so in an Import Complete window, where it will also ask you what you want to do with the photos still in your camera. If you want to keep them there for the time being, click the **Keep** button. If you would prefer to clear up space on your memory card by deleting the images, click the **Delete** button.

The time it will take to import and delete photos from your camera or storage card will vary depending on the number of images on the card. Once the process is complete, however, you will be able to view them all within the main Shotwell window, as well as work with them further, a topic I'll discuss later in this chapter.

13A-2: Transferring Images from Camera to Computer via the File Manager

You can also use the file manager to import photos from your camera, if you prefer. If you happen to have digital movies on your camera's memory card in addition to digital images, then you'll have to go this route (for the movies at least) since Shotwell imports only images. The process for doing this starts pretty much the same as that in Project 13A-1, albeit with a slight twist. Here's how you do it:

1. Plug your camera into one of your computer's USB ports and put your camera into play mode. Within seconds, a window like that in Figure 13-1 will appear. In that window, select **Open Folder** in the drop-down menu button (instead of Shotwell) and then click **OK**.

2. A file manager window will appear, revealing the contents of your camera's storage card. An icon for your camera (looking like a USB drive) will also appear under Devices in the side pane of that window and any other open file manager window (Figure 13-3). And a message will appear at the top of the window telling you that the device you have connected contains digital images, along with a button that you can click to import the images with Shotwell. Since we covered that method already, you can ignore it for now.

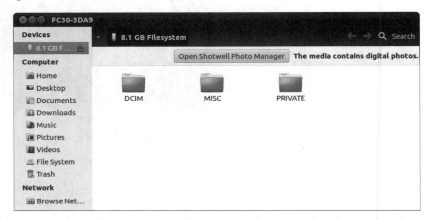

Figure 13-3: You can also drag and drop photos from your digital camera as if it were a USB drive.

3. Double-click your way through the folders on your camera until you find the photos you want to import.

4. Drag and drop, or copy and paste, the images from your camera to any logical spot in your Home folder.

5. When you're done transferring photos, you can click the eject icon next to the entry for your camera in the left pane of the file manager window, or you can just turn off your camera. The file manager window that opened automatically will close, and your camera's entry will disappear from the side pane of any other open file manager windows.

Project 13B: Working with Digital Images in Shotwell

Shotwell not only imports images from your camera to your computer but also acts as a handy photo-organizing, browsing, viewing, and publishing tool, allowing you to easily send images via email without fiddling around with attachments. It also lets you just as easily publish photos to popular online sites such as Facebook, Flickr, and PicassaWeb. In addition, Shotwell serves as a simple photo-editing tool, allowing you to enhance; rotate; crop; remove red-eye from; and adjust the exposure, temperature, and saturation of a photo (Figure 13-4). Just double-click the photo you want to edit and then click the appropriate buttons that appear at the bottom of the window. You can pretty much learn by fiddling around; all the tools are pretty straightforward.

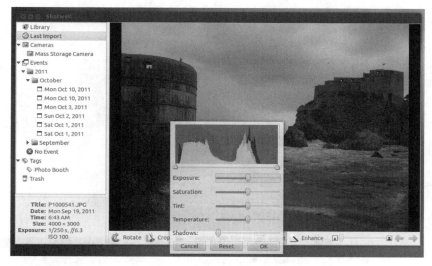

Figure 13-4: Shotwell provides you with basic but useful photo-editing tools.

13B-1: Publishing Images to Online Albums and Galleries

As I mentioned, Shotwell allows you to easily publish images to numerous online sites, much in the way that Windows Live Photo Gallery does. The method I show here for Facebook is essentially the same one you use for the others, and they're all pretty simple. Here's what you need to do:

1. In the Shotwell window, select the photos you want to post online by holding down the CTRL key and clicking each of the photos you want to publish.

2. Once you've made your selection, click the **Publish** button at the bottom of the window. A window like that in Figure 13-5 will appear.

3. The default online site selected in this window is Facebook. If you would like to upload photos to Flickr or PicasaWeb, select that site in the drop-down menu button at the top right of the window. Once you've done that, click the **Login** button.

4. The login page for the site you've selected will then appear in the window (Figure 13-6). Fill in your login information and then click the **Log In** button (or equivalent for the other online sites).

5. In the case of Facebook, you will then be asked to name the machine you are logging in from. Once you have done that, you will need to allow Shotwell to access your Facebook information, something you'll need to do whenever you log in from a new machine.

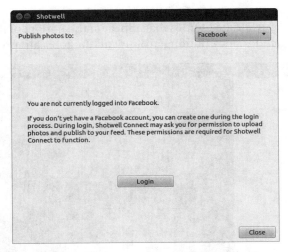

Figure 13-5: Publishing images to online sites such as
Facebook via Shotwell

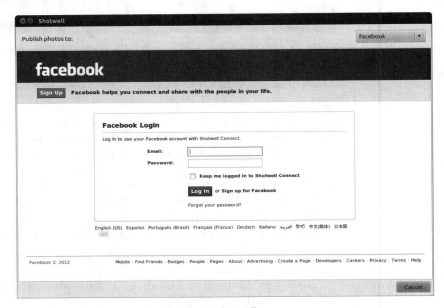

Figure 13-6: Logging into Facebook via Shotwell

6. Once you have done all that, you will be asked to choose an album in
    which to publish the photos you've selected or to create a new album
    (Figure 13-7). Make your choices and then click **Publish**.

7. Once Shotwell has completed publishing your photos, it will tell you so,
    and you can then click the **Close** button. You can then go to your online
    gallery via your web browser to see the results.

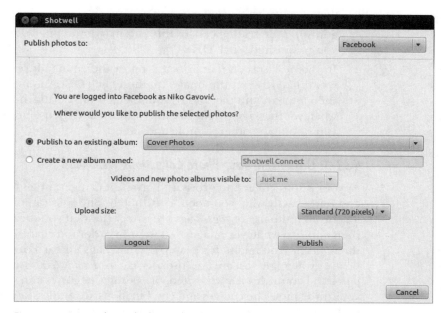

Figure 13-7: Deciding which Facebook album will hold your photos via Shotwell

13B-2: Sending Images by Email via Shotwell

Emailing images via Shotwell is just as easy as publishing images to Facebook—perhaps even easier. It's certainly much easier than having to manually prep the photos as attachments. Assuming you have your Thunderbird set up for sending email as you learned to do in Chapter 5, here is all you have to do:

1. In the Shotwell window, select the photos you want to email by holding down the CTRL key and clicking each photo.

2. Right-click any of the photos you have selected and then select **Send To** in the pop-up menu. A window like the one in Figure 13-8 will appear.

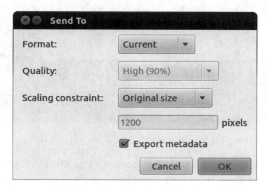

Figure 13-8: Emailing photos made easy with Shotwell

3. Here you can change the size of the photo(s) you are about to send by adjusting the scaling constraints and maximum pixel dimensions. When you're finished, click **OK**.

4. In the next screen that appears, enter the email address of the person you'd like to send the image to, then click **OK**. An email message will then appear, and the photos you selected will be attached. You can write whatever message you like in that window and then send the email just as you would any other. Simple and sweet!

13B-3: Organizing Your Photo Collections with Tags

As your photo collection grows and grows, it can get tough to sort things out and find exactly what you need. Fortunately, Shotwell can make this a bit easier through the use of *tags*. Tags are categories that you create yourself and then apply to whatever images you want in order to organize your collection thematically. You might, for example, create tags for each of your family members, or you might just create a broader tag for *Family*. You could create tags for cities and countries you've visited, providing categories and subcategories for your travel pics. The choices and combinations are endless, and you can decide what they are all are. Once you've applied these tags to your photos, narrowing down your photo searches will be much easier.

The first step is to create a few tags. This is easily done by right-clicking an image and selecting **Add Tags** in the pop-up menu. A small window will appear in which you can just type a single tag or, to kill two birds with one stone, whatever other tags you want to assign to the photo (Figure 13-9). Just be sure to separate each tag with a comma. Once you're done, click **OK**, after which the tags will appear both under the thumbnail and in the left pane of the window.

Figure 13-9: Creating tags in Shotwell

Once you have tags in the left pane of the Shotwell window, adding those tags to other photos is a cinch. Just drag a thumbnail to one of the tags and release your mouse button, and the image will be tagged. If you want to add a second tag, just drag the thumbnail to that tag as well. Once you are done tagging your images, they will be far easier to sort, as you can see in Figure 13-10.

Figure 13-10: Using tags in Shotwell to make dealing with hefty photo collections much easier

Searching for images by tag is perhaps even easier than adding the tags to the images in the first place. Let's say you wanted to find all of your images that you tagged as *Europe*. You would just go to the left pane and click **Europe**. All of the images that were tagged in that category would then appear in the right pane. Sweet.

A Few Other Graphics Apps to Consider

In addition to the graphics applications that come bundled with Ubuntu, still more are available. You can grab all of them via the Ubuntu Software Center. Although you can experiment with what's available, I will point out a few worth noting. If nothing else, these applications will give you an idea of the breadth of stuff out there waiting for you.

RawTherapee

RawTherapee is not some solution for what ails your troubled soul but rather a handy application that allows you to manipulate RAW image files. RAW image files are images that have not been processed by the on-board conversion software in your camera that converts the data it receives from the sensor into a format that your computer is able to deal with (usually JPEG files). For most people, JPEG images work just fine, but many photographers who want to have the best quality results after making adjustments to their images on their computers save their files in RAW image format, or RAW mode. While not all cameras have the option to save files in RAW mode, many advanced amateur and professional camera models do.

Once you load RAW image files onto your computer, the thumbnails for those files will appear as black rectangles. That's because they are essentially blobs of raw data that neither you nor your computer on its own can make heads or tails of. In a sense, they are a digital equivalent of photo negatives.

This is where RawTherapee comes in (see Figure 13-11). Once you open your RAW files with RawTherapee, you will be able to see what they actually look like and then go on to adjust them to your heart's content, usually with much better results than you would get if working on JPEG files. Once you have made your adjustments to the RAW files, you can save them into other, more universally compatible file formats, such as JPEG, while retaining the original RAW file for future use.

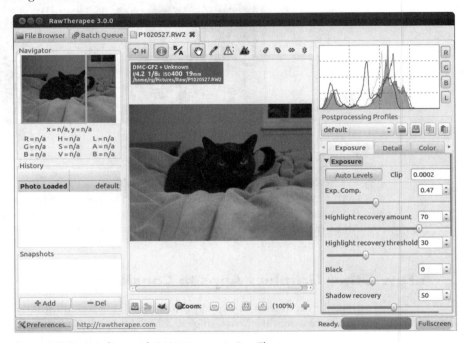

Figure 13-11: Working with RAW images in RawTherapee

Getting Arty with the GIMP

The Windows and Mac worlds may have Photoshop, but the Linux world has the GIMP (see Figure 13-12). Although arguably not as fully featured as Photoshop, the GIMP is a powerful contender, which may explain why it has been ported to both Mac and Windows. The GIMP allows you to create bitmap graphics and, importantly, retouch or completely doctor image files. With the GIMP you can get rid of red-eye in your digital photos, airbrush out unwanted shadows (or even facial blemishes), give your image a canvas texture, change a photo into an oil painting, and even add a bell pepper here and there—with drop shadows no less.

Because not everyone needs or uses the features of the GIMP, the powers that be decided to no longer bundle it on the Ubuntu Desktop CD, thus freeing up space for more frequently run applications. Pity though that might be, you can still install the GIMP via the Ubuntu Software Center.

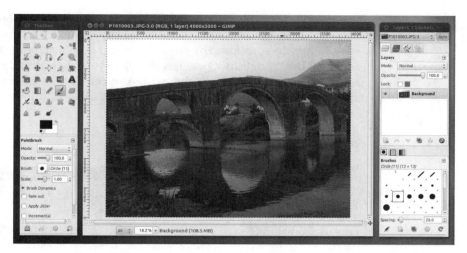

Figure 13-12: Manipulating a digital image in the GIMP

Using the GIMP to Resize Images and Convert File Formats

The GIMP's main strength is in retouching photos. It is also a handy tool for resizing images. You can do this by simply right-clicking an image opened in the GIMP and then selecting **Image ▸ Scale Image** in the pop-up menu. This will open the Scale Image window, where you can set the new size of the image.

The GIMP is also an excellent tool for converting images from one file format to another. You can, for example, open a bitmap (*.bmp*) file and save it as a PNG (*.png*) file, save a JPEG (*.jpg*) file as a GIF (*.gif*) file, and so on. Although this can also be done with other graphics applications, including Shotwell, the GIMP supports an extremely wide variety of file formats, and it even lets you save an image file as a compressed tarball, which makes it a true file conversion king.

To perform a file conversion, just right-click an image opened within the GIMP and then select **File ▸ Save As** in the pop-up menu. You can make the same selection from the File menu if you prefer. Either way, the Save Image window will then appear. In that window, you can specify the new file format by replacing the original file extension in the Name box at the top of that window with the extension for the format you want to convert the image to. If you're not sure what formats are available to you, click the small arrow to the left of the words *Select File Type (By Extension)* at the bottom left of the window and then choose from the options in the pane that appears below. To save a work in progress, use the GIMP-native XCF format so that you can continue working on the image later.

Learning More

It's lots of fun to learn to use the GIMP by just playing around with it for a while. To get you started, most of the fun stuff is located in the Filters menu of any image window. Of course, you should make a backup copy of any file you are planning to experiment with before you alter it.

If you prefer learning via manuals and tutorials to just goofing around, you can download and install the GIMP User Manual via the Ubuntu Software Center by searching for *gimp-help-en* and then installing **Documentation for the GIMP (English)**. Once it is installed, you can access the manual from within the GIMP from the Help menu. You can also view the manual online at *http://docs.gimp.org/en/*, and you can find a series of tutorials at *http://www.gimp.org/tutorials/*.

Phatch Photo Batch Processor

While the GIMP and Shotwell are quite capable of handling the vast majority of your photo-organizing and editing chores, they lack an easy-to-use batch file conversion method that allows you to apply various conversions to a group of files at the same time. For example, let's say you want to convert 100 of your photos so they look like black-and-white snapshots with white borders, are 50 percent smaller than the originals, have a similar thematic filename, and are saved in *.tiff* rather than *.jpg* format. Applying all these changes one by one would be excruciating. Fortunately, Phatch comes to the rescue! (See Figure 13-13.)

Using Phatch is easy—and quite a bit of hocus-pocusy fun.

Figure 13-13: Batch photo file conversions with Phatch

However, its interface might not be obvious for a first-time user. With that in mind, here is a brief rundown on how to use Phatch:

1. Click the + button in the main Phatch window, and the Phatch actions window will appear.

2. In that window, select the action (conversion) you want to apply to your photos and click **Add**. Repeat this process for any other actions you want to apply.

3. Once you have added all the actions you want, click each action in the main Action List and enter the appropriate parameters for each action (size, file format, size of border, output location, and so on).

4. If the actions are not listed in the order you want them to occur, click the action you want to move and change its position using the up and down arrow buttons.

5. Once everything is ready, save your Action List with a meaningful name by going to the Action List menu at the top of your screen and selecting **Save**. This way, you can use it again if need be.

6. Next, click the Execute button (the one that looks like three gears).

7. In the window that appears, select your conversion parameters, making sure to select whether you are converting a whole folder full of files, selected files, or whatever it is you have in the clipboard. I would suggest unchecking the box next to the words *Overwrite existing images* so that you keep your original images intact (Figure 13-14).

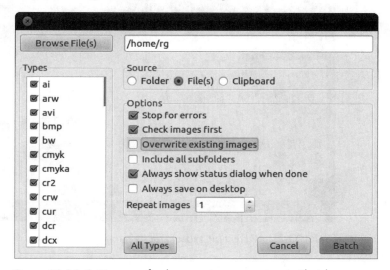

Figure 13-14: Setting your final conversion parameters in Phatch

8. Once you have made your choices, click the **Browse Folder/Browse File(s)** button and then select the folder of files or individual files you wish to convert. Once you have made your selection(s), click **Open**.

9. You will now be back at the window where you selected your parameters. In that window, click the **Batch** button.

10. Another window will then open showing you which files will be acted upon. Click **Continue** in that window.

Phatch will then perform the conversions listed on your Action List in the order listed. It will show you the progress of its work, and a small window will appear to tell you when it's done. You can see the converted product by clicking **Show Images**. If you failed to choose a destination folder, the newly created conversions should appear in a *Phatch* folder on your desktop.

MyPaint

If you prefer to do your electronic artwork with a graphics tablet rather than with a mouse, then MyPaint is for you. MyPaint (Figure 13-15) is designed to work with pressure-sensitive tablets by Wacom and other manufacturers. Despite its simple interface, it features a never-ending canvas (so you can keep on drawing in all directions until you run out of steam), an extensive brush collection, and even a brush-creation and editing tool. If you need a bit of help getting started, check out the online tutorial (*http://mypaint.intilinux.com/?page_id=3*).

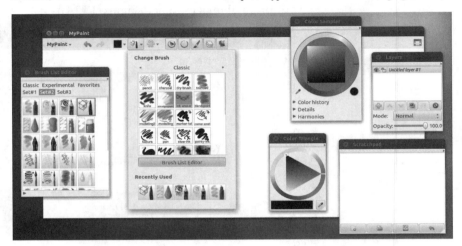

Figure 13-15: MyPaint for Wacom tablet artists

Inkscape

The GIMP, like other so-called paint programs, creates bitmap images in various file formats. In these images, the location and color of every single *pixel* is recorded. Thus, the image is essentially a collection of dots. The file you create is a rather hefty map of these pixels, and this map tells your system where everything in your image is supposed to go when it is displayed or printed.

Vector drawing programs, on the other hand, create vector images, which are actually collections of mathematical formulas representing the various shapes in your image. This may sound arcane, and you may be wondering why you should care. But such drawings have advantages in certain cases. One advantage is that vector image files take up less space on your hard disk than bitmaps. Another, and perhaps the most important, advantage is that shapes in vector images retain their smooth edges when the images are enlarged. A smooth circle created as a bitmap, for example, would begin to show jagged edges ("the jaggies") when enlarged to any extent, while the same circle in a vector image would remain smooth and round no matter how much you increased its size.

If you're interested in giving a drawing program a go, then try Linux's main offering, Inkscape (see Figure 13-16). You can learn how to use Inkscape at the Inkscape home page at *http://www.inkscape.org/*. Be sure to click the **Galleries** link on that page to see examples of what you can create with the program, such as the image shown in Figure 13-16 from *http://focaclipart.net23.net/transporte/*.

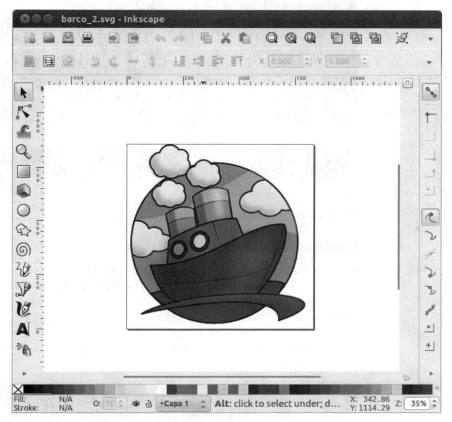

Figure 13-16: Inkscape

gThumb Image Viewer

In earlier editions of Ubuntu, an application called gThumb (Figure 13-17), handy for photo-handling chores, came preinstalled. Some folks wish it still did. It has almost all the same features as Shotwell and a few of its own (such as creating original web album pages and some limited batch conversion capabilities). That said, it all boils down to what you like, and since both gThumb and Shotwell are free and easy to use, there's no harm in trying them both to see which one you prefer.

Figure 13-17: gThumb

Blender

To wrap things up, we turn to Blender, which is perhaps one of the most impressive open source applications available today. Blender (Figure 13-18) is a professional-level 3D modeling, animation, and rendering program. It is rather complex, but that's the source of its power and popularity. (It comes in versions for just about every operating system out there.) If you would like to find out a bit more about Blender before taking the time (and disk space) to install it, go to *http://www.blender.org/*.

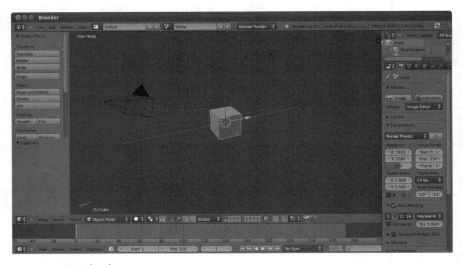

Figure 13-18: Blender

14

TUX ROCKS

Music à la Linux

And now we come to the audio side of things. Yes, Linux does indeed rock, and in this chapter you will find out about the musical talents that your system possesses and how it can work with the musical talents that you possess. You will learn how to rip CDs, create MP3 and Ogg Vorbis files (files that you can recognize by their *.mp3* and *.ogg* filename extensions), add album cover art, change file tags, play music files, and burn files onto audio CDs that you can play in any CD player. You'll also learn about a number of applications that can help the musician within you. If you're interested in learning how to work with your iPod, iPhone, iPad, or other digital media device, or how to convert audio files from one format to another, however, you'll have to wait until Chapter 15.

Where the Apps Are

All of apps in this chapter can be run from the Dash by clicking the Applications lens and then clicking the **Media** filter button. As with all applications, you can also run an app by typing its name in the Dash's search box and then pressing ENTER.

Audio File Formats

Before we go any further, it's probably best to discuss the various formats in which audio data can be stored on your computer. For the longest time, the de facto standards have been WAV (created by Microsoft/IBM and using the *.wav* extension), AU (from Sun/Unix and using the *.au* extension), and AIFF (from Apple and using the *.aiff* extension), all of which are uncompressed formats. Files saved in these formats are, therefore, exceedingly large, with an average WAV file of CD-quality music weighing in at about 10MB per minute. To put that in perspective, back in 1988 my first Macintosh had a 40MB hard disk—more space than I thought I would ever need but not enough space to store a WAV file of Nirvana's "Come as You Are."

As computers underwent their evolution into the multimedia machines they are today, it became clear that something was going to have to be done about those disk space–devouring audio files. Audio compression formats were thus developed. These compression formats work, to oversimplify things a bit, by cutting out the portions of a sound signal that the human ear cannot hear—sort of a dog-whistle approach. The most widely known and embraced of these audio compression formats is *MP3*. Audio files encoded in MP3 format can end up being as little as one-twelfth the size of the original WAV file without any noticeable loss in quality.

Another audio compression format is *Ogg Vorbis*. Ogg Vorbis is a product of the open source community, so, unlike MP3, which has always been used under the shadow of yet-to-be-exercised patent rights, it was free of patent and licensing worries from the get-go. Because of that and the fact that it was the equal of MP3 in terms of quality and performance (if not, as many claim, better), Ogg Vorbis became the darling of the Linux community.

As you rip audio files in this chapter, you are sure to notice yet another encoding option—FLAC. *Free Lossless Audio Codec (FLAC)* is an encoding format that, unlike the MP3 and Ogg Vorbis formats, does not remove any audio information from the audio file during the encoding process. The downside is that FLAC provides space savings of only 30 to 50 percent, much less than the 80 percent neighborhood achieved by MP3 or Ogg Vorbis. The upside, of course, is that the FLAC files should be equivalent to CDs in terms of quality.

Given that retention of audio quality, FLAC is an ideal choice if you are not satisfied with the audio quality provided by Ogg Vorbis or MP3 files. It's also a good choice if you want to create both Ogg Vorbis and MP3 files . . . or if you just don't know which one you want to work with yet. In such cases, you can go ahead and encode it in FLAC format. As I mentioned earlier, once you get to Chapter 15, you will learn how you can convert the FLAC file later, when you know what you want or need.

Installing MP3 Support for Audio Apps

All that talk about Ogg Vorbis and FLAC aside, many people still like or need to deal with MP3 files. You may, for example, already have numerous MP3 files ripped from your music collection, or you may enjoy listening to one of the many Internet radio streams that are broadcast in MP3 format. Unfortunately, MP3 playback and encoding support is not included in Ubuntu because of licensing concerns. Even if you plan on using the Ogg Vorbis format in your future ripping and encoding endeavors, installing MP3 support is a good idea so as to cover all your audio bases. It's also a very easy process. In fact, if you opted to install third-party software support when you originally installed Ubuntu, you most likely already have all the support files you need.

If you did not opt to install third party software when you first installed Ubuntu, then the easiest way to install MP3 playback support is to double-click an MP3 file that you have on your hard disk. A window will appear, asking whether you want to search for the plug-ins necessary to play the file. Click **Search**, after which another window will appear showing you what you need to install (Figure 14-1). Check both boxes in that window, click the **Install** button, and in the confirmation window that appears, click **Confirm**. You will be asked for your password, so provide it and then just wait until the process is complete. Once done, you'll be able to play not only your MP3 audio files but also a variety of other audio and even video formats.

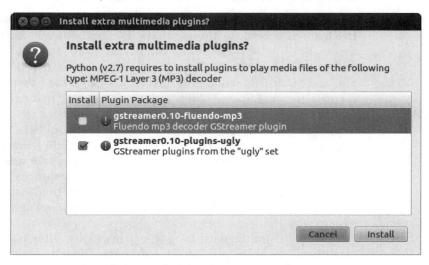

Figure 14-1: Ubuntu helps you find the plug-ins you need.

Rhythmbox—Ubuntu's Default Audio Player

The main audio player in Ubuntu, called Rhythmbox (see Figure 14-2), functions pretty much like a simplified version of Apple's iTunes application. This relatively easy to use player has, despite some quirks, developed quite a following in the Linux world.

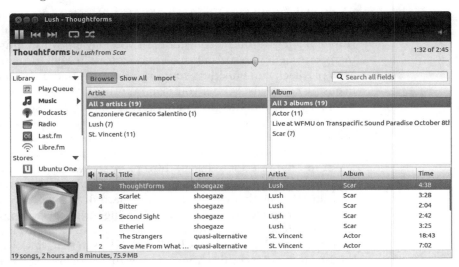

Figure 14-2: The Rhythmbox audio player

Adding Songs and Albums to the Rhythmbox Library

If you are familiar with Apple's iTunes, then you should understand the Library in Rhythmbox because it is essentially the same concept. Rhythmbox should automatically import everything you have in your *Music* folder without any extra work on your part. If it for some reason does not, or if you would like to also add music from another directory, you can do so by going to the **Music** menu, selecting **Import Folder**, and then navigating to the folder for the new album you want to add.

If you prefer things not be so automatic and would like to add only what you want, you can open the preferences window (**Edit ▸ Preferences**), click the **Music** tab, and then uncheck the **Watch my library for new files** box. After that, you can add new albums or groups to your Rhythmbox Library by going to **Music ▸ Import Folder**. If you want to add just a single audio file, you can also do that—select **Music ▸ Import File** and then navigate to the song you wish to add.

If you are not the navigating type, you can also add files and folders by other means. The simplest way is to drag the folder or song you want to add to the Library into the right pane of the Rhythmbox window. You can also add a song to the Library directly by right-clicking the file and selecting **Open with ▸ Open with Rhythmbox Music Player** in the pop-up menu that appears.

Ripping Audio CDs with Rhythmbox

Like iTunes, Rhythmbox allows you to rip songs directly from a CD; convert them to Ogg Vorbis, MP3, or another audio format; and add the ripped tracks to its music library. The steps are as follows:

1. Open the Preferences window (**Edit ▸ Preferences**), click the **Music** tab, and select the encoding format you want to use (Ogg Vorbis is the default). Once you're done, click **Close**. Unless you change encoding formats often, you won't have to do this more than once.

2. If you have selected an encoding format for which you have not yet installed support, such as MPEG Layer 3 Audio (MP3), an **Install additional software required to use this format** button will appear underneath the Preferred format drop-down menu (Figure 14-3). Click that button and install everything suggested, even the unchecked items (to kill as many birds as possible with one stone, so to speak).

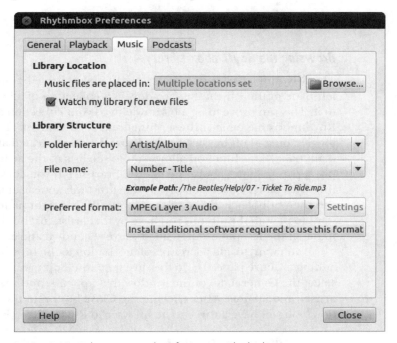

Figure 14-3: Selecting encoding formats in Rhythmbox

3. Once the installation is complete, close the Preferences window and select your audio CD in the left pane of the main Rhythmbox window.

4. All of the tracks and album information will appear in the right pane of the window (Figure 14-4). Check information there, make any corrections you feel are necessary, and then click the **Extract** button at the top left of the pane. Rhythmbox will begin ripping your CD, saving the files to your Music folder while indicating its progress in the lower-right corner of the window.

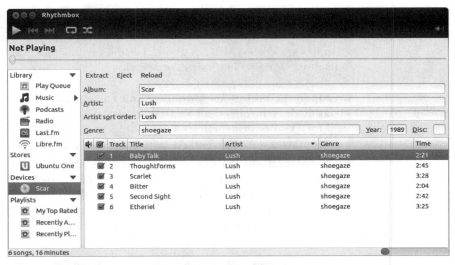

Figure 14-4: Ripping CDs from within Rhythmbox

Browsing the Rhythmbox Library

The Rhythmbox Library, which you can make visible by clicking **Music** in the left pane of the Rhythmbox window, is a collection of all the music you add to it. This can prove to be a bit unwieldy as your collection grows. Fortunately, Rhythmbox has a nice browser function, like the one in iTunes, which can be toggled on and off by clicking the **Browse** button, located at the top left of the main pane. This function allows you to see lists of the artists and albums in two separate panes above the main Library list. If you click a specific artist in the Artist pane, a list of albums by that artist will appear in the right pane. You can then double-click one of the albums in that right pane to play it. If you want to play all the albums you have by that artist, just double-click the artist's name in the left pane. All in all, it's a very handy feature.

If you want to add a layer of categorization to the browser, you can do so by adding a Genre pane. To do this, just go to the **Edit** menu, select **Preferences**, select the **General** tab of the window that appears, and then select **Genres, artists, and albums**. After clicking the **Close** button in the Preferences window, you will have a three-pane browser in Rhythmbox (Figure 14-5).

Creating Playlists in Rhythmbox

Of course, you can tailor things even further to match your every situation and every mood. There are days, after all, when you're feeling a bit too ethereal for Adam Lambert (and thank goodness for that). To prepare for such moments, you can create *playlists*, which are lists of songs to be played in a predetermined order. Just think of each playlist as an all-request radio station . . . where all the requests are your own.

Figure 14-5: The Rhythmbox browser with expanded categories

To create a playlist in Rhythmbox, select **Music ▸ Playlist ▸ New Playlist**. When the Playlist icon appears in the left pane of the Rhythmbox window, type a name for the list and press ENTER. Click the music icon in the left pane to show the contents of your music library. Then add the songs you want by simply dragging them from the Library pane to the Playlist icon. The songs themselves will remain in the Library, so you aren't really moving anything— just creating aliases.

You can also create *automatic playlists*, which are lists that automatically scan the Library for songs that match your creation criteria. For example, you might choose to create a list for the all the songs in your Library by a particular artist or of a specific genre. To do this, select **Music ▸ Playlist ▸ New Automatic Playlist**. A window will appear in which you can specify what the list is to contain. You can even specify how many songs you want in the list.

Once you've created your lists, you can play one by clicking the list once and then clicking the **Play** button near the top of the window (or by just double-clicking the list).

Ubuntu One Music Store via Rhythmbox

Similar to the iTunes store, Rhythmbox provides you with access to the *Ubuntu One Music Store*, which provides music by major artists from the 7digital catalog. The songs sold there are free from the digital rights management (DRM) limitations found in many songs purchased from other online stores. The Ubuntu One Music Store is also cloud enabled, so whatever you buy is delivered to your Ubuntu One cloud, from where you can then download your purchases to your other devices. (An Ubuntu One account is required, but you can get one, with 5GB of free storage, for free.)

Other Cool Features in Rhythmbox

Rhythmbox includes a couple more cool features worth noting. One of these is the ability to automatically download and display the lyrics of the song you are currently playing. To use this feature, you must first activate it by going to the **Edit** menu and selecting **Plugins**. In the Configure Plugins window that appears (Figure 14-6), check the **Song Lyrics** box and then click the **Preferences** button that appears. When the Song Lyrics preferences window appears, check all the boxes there and click the **Close** button. You can then close the Configure Plugins window. After that, to start playing a track, go to the **View** menu and select **Song Lyrics**. Rhythmbox will search the Internet for the lyrics of the track you are currently playing and display them in a separate window (Figure 14-7).

Figure 14-6: Activating Rhythmbox's lyrics retrieval and display plug-in

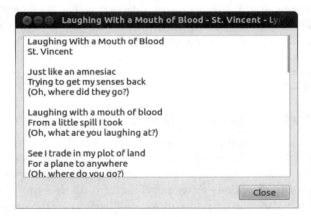

Figure 14-7: Rhythmbox displays the lyrics of the track currently playing.

Another cool feature is Rhythmbox's ability to display album art for the songs you have in your collection. The art is displayed in the bottom left corner of the window and in the notification that pops up momentarily in the top-right corner of your screen. Unfortunately, at the present time this works only with those songs in your collection that already have album art information embedded, such as those you have purchased online. The ability to download and display album art for those tracks you ripped yourself is still broken and has been since the switch to the Unity desktop environment. A solution is still being sought, so this functionality might well work again after a future update.

Project 14: Listening to Streaming Media with Rhythmbox

In addition to allowing you to play audio CDs or the music you have stored on your hard disk, Rhythmbox also allows you to play Internet radio streams in either MP3 or Ogg Vorbis format. To listen, just click **Radio** in the left pane and then find a stream to play in the main pane. Once you've made your selection, you can start playing it by either double-clicking or selecting it and then clicking the green play button at the top left of the window.

14-1: Adding Radio Streams to Rhythmbox

It is also possible to add streams to Rhythmbox. To get started, let's try adding FIP, a French music station specializing in the eclectic. The process for adding FIP is essentially the same for adding any other stream. Here are the steps:

1. Click **Radio** in the left pane of the Rhythmbox window.
2. At the top left of the main pane, click the **Add** button.
3. In the window that appears, type `http://www.tv-radio.com/station/fip_mp3/fip_mp3-128k.m3u` and click **Add**.
4. Double-click the new entry for your stream to play it.

14-2: Changing a Stream's Title and Information in Rhythmbox

The only problem with what you've just done is that the title of the stream that appears in the Rhythmbox window is the URL you entered, and the genre appears as *unknown*. Needless to say, this isn't all that handy a way to have things, especially once you have more than a couple of streams listed and have to go wading through them to figure out what is what.

Remedying this state of affairs is a simple process. Just right-click the stream and select **Properties**. In the window that appears, change the content of the Title and Genre boxes so that they're more meaningful to you. As you can see in Figure 14-8, I used *Radio France - FIP* for the title and *Eclectic* for the genre.

Figure 14-8: Changing a stream's title and genre properties in Rhythmbox

Creating Audio CDs

All this talk about encoding and listening to MP3 and Ogg Vorbis files on your computer is fine and dandy, but no doubt you sometimes would like to have your songs on a plain audio CD that you can play while you slog your way to work on the New Jersey Turnpike or the Ventura Freeway. Luckily, this is easy enough to do, and there are a couple of ways to go about it.

Burning Audio CDs with Rhythmbox

For Rhythmbox users, the easiest way to go about things is to do it all from within Rhythmbox. To do this, first create a playlist with the songs you want to burn to CD, then click the icon for that list in the left pane, and then click the **Burn** button at the top of the main pane. Brasero, the disc-authoring application that we first discussed in Chapter 7, will now take over, opening a window that shows the files to be burned (Figure 14-9). Place a blank disc in your drive and click the **Burn** button. In the Properties window that appears, just click the **Burn** button, and the process will begin. You can follow how the burn is progressing in the small window that appears. When the process is done, the progress window will vanish, and your new audio CD should pop out of your drive. Simple.

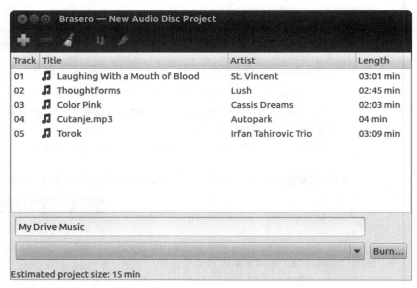

Figure 14-9: Burning an audio CD with Rhythmbox and Brasero

Burning Audio CDs Directly with Brasero

You can also create a "play-anywhere" audio CD from your ripped MP3 and Ogg Vorbis files directly from Brasero, thus bypassing Rhythmbox. To go this route, run Brasero from the Dash and place a blank CD in your drive (and close any window that pops up asking how to handle it). When Brasero appears, click **Audio project**. Now add any mix of songs (in any mix of audio formats) to the blank area of the window. You can do this by clicking the add button (which looks like a green plus sign) and then navigating to the songs you want to add. You can also just directly drag files from any open file manager window to the Brasero window.

As you add songs to the Brasero window, a bar at the bottom of the window (visible in Figure 14-9) will show you how much more space is available on the disc. Keep an eye on that so as not to queue up more than your disc can hold. Once you are ready, the process is just as described in the previous section: Click the **Burn** button and then click **Burn** in the setup window that appears after that. A progress window will appear, and once the burn is complete, Brasero will let you know and eject your disc. You can then plop the disc in your car stereo or wherever else you want to play it and enjoy the results.

Other Cool Audio Apps

The applications I have covered so far are only a taste of what Ubuntu has in store for you. You can see what else is available by browsing through the offerings listed in the Ubuntu Software Center. Try them and keep them if you like them or remove them if you don't. After all, it doesn't cost you anything in Linux.

To give you a starting point, I'll mention a few applications that I think might be worth investigating.

Alternative Players

If the music players that I've covered in this chapter have whetted your appetite for more, you are in luck—there are plenty of others, as a browse through Ubuntu Software Center's Sound & Video category will reveal. Check out Exaile, Banshee, Audacious, and Listen to get started. Oh, and as you'll find out in Chapter 16, if you haven't discovered it already, Movie Player, which comes with your system, also doubles as an audio player. Wow.

Streaming Music with Streamtuner2

If you are an Internet radio junkie, probably no application is handier than Streamtuner2 (Figure 14-10). Streamtuner2 is, as its name implies, an online radio stream tuner. It works by downloading lists of available streams from a variety of sources, which you can then easily browse. When you find something you like, just double-click the stream (or just select the stream and then click the green play button at the top left of the window), and the stream will open in the player of your choice.

The default player for most streams is Audacious, but that app does not come with Ubuntu (though it is available for download from the Ubuntu Software Center), so you'll have to pick an alternative. You can make this choice the very first time you run Streamtuner2, since the first window you'll see is the settings window. In that window, change the default entries from Audacious to whatever audio player you prefer. The name of the player is usually represented by the name of the application in all lowercase letters.

Figure 14-10: Browsing Internet radio streams with Streamtuner2

For example, I like to use the Movie Player application, which, as you'll learn in Chapter 16, not only plays movies but also does nicely with audio. In this case, I change all the entries of audacious to **totem**, which is the project name of Movie Player. (I leave the entries for VLC as is. You'll be learning about this useful application in Chapter 16.)

You'll also need to change the Web Browser setting, since the browser specified is also not bundled in Ubuntu. Change that entry to **firefox** or, if you've installed it, **chrome**. Your window should then look something like Figure 14-11. Once done, click **Save**. If you want to change your settings again in the future, you can access this window by going to the **Edit** menu and selecting **Properties**.

Configuration Settings

	Format	Audio Player
Player	audio/mp3	totem
	audio/ogg	totem
Display	audio/aac	totem
	audio/x-real	vlc
	audio/*	totem
System	*/*	vlc %srv

Here %u or %pls return a direct URL to the shoutcast link.

And %g or %m3u provide a local .m3u file for the audio player, what's usually better.

Recording

audio/* | x-terminal-emulator -e streamripper %sr

Web Browser

url/http | chrome

cancel | save

Figure 14-11: Changing settings in Streamtuner2

You'll be happy to know that you can rip the streams you are listening to (and even those you aren't listening to) and save them as MP3 files. Streamtuner2 is set up to do this though a background app called Streamripper, which you have to install separately. (Just search for it in the Ubuntu Software Center and install normally.) Once it's installed, you can record a stream from within Streamtuner2 by right-clicking the target stream and then clicking the red record button at the top of the window.

Ex Falso and EasyTAG

For the true audio geek, there are a number of applications that allow you to alter the tags of your MP3 and Ogg Vorbis music files. EasyTAG is the more full featured of the two, but Ex Falso (Figure 14-12) has a friendlier user interface. Give 'em both a try and see what you think.

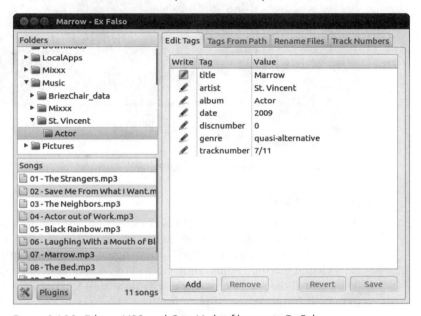

Figure 14-12: Editing MP3 and Ogg Vorbis file tags in Ex Falso

Apps for Music Makers

The audio apps I have mentioned up to this point are really oriented to the listening side of music. There are also a number of applications for those who like to make music. In this section, I'll introduce some of the most useful or at least most interesting of these.

Audacity

Although not purely a music-making application, Audacity (Figure 14-13) is the king, in terms of numbers of users, of the sound-recording and editing apps, not only in the Linux world but to a large degree in the Mac and Windows worlds as well. Audacity allows you to record sound files and then edit them, raising pitch, increasing and decreasing speed, adding echo and other effects, and . . . well, all sorts of other neat stuff. You will probably find yourself using Audacity for more than you ever imagined.

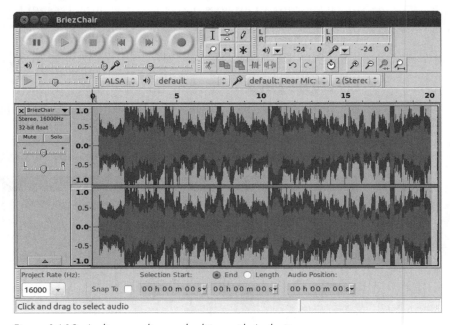

Figure 14-13: Audio recording and editing with Audacity

Ardour and LMMS

Ardour (Figure 14-14) and LMMS are the two most commonly used Linux digital audio workstations, both in the genre of the popular professional digital audio workstation, Avid Pro Tools. Digital audio workstations are basically virtual mixing rooms, allowing you to record, edit, and play back music. They also allow you to create music from within the program itself. I'm no expert with this type of application, but many people say that LMMS is stronger in the creation department while Ardour is stronger in the recording/editing area. Of course, the easiest way to figure out which one is best for your needs is to try them both out.

MuseScore

If you need to print out musical scores, you can turn to the straightforward and very capable music notation program MuseScore. MuseScore (Figure 14-15) allows you to create sheet music, by either mouse, keyboard, or midi device, with up to four voices per staff. It also allows you to play back the compositions you've put on the page. This is a great feature for folks like me who can't read music but find themselves wanting to figure out a melody based on its score. Just copy the notes to a page in MuseScore, click the play button, and the elusive melody is there before your ears (as well as your eyes).

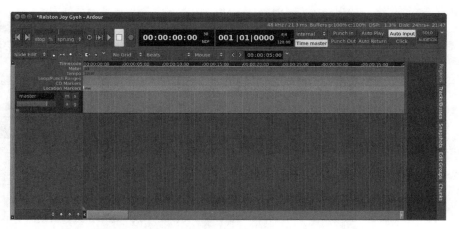

Figure 14-14: Ardour, a Linux digital audio workstation

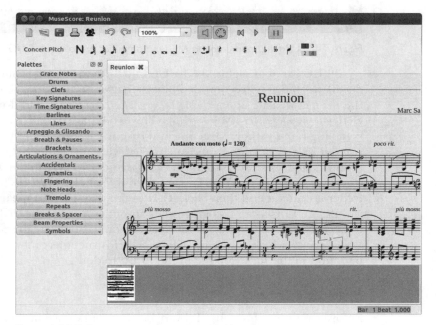

Figure 14-15: Putting notes on paper with MuseScore

Amping It Up with PLUG

The guitar players among you, particularly those of you with Fender Mustang amplifiers (I–IV), will be disappointed to learn that Fender's Fuse software that normally comes with your amp is not compatible with Linux. The good news is an answer in the form of the application PLUG (Figure 14-16). Like Fuse, PLUG can be used to create and edit amplifier presets and upload them to your amplifier. Using PLUG is like creating and modifying your own pedal, just virtually rather than on the floor in front of you. You can also apply firmware updates for your amplifier via PLUG.

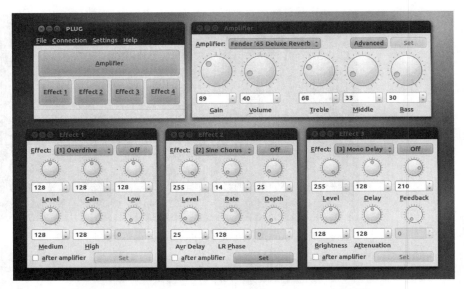

Figure 14-16: Editing and creating Mustang amplifier presets with PLUG

PLUG is not available via the Ubuntu Software Center, but it is easily downloadable as a precompiled binary that works just fine. Get PLUG from the project website at *http://piorekf.org/plug/download/* and download the Generic package for 32-bit systems. This is a binary tarball, so you won't be installing it but rather extracting and running it from your Home folder, as you did with some of the apps you worked with in Chapter 8. Once the tarball is downloaded, extract it to the *LocalApps* folder you created in Chapter 8 (or wherever else you prefer). To run it, double-click the *PLUG* file within the folder it came in and then click **RUN** in the dialog that appears.

Before PLUG can recognize your amplifier, you'll have to do a little work to get around the fact that Ubuntu allows only root users to access unknown USB devices, which your amp will be. The instructions on how to do this can be found in the *README* file in the *PLUG* folder.

Hydrogen & Mixx

Before wrapping things up, I'll very briefly mention a couple more applications that deserve mention if for no other reason than they are pretty cool at what they do. One is Hydrogen (Figure 14-17), which is a digital drum machine for Linux. It aims to provide, as the project page puts it, "professional yet simple and intuitive pattern-based drum programming." The other is Mixx (Figure 14-18), a cross-platform, full-featured digital dual-deck DJ mixer.

Figure 14-17: Hydrogen, a digital drum machine

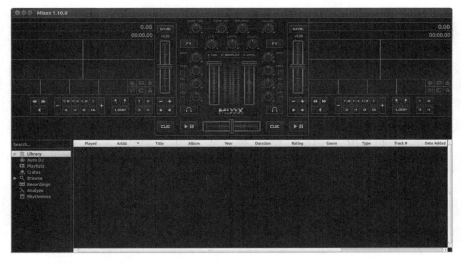

Figure 14-18: Mixx, a cross-platform DJ mixer

15

PLUGGIN' IN THE PENGUIN

Working with Your iPod, iPhone, and Other Digital Media Devices

With all the talk in the previous chapter about ripping, encoding, and playing back audio files, you may be wondering whether Ubuntu will allow you to transfer any of those files to your digital media devices, such as your MP3 player, cell phone, or iPad. Well, you will be happy to know that using your device with your Ubuntu system is quite easy—easier than ever, in fact. No longer do you have to mess around with mount and unmount commands or edit system tables, and if you don't know what I'm talking about, consider yourself lucky. Just plug in your device, and Ubuntu will do the rest.

Knowing Your Limits

Assuming Ubuntu helped you to download and install all the audio codecs and support files for the applications mentioned in Chapter 14, you shouldn't encounter any problems handling any of the media files on your digital media device. Even if you didn't install those codecs and files, Ubuntu will automatically help you find the necessary items if you try to play a file it hasn't already installed support for. Nevertheless, not all formats will work with equal degrees of comfort or success—it depends on your device and the file format's compatibility with Ubuntu. As a general rule of thumb, most players will be able to handle MP3 files and unlocked AAC (*.m4a*) files. Check your device's manual for specifics about other file formats (or just give them a try).

As far as Ubuntu goes, it can work with all the file formats mentioned—with the exception of locked AAC files. And you will learn a way to deal with them later in the chapter.

NOTE *Although working with your digital media devices in Ubuntu has become increasingly simple, it's always worth using a bit of caution. Make sure to have backups of the files on your device before working with it on Ubuntu.*

Mounting and Ejecting Your iPod, iPhone, or iPad

Working with your iPod, iPhone, or iPad is extremely simple. Basically, just connect the device to your computer via a USB connector, and Ubuntu will mount the device so you can access it. An icon for your device and another for Documents will then appear in the left pane of any file manager window you happen to have open. Ubuntu will also place icons for your device and Documents in the Launcher.

In addition, two of those what-do-you-want-me-to-do-with-this-stuff types of displays will appear. (These are the same kind of displays that show up when you insert a music CD or DVD into your drive or connect a digital camera to your machine via USB cable.) You'll see one for music and podcasts and one for photos (Figure 15-1), and they'll usually be stacked one directly above the other. You can select Rhythmbox for music-handling chores in one and Shotwell for photo handling in the other. Then click **OK** in each window to work with your device through those two applications. Or you can just close both of those windows for now and then open either Rhythmbox or Shotwell, or both, later on by clicking the icon for your device in the left pane and then clicking either of the two buttons that appear in the file manager window for your device (Figure 15-2).

To "eject" your iPhone or other "i" device, click the eject button next to the icon for your device in the side pane of the file manager window or right-click the Launcher icon for the device and then select **Unmount**.

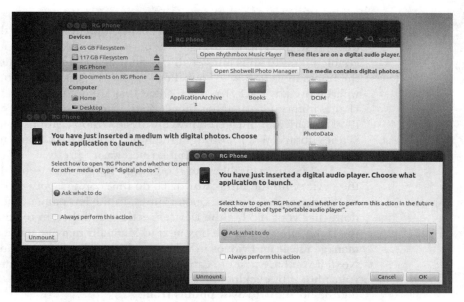

Figure 15-1: Ubuntu instantly recognizes your iPod, iPhone, or iPad.

Figure 15-2: Launching Rhythmbox and Shotwell for working with the audio and image files on your device

(Not) Auto-updating Your iPod or iPhone

With the simple instructions as to how to use your iPod or iPhone with Ubuntu out of the way, it's worth thinking about a couple of other things. Most important of these is the device's auto-updating settings. When you enable auto-update on your iPod or iPhone via iTunes, the function is set up within the device itself. You can use your iPod in Windows, Mac OS, or Linux—or all of them interchangeably. If you set up your iPod to auto-update songs and playlists, however, you are leaving yourself open for trouble unless you have exactly the same music collection on all of your machines.

Here's why: Although iTunes allows you to add files *to* your iPod, it does not allow you to copy files *from* it. The auto-update feature is thus strictly a one-way street. This means that whenever you hook up your auto-update–enabled iPod to an iTunes-enabled computer, iTunes will automatically add the tracks in its library to your iPod—so far, so good. More frighteningly, it will remove any tracks from your iPod that are not present in that machine's iTunes library. I learned this the hard way when I took my now ex-wife's loaded iPod to work and plugged it into my office Winbox with its completely empty iTunes library. When I brought the little Podster back home to her with nothing at all on it, well . . . what ensued wasn't pretty.

Make sure to disable your iPod's auto-update function before bringing the device into the Linux world. To do this, connect your iPod to your Mac or Windows machine and open iTunes. In the left pane of the iTunes window, click your iPod in the Devices section, and then in the **Summary** tab in the right pane, check the box next to **Manually manage music** (or **Manually manage music and videos** in video-capable iPods), as shown in Figure 15-3. Next, if you have a photo-capable device, repeat nearly the same process for your photos by clicking the **Photos** tab in the right pane and then unchecking the box next to **Sync photos from**.

Figure 15-3: Disabling the auto-update function on your iPhone/iPod in iTunes

Working with Android-Based Devices

Although the iPhone continues to be the king of the smartphone hill, phones and tablet computers running Google's Android operating system are starting to give Apple a run for its money. Fortunately, working with any

Android-powered device in Ubuntu is quite simple, and it's only slightly different from working with one of Apple's "i" devices. Basically, this is the process:

1. Connect your Android-powered device to your computer using the USB cable that came with it.

2. In the dialogue that appears on your Android device, asking you what you want to do now that you are connected to an external device, press the **Mass storage** button.

3. In the next screen that appears on your Android device, press **Connect storage to PC**.

4. The first time you do this, another small window will then appear on your device telling you that some apps might not work when your device is connected as a USB storage device. Click **OK**.

NOTE *Because different versions of the Android system are in service, it is possible that the details of the process described here might be slightly different from what you need to do with your phone. You should still be able to follow along.*

Similar to what happens in the case of the iPhone, iPod, and iPad, one or more windows will then appear asking you what you want to do with the photos and music files on your device, and an icon for your device should appear in the side pane of any open file manager window and in the Launcher.

To "eject" your Android device, right-click either the file manager or Launcher icon for the device and then click **Eject** in the pop-up menu. Then on your phone, press **Disconnect storage from PC**.

What About Kindles, NOOKs, and Android 3.0+ "Honeycomb"-Based Devices?

In the very recent past, getting Kindles or NOOKs or tablets with the newer Android 3.0+ operating system (known as "Honeycomb") to work with Ubuntu involved a lot of tinkering around from the command line. The reason was that these devices did not use the USB protocol that most of the other devices in this class use. Instead they used a file transfer protocol called MTP (Media Transfer Protocol) which was not Linux (or even Mac) friendly. The good news is that while these devices still use the MTP file transfer protocol, Linux, as of this Ubuntu 12.04 release, has no problems working with these devices. This means that all those connection and file transfer problems are gone, and your device should work with Ubuntu just like all the others mentioned in this chapter.

Working with Other Digital Media Players and Cell Phones

Although the iPod may be the most popular digital media player out there and the iPhone holds the crown in the smartphone market, they are by no means the only games in town. As I have already shown, Android-based phones are quite popular, and there are still other devices available, like the simple $10 USB MP3 players you can find in just about any big-box department store.

How to work with these devices in Ubuntu can vary by device, but for the most part, they will work in either the same manner as an iPod or Android device or the same manner as a USB data device. The simplest way to see how your device will work is to connect it to your computer via a USB cable. If windows asking you how to deal with the device do not appear, open a file manager window to see whether you find an icon for the device there. If so, you can work with your device using the tried-and-true drag-and-drop method. You can also use Rhythmbox to work with the audio files on your generic device by doing the following:

1. In Rhythmbox, go to the Music menu and select **Check for New Devices**.

2. If your device does not show up in the left pane, then import the folder on your device where the audio files are stored by clicking the **Import** button above the main pane in the Rhythmbox window.

3. In the Import Folder into Library window that appears, click your device in the left pane. Then navigate to the folder that holds the audio files in the right pane (Figure 15-4).

4. Click that folder in the right pane to select it and then click **Open**.

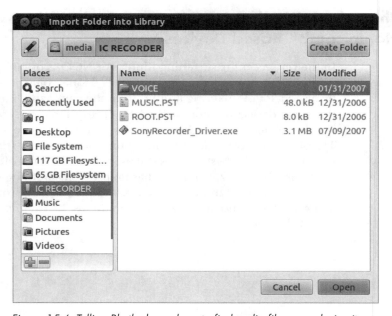

Figure 15-4: Telling Rhythmbox where to find audio files on a device it doesn't spot

Managing Your Audio Device's Audio Files with Rhythmbox

As I've already mentioned, Rhythmbox is set as the default application for iPhones, iPods, iPads, Android-powered devices, and, one way or another, any other music player in Ubuntu. Once Rhythmbox is up and running, things work pretty much as they do in iTunes.

- To view the contents of your iPod or other device, click the icon for the device in the left pane of the window. The contents of the device will then appear in the right pane of the window.

- To copy a song from your library to your device, just click **Music** in the Library section of the left pane and then drag the artists, albums, or single tracks you want from the right pane to your device's icon in the left pane.

If dragging files to your device seems a bit tedious, it is possible to sync your device to the Rhythmbox music library. Just click the icon for your device in the left pane of the Rhythmbox window and then click the **Sync with Library** button above the main pane. A window, like that in Figure 15-5, will appear. Check the items you want to sync in the top portion of the window and then click **Sync with the device**. Rhythmbox will begin the synching process, copying all the music and podcasts in the library (if you chose that option) to your device and showing the progress of the transfer in the bottom right corner of the window.

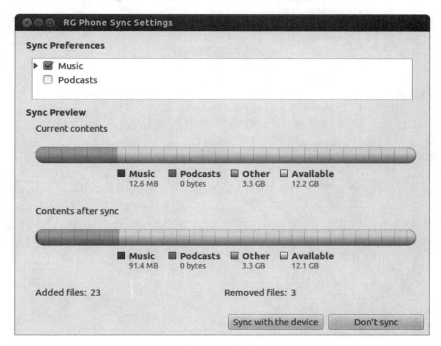

Figure 15-5: Synching your audio device with Rhythmbox

Copying Songs from Your Audio Device to Your Hard Disk

One feature of most digital media players that isn't available in iTunes (at least not without the installation of a special freeware plug-in) is the ability to copy songs from your iPhone/iPod to your hard disk (or even to an external USB drive). Luckily, Rhythmbox allows you to do this easily.

To copy music from your iPhone/iPod/iPad, Android-based phone, or other digital media device with Rhythmbox, select the tracks you want to export (hold down the CTRL key to make multiple selections or use the tabs to select whole artists or genres if you like) and drag the selected items to your desktop, music folder, or wherever you want them. The only catch with this mostly simple approach is that when copying files from an iPod/iPhone, you end up with files on your hard disk with funky filenames, such as *ZPAD.m4a* or *ATDT.mp3*, rather than the name that appeared on your iPhone/iPod or within Rhythmbox. This means you'll have to rename the files once they have been transferred to your hard disk. This isn't too much of a chore unless you're dealing with lots and lots of files or if you've forgotten which file is which. In the latter case, right-click the file, click **Properties**, and then click the **Audio** tab, where you will find the original filename (Figure 15-6). Once you know the filename, click the **Basic** tab, type the correct name in the Name box, and then click **Close**.

Figure 15-6: Finding the filename properties of a mislabeled audio file

Ejecting Your iPod or Other Digital Device from Within Rhythmbox

When you're done working with your iPod or other digital device in Rhythmbox, you can eject it in one of two ways. Either click its entry in the left pane of the Rhythmbox window and then click the **Eject** button near the top of the window, or right-click its icon in the left pane and select **Eject** in the pop-up menu that appears. If Rhythmbox is closed, this right-click-to-eject approach also works from within a Nautilus window or with the Launcher icon for a mounted device.

Problems Writing to Your iPod

If you have an iPod (iPhone, iPod Touch, and iPad not included) that you were last using in conjunction with a Mac, you may find that although you can read the files on your iPod, you cannot write files to it. If this is the case, most likely your iPod is formatted in Apple's native HFS+ filesystem—although this in itself is not a problem. The problem is that HFS+ formatted iPods have journaling enabled. *Journaling* is an HFS+ feature that acts to protect the filesystem from damage due to power surges, power failures, or hardware breakdowns.

As fate would have it, however, the Linux kernel doesn't deal well with journaling-enabled, HFS+ formatted devices. Fortunately, the tweak to fix this is quite simple, and it isn't even particularly geeky: You just have to disable journaling on your iPod.

Disabling journaling on an HFS+ formatted iPod is easy if you have a Mac nearby. Just plug your iPod into a Mac, close iTunes when it automatically opens, and then run Disk Utility (in the Utilities folder within the Applications folder). When Disk Utility opens, select your iPod (by name) in the left pane of the window, press the OPTION key, and then choose **Disable Journaling** in the **File** menu. After a moment, journaling on your iPod will be disabled without any loss of data. If you connect your iPod to your Linux machine again, you will be able to use it more or less like normal.

Working with Photos on Your Digital Device

As I already mentioned, if your phone or digital device is photo capable and Ubuntu automatically recognizes it, you will be led to Shotwell, just as you are when you hook up your digital camera to your Ubuntu machine. In the same way, Shotwell takes stock of what you have on your device and then allows you to copy photos to your hard disk.

As you can see in Figure 15-7, you first select the photos you want to copy to your hard disk, add a tag if you like, and then click **Copy**. After the photos are copied to your disk, they will appear in the Shotwell Library, from which you can work with them as you see fit.

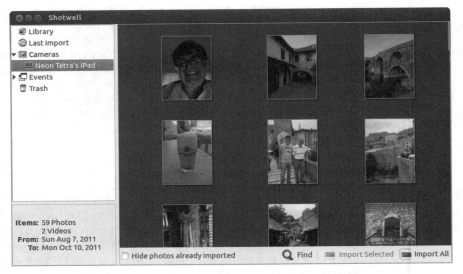

Figure 15-7: Importing photos from your iPhone/iPod/iPad or other digital device with Shotwell

Converting Audio File Formats

As I pointed out at the beginning of the chapter, there may be some points of incompatibility when it comes to certain audio file formats, your hardware, and Ubuntu. Fortunately, SoundConverter (shown in Figure 15-8) makes it easy to convert Ogg Vorbis files to MP3 format, or vice versa. It can also convert AAC files to MP3 or Ogg Vorbis format, if that is of interest to you. Because SoundConverter does not come bundled with Ubuntu, you will have to install it from the Ubuntu Software Center.

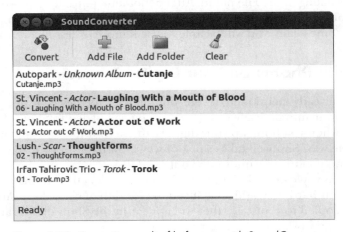

Figure 15-8: Converting audio file formats with SoundConverter

To use SoundConverter, add the songs you want to convert to the main pane by clicking either the **Add File** or **Add Folder** button. You can also drag audio files from your *Music* folder (or wherever else you store them).

Once you've chosen the files to convert, you need to choose which format to convert them to. You can do this by selecting **Edit ▸ Preferences** and then making your choice in the Preferences window (Figure 15-9). While you're there, it's also a good idea to tell SoundConverter to place your converted files in a location other than the folder where the original files are stored. Doing this prevents having to deal with duplicates in Linux audio playback applications that automatically scan your *Music* folder, such as Rhythmbox. You might also want to check the **Create subfolders** box to keep things organized.

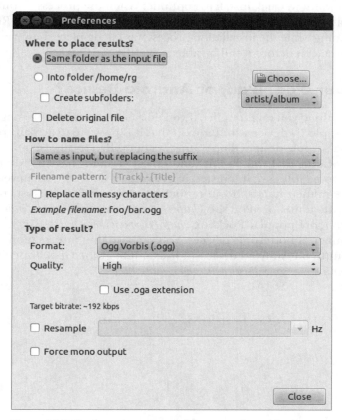

Figure 15-9: Setting conversion preferences in SoundConverter

Once you have set things up and are ready to convert, click **Close** in the Preferences window and then click **Convert** in the main window. Sound-Converter will begin doing its stuff.

Playing Locked AAC (M4P) Files

If you purchased music from the iTunes Store before Apple did away with digital rights management (DRM) in its music, chances are you are in possession of some locked AAC files, which you can recognize by the *.m4p* extension. These files can be played only on registered machines through iTunes. As you may have already discovered, you cannot do much with such files on your system as is. All you will get when you try to play one is an error message and an option to have Ubuntu search for the missing plug-in. Accepting that option is the easiest way to get the support you need to play such files within Ubuntu.

Once you accept, Ubuntu will search for the plug-in and necessary support files. Once Ubuntu finds them, it will show the result of its search in a new window. Click **Install** to continue. When the process is complete, you will be able to play previously locked AAC files on your system. If Rhythmbox was running while the installation process was taking place, however, you will need to restart it before it will be able to handle the files.

Linux on Your iPod, iPad, or Android Device?

One thing you might notice if you do a Google search on using your Android or Apple "i" device with Linux is that it is possible to actually replace your iPod's Apple-designed operating system with a form of Linux. Now, I'm not advocating that you do this (and I most certainly have not done so myself), but some folks are interested in geeking around with whatever gadget they have in their hands. If you're such a person or if you're just curious, check out the Linux on iPod site (*http://ipodlinux.sourceforge.net/index.shtml*) or the even more popular Rockbox (*http://www.rockbox.org/*), which also runs on a number of non-Apple devices. You can also find information on installing Ubuntu on Android devices, for example at the Geeknizer site (*http://geeknizer.com/install-run-ubuntu-on-android/*).

16

COUCH PENGUINS

Video and DVD Playback in Ubuntu

Now that I've covered much of what Ubuntu can do in terms of audio, it's time to turn to the equally important area of video. Ubuntu is quite capable in terms of video, allowing you to view DVDs, video CDs (VCDs), video files you download from the Internet, and some Internet video streams. It also allows you to download video movie files from your digital camera, or to capture movies from tape-based digital video cameras and then edit them.

Where the Apps Are

All of the apps in this chapter can be run from the Dash by clicking the Applications lens and then clicking the **Media** filter button. As with all applications, you can also run an app by typing its name in the Dash's search box and then pressing ENTER.

DVDs

Your system allows you to play DVDs; however, due to licensing concerns, playback is limited to unencrypted discs by default. Unfortunately, this rules out a vast majority of the DVD movies you buy or rent at your local video shop and leaves you with a limited choice of films to play on your computer. Given the limited offerings in the unencrypted DVD world, you will no doubt want to enable your system to play the encrypted variety.

Project 16: Installing Support for Encrypted DVDs

As I already mentioned, Ubuntu does not allow you to play encrypted DVDs from the start, unless you opted to install third-party software support when you installed Ubuntu. If you did not do that, then for you to watch such DVDs (and that would be the vast majority of them), you need to install a whole bunch of stuff—most crucially the package *libdvdread4*. Fortunately, this has become quite easy to do now that Ubuntu tells you what you need when you need it, just as it did in the previous chapter.

The first step is the easiest: Insert a DVD movie disc in your disc drive. In few moments, a window will appear telling you that you have inserted a DVD (duh!) and asking you what you want to do. In the drop-down menu, select **Movie Player** and click **OK**. A new window will appear as Ubuntu figures out what you need to install before you can start playing DVDs. Once it is done, accept the default packages suggested in the window that appears by clicking **OK** and then entering your password. Then sit back for a minute or less until the installation process is complete. Once it is, you will have successfully installed *libdevread4* and a bunch of other necessary files. So now you're ready to play your DVD, right? Well, not quite.

With just about any other application, you would be done at this point, but as you will notice, Movie Player will be open but your DVD will still not be playing. The reason is that *libdvdread4* requires that you also run an installation script that comes with it in order to get the job done. To run the script, open the Terminal, type the following, and then press ENTER:

```
sudo /usr/share/doc/libdvdread4/install-css.sh
```

You will soon be prompted for your password, so type it in and press ENTER. Once the Terminal returns you to the user prompt, the process will be done. Close Movie Player, reinsert the DVD movie disc in your drive, and once again select Movie Player in the window that pops up. Once you click **OK**, Movie Player should open and start playing the DVD. (You'll learn more about Movie Player soon.)

Can I Play Foreign DVDs?

Your computer can play DVDs of any broadcast standard (NTSC, PAL, or SECAM) and of any regional encoding. This is a better setup than the DVD player you have hooked up to your TV, because the vast majority of stand-alone DVD players in the United States (I would venture to guess 99.9 percent) do not allow you to play anything other than Region 1 NTSC discs (NTSC being the broadcast standard in the United States and what US televisions are designed to display, and 1 being the DVD region). This information is usually provided on the back of DVD packages (see the examples in Figure 16-1), though the packaging for most discs produced for the US market does not include it.

Figure 16-1: Examples of regional encoding labels on DVD packages

Despite the wonderful, everything-goes nature of your computer in terms of DVD playback, there is a serious caveat to bear in mind. Depending on the manufacturer of your DVD drive, you will be able to switch back and forth between DVDs of differing regional encodings only four or five times. After that, the drive will be locked into the regional encoding of the disc you were playing at that time . . . *forever*. This is unrelated to your operating system—it is strictly a hardware matter. The only exception to this region-lock rule are those DVDs labeled *Region Free* or *ALL* (sometimes inaccurately labeled *Region 0*), which can be played on any DVD player in any region and thus do not register as a regional encoding switch when you plop one of them in your computer's DVD drive.

If your drive does eventually lock into one regional encoding, especially one for which you have few DVDs, there is some good news. That comes in the form of Videolan's *libdvdcss2*, the library that is included in the *libdvdread4* package you installed in Project 16A. The *libdvdcss2* library allows you to play back encrypted DVDs. In addition to that primary function, *libdvdcss2* also, in theory, allows you to play back DVDs from multiple regions even if your DVD drive is already locked into one region. It does this by performing a cryptic attack (to use Videolan's term for it) on your drive until it can find the disc key for that drive. Of course, this process of cryptic bombardment can take several minutes, so it is not the optimal way of going about things. It's better than being stuck, though. Whether this process of bypassing regional encodings is legal remains a subject of debate, so if you are concerned about such things, you should do a little research.

Watching Video Files with Movie Player

A number of video players are available in the Linux world. The one that comes bundled with Ubuntu is called, appropriately enough, Movie Player. As you can see in Figure 16-2, Movie Player has a very simple interface and is equally simple to use.

Figure 16-2: Movie Player

Using Movie Player to Play DVDs, VCDs, and Other Multimedia Files

Because Movie Player is the default video player in Ubuntu, you can play a DVD with it by simply placing a DVD in the drive, selecting Movie Player when prompted, and clicking **OK**. If you've got a copy of *Red Detachment of Women* on VCD that you're aching to watch, you can do so in the same way. Just pop the VCD in your drive, follow the same steps, and Movie Player should start up and begin playing the disc.

Not only does Movie Player play discs, DVDs, and VCDs, but it can also play MPEG and WMV files. Just double-click the files directly or go to the Movie Player **Movie** menu, select **Open**, and then navigate to the video file you want to view. If you have not already installed the necessary libraries to play such files, Ubuntu will let you know, tell you what you need, and allow you to install them at that point. Easy.

Movie Player as an Audio Player?

You may have noticed while on the Display tab of the Preferences window that there was a Visual Effects section. Well, those visual effects aren't for the videos you play but rather are visualizations to accompany your audio files when they are played via Movie Player (Figure 16-3). Yes, Movie Player not only does video but also does audio. You can play such files from the Movie

Player **Movie** menu by selecting **Open** and then navigating to the songs you want to play. If you have a CD in your disc drive, you can even use Movie Player as a CD player by going to the **Movie** menu and selecting **Play Disc 'Audio Disc'**.

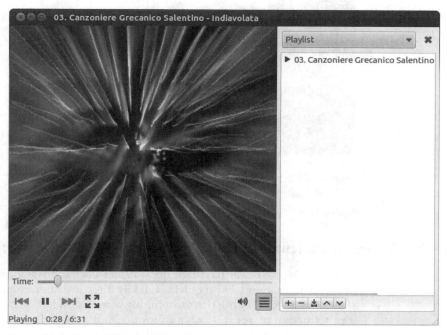

Figure 16-3: Movie Player as an audio player

A Couple of Other Cool Movie Player Features

Movie Player has a couple more cool features that you might like to know about. One is its ability to perform screen captures of whatever video you happen to be viewing at the time. Just select **Edit ▸ Take Screenshot**, and you've got yourself a screen capture—a still image taken from a video file.

Another feature worth mentioning is Movie Player's sidebar. As you no doubt noticed, at the bottom-right corner of the Movie Player window is a sidebar button. If you click that button, a new pane will open at the right side of the Movie Player window. In that pane you can select and listen to BBC podcasts; search for and watch YouTube videos (Figure 16-4); and load, create, and save playlists. You can select these various functions from the drop-down menu at the top of the sidebar.

The playlists you create can consist of any combination of supported video or audio files, thus providing you with the whole multimedia banana. Any time you play a file in Movie Player, that file appears in the Playlist pane, but you can also add items to the list by simply dragging the files there from your desktop or any Nautilus window.

Figure 16-4: Viewing YouTube videos in Movie Player

An Alternative (and Arguably Better) Video Player: VLC

Although Movie Player has made great strides since it first appeared, many users find it temperamental and quirky. Luckily there are alternatives, with a media player called VLC being the most highly recommended. VLC (Figure 16-5) is a very capable player with a big following, not only in the Linux world but in the Mac and Windows worlds as well. Like Movie Player, VLC handles audio files as well as video and audio streams, including YouTube. Unlike Movie Player, however, VLC just seems to work right, especially with DVDs. That's the way things are supposed to be.

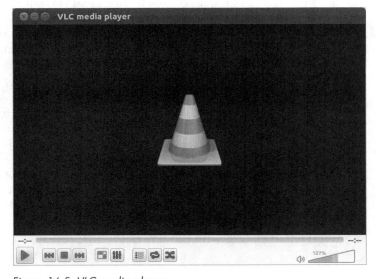

Figure 16-5: VLC media player

VLC is not bundled with Ubuntu, so you will need to download it yourself from the Ubuntu Software Center. I'm pretty sure you won't be disappointed.

Transferring Movies from Your Digital Camera to Computer

Digital video cameras have been around for a number of years now, though the impressive strides in video capabilities of still digital cameras and phones have resulted in many video enthusiasts not bothering with dedicated video cameras at all. This means that people are creating their own videos more than ever, and now with the ability to share video creations with family, friends, and the rest of the world via YouTube, it's fair to say that home digital video is just about ubiquitous.

Before you can work with your videos on your computer, you will have to transfer them from your camera. Fortunately this is pretty easy, though the process will vary slightly depending on the type of device you used to record your videos. Different devices store videos in different ways.

Transferring Video Files from a Camera with a Storage Card

Most digital cameras and dedicated digital video cameras today store your videos as files on a memory card, the most common being an SD card. Transferring your files from devices with these cards to your computer is straightforward, and there are a number of ways of going about it. While many video types can be imported via Shotwell in the same way you import photos, this sometimes does not work, depending on the file format in which the video is saved on your camera. One way that always works, however, is to just transfer the video files from your camera to computer as you would transfer files from a USB drive. Here is what you do:

1. Connect your camera's USB cable to your computer.
2. Turn on your camera in play mode.
3. In the dialog that soon appears, select **Open Folder** and click **OK**.
4. A file manager window will appear. Double-click through the folders there until you find your video files. You can recognize these by the file extensions, usually *.avi, .mp4, .mts,* or *.m2ts.*
5. Drag the files you want to copy to *Videos* in the left panel of the window and release the mouse button. The files will then be copied to your *Videos* folder.

Transferring Video Files from a Cell Phone or Another Mobile Device

Most cell phones and other portable computing devices are now able to take good-quality video, and these files, usually in a modified MPEG4 format (with a *.3pg* file extension) can also be transferred to and edited on your computer. Although the process for transferring such files is usually simple, the exact steps can vary greatly from device type to device type. To find out how to transfer files from your phone or other portable device, please refer to Chapter 15.

Capturing Digital Video from Cameras with Tape Storage

The transfer methods we've covered so far are easy to understand and deal with—you're basically just finding your files and then copying them from your camera to your computer. When you want to transfer a video clip to your computer from a digital video (DV) camera that saves its data on tape or from a video stream, however, there is no way to simply drag the file from one place to another. You have to capture the video stream to disk while you play it, and to do that, you need some sort of software solution. This is usually found in the form of a video editor; however, not all video editors have this capability. One that does have this capability and does the job easily is Kino (Figure 16-6).

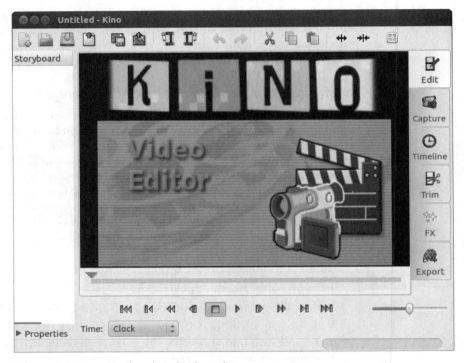

Figure 16-6: Kino, another digital video editor

Kino does not come bundled with Ubuntu, so you'll need to download and install it from the Ubuntu Software Center. Once you have done that, you are ready to capture video from your camera. To do this, connect your camera to your computer (if it isn't already connected), turn on your camera to Play mode, start up Kino, and then follow these steps:

1. Click the **Capture** tab to the right of the playback pane.

2. The control buttons at the bottom of the playback pane will now control the functions of your camera. Start by clicking the **Rewind** button until you get to the beginning of the video segment you want to capture.

3. Click the **Play** button. You will be able to see the video on your camera play back within the Kino window (Figure 16-7).

Figure 16-7: Capturing video from your digital camera with Kino

4. When you reach the point at which you want to start capturing, click the **Capture** button just above the playback controls in the Kino window. Kino will start saving your video to your computer's hard disk.

5. Click the **Stop** button when you would like to stop capturing.

The captured video will now be on your disk (in your Home folder by default). To keep things easy to manage later on, the captured video stream will be automatically split into several smaller files, the number of which depends on the length of the video played.

You can view the captured video by clicking the **Edit** tab and then using the playback controls at the bottom of the playback pane. You can also view the video in Timeline view (Figure 16-8) to navigate between various segments of the video. Just click the **Timeline** tab, click the segment you want to view, and then use the playback controls below the playback pane.

If you feel like getting a bit arty, you can also try the effects available in Kino (some examples are shown in Figure 16-9) by clicking the **FX** tab and then playing around with the various effects in the drop-down menu below the words *Video Filter*. After you choose an effect, specify the segment you'd like to convert (or at least experiment with) by typing the beginning and ending frame numbers in the boxes below the word *Overwrite*. To see the results of the filter without saving the changes to disk, click the **Play** button.

If you decide you want to convert the segment to keep the effect, click the **Render** button, and Kino will create a new file of just that segment. You can also double-click those files (as well as the original captures) to view them in Movie Player, which is better suited to viewing videos than Kino.

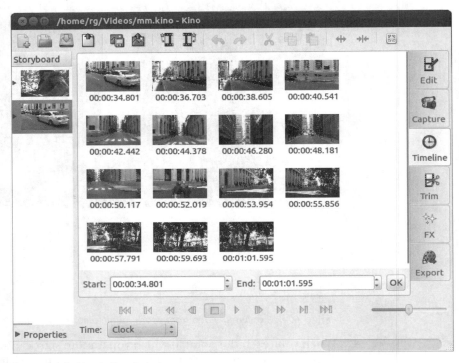

Figure 16-8: Kino's Timeline view

Figure 16-9: Examples of Kino's video effects, before and after

Editing Digital Video with PiTiVi

Now that you have learned how to get your video files from camera to computer, you can view them just by double-clicking any of them and watching them in Movie Player (or any other video player). Many people, however, want to edit movies by splicing clips together or cutting bits out. Others like to add transitions and other effects as well, and although Kino has some of these features, the application PiTiVi (Figure 16-10) has more of them and is generally easier to use. Like Kino, PiTiVi is available from the Ubuntu Software Center.

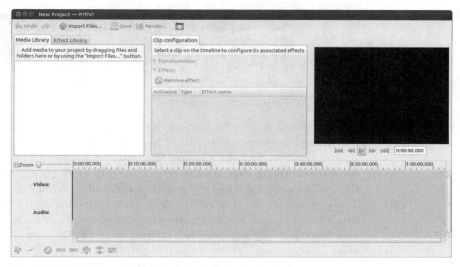

Figure 16-10: PiTiVi video editor

As you will immediately see, PiTiVi lacks the bells and whistles of applications like iMovie or, to some degree, Windows Live Movie Maker. PiTiVi does allow you to apply some effects and fairly basic transitions between film clips, and it does allow you to work with audio tracks. However, it lacks one of the most basic functions a consumer-oriented video editor should have, titles and captions, though these are promised for the future.

Limitations and peculiarities aside, the actual editing process in PiTiVi is relatively straightforward. First you start a new project and decide its name and settings (**Project ▸ Project Settings**). Then you add files to that project, either by dragging and dropping from your Home folder to the PiTiVi window or by clicking the **Import clips** button and then selecting the files you want to add via the Import a clip window that appears. The files, now called *clips*, will appear in the Clip Library pane of the PiTiVi window. From that pane, you can drag the clips you want to work on to the timeline below and then split the clips, delete the embarrassing or boring bits, and combine files (Figure 16-11). Be sure to save your project as you go along.

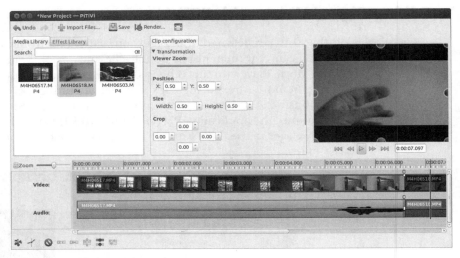

Figure 16-11: Editing video with PiTiVi

Once done with your editing, you can produce your new film by clicking the **Render project** button, after which a Render project window will appear. In that window, click the **Choose File** button and give your new film a title in the **Choose file to render to** window. This will be the name of the actual file that will be produced. Once done, click **OK** and then click the **Render** button. The progress of the rendering process will be shown in the Render project window, and when it is done, the words *Rendering Complete* will appear. You can then close the Render project window and PiTiVi as well. Be sure to save your project when prompted to do so.

For more detailed information on using PiTiVi, have a look at the user manual, which is available from the PiTiVi site at *http://www.pitivi.org/*.

Other Video Apps

I've covered the main video applications in Ubuntu, but there are still others that you might want to consider, all of which are available via the Ubuntu Software Center. If you are interested in yet another alternative video/DVD player, you can try GNOME MPlayer, which has long had a significant following because of its ability to handle numerous video formats.

Another cool application for video streaming enthusiasts is Miro Internet TV (Figure 16-12), which allows you to easily search, download, and play online video streams. Just perform an Ubuntu Software Center search for *miro*.

If you have a webcam, you might want to try an application called Cheese, which allows you take pictures and videos from your webcam and add cool graphical effects. Camorama is another webcam viewer/capture application to consider.

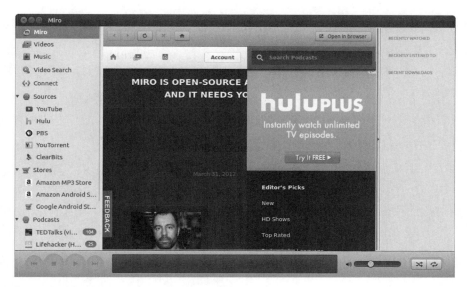

Figure 16-12: Miro, a videostreaming enthusiast's dream

If you're looking for an alternative to PiViTi and Kino, you can try Avidemux. One very handy feature makes it worth having, even if you don't use it as your main video editor: It can rip audio tracks from video files. If stop-motion animation video is your thing, then be sure to also check out Stopmotion.

For those of you interested in ripping DVDs, DVD:Rip, AcidRip DVD Ripper, and the less daunting Thoggen DVD Ripper are worth checking out. You might also be interested in DVD95 and the more highly configurable K9copy, which are the Linux world's answers to DVDShrink. These applications allow you to rip dual-layer DVDs (DVD9) and compress the output so that it will fit on a single-layer blank DVD disc (DVD5). For creating your own DVDs from scratch (as you would with iDVD), a couple of applications are worth considering: DVD Styler and Bombono DVD.

17

FEATHERED FLIPPERS

Linux Gaming

Many people hate to admit it, but games are a big attraction for almost everyone at the helm of a personal computer. Even those who deny being gamers often find themselves caught in the act of knocking off a quick round of solitaire between work projects. As a Linux user, you will most likely find that one of the most common questions users of other operating systems will ask you about Linux is "What games does it have?" Well, although there might not be as many games in the Linux world as there are on Planet Windows, Linux still has plenty to choose from. In fact, most Linux distributions come bundled with a number of games.

Ubuntu, for example, comes with the games AisleRiot Solitaire (a collection of more than 80 solitaire card games, shown in Figure 17-1), FreeCell Solitaire (a standalone version of one of the most popular solitaire games around), Mahjongg (a tile-matching game similar to the Xmahjongg game introduced in Chapter 8), Mines (the Linux world's answer to Minesweeper), and Sudoku (the Japanese number puzzle). Many other free games are available via the Ubuntu Software Center (and other sources), some of which you will learn about in this chapter.

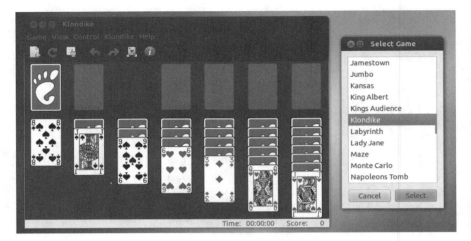

Figure 17-1: AisleRiot

Where the Apps Are

The majority of apps in this chapter can be run from the Dash by clicking the Applications lens and then clicking the **Games** filter button. Any exceptions are noted in the relevant sections. As with all applications, you can also run an app by typing its name in the Dash's search box and then pressing ENTER.

Project 17A: Expanding Your Game Collection via the Ubuntu Software Center

Expanding your gaming repertoire is quite easily done via the Ubuntu Software Center. In this project, you'll plug a few gaming holes by installing some classic Linux games. The steps in this project are basically a review of what you learned in Chapter 6, so there will be no challenging work involved—just fire up the Ubuntu Software Center and click away.

17A-1: Installing Classic GNOME Games

Older versions of Ubuntu used to come with a collection of games that were part of the GNOME desktop environment. These included several traditional favorites, such as the puzzlers Klotski (Figure 17-2), a challenging block-moving exercise, and Tetravex (Figure 17-3), which you can think of as a triangular form of dominoes. Others included Same GNOME (a GNOME version of the Japanese marble-matching game Same Game), Tali (an ancient Roman form of poker played with dice), Iagno (a GNOME

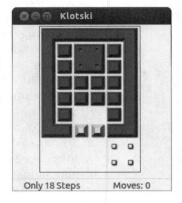

Figure 17-2: Klotski

clone of Reversi), Nibbles (one of those old-fashioned snake games), Five or More (a matching game based on the old Windows game Color Lines), Robots (a weird little "classic," in which you run around avoiding robots), Blackjack, and Chess.

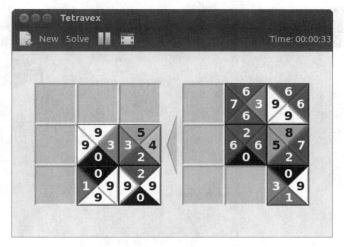

Figure 17-3: Tetravex

All of these can now be downloaded and installed individually from the Ubuntu Software Center, so you can now just install only those you actually like, or none at all.

17A-2: Installing Some Linux Classics: Frozen Bubble, Tux Racer, and Pingus

Several other games might be called Linux classics, either because they're Linux originals or because they are penguin themed, in honor of Linux's cuddly penguin mascot Tux. One of the most well-known and well-liked of these is Frozen Bubble (Figure 17-4). Frozen Bubble qualifies as the ultimate Linux classic: It was written for Linux, it's Linux (penguin) themed, and Linux versions are always released first. It has since been ported to Mac OS, Windows, and even iPhone and Android systems, but Frozen Bubble's soul is pure penguin.

The objective of Frozen Bubble is simple: Clear the screen by matching like-colored bubbles so you can move on to the next level. This may sound boring, but never fear—you'll be hooked in no time.

Another Linux-themed game you might be interested in is Pingus (Figure 17-5), a traditional maze game based on the old classic Lemmings. Your goal is to lead your group of adorable little penguins safely to the end of each level, without letting them be dashed to bits on the dangerous obstacles awaiting them. The game includes 22 playable levels, and if you're feeling adventurous, you can try playing some of the untested levels—there are more than 200 of them! For instructions on playing these extra levels, visit *http://pingus.seul.org/faq.html*.

Figure 17-4: Frozen Bubble

Figure 17-5: Pingus

3D Games

Most of the games I've mentioned so far are a little, well . . . two-dimensional. Sure, 2D games can be fun—I've certainly lost a significant portion of my life to Sudoku—but they don't have the excitement factor that you get from shooting hordes of aliens or crashing a high-powered sports car into a wall. Unfortunately, game designers have traditionally neglected Linux to concentrate on the significantly larger Windows market, so up until a couple of years ago, there were few Linux-friendly 3D games to choose from. As the penguin has grown in popularity, however, people have started to take notice, and more Windows games now come with a Linux version.

The open source gaming community has grown by leaps and bounds too, and there are some really high-quality games now. In this section, I'll run through a few of my favorites, after first making sure that your computer can handle the strain of 3D graphics.

Checking for Hardware Acceleration

To play 3D games, you need a graphics card that can handle *hardware acceleration.* Without hardware acceleration, your computer's processor has to try to do all of the fancy graphics rendering itself (a task for which it just isn't designed), so your games end up running at a snail's pace, if at all. Most modern graphics cards have hardware acceleration support built in, but whether it is enabled will depend on the state of the Linux driver for your card. You can find out how good 3D support is for your graphics card at *https://wiki.ubuntu.com/ HardwareSupportComponentsVideoCards/*.

If you just want to know whether you have the minimum level of acceleration required to play games, then bring up the Dash, open a Terminal, type `glxinfo | grep rendering`, and press ENTER. (That vertical line is the "pipe" symbol and can normally be inserted by pressing SHIFT and \ on your keyboard.) If you get a message telling you that glxinfo isn't installed, use the Ubuntu Software Center to install *mesa-utils* and then try again.

If hardware acceleration is enabled, you'll see `direct rendering: Yes` appear in the Terminal. That's good news, because it means you can skip to the next section and sink your teeth into some 3D gaming goodness.

If you received the message `direct rendering: No` instead, you'll need to install different graphics drivers for hardware acceleration to work. See "Games/Unity Don't Work: Installing Accelerated Graphics Drivers" on page 392 for instructions.

NOTE *Many of the default graphics drivers for Linux can't handle anti-aliasing, a feature that removes jagged edges from graphics, making them look smoother and more lifelike. If you can't live without anti-aliasing, see Chapter 22 for information on installing a better graphics driver.*

Shooting Games

Like many people, my first real 3D gaming experiences were with first-person shooter (FPS) games. In fact, I still have a soft spot for Doom, arguably the granddaddy of all FPSs. What could be more fun than battling endless waves of hellish monsters in a military outpost on Mars? Nothing!

Doom looks a little dated nowadays, but if you have similarly nostalgic thoughts of this classic game, you'll be pleased to know that a version is available for Ubuntu. It's called Freedoom (Figure 17-6), and you can install it from the Ubuntu Software Center (like all the games in this section).

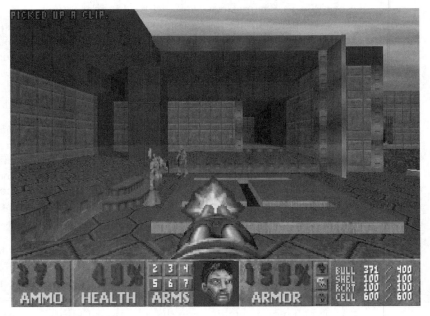

Figure 17-6: Freedoom

The gameplay in Doom may have aged gracefully, but the graphics sure haven't. If pixilated blobs are failing to intimidate you, why not try something a little smoother in the form of Nexuiz (Figure 17-7)? In terms of gameplay, Nexuiz feels similar to Unreal Tournament—you collect a wide array of weapons and power-ups as you run around dimly lit levels, shooting at opponents of varying levels of (artificial) intelligence. As with most death match–style games, the aim is generally to be the last one alive, but there are other game modes, like "capture the flag." There's also an online multiplayer option if you're finding that the computer-controlled opponents aren't providing enough of a challenge.

Tremulous (Figure 17-8) is another popular open source FPS, although its gameplay also contains elements of real-time strategy. You play online, taking the side of either humans or aliens. As you work to destroy the opposing team, you build structures and collect power-ups to gain as much of an advantage as you can. It can get quite involved, so I recommend that you read the notes at *http://www.tremulous.net/* before you begin playing.

Figure 17-7: Nexuiz

Figure 17-8: Tremulous

Plenty of other FPSs are available: AssaultCube, Open Arena, Red Eclipse, and Alien Arena immediately spring to mind. Check out the **Games ▶ Arcade** section in the Ubuntu Software Center to see what else you can find.

Strategy Games

I enjoy first-person shooters, but sometimes my reaction times aren't quite up to scratch. If the thought of running around a virtual world and shooting at things leaves you feeling cold (or clumsy), perhaps a strategy game is more your style. Plenty of these are waiting to be discovered in the Ubuntu Software Center, but I thought I'd mention a couple of good ones here.

Warzone 2100 (Figure 17-9) is broadly similar to the Command and Conquer series of games. You start off on a battleground with a small collection of vehicles, which you must command to build a base and defend it from enemies. Once your base is in good shape, you can build new units and send them to attack your foes. Your opponents are doing the same, however, so battles can turn into subtle tactical affairs, where your ability to launch successful attacks must be balanced against the limited availability of resources and the constant threat that the enemy will destroy your base.

Figure 17-9: Warzone 2100

If you're struggling to find the time to mastermind an entire military campaign, perhaps Hedgewars (Figure 17-10) is more your thing. It's a clone of the popular Worms game, which sees you in command of a small team of heavily armed worms (or, in the case of Hedgewars, cute little hedgehogs) scattered around an oddly shaped landscape. You take turns, using your over-stocked arsenal to remove opponents from the map in elaborate ways before they can do the same to you. It's definitely worth playing, if only for the interesting sound effects. . . .

Figure 17-10: Hedgewars

A few other strategy games worth looking out for include 0 A.D. and Widelands, where you command an ancient civilization as it settles (and battles) the rest of the known world; Bos Wars, which is similar to Warzone 2100; and The Battle for Wesnoth, which has more of a fantasy vibe.

Simulators

Waging war isn't everyone's idea of escapism, which is why an extensive collection of simulation games is available for Linux. I've tried to cover as many bases as possible in this section, but as always, you should peruse the Ubuntu Software Center if you don't see something here that appeals to you.

When I think of simulation games, my mind immediately jumps to Sim City, the venerable city-building game. As the mayor, you're in charge of running your city: You plan construction work, build and maintain transport links, and set budgets and taxes. Throw the odd natural disaster into the mix, and you have a challenge on your hands! The Linux equivalents of Sim City are LinCity-NG and OpenCity. I prefer LinCity (Figure 17-11)—the graphics seem friendlier and more cartoonish—but you should try both and decide for yourself. The original Sim City game is available too, if you don't mind playing a game with old-fashioned graphics. Just search for *Micropolis* in the Ubuntu Software Center (it was renamed for legal reasons). Finally, if managing a whole city sounds like a bit of a chore, you could always take a look at OpenTTD instead. It's a clone of Transport Tycoon, which "merely" has you running the transport network.

Figure 17-11: LinCity-NG

The hardcore flight-simulator enthusiasts among you will want to take a look at FlightGear (Figure 17-12). The focus is definitely on realism, with all sorts of cockpit controls and aircraft for you to play with. If you really want the full experience, there's even an Earth-sized online multiplayer map to fly around. If you're not already in possession of a pilot's license, then it might be a good idea to read the manual before you play; you can find it at *http://www.flightgear.org/Docs/getstart/getstart.html*. For something a little less involved, and a little more warlike, check out gl-117, a combat flight simulator. Or, the humanitarians among you might prefer Search and Rescue, in which you pilot aircraft on various rescue missions.

A little less serious than FlightGear is Torcs, a motor-racing game (Figure 17-13). It's a pretty standard track racer in which you speed around a circuit against computer-controlled opponents. It has a good choice of cars, tracks, and race styles, and more are available on the Torcs website at *http://torcs.sourceforge.net/*. If off-road racing is more your style, take a look at the Trigger rally game. It's not as well developed as Torcs, but it makes for a change.

If you'll permit me to stretch the definition of *simulator* just a little, there is a neat rock-star simulator called Frets on Fire (Figure 17-14). The gameplay is very much like that of Guitar Hero, but with one major difference: You use your keyboard to play notes, rather than a guitar-shaped controller. However, if you don't mind doing a little tinkering, you can get your Guitar Hero controller to work with Frets on Fire. (See *http://fretsonfire.wikidot.com/using-guitar-hero-controller/*.) Plastic guitar or not, it's an addictive game. Or, if karaoke is more your style, there's always Performous.

Figure 17-12: FlightGear

Figure 17-13: Torcs

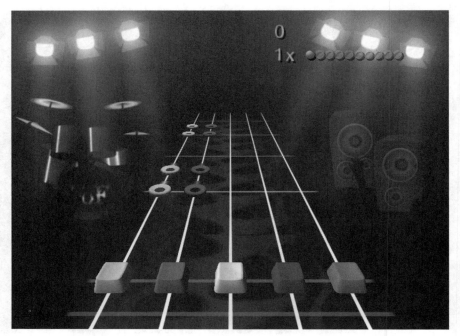

Figure 17-14: Frets on Fire

Beyond the Ubuntu Software Center

I hope you've found something agreeable among my recommendations so far, but it's hardly an exhaustive list. Hundreds of games that do run on Ubuntu but haven't made their way into the Ubuntu Software Center yet are packaged as Ubuntu-ready DEB files all the same.

PlayDeb (*http://www.playdeb.net/*) is a good place to find extra games. Everything on PlayDeb is available through its own Ubuntu-friendly software repository, so you'll be able to install its games through the Ubuntu Software Center once you've added the PlayDeb repository to your list. See "Adding Extra Software Repositories" on page 88 for full details—the APT line that you need is `deb http://archive.getdeb.net/ubuntu precise-getdeb games`.

Another option worth exploring is the PPA section of Launchpad. To see what's available, head over to *https://launchpad.net/ubuntu/+ppas?name _filter=game* and browse through the rather lengthy list. Many of these are games in the home-brew tradition, so don't expect much polish in most of what you find, but there are a few gems here. You can find instructions on how to install PPAs in "Project 6B: Installing Software from a PPA—Turtle Arena" on page 90.

Commercial Games

All of the games that I've mentioned so far in this chapter are free and open source, in keeping with Ubuntu's usual mode of operation. But plenty of commercial games are available for Linux too; it's just a matter of knowing where to look for them.

Some, like Doom III, Unreal Tournament, and Enemy Territory, come with a Linux installer right out of the box. The installation instructions, which you can generally find somewhere on the install CD/DVD, usually amount to little more than running an install script from the Terminal. The availability of a Linux installer on the same disc as the Windows version is still something of a rarity among blockbuster titles though, so it's often necessary to look online for one. A list of commercial games, some free and some for a price, along with helpful links to their Linux installers, can be found at *http:// icculus.org/lgfaq/gamelist.php*. Wikipedia also has a few lists of Linux games that are kept up-to-date: Start at *http://en.wikipedia.org/wiki/Linux_gaming* and see where the links take you. . . .

If spending the whole afternoon scouring the Web for decent games doesn't sound too appealing, how about letting someone else collect the real gems for you? That's what the rather splendid *Humble Bundles* are all about: They're collections of cross-platform games (all of them can run on Linux, Windows, and Mac OS) that are occasionally made available on a "pay what you want" basis. Depending on how much you choose to pay, you might also get access to bonus games and features. As an added incentive, every so often some of the games in the bundle are open sourced if sales of the bundle are sufficiently good. That's what happened to Gish (in which you play a happy little blob of tar slipping and rolling through various levels and mini games) and Lugaru (Figure 17-15), which features a rabbit, skilled in the martial arts, on a quest to avenge the deaths of his family and friends against wolves and rabbit conspirators. Both of these are now available in the Ubuntu Software Center for free.

Figure 17-15: Lugaru, where you play an angry, karate-kicking rabbit

To get your hands on a Humble Bundle, you'll have to be quick—typically, the offers are only available for a short time—and you'll only be able to buy the games individually, at a fixed cost, after that. For details on upcoming bundles, take a look at *http://www.humblebundle.com/*. There's also a list of all the previous collections on Wikipedia (*http://en.wikipedia.org/wiki/Humble_Indie _Bundle*); while you can't buy those bundles directly anymore, it's still a useful list of good, Linux-friendly games that you might want to explore.

Another potential source of commercial games is the Ubuntu Software Center. It's only recently started accepting paid-for titles into its listings, but the number of commercial games that you can obtain through its familiar interface is growing all the time. To see what's on offer, fire up the Software Center and click the small downward-facing arrow immediately to the right of the All Software button. From the menu that pops up, select **For Purchase**; then browse through the list that appears in the main pane of the Software Center window. As I write this, most of the software in the list consists of games (though other types of commercial software are available here too), with the majority priced from $5 to $20. For example, the award-winning puzzle game World of Goo, which sets you the challenging task of building wobbly structures out of blobs of black gloop, comes in at a pretty reasonable $19.95 (a demo version is available as a DEB package if you'd like to try before you buy; check out *http://worldofgoo.com/dl2.php?lk=demo*). Another top-notch puzzler is Braid (a bit cheaper at $10), in which you must solve puzzles by modifying the flow of time itself. As you saw in Chapter 6, installing commercial software is very similar to installing anything else from the Software Center, except for an additional payment step. See "6A-4: Commercial vs. Free Software" on page 83 to get the full story.

In Chapter 19, I'll explain how you can also run Windows games in Ubuntu using Wine. Indeed, this is how many people enjoy big commercial titles that don't have Linux versions: Guild Wars, Spore, and Call of Duty are just a few examples of games that can be run flawlessly in this way. If this sounds like your sort of thing, "Project 19C: Running Windows Programs" on page 329 will be of particular interest to you; there you'll learn how to use a neat little app called PlayOnLinux, which can be used to handle most of the fiddly configuration stuff that is often required to get less well-supported games running under Wine.

Project 17B: Installing a Java-Based Game: Schnapsen

As you can see from most of the games discussed thus far in this chapter, the Ubuntu Software Center is a great one-stop shop for most Linux games. As you have also learned, however, there are also many games beyond those in the Ubuntu Software Center. These include the games you worked with in Chapter 8 that were written in scripting languages, such as the Python-based pyWings and the Tcl/Tk-based Briscola, but it just wouldn't be right to leave out games written in what might be considered the mother of all scripting languages—Java. In this project, you'll learn how to install the Java Runtime Environment and how to install and run the Java-based version of a classic Austrian card game, Schnapsen.

17B-1: Installing the Java Runtime Environment

To run Java-based applications, or *scripts*, you need to first install the Java Runtime Environment. If you opted to install third-party software during the installation of your system, you already have the Java Runtime Environment installed, so you can skip this part of the project and go on to 17B-2. If not, then you can download it now via the Ubuntu Software Center. Just search for and install *openjdk java 6 runtime*. The whole set of Java packages is pretty hefty in terms of download weight, so don't get freaked out if this download takes longer than usual. When the process is complete, close the Ubuntu Software Center and move on to the next step.

17B-2: Getting and Extracting Schnapsen

Once you've installed the Java Runtime Environment, you need to run a Java application in order to see it at work. The application you'll be installing is one I had been searching for ever since I moved to the world of Linux, a 20-card Austrian card game called Schnapsen, shown in Figure 17-16.

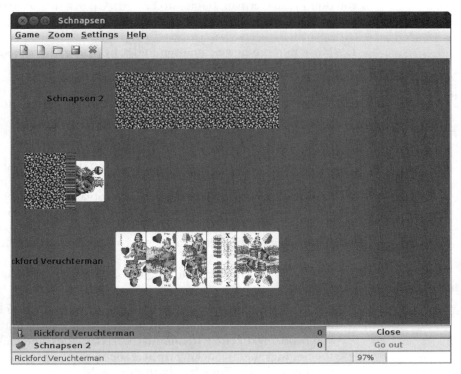

Figure 17-16: A Java version of the Austrian card game Schnapsen

To get started, you will need to download and extract Schnapsen. Here's what you need to do:

1. Open your web browser and go to *http://projects.hagru.at/tjger/en/*.
2. On that page, click the **Schnapsen** link in the left frame.
3. In the right frame, click **Schnapsen.zip**. Continue to follow the Schnapsen links until you get to the download page.
4. Once you've clicked your way to the download page, an Opening Schnapsen_1.00.zip window will appear. Accept the default, *Open with Archive Manager*, by clicking **OK**.
5. When the Archive Manager window appears, click the **Extract** button, which will open the Extract window.
6. In that window, click the **Create Folder** button and create a folder within your Home folder called *Schnapsen*.
7. Click the **Extract** button in that window and, when the extraction process is complete, click **Quit** in the progress window.

17B-3: Running and Anglicizing Schnapsen

Now that Schnapsen is in your Home folder, it's time to run it and, assuming you don't read German, put it into English. Open a new terminal window and do the following:

1. Move into the new Schnapsen folder by typing `cd Schnapsen` and pressing ENTER.
2. Type `java -jar Schnapsen.jar` (be sure to place a space between java and -jar and use a capital *S* at the beginning of Schnapsen) and press ENTER. Schnapsen will soon appear, after which you can start playing . . . if you read German.

In case you're wondering, here's what you did in that last line: The first part of the command string, java, calls the Java Runtime Environment into action; the -jar flag after that tells Java that you are going to be running a JAR file, which is what a Java script is called; and the last part is the actual file you are going to run, *Schnapsen.jar*. (In the future, if you choose to run other Java-based applications, just follow the same pattern: java -jar *application_name*.jar.)

1. To switch the interface into English, go to the **Einstellungen** menu and select **Sprache ▶ Englisch**.
2. If you are not familiar with the German card faces and suits (referred to as Traditional in this game), you can switch them over to the French suits you probably do know (diamonds, hearts, spades, and clubs) by going to the **Settings** menu, clicking **Appearance**, and then in the Appearance window selecting **French** in both the Cards' set and Trump sign menus (Figure 17-17).

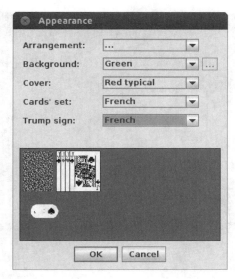

Figure 17-17: Switching from German to French suits and card faces in Schnapsen

You are now set to play. There are some basic rules in the Help menu, but you can also learn the rules of Schnapsen (and any other card game in the world) in greater depth at *http://www.pagat.com/*. Have fun!

Online Gaming

With all this talk of installing games, it's easy to forget that there are many games that you don't have to install at all. Numerous websites allow you to play games online for free, as long as you have the proper browser plug-ins installed. (See "Multimedia Plug-ins" on page 62 for help installing plug-ins.) For example, check out *http://www.popcap.com/*, *http://www.freeonlinegames .com/*, and *http://gametrick.net/* for some great online time wasters. You can also play any of the games found on Facebook or other social networking sites, such as Farmville and Mafia Wars, without ever leaving the comfort of your Ubuntu desktop.

Searching for More Games

There are lots of other great games for Ubuntu that I haven't covered, but rest assured that they're out there. Some are available as DEB files and can be installed in the same way you installed Google Earth in Chapter 6. A good example is SDL Hana (Figure 17-18), a Linux version of the Japanese flower card game Hanafuda, which is available from *http://sdlhana.nongnu.org/*.

NOTE *SDL Hana must be run from the Terminal. Just type* **sdlhana** *in a Terminal window and then press* ENTER.

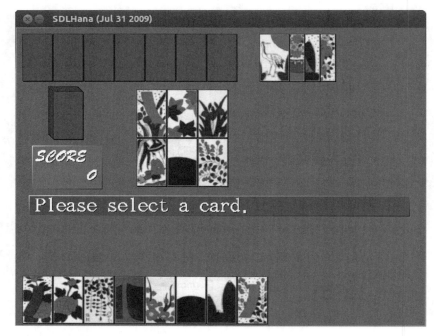

Figure 17-18: SDL Hana

Still more are available from the Ubuntu Software Center: Some of my old-time favorites include the Czech maze game, Fish Fillets (Figure 17-19), in which you guide two fish through all sorts of cumbersome, but very attractive, underwater locations, and the Serbian Pac Man clone Njam (Figure 17-20).

Figure 17-19: Fish Fillets, the underwater maze game

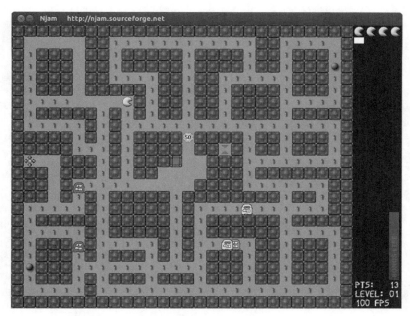

Figure 17-20: Njam, a Serbian Pac Man clone

Plenty more are available on the 3D side of things. In the beautifully designed Yo Frankie! (Figure 17-21), you play an evil, sheep-throwing squirrel called Frank who runs through idyllic landscapes being chased by unfriendly animals—kids (and aesthetes) will love it. You can also lose yourself in the Balazar role-playing game, with plenty of magic and monsters to keep you company, and fly a space fighter in 4D in Adanaxis (yes, they managed to squeeze an extra dimension in there, sort of).

Figure 17-21: Yo Frankie!

Of course, you can see what else is in store for you just by browsing the Ubuntu Software Center's Games category. There's a whole world of games out there, so enjoy the search.

18

SWEET HOME ANTARCTICA

Linux Around the House

So far you've been introduced to a good number of the applications that either come bundled with Ubuntu or are available from the Ubuntu Software Center, and many of those could be considered "around-the-house" sort of applications. There are, however, other applications and even some extensions that you can add to your system that will provide still more around-the-house functionality. These include things that might not fit clearly in any of the preceding chapters but do fit under the home banner. Here you'll learn about a number of these applications that can make your Ubuntu-powered machine a more thoroughly functioning part of your home life. All are available from the Ubuntu Software Center unless otherwise noted.

Where the Apps Are

The apps in this chapter fall under a number of different categories. Instructions on how to find each of them in the Dash will be provided in the relevant sections. As with all applications, you can also run any of these apps by simply typing its name in the Dash's search box and then pressing ENTER.

HomeBank

Money makes the world go round, as the saying goes, and nowhere is that awareness more keen than at home. If you are looking for personal financial management software to make household budgeting a bit easier to deal with, then you'll be happy to know that there are quite a few Linux offerings for you. The one that is probably easiest to use is called HomeBank (Figure 18-1), which is also available for Windows and Mac OS systems. HomeBank sports a number of features, including the ability to show multiple accounts and generate reports and graphical charts. It can import and export files created by the popular finance programs Quicken (*.qif*) and Intuit (*.qfx*), and it can also import spreadsheet-generated comma-separated values (*.csv*) files. Because it is a cross-platform application, it has a pretty good-sized user community out there, so you should be able to find help online easily if necessary. In fact, there are links to the HomeBank user manual, tutorials, FAQs, and community LaunchPad forum at *http://homebank.free.fr/*.

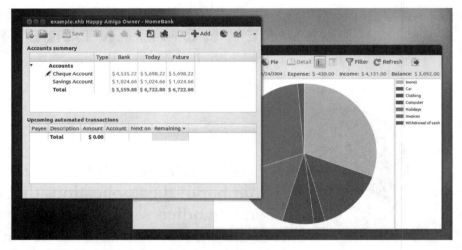

Figure 18-1: Home money management with HomeBank

You can run HomeBank by going to the Dash and typing **homebank** and pressing ENTER or by clicking the Application lens in the Dash and then clicking the **Office** filter button.

Project 18A: Installing a Recipe Lens

Since we are on the topic of home, and no room signifies *home* as much as the kitchen, we are going to make a little diversion into that sphere. As you learned in Chapter 3, it is possible to install additional lenses on the Dash to allow more specific searches, particularly on the Internet. In this chapter, you will learn how to install a recipe lens, which will allow you to easily search for recipes directly from the Dash. This requires adding a new repository to the ones that your system already uses when looking for updates and new software; you learned how to add repositories in Chapter 6. Here is what you need to do:

1. Start by opening the Terminal (from the Dash, type **terminal** and press ENTER).

2. In the Terminal, type **sudo apt-get-repository ppa:scopes-packagers/ppa** and press ENTER in order to add the new repository.

3. Type your password when prompted to do so and then press ENTER.

4. After a second or so, you will be asked to press ENTER to continue—do so.

5. Now update the repository database by typing **sudo apt-get update** in the Terminal and then pressing ENTER.

6. Fetch and install the lens by typing **sudo apt-get install unity-lens-cooking** and pressing ENTER.

7. Type **y** (for *yes*) when asked if you want to continue and then press ENTER.

8. Finally, log out and log back in again.

Once you have logged back in, open the Dash, where you will find your new lens in the middle of those that were there before (it looks like a cross between a bull's-eye and Pac-Man). Just click it and start searching away. The results will then appear, as in Figure 18-2.

Figure 18-2: Searching for recipes online via a Recipe lens for the Dash

Personal Health

Since we were just talking about recipes and you are what you eat, this is a perfect chance to segue to some of Ubuntu's offerings in the field of personal health. One of these is Pytrainer (Figure 18-3), which allows you to keep a record of all your various exercise activities, including by importing data from GPS devices. Another such application is Pondus (Figure 18-4), which allows you to keep a record of your current weight-loss progress in both numerical and graphical forms. Finally, there is QuitCount (Figure 18-5), which shows you a daily update of how much money you have saved and how many weeks you have added to your life since you quit smoking.

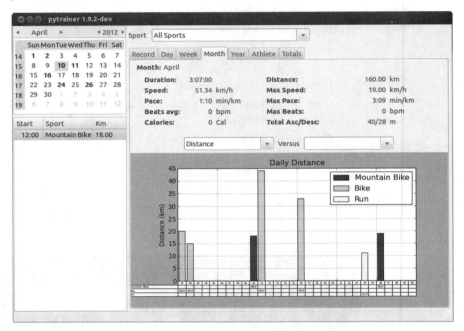

Figure 18-3: Keeping track of your exercise regime with Pytrainer

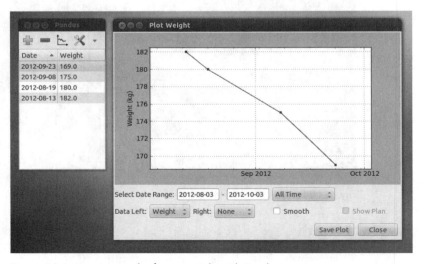

Figure 18-4: Keeping track of your weight with Pondus

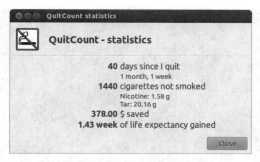

Figure 18-5: Tracking your savings and increased longevity after quitting smoking with QuitCount

These apps can be run from the Dash by typing **pytrainer**, **pondus**, or **quitcount**, respectively, and pressing ENTER. You can also click the Dash's Applications lens and then run Pondus and QuitCount by clicking the **Accessories** filter button, or Pytrainer by clicking the **Office** filter button and finding the app in the results.

Fun (but Educational) Stuff

Ubuntu has a lot of applications that are educational and appropriate for people of all ages. Different apps address a variety of interests and learning needs. In this section, we'll look at the Marble Virtual Globe (Figure 18-6), which allows you to look up cities and find their locations on the globe; the desktop planetarium, Stellarium (Figure 18-7), which allows you to see the skies at various times of day and night from different locations on Earth and in different modes (naked eye versus telescope, for example); and gbrainy (Figure 18-8), a brain-twisting quiz program with four types of games (logic puzzles, mental calculation, memory training, and verbal analogy) to help keep your brain in gear.

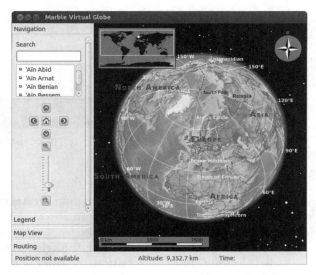

Figure 18-6: Finding places using Marble Virtual Globe

Figure 18-7: Viewing the heavens with Stellarium

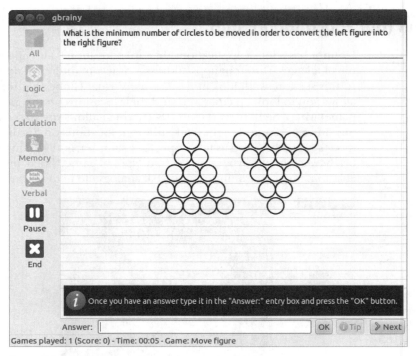

Figure 18-8: Keeping your brain sharp with gbrainy

These apps can be run from the Dash by typing `marble`, `stellarium`, or `gbrainy`, respectively, and pressing ENTER. You can also click the Dash's Applications lens and then run Marble Virtual Globe by clicking the **Education** filter button, Stellarium by clicking the **Science & Engineering** filter button, or gbrainy by clicking the **Games** filter button and finding the app in the results.

Kids' Stuff

To be sure, Ubuntu has a good number of games available for people of all ages, including children, and a good number of these are educational as well. These include the Tux applications, Tux Typing (Figure 18-9) and Tux Math (Figure 18-10), which allow children to learn typing and math skills in a fun, gamelike atmosphere.

Figure 18-9: Learning how to type with Tux Typing

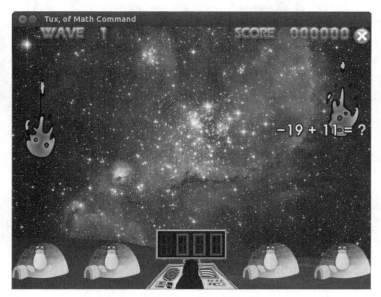

Figure 18-10: Practicing math skills with Tux Math

Both Tux Typing and Tux Math can be run from the Dash by typing **tux typing** or **tux math**, respectively, and then pressing ENTER. They can also both be found from the Dash by clicking the Applications lens and then clicking the **Education** filter button.

NOTE   *Both Tux Typing and Tux Math, by default, run in full-screen mode. You can instead run them in their own window from the Terminal by typing* **tuxtyping -w** *or* **tuxmath -w** *and pressing ENTER.*

Another nice Tux application is Tux Paint (Figure 18-11). Children find its big, colorful buttons and fun and funky tools easy to handle and a lot of fun. The best of Tux Paint's features (at least in my opinion) are its stamps of everything from apples to seahorses to euro coins! Oh, yes, and it talks to you. Click a duck stamp, and not only will you hear a voice say "duck," but you will also hear the "quack quack" of our waddling friends. You can find Tux Paint in the Dash by clicking the Applications lens and then clicking the **Education** filter button or by typing **tux paint** in the Dash and pressing ENTER.

Figure 18-11: Tuxpaint

Finally, there is Turtle Art (Figure 18-12), which is designed to allow children (or their parents) to learn the basics of programming while creating art, all by snapping together programming elements in graphical form. You can run Turtle Art from the Dash by clicking the Applications lens and then clicking the **Education** filter button or by typing **turtle art** in the Dash and pressing ENTER.

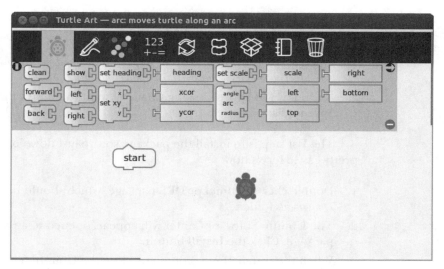

Figure 18-12: Learning programming basics with Turtle Art

Project 18B: Installing Parental Controls

One major concern of most parents is how long their children are spending on the computer. Most systems provide parents with a way to monitor this through parental control settings. There are a couple of parental control packages for Ubuntu. One, called Nanny, is in the Ubuntu Software Center but does not yet work with the new Ubuntu 12.04 release. Another, timekpr, can work after a bit of trickery at the command line but is not included in the Ubuntu Software Center. Nanny is useful in that it allows you to control web access, but since we want something that will work, we'll settle for timekpr for now and just hope that Nanny is fixed in the near future (keep checking).

Before you can use timekpr, you will need to have separate standard (not administrator) accounts for your kids; otherwise, timekpr will not work. So, if you have not yet created user accounts for the kids, do that first (see Chapter 9 if you need a review).

Once you've done that, you can move on to the first part of the project: creating a symbolic link that diverts timekpr from the support file it needs and is looking for (called GDM), which is no longer in Ubuntu, to another support file that is essentially the same thing, albeit with a another name (LDM), and *is* in Ubuntu. This is necessary because the version of timekpr you will be installing was prepared for the previous version of Ubuntu (Oneiric Ocelot). But don't worry, the fix works, and it's not difficult. Here are the steps:

1. Open the Terminal (from the Dash, type **terminal** and press ENTER).
2. Create the symbolic link by typing **sudo ln -s /etc/mdm /etc/gdm** and pressing ENTER. Type your password when prompted and then press ENTER.
3. You can now close the Terminal.

Since the timekpr package is not available in the Ubuntu Software Center, the next step is to download the package:

1. Open a web browser and go to *https://launchpad.net/~timekpr-maintainers/ +archive/ppa/+files/timekpr_0.3.2~ppa1~ubuntu2_all.deb*.

2. A window will appear, asking what you want to do with the file. Choose **Save to disk** and press ENTER.

The last step is to install the package you've just downloaded, which is pretty easy. Here's how:

1. Double-click the timekpr DEB package, which should be in your *Downloads* folder.

2. The Ubuntu Software Center will appear, opened to a page for your package. Click the **Install** button.

3. When the installation is complete, close the Ubuntu Software Center.

You can now run timekpr from the Dash by typing `timekpr` and pressing ENTER or by clicking the Applications lens and then clicking the **System** filter button. Before the timekpr window opens, you will be prompted for your password, so type that in and then press **OK**. timekpr (Figure 18-13) will then appear, and from there you can decide how long each of your children can be online and when they can be online.

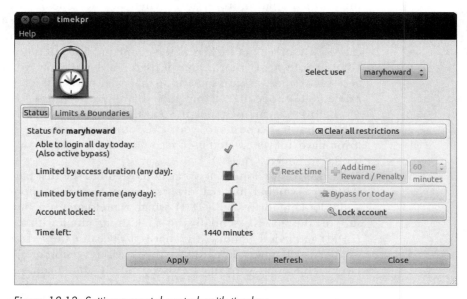

Figure 18-13: Setting parental controls with timekpr

Other Home-Related Applications

There are, of course, many other applications that are home related, so we'll finish up this chapter with three that are completely unrelated to one another but are both useful and a good representation of the diverse range of applications available for Ubuntu. First is the application called Gramps (Figure 18-14), which allows you to record information about your ancestors (even photos) and then view the information through a variety of report types and/or family trees. Gramps also allows you to import or export GEDOM files, which is the industry-standard file format for genealogical software, so you can easily share information with other genealogists. Documentation and additional information on Gramps are available at *http://gramps-project.org/*.

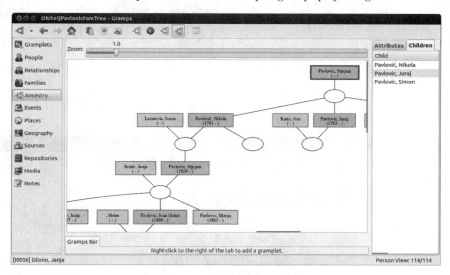

Figure 18-14: Keeping track of your ancestors with Gramps

You can run Gramps from the Dash by clicking the Application lens and then clicking the **Office** filter button. You can also just type `gramps` in the Dash and press ENTER.

Another useful application is Sweet Home 3D (Figure 18-15), which is a 2D interior-design program with a 3D preview. It allows you to play around with various room layouts by dragging and placing pieces of furniture and other items into customized rooms. Documentation and other information are available at *http://www.sweethome3d.com/index.jsp*.

To run Sweet Home 3D, go to the Dash, type `sweet home`, and press ENTER. Alternatively, click the Dash's Application lens and then the **Graphics** filter button.

Finally we come to Brewtarget (Figure 18-16), which is designed to allow you to create and manage beer recipes. What could be better! It is also compatible with the home-brewing software BeerSmith.

You can run Brewtarget from the Dash by typing `brewtarget` and pressing ENTER or by clicking the Application lens in the Dash and then clicking the **Education** or **Science & Engineering** filter buttons.

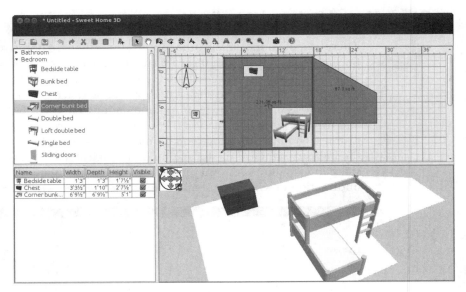

Figure 18-15: Designing your room with Sweet Home 3D

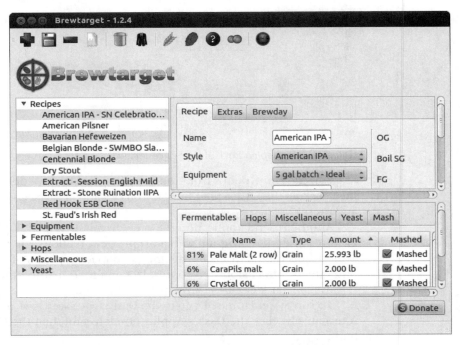

Figure 18-16: Managing and creating beer recipes with Brewtarget

19

PENGUINS AT THE GATES

Working with Ubuntu in a Windows World

Despite the rapidly growing popularity of Linux, it's still very much a Windows world. If you're anything like me, you'll often find yourself working with people who use Windows, so it's important to know how to make Ubuntu happily coexist with Microsoft's ubiquitous OS. Fortunately, Linux is just about the most accommodating operating system available and has no problems sharing files, reading Windows disks, and so forth. In fact, your Ubuntu programs probably support a wider range of file formats than their Windows equivalents; on more than one occasion I've tried to open a file in Windows, failed, and then booted into Ubuntu where I could open it effortlessly.

Of course, sharing files with others may not be your only Windows-related worry, especially if you're a dual-booter. Plenty of people decide to run both Windows and Linux on their computer, so it pays to know how you can minimize the bureaucracy involved in switching between the two. If you kept Windows for the sole purpose of running a specific application and you can't find a Linux-compatible equivalent to it, perhaps you can save the effort of dual-booting altogether and simply install the program directly onto Ubuntu. I told you Linux was accommodating . . . it'll even adopt Windows programs as its own!

Over the course of this chapter, you'll learn how to make the most of your double operating system setup: You'll install some Windows fonts, install some Windows programs, and share files on a Windows network. And if that isn't quite enough Windows for you, you'll even see how to run Windows (in a window!) in Ubuntu. You might want to sit in a dark room for this one—if you're not tired of "windows" already, you will be by the end of the chapter!

Project 19A: Accessing Files on Your Windows Partition (for Dual-Booters)

If you decided to dual-boot with Windows when you installed Ubuntu, then you'll have a partition lurking somewhere on your hard disk filled with your Windows files and programs (see Chapter 2 if you need a refresher on how partitions work). You can access files on Windows by *mounting* the partition from within Ubuntu. When you mount a partition, the files are made available to you through Nautilus (and other programs)—mounting is just Linux's way of recognizing a partition and preparing it for use.

19A-1: Mounting Your Windows Partition

Mounting your Windows partition in Linux used to be a bit of a chore, but that isn't the case anymore (at least not in Ubuntu). In fact, all you have to do is open a Nautilus window and click the Windows partition in the sidebar.

You might find more than one hard disk icon in the sidebar, so it is possible that you won't be sure which one your Windows partition actually is. Just remember that your Linux partition is represented by the hard disk icon named *File System*, which is listed under the Computer section in the Nautilus sidebar. Things aren't so simple for the Windows partition, unfortunately. It should be listed under Devices, rather than Computer, but it could be labeled *OS* (as shown in the sidebar in Figure 19-1) or with the size of the partition followed by the word *Media* (for example, if your Windows partition is 80GB in size, it might appear as *80GB Media* in the sidebar). Or, it might be something else entirely. Guess which one it is, if necessary—it won't hurt if you get it wrong.

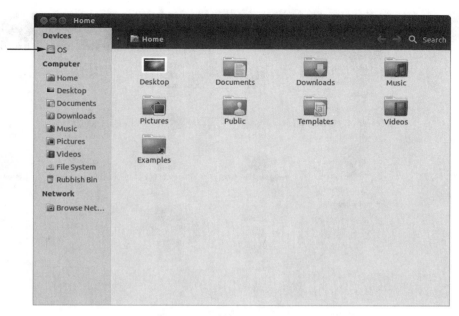

Figure 19-1: Mounting a Windows partition in Nautilus

Now that you know which disk icon is which, it's time to get it mounted! Just click the icon for the Windows partition in the Nautilus sidebar. An Authenticate window may appear; if it does, type your Ubuntu password and click the **Authenticate** button. A new window showing the contents of your Windows partition will then appear.

NOTE *If you hibernated rather than quit Windows, you will most likely receive a "Cannot mount volume. You are not privileged to mount this volume." error message when trying to mount your Windows partition. Some hibernated Windows partitions cannot be safely mounted for reading and writing in Linux, because adding new files while Windows is hibernated could seriously confuse it when it starts up again. To get full access to the drive, be sure to shut Windows down rather than hibernating.*

19A-2: Unmounting Your Windows Partition

You can unmount your Windows partition immediately after finishing your work with it, or you can just wait until you shut down your system, whereupon it will be automatically unmounted. Before you can unmount it yourself, you must first make sure that none of your programs are accessing files or folders on the partition. Nautilus and the Terminal are the usual suspects, so before unmounting, close any Nautilus or Terminal windows that are browsing that partition. Once you've done that, click the little eject icon next to the Windows partition in the sidebar of a Nautilus window (Figure 19-2) or right-click the eject icon and select **Unmount**.

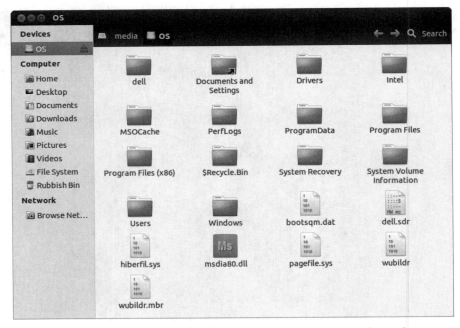

Figure 19-2: The Windows partition "OS" in the Nautilus side pane, complete with eject icon

Accessing a Linux Partition While Running Windows

Viewing your Windows files in Ubuntu isn't too stressful, as you have just found out. But what about going the other way and getting Windows to recognize your Linux partition? Unfortunately, Windows isn't too helpful in this respect—it can view only FAT or NTFS-format partitions and has no built-in support for the ext format normally used by Linux. As such, if you need access to your Linux files in Windows, it's probably easiest to create a separate FAT partition to be shared by both operating systems (see Appendix C). Hmm, not exactly convenient.

An alternative is to add support for Linux partitions into Windows by installing some extra software. Unfortunately, the state of such software is pretty dire: Support for the old-fashioned ext2 format is pretty good, but Ubuntu uses ext4 nowadays, which is a different beast entirely. As far as I can tell, the best that people have managed to do is to get an ext4 partition mounted in Windows in read-only mode. Although you won't be able to add new files to the partition, at least you'll be able to see what's in there and copy them into Windows. To try this for yourself, download Linux Reader from *http://www.diskinternals.com/linux-reader/*. It seems pretty usable and has the distinct advantage of being free!

Project 19B: Installing Microsoft Windows Core Fonts

Like it or not, the computing world is still pretty much a Microsoft world, and that means the vast majority of users, even Mac users, are using Microsoft fonts. Thus, you will inevitably have to deal with documents using fonts such as Georgia, Verdana, Times New Roman, and Courier, to name a few. Of course, your system can substitute the fonts it has for those used in the document. But for you to see things precisely as they were intended and to allow others to see your documents the way you intended, it will behoove you to install those Microsoft core fonts on your own system.

Fortunately, there are two ways to get these fonts. One is to download and install them via the Ubuntu Software Center, while the other, for those of you with a dual-boot setup, is to simply copy them from your Windows partition. In the former case, all you need to do is install the Microsoft Core Fonts package using the Ubuntu Software Center. To do this, search for *mscorefonts* in the Software Center and install the Installer for Microsoft TrueType core fonts package (it should be the only result). Note that this is the older set of fonts from Windows XP, so installing this package won't get you any of the swishy new fonts that are bundled with later Windows versions. Once the installation process is complete, your new Microsoft fonts will have been successfully installed and made ready for immediate use by every user account on your machine.

If you're a dual-booter, you can copy the fonts directly from your Windows installation. This has the advantage of getting all your Windows fonts into Ubuntu, even the newer ones (if you have Vista, Windows 7, or Windows 8 installed). Here's what you need to do:

1. Mount your Windows partition, as described in "Project 19A: Accessing Files on Your Windows Partition (for Dual-Booters)" on page 322.

2. Open the Windows partition in Nautilus and browse to the *Windows/ Fonts* folder.

3. Now for a little trick: Select **Edit ▸ Select Items Matching**, type ***.ttf** in the box that appears, and click **OK** (Figure 19-3). This will select all the files in the folder with names ending in *.ttf*, which are all TrueType font files.

Figure 19-3: Selecting all the TrueType fonts in the Windows/Fonts *folder*

4. Copy the files to a convenient location (somewhere in your Home folder should do it).

5. Now, go back to the *Windows/Fonts* folder and select **Edit ▸ Select Items Matching** again. This time, however, type ***.TTF** in the box (note the capital letters this time). This will select the rest of the font files—the item selection feature is case sensitive, and the filenames use different cases for some reason. Copy the selected files as you did previously.

6. With all the font files copied over into Ubuntu, you can now install them as you would any other font. At its simplest, this involves copying the files into the hidden *.fonts* folder in your Home folder, but you should see "Project 10: Installing TrueType Fonts" on page 190 for the full details.

Dual-Booting: Changing the Boot Order and Timeout

If you chose to install Ubuntu alongside Windows in a dual-boot setup, you'll be used to seeing the GRUB boot menu screen by now (Figure 19-4). This is the screen that appears every time you start up your computer and gives you the option of running either Windows or Ubuntu.

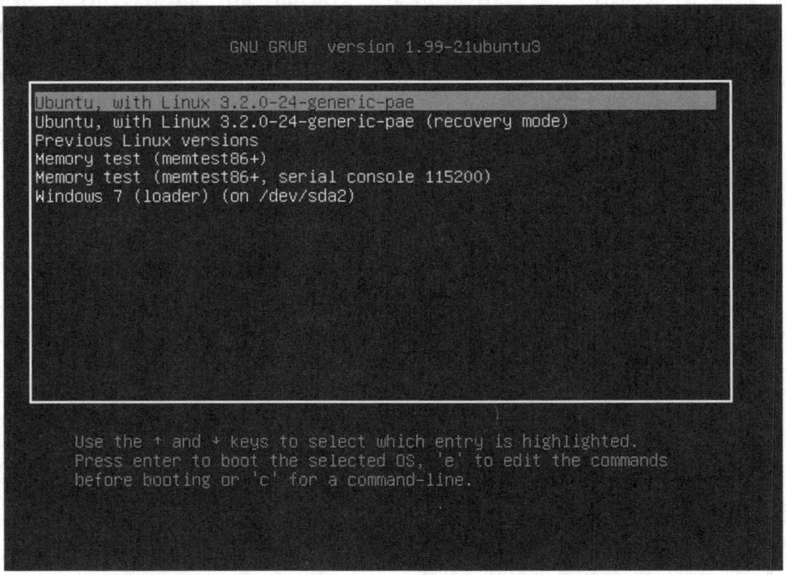

Figure 19-4: The GRUB boot menu screen

Ubuntu is started automatically if you don't select a different option after a few seconds. This is fine for people who want to use Ubuntu for almost everything but need to dip into Windows from time to time. If you spend more time in Windows, however, you might prefer to use that as the default operating system. To make the change, you'll first need to install a neat little app that goes by the name of Grub Customizer. Alas, it's not yet available from the regular Ubuntu software repositories, but you can get it from a PPA instead without much fuss. As you might recall from Chapter 6, PPAs are a way for third-party application developers to make their software available to the wider Ubuntu-using world. The ins and outs of finding and enabling PPAs were covered in "Project 6B: Installing Software from a PPA—Turtle Arena" on page 90, but here's a quick reminder of what to do to save you a bit of page flipping:

1. Open the Software Center, click **Edit ▸ Software Sources** and then click the **Other Software** tab in the Software Sources window that pops up.

2. Click **Add** and type `ppa:danielrichter2007/grub-customizer` into the box provided. This is the name of the PPA for Grub Customizer.

3. Click **Add Source** and, if prompted, enter your password. The PPA will be added to the Other Software list.

4. Close the Software Center and wait a little while; the PPA will be enabled in the background. (Annoyingly, it won't tell you when it's finished—see Chapter 6 for more on this).

Once the PPA has successfully been added to your system, open up the Software Center and search for Grub Customizer. Install it (as you would any other application) and then head over to the Dash and open it up. You'll probably be asked to enter your password, so do that and then wait a little while as it loads. Once that has finished, follow these instructions to set Windows as the default operating system:

1. In the Grub Customizer window, click **Preferences** and then go to the **General** tab in the settings window that pops up (Figure 19-5).

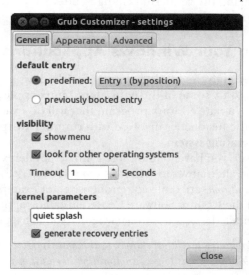

Figure 19-5: Changing boot options with Grub Customizer

2. Select Windows from the **predefined** drop-down list under the *default entry* heading. The actual name of the Windows option will differ depending on which version you have installed—mine says *Windows 7 (loader)*, for example.

3. Close the settings window and then click the **Save** button. The window will turn gray for a little while, during which time the boot menu settings will be updated.

4. When the window returns to normal, the process is complete. From the next time you restart onward, Windows will boot automatically instead of Ubuntu.

NOTE *If you apply a major update to Ubuntu at some point, you may find that Windows is no longer the default the next time you start the computer. This is because the update will have added a new entry to the boot list, causing the Windows item to slip down the list, where it won't be recognized as the default any more. To fix this problem, open Grub Customizer and reselect Windows as the default operating system.*

Grub Customizer lets you change the boot timeout too. By default, GRUB waits for 10 seconds before loading your default operating system, but I'm impatient and find this far too long to wait—so impatient, in fact, that I changed the Timeout option (also on the General tab of the settings window) to 1 so the menu is displayed only for a second. This might sound fast, but when I want to get into Windows, all I do is press the down arrow key a few times while my computer starts up. GRUB stops the timer when you press a key and just keeps the menu on the screen. Once that has happened, I'm free to choose the Windows option at my leisure.

Once you're happy with your revised boot timeout and/or default operating system, click **Save** to apply the settings. Grub Customizer will spend a few seconds making the requested changes, after which you can safely close the window. Restart the computer to see the updated boot menu in action.

Linux Equivalents to Your Windows Applications

Before going through the trouble of running Windows programs in Ubuntu, it's a good idea to try some of the equivalent Linux applications. More often than not, there's a native Linux program that will do exactly what you need without any of the headaches involved with running an application designed for another operating system.

First, however, you have to find those Linux equivalents. Luckily, plenty of websites list good alternatives to Windows software: *http://www.osalt.com/* and *http://www.linuxalt.com/* are quite comprehensive, for example. Or you can simply root around the Ubuntu Software Center, installing applications that tickle your fancy. After all, the best way to see whether you like a program is to try it!

NOTE *Some Windows programs don't have direct equivalents in Ubuntu, so you might need to install a couple of programs to get functionality like that of your Windows software. In the rare cases where there aren't any suitable alternatives, you can try using Wine or installing Windows on a virtual machine, which I'll talk about next.*

Project 19C: Running Windows Programs

In Chapter 6 you learned a host of ways to add applications to your system, but you may not have considered one other method—installing Windows applications. Despite there being Linux equivalents for most of the Windows programs that you need, you may miss one or two programs. Fortunately, it is possible to run some Windows applications from within Linux with the help of a program called Wine. Wine works by fooling applications into thinking they're running on Windows. It does this by providing all of the libraries and support files that programs expect to find on Windows, without any need for Windows to actually be installed. The list of compatible software includes the likes of Microsoft Office, Internet Explorer, Adobe Photoshop, and a whole host of games, so if you're desperately missing a particular program, then Wine is definitely worth a look.

It is only fair to point out that Wine continues to be a work in progress. It works well with some programs and not at all with others. Things are improving, however, and Wine now seems to work better with more applications. If you are curious about which apps are known to run under Wine and how well, check out the Wine home page at *http://www.winehq.org/* and click the **AppDB** link. The AppDB entries for programs often contain helpful advice on getting them to run in Wine, so check there first if you run into problems.

19C-1: Installing and Testing Wine

You can get Wine via the Ubuntu Software Center by doing a search for *wine* and installing the Microsoft Windows Compatibility Layer (it should be the first search result). Once the installation is complete, you can test it by opening the Dash and searching for Notepad. When the results are in, click the icon for the Notepad application (the one with a wine glass on it) and, after a few seconds (longer the very first time you use Wine), the Windows Notepad will appear (Figure 19-6).

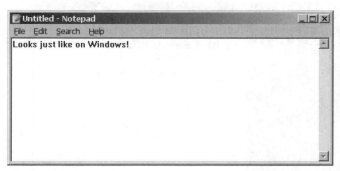

Figure 19-6: Windows Notepad running under Wine

19C-2: Installing a Windows Application in Wine

Now that you've seen one Windows application in action under Wine, you might as well learn how you can install more yourself. I will point you to one application that will definitely work—a pretty cool text editor called NoteTab Light (Figure 19-7).

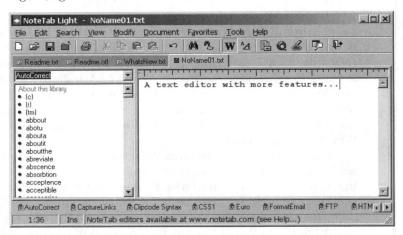

Figure 19-7: NoteTab Light running under Wine

To get NoteTab Light, go to *http://www.fookes.com/ftp/free/NoteTab_Setup.exe*, select **Save File**, and click **OK** in the window that appears to save the file in your *Downloads* folder.

When the download is complete, go to the *Downloads* folder, right-click the *NoteTab_Setup.exe* file, and select **Open With ▸ Wine Windows Program Loader** from the pop-up menu. A few moments later, the same sort of setup wizard that you would see if you were installing NoteTab in Windows will appear (Figure 19-8). Go through the wizard, accept the license agreement, and then accept all the defaults along the way until the installation is complete.

Figure 19-8: A Windows installation wizard running under Wine

Running NoteTab Light is easy because it provides you with a desktop launcher. Double-click that launcher (it looks like a notepad with a Swiss flag on the front), and NoteTab Light will soon appear, just as a regular Linux app would. (The other file that was put on the desktop, ending with *.lnk*, can be safely deleted to reduce clutter.) You can also run NoteTab Light and other Windows applications installed under Wine simply by searching for them in the Dash, just as you would any other application.

19C-3: Getting Windows Apps to Work in Wine with PlayOnLinux

Some Windows software stubbornly refuses to work in Wine unless you have things set up in a specific way. The Wine website is full of tips on how to tweak settings until you hit on the magic formula that seems to work for a given program (settings that are practically guaranteed not to work for other programs you installed with Wine). Some instructions even ask you to install different versions of Wine for different programs! Fortunately, there's a neat way to sidestep these issues called PlayOnLinux. It handles all the settings tweaks for you and supports many commonly used Windows programs (and an especially large number of games). You can install PlayOnLinux in the usual way from the Ubuntu Software Center.

Once it's installed, start PlayOnLinux by searching for it in the Dash. When it opens, a PlayOnLinux first-use window will appear. Click **Next**. It'll spend a minute or two updating its database of supported programs. Once it's done, click **Next** again, and it will leave you at the main PlayOnLinux window (Figure 19-9). In that new window, click **Install** and use the category pane or the search bar in the window that appears to look for a Windows program of your choice.

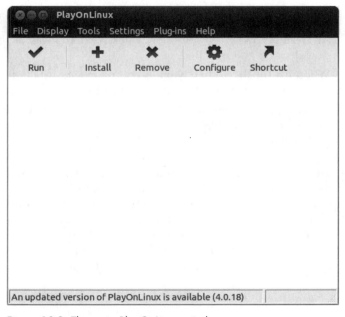

Figure 19-9: The main PlayOnLinux window

In this example, you'll install the delightful Crayon Physics game:

1. Select the **Games** category and find the Crayon Physics entry in the list (not the Deluxe version).

2. Select **Crayon Physics** (as in Figure 19-10) and click **Install** to start the installation process.

Figure 19-10: Selecting a Windows application to install in PlayOnLinux

3. An installation wizard will open. Click **Next** and wait as the game is downloaded and installed.

4. When it's finished, click **Next** to complete the installation. You will be returned to the main PlayOnLinux window.

5. To start playing, double-click the Crayon Physics entry in the list of programs in the main PlayOnLinux window or select the game from that list and click **Run**.

Assuming that the game was installed successfully, you'll be met with a Crayon Physics window. Click anywhere in that window, and you'll see a landscape scrawled onto your display in crayon, similar to the one in Figure 19-11. The aim of the game is to draw boxes on the screen with your mouse that land in such a way as to roll a ball onto a star. Every time you get the star, you move to the next level, where you'll be forced to come up with a more ingenious ball-rolling strategy. It sounds simple, but it's addictive!

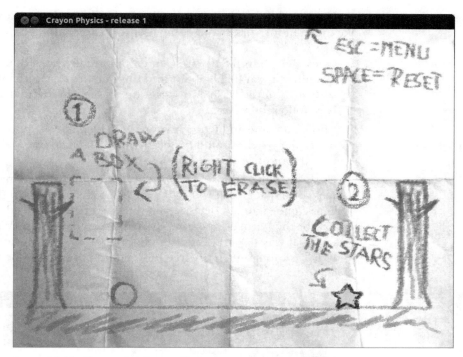

Figure 19-11: Playing the Crayon Physics game, courtesy of PlayOnLinux

Installing Windows Inside Ubuntu

One of the weirder things you can do with a computer is to run a simulation of a computer inside it. This simulation, known as *virtual machine (VM)* software, allows you to install one operating system inside another so you can run both at once without having to reboot. This is handy if you need to run Windows for some reason, perhaps for some specialized software, but are too comfortable working in Ubuntu to even contemplate going through the somewhat time-consuming rebooting procedure that dual-booters must follow to get back into Microsoft territory. You can even get Windows to sit there in, well, a window, which can be opened and closed at will just like any other program.

There are some caveats. First, the virtual machine has to share your computer's resources with all your other programs, so it can slow things down if you're doing anything computationally strenuous. Second, it doesn't have the same access to your computer's hardware as the "real" operating system, so you probably won't be able to get Windows-only devices working through the virtual machine very easily. Finally, and perhaps most awkwardly, you need a Windows installation CD to be able to put Windows into a VM, but most computers only come supplied with a recovery CD, which won't do the trick.

If you do have an installation CD, getting Windows into a VM doesn't take much more work than getting it onto a real computer:

1. Open the Ubuntu Software Center and install VirtualBox. Other virtual machines are available, but I find this one the easiest to use. Search for *VirtualBox* in the Dash and start it up. In the window that appears, click **New** followed by **Next**.

2. Choose a name and type for your VM. The name is up to you, but the operating system should be set to Microsoft Windows. Make sure you pick the right version of Windows too.

3. Click **Next** and choose the amount of memory (system memory, not hard disk space) that you'd like the VM to have access to (Figure 19-12). This can be a tough decision; on the one hand, you need enough memory for the "virtual" operating system to be able to run (Windows XP needs at least 128MB, for example), but on the other hand, you want to leave enough memory free for Ubuntu programs to be able to use it. VirtualBox normally suggests something sensible.

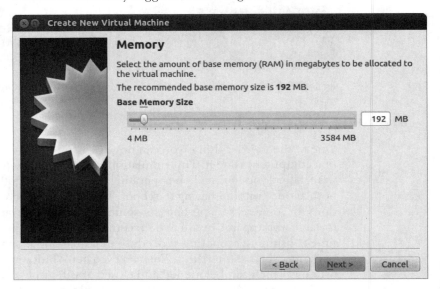

Figure 19-12: Choosing how much memory to allocate to the virtual machine

4. Click **Next** again and choose **Create new hard disk** (Figure 19-13). Make sure that **Boot Hard Disk** is checked too. Then click **Next** to open the Create New Virtual Disk window.

5. Run through the Virtual Disk Wizard, clicking **Finish** when you're done; the defaults should be fine for most of the options, but you might want to choose the size of the virtual disk yourself. This will be used as the hard disk of the virtual machine and is stored as a file in a hidden folder inside your Home folder. Again, choose a size that's big enough to run the virtual OS but small enough that it doesn't engulf your entire hard disk.

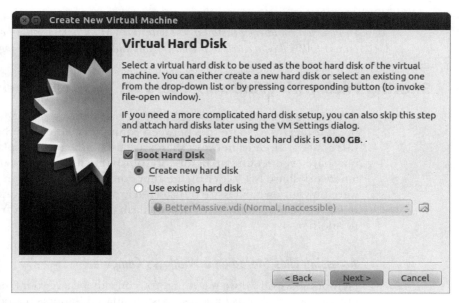

Figure 19-13: Creating a new virtual hard disk

NOTE   *If you choose* Dynamically expanding storage *as the storage type, the virtual disk will start off small and grow in size as you add more files in the virtual machine. This is a handy way to save on disk space.*

6. With the virtual disk setup finished, you'll be taken to a summary page where you can click **Finish** to create the virtual machine.

So far, so good. With a VM ready and rarin' to go, it's now time to install Windows. I'm going to leave the Windows specifics up to you (they're a little outside the scope of this book, don't you think?), but here's what you need to do to get things started:

1. Insert the Windows installation disc into your CD drive and close any windows that open and ask what to do with it.

2. Back in the main VirtualBox window, select your VM from the left pane and click **Start**. A black window will open, along with a First Run Wizard; click **Next**.

3. Make sure that CD/DVD-ROM Device is selected under Media Type and click **Next** again.

4. Click **Finish**, and the VM should try to boot from your Windows CD. After a few seconds, you should be face-to-face with the Windows Installer. Have fun with that!

5. Once the Windows installation has finished, the VM will restart. Remove the CD when prompted, and, after a few more minutes of setup, you should be staring a Windows desktop in the eye. Phew, hard work over!

NOTE *You can install Linux and other operating systems besides Windows in virtual machines. In fact, you could even install a VM within a VM, although you'd probably have to budget half a day to check your email if you had both of them running at once.*

Sharing Files with Windows Users on Your Network

One of the main reasons for connecting to a network (apart from accessing the Internet) is to share files between computers. You might be familiar with this concept already; network shares are used in many workplaces, and you may have even set one up before on your home network. For the uninitiated, a network share is a folder on another computer that you can access as if it were on your own. Files are transferred around on the network, so there's no need to use a portable hard disk or flash drive to get them from one place to another.

Accessing Files Stored on a Windows Computer

Network shares are a two-way thing: You can either share your files with others by creating a *shared folder* or access existing shared folders created by other people. If you're connected to a network of Windows computers, then you probably have some network shares already. I talked about browsing network shares in some depth in "Using Nautilus as a Network Browser" on page 106, but to save you the anguish of flipping back so many pages, here's a quick outline of what you need to do to access a share from Ubuntu:

1. Open Nautilus by clicking its orange folder icon in the Launcher. Click **Browse Network** in the Network section of the sidebar and then double-click **Windows Network** to see a list of all the Windows computers connected to the network. Double-click one of the computers to see its shared folders. If no computers are listed, try opening one of the folders with a network icon on the front (like the one in Figure 19-14) and look for computers in there instead.

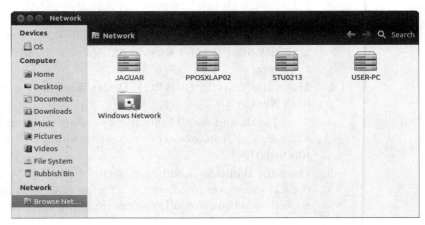

Figure 19-14: A folder containing links to Windows computers on the network

2. Pick a shared folder and double-click it to access the files inside. Depending on how the shared folder has been set up, you may be asked to enter a username and password for the computer that it's hosted on.

Making Your Files Accessible from a Windows Computer

Since your Windows computers have so gladly made their files available on the network, let's have Ubuntu reciprocate by sharing a folder of its own:

1. Open Nautilus and find the folder you want to share; then right-click it and select **Properties**.
2. Go to the **Share** tab and check **Share this folder**.
3. You'll be told that the sharing service is not installed—click **Install service**, then **Install** in the window that appears. Enter your password if prompted and wait for the installation process to finish. You may be asked to install other packages, so click **Install** when prompted for those too.
4. Once installation has finished, you'll be prompted to restart your session. Click **Cancel** for now; you'll need to log out, then log back in again later.
5. Back in the Folder Sharing window (Figure 19-15), choose a name for the shared folder and type a comment if you like.

Figure 19-15: Sharing a folder on the network

6. Check **Allow others to create and delete files in this folder** if you want other people on the network to be able to modify the files you have there. If you don't check this option, others will only be able to read and copy these files.

7. By default, only people with a user account on your computer can access your shared folders. To make it so anyone on the network can access your shared files, check the **Guest access** option.

8. Click **Create Share** to finish up.

9. To complete the process, you need to restart your session. So save all of your work and log out of your user account. Then, log back in again.

Go to your Windows computer and try to access the newly created share. Shared folders on Ubuntu computers can be accessed in the same way as any other share, so do whatever you would normally do to find it. (In Windows XP, for example, you'd find it in your *Network Shares* folder.) If you can open a file in the shared folder, you'll know that everything was set up correctly.

If you don't want to share a folder anymore, right-click it in Nautilus, click **Properties**, and uncheck **Share this folder** under the **Share** tab.

20

DEFENDING THE NEST

Security

Many a Windows user has entered the Linux fold after a host of bad experiences with *malware* in the Windows world—viruses, spyware, and all sorts of other malicious bits of software too numerous to imagine. Windows is also plagued by a seemingly endless array of security vulnerabilities, leaving the system easy prey to invaders with less than noble intentions. Every trip into cyberspace thus becomes something like a run through the infectious diseases ward of a hospital. For a Windows user, it can sometimes seem that more time is spent ridding the system of viral pests and defending it from invaders than actually getting things done.

Fortunately, Linux does not suffer greatly from such problems, leading to the much-touted claim that Linux is practically virus free and quite secure. Numerous lines of reasoning have been proffered to explain Linux's malware- and exploit-resistant nature. One reason is simply popularity—or lack thereof. Because Linux is not as widespread a system as Windows is, it is also a much less attractive target for digital evildoers, who very often seem to be motivated by the challenge and headline-catching glory that comes with creating a truly global virus or finding a theretofore unknown backdoor.

Another reason is that Linux users, as a general rule, work on their computers in a nonprivileged mode, one in which the user does not have the right to install software without a password. This is not the case in some older versions of Windows. A virus or other form of malware attached to an email or piggybacked upon another file or application cannot, therefore, install itself in your Linux system without that password . . . well, theoretically, at least. Of course, now that more recent versions of Windows use a privilege structure similar to this by default, this point is a bit less of an issue.

There is also the matter of structural design. Every system has security holes that can be exploited by digital and human foe alike. Windows might well be called the Swiss cheese of operating systems in this regard. Of course, Linux has its holes too, though apparently far fewer of them than Windows does, and Linux generally plugs them through downloadable updates faster once they are found.

Finally, Ubuntu's preconfigured security policy brings a defensive edge—a firewall is turned on by default. This means your Ubuntu Linux system is even less susceptible to unwanted intrusions.

Does My System Need Protection?

So, with all this talk about Linux's great security, you may wonder whether you need to bother worrying about vulnerabilities at all. Well, if you take a look at the Ubuntu forums, you might find yourself a bit confused. When asked whether Linux users need to install antivirus software or firewalls, most users answer with an emphatic *no*. On the other hand, you'll find that an awful lot of people have installed or are trying to install that software. Hmm.

So, what's a Linux user to do?

If you are on a network where you transfer a lot of files among a lot of Windows machines, you might want to think about installing some antivirus soft-ware, if to achieve nothing more than the good of the Windows systems involved and the users of those systems—your unenlightened (that is, Windows-using) email pals, for example. You might also want to give it a go if you are, by nature, on the cautious side of the spectrum. Basically, if it makes you feel safer to install some protection, go ahead. If it makes you feel safer to go whole-hog and install the full line of defense mechanisms I cover in this chapter, go ahead. After all, either way, it isn't going to cost you anything, and it certainly isn't going to hurt you. On the other hand, you'll probably be fine without installing any of the software described here too.

The First Line of Defense

Regardless of the system you happen to be using (though I am assuming that you have become a Linux devotee by now), the first line of defense for any computer permanently hooked up to the Internet is a *router*—an electronic device that allows a number of computers on a local network (such as in your home or at your office) to connect to and share a single connection from your Internet service provider (ISP). The router is connected to your Internet connection via cable, but the connection from the router to the computers on your local network can be wired, wireless, or both.

What does a router have to do with the defense of your computer? Well, most routers include a *firewall*, which essentially functions to keep all of the bad stuff on the Web away from your computer, much in the way that the firewall in your car keeps the heat, fumes, and noise from your engine out of the passenger compartment. This built-in firewall is one reason that even people with only one computer, who could just as easily connect directly to a cable or DSL modem, use a router. Of course, just how much security the firewall in your router provides depends on which filters you select in the firewall setup software. For example, a very common and useful filter (particularly for those with a wireless network) limits Internet access to those computers specified on the firewall's access list. This prevents your next-door neighbors from hitching a wireless ride via your ISP connection. They aren't paying the bill, after all.

The setup software for a router is built into the router, so you don't have to worry about software installation and system compatibility. Using your router with Linux is no different from using it with Windows. You can access the software and modify your settings via a simple web browser, as you can see in Figure 20-1. Just type the IP address of the router (usually provided in the owner's manual) in the browser's location bar, press ENTER, and you'll be ready to go.

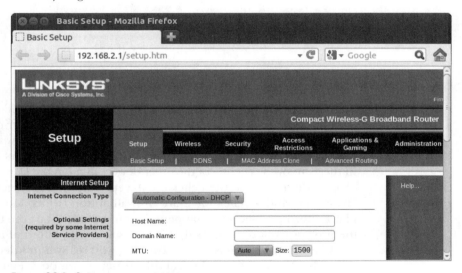

Figure 20-1: Setting up a router

Software Firewalls

If you don't have a router and don't plan on getting one, or if you have one but are bordering on paranoia, you might want to consider using a software firewall, in particular one of the most popular software firewalls available for Linux, Firestarter.

You can get Firestarter via the Ubuntu Software Center by searching for *firestarter* and installing it. Once it is installed, open Firestarter from the Dash (you might be asked for your password). Firestarter will open with a self-explanatory setup wizard the first time. Just read each screen carefully; make whatever selections are suggested, if any (the defaults should be fine), and click the **Forward** button in each of the wizard screens until you get to the last one (shown in Figure 20-2). On that screen, make sure that the box next to *Start firewall now* is checked and then click the **Save** button. The wizard window will close, and the main Firestarter window will appear. Assuming the correct network device was detected and selected and the correct wizard choice made, the firewall will be up and running.

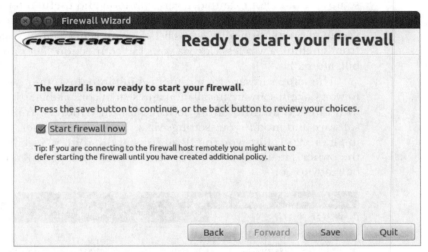

Figure 20-2: The last screen of the Firestarter setup wizard

If the wrong network device was selected, a warning window will appear telling you so. In that case, you can do a bit of trial-and-error manipulation by selecting **Edit ▸ Preferences** in the main Firestarter window and then clicking **Network Settings** in the Preferences window that appears (Figure 20-3). In that window, select one of the other devices listed in the Detected device(s) drop-down menu and then click the **Accept** button. Once back at the main Firestarter window, click the **Start Firewall** button (which looks like a blue Play button) and see what happens. If you still can't start the firewall, repeat the process I've just described, this time selecting a different network device.

Once your firewall is up and running, you really don't need to do anything else. You can simply look at the Firestarter window (Figure 20-4) to see what is going on network-wise on your computer—which active connections you have; how much information has been coming and going; and whether there have been any events in which, for example, the firewall has blocked an intruder. If you click the **Events** tab, you can then see the details of those events, such as what connection attempts were blocked, where they came from, and when they happened.

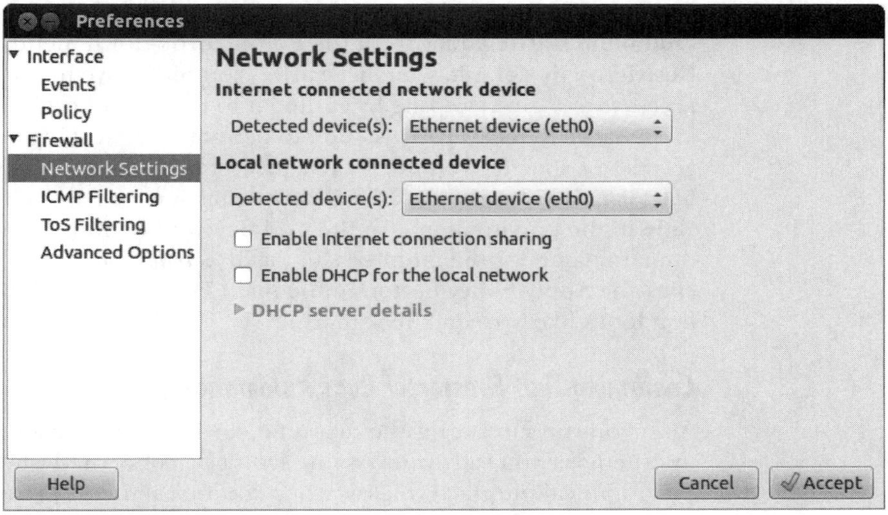

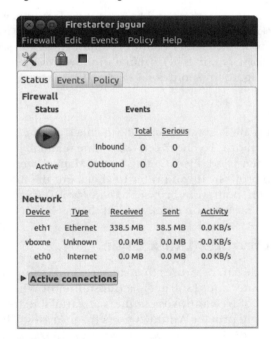

Figure 20-3: Selecting network devices in Firestarter

Figure 20-4: Firestarter in action

Taking Control of Firestarter

You can control how Firestarter deals with various network events by creating your own *policies*. The default policy set in Firestarter allows you to do whatever you normally do via the Internet, while it blocks new connections to your computer from the Internet or any other computer on your network.

To make things a bit more draconian, you can click the **Policy** tab, choose **Outbound traffic policy** from the Editing drop-down menu, and then select **Restrictive by default, whitelist traffic**. You then have to specifically allow access to any given website by adding it to the list of hosts. This sounds like a lot of hassle to me. If you just want to deny anyone working on your computer access to a specific website, for instance, simply select **Permissive by default, blacklist traffic**; right-click the **Deny connections to host** field; and select **Add Rule** in the pop-up menu. In the Add new outbound rule window, enter the domain name for the targeted site (as in *example.com*), click **Add**, and then click the **Apply Policy** button in the main Firestarter window (it's the one that looks like a green check mark).

Confirming That Firestarter Runs Automatically

After you run Firestarter the first time, it will set itself to automatically start up whenever you start your system. Don't be concerned when you don't see the graphical interface you saw when you first started it; Firestarter will be running in the background, silently protecting your computer.

If you are the doubting type, you can check to see whether Firestarter actually is running in the background by opening a Terminal window, typing `sudo /etc/init.d/firestarter status`, and then pressing ENTER (then entering your password, if prompted). If Firestarter is running, you will see the message `* Firestarter is running...` in the Terminal window. Worries over. If Firestarter isn't running, the response will read `* Firestarter is stopped`.

Finding Out More

If the world of firewalls is new to you, you can check out the Firestarter home page to learn a bit more. To check out the online manual, just to go to the Firestarter **Help** menu and select **Online Users' Manual**, which will open the page in your web browser. If you prefer to check out the manual before installing Firestarter, point your browser to *http://www.fs-security.com/docs.php*. You will also find a pretty good quick tutorial there.

ClamAV: Antivirus Software, Linux Style

Despite a relative dearth of viruses that can wreak havoc upon your Linux system, your computer could still act as a transmitter of Windows viruses. As a result, a number of free antivirus scanners are available for Linux users interested in helping protect Windows users from viruses. These include Panda Desktop Secure (*http://www.pandasecurity.com/usa/homeusers/downloads/desktopsecure/*), F-PROT (*http://www.f-prot.com/*), avast! (*http://www.avast.com/linux-home-edition/*), and numerous others. For most Linux users, however, the virus scanner of choice is the open source contender: *ClamAV*.

Although it can be used on a number of operating systems, ClamAV is considered to be *the* Linux antivirus software package. It is open source and totally free, and you don't have to worry about licenses or suffer the bother of renewing them. Unfortunately, on its own, ClamAV is a command-driven application, which makes it a bit less user-friendly. Fortunately for all involved, a graphical interface, albeit a simple one, is available; it goes by the name of ClamTk. Both ClamAV and ClamTk are available via the Ubuntu Software Center— just search for and install *ClamTK*. The Ubuntu Software Center will then automatically install ClamAV and all other packages it needs in order to run.

Once ClamAV is installed, you can perform a virus scan by opening ClamTk from the Dash. This will open the ClamTk Virus Scanner window (Figure 20-5).

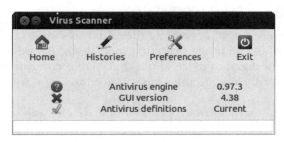

Figure 20-5: ClamTk, the graphical interface for ClamAV

Now that ClamAV is up and running, you can scan your system on demand from the Scan menu. To scan a single folder, select **A Directory**. To scan a directory and everything within it, choose **Recursive Scan**. In either case, the Select a Directory window will appear. Select the folder or disc you want to scan and click **OK**. ClamAV will start scanning your system. ClamTk will let you know what it is scanning at any given moment in the empty space just below the button bar. If it finds anything suspicious, it will list that item in the main pane of the window.

ClamAV is set up by default to check for *signature updates* when it starts. These signature updates tell ClamAV what new viruses to be on the lookout for. If you leave your machine on for days and days at a time, it is probably also a good idea to set things up so that ClamAV will automatically check for signature updates daily rather than just on startup. To do this, go to the **Advanced** menu and select **Scheduler**. In the Schedule window, select a time for ClamAV to do its update check in the bottom half of the window. Click the **Add** button when done (it looks like a plus sign). You can also use this window to set up a time to regularly scan the system—just select the time you'd like the scan to occur and click **Add**. When you're finished, click **Close**.

As I mentioned, the only viruses you are likely to encounter during a virus scan are those designed for Windows systems, which cannot affect your Linux system. Although scanning your entire system for viruses won't hurt anything, it's probably better to focus your virus-scanning activities on your Windows partition, if you have one, and on any files that you will be sending as email attachments, particularly to Windows users.

Project 20A: Encrypting Your Files

Protecting yourself against Internet nasties is all well and good, but what if someone gains physical access to your computer? Data theft is a serious business, so if you have any sensitive files, you should think about protecting them. A good way of doing this is to *encrypt* your sensitive files. Encryption is a way of taking a file and scrambling it in such a way that only a person with the right *decryption key* will be able to recover the original information. If someone tries to look at the file while it's still encrypted, all he will be able to see is a bunch of nonsense characters.

20A-1: Creating an Encrypted File Folder

Ubuntu has a nice way of encrypting files, but you should take care when using it! The whole point of encrypting your files is that no one but you will be able to access them, so there's little chance of recovering them if you forget your password. Here are the steps you need to follow to get encrypted:

1. Open the Ubuntu Software Center and search for and install *ecryptfs-utils*.
2. Once installation has completed, open the Dash and search for Terminal. When the Terminal window appears, type **ecryptfs-setup-private** and press ENTER.
3. You'll be prompted for the password that you use to log in to Ubuntu. Type it and press ENTER. (The letters won't show up on the screen, but that's normal.)
4. You'll be asked to enter a mount passphrase (password). Pick something *very* memorable—there's no recovering this password if you forget it! Press ENTER, retype the password (to make sure there were no typos), and press ENTER again.
5. Close the Terminal window, log out of your user account, and log back in again.
6. When you log in, an Update information window will appear (Figure 20-6). Click **Run this action now**, type your login password into the window that appears (it will look as if nothing is being typed again), and press ENTER.

NOTE   *The Update information window may not appear when you log in again. If this happens, restart your computer and then log in—it should pop up this time.*

7. Your mount password (also referred to as *encryption passphrase*) will be displayed on the screen. Make a careful note of it, press ENTER, and then click **Close** in the Update information window to continue.

If you open your Home folder, you'll now see a folder called *Private*. Anything you put in this folder will be encrypted and will be safe from prying eyes. This is especially useful if your computer gets stolen—only someone with your mount password will be able to look at the files, and ideally the only person who knows it is you!

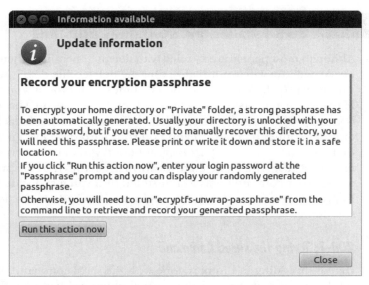

Figure 20-6: Checking your encryption passphrase

20A-2: Recovering Encrypted Files If Something Goes Wrong

If you have problems with your computer and need to recover the files in the encrypted *Private* directory, use the following steps after you get Ubuntu up and running again. If you don't feel confident following these instructions, you should definitely ask for advice on the Ubuntu forums first.

1. Open a Terminal, type `sudo mount -t ecryptfs /home/`*username*`/.Private /home/`*username*`/Private` (note the period in the first path) and press ENTER. You should, of course, replace *username* with your own username.

2. You'll be asked for your passphrase. Type your mount passphrase (password) and press ENTER.

3. Now you'll be prompted a few times to make a selection. Hit ENTER a few times until you're given a `WARNING` message.

4. Type `yes` and press ENTER; then type `no` and press ENTER.

5. If you entered the right mount password, the *Private* folder will be decrypted, and you'll be able to access your files. Copy them from that folder to somewhere safe!

If you have no luck recovering your files, take a look at *https://help .ubuntu.com/community/EncryptedPrivateDirectory/* to see whether there's anything further you can try.

Project 20B: Shredding Documents Digitally

Although most people are satisfied with deleting their files when they no longer need them, they may not realize that the deleted file data is still retrievable. This may pose little concern when it comes to photos of your summer trip to Maryland or reports you may have written for a class on Thai cooking, but it is a completely different situation if you've been storing bank account details or other confidential information on your hard disk. Even if you reformat that disk, the data stays. That is great news if you want to retrieve any files you may have accidentally deleted (or formatted away), but it isn't such good news if your computer gets lost or stolen or if you just decide to give it away. In preparation for such cases, it might not be a bad idea to do some digital shredding.

20B-1: Trying the shred Command

Digital shredding in Linux is done with the shred command. Its usage is very similar to the rm command you learned to use in Chapter 8, though in terms of removal, shred is much more thorough. To give it a try, create a dummy file by going to the File menu of a Nautilus window and selecting **Create New Document ▸ Empty Document**. Name the new document *myShredExp.txt* and

then double-click the file. This will open gedit. Type a couple of sentences in the document—anything will do—and save it. Close gedit. The first couple of words you typed should now appear on the icon of the new dummy file you created (as shown in the example on the left side of Figure 20-7).

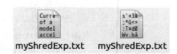

Figure 20-7: Files change their appearance after being shredded.

With your new file in hand and placed in your Home folder to make it easier to follow along, you are ready to try shred. Open a Terminal window, type **shred myShredExp.txt**, and press ENTER. If you look in your Home folder, you will notice the difference right away: Your original file is still there, but the text on the icon now looks like gibberish (as you can see in the example on the right side of Figure 20-7), which is what your file has become. If you double-click the file, gedit will open as it did before, but this time around, it won't be able to read your file and will tell you so (Figure 20-8).

So, now you've got yourself a shredded file sitting in your folder, but it sure would be handy to get rid of the file rather than just have it sit there littering things up, wouldn't it? Of course, you can remove the file via the Terminal by using the rm command, but it would be easier if future shredded files were deleted immediately after being shredded. Fortunately, this is easy enough to do by using the shred command with the -u flag. You can try it on the file you've already shredded by opening a Terminal window, typing **shred -u myShredExp.txt**, and pressing ENTER. Your file will then be further shredded and deleted.

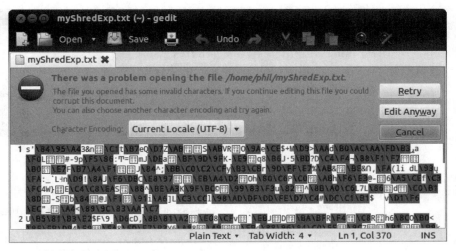

Figure 20-8: gedit can't open your shredded files.

20B-2: A Graphical Equivalent to the shred Command

Although using the shred command isn't all that difficult, most average users would prefer to do things graphically. After all, you don't *have* to type commands to delete or move a file, right? That's where BleachBit comes in. BleachBit (Figure 20-9) is an application that helps guard your privacy in a number of ways—not least by shredding all manner of things for you. Here are the steps you need to follow to shred a file:

1. Install BleachBit from the Ubuntu Software Center. When installation has finished, open it up via the Dash.

2. When the BleachBit window opens, you'll be greeted by a preferences window. The defaults are good enough for our purposes, so just click **Close**.

3. Assuming you don't want to do anything fancier, let's shred a single file. Click **File ▸ Shred Files** and choose the file you want to shred (hold down CTRL to select multiple files). Take care not to select the wrong file, since you won't be able to recover it post-shredding! Click **Delete**. You'll be asked to confirm the deletion. This is the point of no return so, if you're happy to proceed, click **Delete** to finish the job.

4. The file will vanish, shredded into oblivion and safe from recovery.

As I mentioned, there's a lot more that you can do to guard your privacy with BleachBit, aside from shredding the odd file. The list on the left of the main BleachBit window contains all sorts of weird and wonderful ways of securely deleting some of the personal information that's probably lurking on your computer. Take Firefox, for example: Click the Firefox list item in the BleachBit list, and an information page will appear in the main pane, telling you how BleachBit can securely remove various information kept by Firefox.

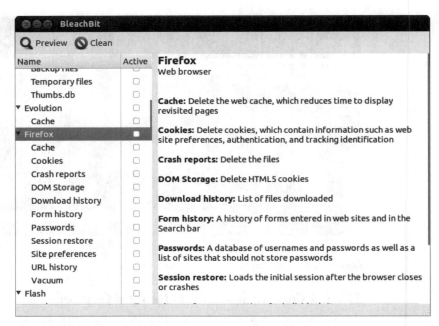

Figure 20-9: Using BleachBit to guard your privacy

For example, you could check the Cookies list item. With that selected, all you'd have to do is press the Clean button at the top of the window to delete all of the web cookies that Firefox has accumulated. Easy, huh?

NOTE *Cookies are fragments of text that your web browser uses to store information about websites. Websites use cookies as a way of recording that you have visited them. For example, if you log in to a website, it will store a cookie with your username in it so that it will remember who you are next time you visit.*

21

A COLONY OF PENGUINS

The Ubuntu Community

One thing that really sets open source software apart from the commercial software world is the importance placed on *community*. This can include pretty much anyone who has anything to do with the software: The people who use it, the people who design it, the people who help others with problems . . . every last one of them is a valued community member.

Consider the commercial software world, where things tend to be quite top-down. When you have a problem, you go to some company that provides you with support. This company probably also designed and sold you the software, and you probably played no part in that process—you're the customer; it's the vendor. Open source is different: Rather than one business managing everything, everyone pitches in together and helps each other. People write software and fix faults because doing so helps other people and because they want to help. Everyone can play a part in offering feedback and suggestions and helping others with problems, and no one is in absolute control of the whole process. All in all, it's much more democratic and, in my opinion, much more fun!

The Ubuntu community in particular is large, vibrant, and notoriously friendly. In this chapter, you'll learn how to get the most out of it and how you can play your part by joining in and giving something back (if you like).

Take Me to Your SABDFL

Open source communities tend to have a well-defined structure, and Ubuntu is no exception. At the top of the pile is Ubuntu's founder, Mark Shuttleworth, whom you met in Chapter 1. He's the Self-Appointed Benevolent Dictator For Life (SABDFL), and according to *http://www.ubuntu.com/project/about-ubuntu/ governance/*, his role is to "provide clear leadership on difficult issues and set the pace for the project." This doesn't mean that he makes all of the plans and decisions—that's more the job of the Technical Board, a group of senior Ubuntu contributors who figure out what shape the next Ubuntu release will take. Mark is just there to step in if no one can agree.

There's also the Community Council, which oversees the teams of contributors who make up the bulk of the project. There are lots of teams with all sorts of responsibilities: The Documentation Team writes the documentation for each release of Ubuntu, the Installer Team looks after the software used for installing Ubuntu, and so on. You can find a list of them at *https:// wiki.ubuntu.com/Teams/*. Teams consist of members from all over the world (Figure 21-1), and people on the team may have all sorts of responsibilities. Developers, for example, are the people who write and update the software. Last, but certainly not least, are the millions of Ubuntu users worldwide who form the biggest part of the community. This group includes you!

Figure 21-1: A world map showing the locations of the members of the Ubuntu Documentation Team

Everyone who participates is expected to abide by the Code of Conduct (*http://www.ubuntu.com/project/about-ubuntu/conduct/*), and people who make changes to the project (like developers) are asked to sign a copy of this document to show their commitment to the principles of Ubuntu. One final note: Ubuntu is a *meritocracy,* in which the people who've contributed most to the project get the biggest say. The most prolific contributors are awarded with *Ubuntu membership* (if they apply for it) and benefit from such perks as an *ubuntu.com* email address.

Launchpad: Your Passport to the Ubuntu Community

Every open source software project needs a place to call home. In Ubuntu's case, this is Launchpad, a sort of project information website on steroids. Whether you want to report a problem, ask for help, design a cool new feature, or write your own program, Launchpad is where you go.

Fire up Firefox and browse to *http://www.launchpad.net/*. Unless you've signed up before, you'll want to register for an account, so click **Log in / Register** at the top of the page, click **Create a new account**, and answer the questions on the form that appears. Hit **Continue** and go check your email for details on how to finish signing up. When the message arrives, click the first link, fill in your details, and click **Continue** on the page you get sent to so you can start using your account.

Once that's all done and dusted, go back to *http://www.launchpad.net/* and click your name in the top right of the page to see your profile. It's probably looking pretty empty at the moment, apart from a bunch of three-letter acronyms and a mysterious invitation to change your "branding." Click one of the round, yellow pencil icons to start changing your details. You can put as much or as little information on your account as you want—for example, if you'd like people to be able to find you on IRC (see "Chatting on IRC" on page 364), make sure you enter your nickname on the page (Figure 21-2). Otherwise, you can leave most things blank.

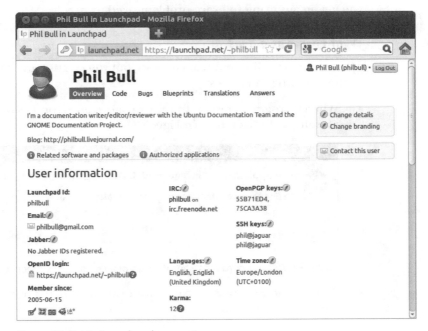

Figure 21-2: My Launchpad account page

If you've just created your account, you might notice a sad little zero hanging around in the "Karma" section. Fortunately, it's not karma of the metaphysical sort, and your eternal soul isn't in any danger. Rather, it's a points system for recognizing people who have helped make Ubuntu better. The more you contribute, the more karma points you get, and hence the greater your bragging rights over your Ubuntu-obsessed friends (that's all of them, right?). Check out *https://help.launchpad.net/YourAccount/Karma/* for details on how it all works.

Bugs, Bugs, Glorious Bugs

The computers of yesteryear were enormous, complicated beasts, filling entire rooms with delicate electronics and whirring tape drives. Renowned computer scientist Grace Hopper, on retrieving a moth from a relay in one such giant, taped the offending insect into her logbook and remarked that she had found a "bug" in the computer. Well, computers may have changed a lot since the 1940s, but some of the terminology hasn't. Whether it's as major as a program crashing or freezing or as minor as a missing icon, any problem that you find with a piece of software is still referred to as a *bug*.

You've almost certainly come across a bug before—no software, whether commercial or open source, is ever perfect. The difference with open source is that you're strongly encouraged to report problems wherever you see them. Developers need feedback in the form of bug reports so they know what needs fixing, and problems get fixed more quickly if they're reported sooner. Filing a bug report is a relatively easy way of giving something back to the community; it doesn't take long, it helps to improve the software for everyone, and you get an annoying software problem fixed for free!

What Counts as a Bug?

There are lots of different types of bugs, but you can usually fit them into one of the following categories:

- When a program crashes, freezes, or shows an error message for no good reason (as, for example, in Figure 21-3)

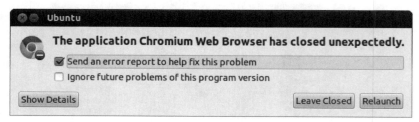

Figure 21-3: If a program crashes (like Chromium here), it's probably got a bug.

- When something doesn't work (for example, when a button does nothing when you click it)

- When hardware (such as a printer or your sound card) misbehaves or doesn't work at all

- Typos, missing icons, and other cosmetic mistakes

If your problem fits any of these descriptions, then you likely have a bug on your hands! You should be aware of a few notable exceptions, though. First, if a program is missing a feature, that's not really a bug. You can still report it as a bug, but it probably won't get much attention; try discussing it on the Ubuntu Forums first. Second, you shouldn't ask for help with software by reporting a bug, since you probably won't get a response. Use the forums, Ask Ubuntu website, or IRC instead; find out more on those in "The Ubuntu Forums" on page 361 and "Ask Ubuntu" on page 363. Finally, it's important that the bug be *reproducible*. This means that you can provide a set of instructions for someone else to follow, and they will experience the same problem as you. Sometimes computers just do one-off weird things, and if the problem's not repeatable, there's little chance that it can be identified and fixed.

Reporting a Bug

If you're confident you've found a bug, it's time to tell someone about it! If it happened in a specific program, select **Help ▶ Report a Problem** in that program's menu, if that option exists, and skip to the next paragraph. If that option isn't there, you'll have to get your hands a little dirty. First you need to find the command name for the offending program. This isn't always the same as the name that appears in the title of the window, so you may have to apply a little guesswork:

1. Press ALT-F2 to bring up the Run a command view in the Dash. Using all lowercase letters, begin typing the name of the application. After you've typed a few letters, the icon for the application will hopefully appear; the command name is simply the text under the icon (for example, tomboy is the command name for Tomboy, as shown in Figure 21-4).

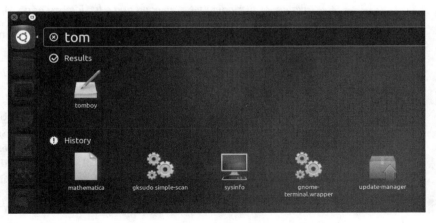

Figure 21-4: Finding the command name for Tomboy using the Dash

2. If you don't find the icon for the program you're looking for, try installing the Main Menu application from the Software Center. Once it's installed, start Main Menu and find the application you're looking for by navigating through the menus. Then right-click the name of your program and choose **Properties** from the menu that pops up. When the Launcher Properties window appears, take a look at the contents of the Command box—for Tomboy it should say tomboy --search (Figure 21-5). You can ignore everything after the first space (only the first part matters), so in this case, the program's command name is tomboy.

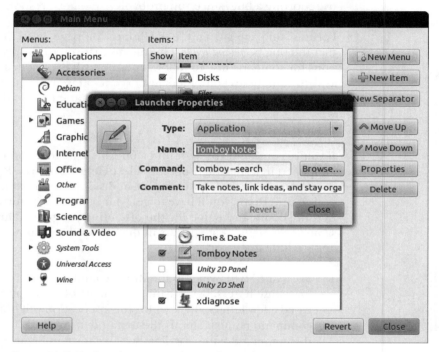

Figure 21-5: Finding the command name for Tomboy using Main Menu

3. With the command name in hand, press ALT-F2 to open the *Run a command* view of the Dash again.

4. Type **ubuntu-bug** *tomboy* (replacing *tomboy* with the command name for your program) and press ENTER.

The bug-reporting tool will start and collect some information about the program (such as what version you're using). Next, it'll ask whether you want to send this report to the developers—you do, so click **Send Report**, and a web page will open (log in to Launchpad if you haven't done so already). Type a brief description of your problem, being as specific as possible, and click **Next**.

Has It Already Been Reported?

Lots of people are using the same programs as you, so there's a good chance that someone has gone to the trouble of reporting your bug already. Launchpad will go off to look for existing bugs that it thinks match the description you gave, so take a look at the list that appears and see whether any of the results sound familiar (Figure 21-6). If you find one that does, click the arrow next to it, read the description to make sure, and click **Yes, this is the bug I'm trying to report**. This could be a good sign, because someone just might be working on a fix already!

Figure 21-6: A list of bugs that Launchpad thinks are similar to the one you're reporting

Choose **Just mark the bug as affecting me** and click the green check button to go straight to the bug page (the alternative option, Subscribe me as well, means that you will receive an email every time someone posts a comment about the bug). Take a look at the comments that others have made about the bug and see whether anything could help you work around the problem. Comments are sometimes technical in nature, so it might be necessary to ask around on the forums for help with some of the more cryptic instructions. If you can't see anything helpful, you can try to provide some more details on the problem to help a developer track it down. The developer will often ask for you to provide a copy of the output of some command, which can help determine what's going wrong. If you think you can help, scroll down to the bottom of the bug page and put what you know in the comment box.

A New Bug

If no one else seems to have the same problem, then you've got a live one! Click **No, I need to report a new bug** at the bottom of the page where the list of suggested bugs appeared and write a description of the bug in the Further information box. Here are some tips on how to write a breathtakingly beautiful bug report:

Report only one problem per bug.   If you report more than one problem at a time, it will be difficult for the developers to keep track of what they've fixed and what they haven't.

Describe what you were doing at the time the bug occurred.   Context is important, so you should describe what you were doing when you experienced the problem. For example, if your music player crashed when you plugged in your iPod, then you should mention that.

Mention which version of the program you're using.   The bug-reporting tool should have automatically provided information about software versions, but it's a good idea to make a note of them yourself too. Selecting **Help ▸ About** in the program's menu will usually give you the version number of the program, and you can find out which Ubuntu version you're running by clicking the power button on the top panel and selecting **System Settings** from the pop-up menu. Double-click **Details** in the window that appears, and the Ubuntu version will be listed in the Overview section.

Describe how to reproduce the bug.   Developers need to see how the bug happens in order to fix it. Provide a step-by-step list of instructions that describe how someone could make the same problem happen on their computer. If you don't know how to make the bug happen again, just describe in as much detail what you clicked or changed when the bug happened.

Once you've packed the report with information, click **Submit Bug Report** to finish the process.

What Happens Now?

You'll receive an email from Launchpad confirming that your bug was reported successfully, but this isn't the end of the story. Let's take a look at a typical bug to see how things pan out: Open Firefox and head over to *https://bugs.launchpad.net/ubuntu/+bug/121853/* to see a bug I reported for the Rhythmbox music player back in 2007. The first thing to note is the information at the top of the page (Figure 21-7): The *Affects* column lists which packages are affected by the bug, *Status* tells you how far the bug has made it on the road to being fixed, *Importance* tells you how serious the bug is, and *Assigned to* is the name of the developer or team responsible for fixing the bug. These details are changed by developers as progress is made on identifying and fixing the problem.

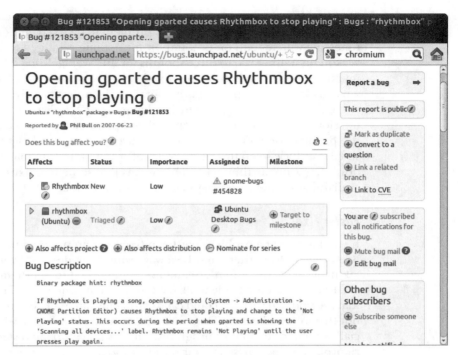

Figure 21-7: The Launchpad bug report page for my Rhythmbox bug

NOTE   *It's bad practice to change the status or importance of your own bug, since people often overestimate the importance of their problem. Leave it up to an Ubuntu developer or another community member.*

Farther down, you'll see my original bug report followed by a question from superstar Ubuntu developer Sebastien Bacher. There's a bit more to-and-fro until the bug gets sent *upstream*—that is, to a different open source project that handles the bugs for Rhythmbox. From there, I just had to wait for the Rhythmbox developers to fix the problem.

If you've reported a bug, keep an eye on your email. You'll be notified every time the bug is changed or a comment is made. If someone asks for more information on the problem (as Sebastien did with mine), all you need to do is reply to the email. Your reply will be automatically added to the bug report for everyone to see. The more information the developers have, the faster they will be able to fix the problem.

When Will My Bug Be Fixed?

Hundreds of new bugs are reported for Ubuntu every day, which isn't surprising when you think about the 40,000-odd packages available to install. The sheer volume of bugs isn't easy to cope with, and dealing with them has been likened to "drinking from a fire hose." To calm the chaos, an army of volunteers called the Bug Squad pore over all the new bugs, categorizing them, identifying ones that have already been reported, asking for details on how the bugs happen, and generally trying to get enough information together for a developer to be able to swoop in and fix the issue. In practical terms, this means it can take quite a while for a problem to be fixed, although the actual timescale will depend on how important the bug is judged to be. I normally reckon on waiting two to three months for an "average" bug. Having said that, my Rhythmbox bug hasn't been fixed yet—five years later! (To be fair, it was a particularly minor problem that few people are ever likely to experience.)

Once a bug is fixed, its status is changed to Fix Released, and the Ubuntu developers will often provide an updated package that you can install to fix the problem on your computer. Fixes aren't made available straight away, since they have to go through a series of stringent tests to make sure that they don't screw up anything else. This means that some bug fixes might not be available until the next version of Ubuntu is released.

Faster Fixes

If you know that a problem has been fixed but an updated package hasn't been released yet, there may be a way around the delay—if you don't mind taking a small risk. When updates are being tested to get them ready for official release, they are made available online for anyone to try. There's a chance that the updated versions could cause problems (after all, they're being tested!), but they're usually fine. There are also *backported* packages, which are unofficially updated versions of programs. These will have been tested, just not very rigorously, so use these at your own risk too.

To gain access to these less stable packages, open the Ubuntu Software Center, click **Edit ▸ Software Sources**, and bring up the **Updates** tab. Make sure that **Proposed updates** and **Unsupported updates** are checked (as in Figure 21-8) and click **Close**. Now, go to the Dash, open up the Update Manager, and click **Check** to see which packages can be updated.

Figure 21-8: Using the Software Sources tool to enable proposed and unsupported updates

WARNING *You really do need to be careful when using untested updates. One package that commonly causes problems is the Linux kernel itself—scroll down the list of packages in Update Manager and look for the "Proposed updates" section, if there is one. If you find a package that has a name like* linux *or* linux-generic *in there, consider unchecking the box next to it to prevent it from being updated for the time being.*

THE HACKER CULTURE—A BRIEF ASIDE

If Linus Torvalds hadn't shared his hobby project with the world, we wouldn't be here talking about Ubuntu, or any form of Linux (see Chapter 1 if you want a refresher on the history). The open source movement is founded on the hard work and ingenuity of people like Linus, who are affectionately known by the community as hackers. By this, I vehemently don't mean the people who break into computers, write horrible computer viruses, or otherwise spoil the party for everyone. Another meaning of the term hacker goes much further back in computing history: Put simply, it means someone who writes computer programs as a pastime. The guys who founded Microsoft and Apple were hackers—enthusiasts playing around with early desktop computers in their respective garages.

The hacker culture extends beyond computers to all sorts of activities. It's about experimenting, coming up with cool ideas, and then sharing them with similar-minded people, and it's this philosophy that has made the open source movement possible.

The Ubuntu Forums

An online *forum* is a place where you can post messages about some topic that other forum users can read and respond to publicly. There are thousands of forums on the Web, bringing together people from all over the world to talk about all sorts of stuff. The Ubuntu forums are a great place to ask questions, get help, and converse with other people using Ubuntu. There are around 50,000 active users, and more than a million posts have been made to date. If you do have a question, there's a good chance that it's already been answered somewhere or that someone will be able to answer it for you.

Dust off your explorer's hat, and let's go take a look around the forums. Head over to *http://www.ubuntuforums.org/*, and the first thing you'll notice is the many different categories on the front page. Choosing the right category is pretty straightforward—people seeking help with computer problems will post their questions in one of the Main Support categories, for example. For now, let's check out the part of the forum set aside for new Ubuntu users. Click the **Absolute Beginner Talk** link and scroll down to the bit that says *Sticky Threads* (Figure 21-9).

A *thread* is a collection of messages about the same topic. You can post replies to existing threads or start new threads yourself. A *sticky* thread is one that the forum moderators (the head honchos who make sure everything runs smoothly) deem important enough that it should stick around permanently, for everyone to read. Normal threads don't stick around and slowly make their way down the list as new threads are started and added to the top. To read a thread, just click its name.

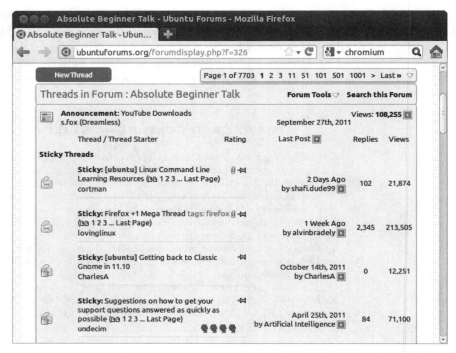

Figure 21-9: Viewing the sticky threads in the Absolute Beginner Talk forum

There are so many threads on the forums that sifting through them manually would take a lifetime. Luckily, there's a pretty good search feature. Just click the **Search** link at the top of the page, type some search terms in the box that appears, and click **Go** to see what turns up.

Replying to a Post

You can read any of the threads on the forums without a user account, but you do need to be logged in to reply to one of them. Click the **Register** link at the top of the page to create an account. You'll need to click through a couple of pages, entering your details as you go, but registration should be quite straightforward. Click **Complete Registration** when you're finished and go check your email. Once the confirmation email arrives, click the first link that it contains to finish setting up your account. Then log in using the form at the top right of the page.

Now that you're logged in, find the thread you want to reply to and click the **New Reply** button at the top (or bottom) of the page. Type your message and click **Submit Reply**, and your post will be added to the end of the thread. If you realize that you made a mistake in your reply, you can go back to the thread and click the small **EDIT** button in the bottom-right corner of your post.

Creating Your Own Thread

If you search through the forums but can't find anything relevant to your problem, why not create a new thread? The first step is to find the category that best fits the topic you want to discuss. Head back to the forum front page and browse through the list until you find something that looks suitable. If you have a burning question about your wireless connection, for example, you'd click the **Networking & Wireless** category under the "Main Support Categories" heading.

Once you've found a category, click its name to view all of the threads it contains. Click the **New Thread** button at the top of the page to start writing. Make sure that you choose a descriptive title for your new thread, and include plenty of details if you're asking a question about a problem you're having. To finish off, click **Submit New Thread**. Then just wait for the replies to roll in!

What's All This Bean Business?

You might have noticed a lot of talk about coffee and beans on your travels through the forums. Don't worry—you haven't wandered into a caffeine-addiction support group. Beans are just a way of keeping track of how many posts a person has made. (It's supposedly an inside joke, referring to geeks' love of coffee, but personally I can't stand the stuff!) You're given a bean for every reply or thread you make, and as you collect more beans, you'll find that the description that appears under your name will change. As of this writing, I'm informed that my beans are green, with the chances of my ever becoming an "Ultimate Coffee Grinder" looking slimmer by the day.

Ask Ubuntu

A relative newcomer to Ubuntu's growing stable of help and support channels is Ask Ubuntu, a simple website for getting your Ubuntu-related questions answered. Although it's not as established as the Ubuntu forums and doesn't have the same friendly community chitchat, it's a useful place to go if you're trying to answer a specific question or solve a problem. You can check it out by visiting *http://www.askubuntu.com/*.

On arriving at the Ask Ubuntu front page, you'll notice a list of "Top Questions" running down the page, ranked by their number of "votes." Users of the site ask questions, which other users can then vote up or down in importance. The most important, interesting questions, as determined by the community, bubble up to the top of the list, get the most attention, and are thus more likely to get answered. You may have seen a similar sort of system in place on news websites and sites like YouTube; insightful comments receive lots of votes and appear at the top of the list, whereas less useful comments are buried further down the page.

Click any of the questions at the top of the Top Questions list, and you'll find, in addition to the original text of the question, a number of comments discussing possible solutions. Some of these are marked as "answers," which directly propose a solution to the question. Other users can vote answers up or down, so the best answer will (in principle) also bubble to the top. All in all, Ask Ubuntu is an efficient way of getting the information you need if you have a specific problem or question. If you're not sure exactly what you're looking for, however, the Ubuntu Forums are probably a better bet.

If you want to give Ask Ubuntu a go, the first thing to do is log in. Click the **log in** link right at the top of the page and then click to log in with Launchpad (or you can log in with your Google or Facebook account if you prefer). Then follow the instructions onscreen to create a new account. Once that's done, you'll be returned to the Ask Ubuntu website. From here, you can click **Ask question** to ask a new question and go through the whole voting/commenting/answering cycle that I explained above.

Chatting on IRC

Internet Relay Chat (IRC) is where Ubuntu users can go to talk to one another online. Chats happen in real time, and using IRC is very similar to using an instant messaging service. Chatting is a particularly good option if you want to talk to someone as soon as possible about a question you have without waiting for a reply on the forums.

IRC can be daunting at first, so let's walk through a typical session. First, you'll need to make sure you have the right chat software. Open the Ubuntu Software Center, search for *XChat IRC* (not to be mistaken for XChat-GNOME), and install it. Once you've done that, limber up your clicking finger and follow these steps:

1. Bring up the Dash and open XChat. A Network List window like the one in Figure 21-10 will appear.

2. Make a few choices for your nickname. Your nickname is how other users will be able to identify you, so choose something that befits your uniqueness (mine is *philbull*). You should try a few alternatives in case someone has already used your first choice—adding random numbers to the end of your first choice seems to work well. Just make sure not to use spaces in your nickname.

3. Make sure that *Ubuntu Servers* is selected in the Networks list and then click **Connect**.

Figure 21-10: XChat's Network List window

4. A load of text will flash across the screen as you are connected to the IRC server. After a few seconds, you'll be switched over to the *#ubuntu* channel.

Don't panic if things look confusing; you'll figure it all out right now. Call it a crash course in IRC!

A *channel* is just a place where you can go to talk to other people. There are lots of them on IRC, each one dedicated to a different topic. In XChat, the channels that you're connected to are listed in the pane on the left side of the window, so you should be able to see that you're currently in *#ubuntu*, which is for general Ubuntu help and support. You could select **Server ▸ Join a Channel** to connect to a different channel, but for now there's no need since we're already in the right channel. In the right pane is a list of other users who are currently connected to the same channel; *#ubuntu* is very popular, so there are probably quite a few of your fellow users out there.

When you entered the channel, a bunch of messages passed by in the pane in the center of the screen. The first few are automated messages that describe what the channel is for, set some ground rules, and so forth, but by now you should see messages from other people scrolling up the screen too (Figure 21-11). The nickname of the person talking is to the left of the vertical dividing line, and his message is on the right. Everyone in the channel can see the same messages, and typically several conversations are going on at once. You'll also see messages in different colors when someone joins or leaves the channel. People are coming and going all of the time, so you can just ignore these messages.

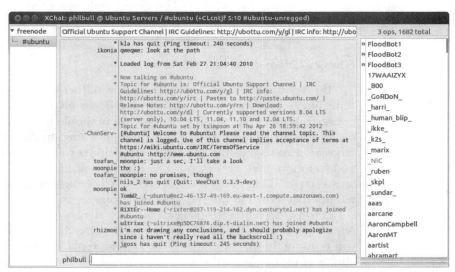

Figure 21-11: Other users chatting in the #ubuntu IRC channel

If you want to send a message, type it into the message box next to your nickname at the bottom of the screen and press ENTER. You'll see your message appear in the center pane, and so will everyone else who's in the *#ubuntu* channel. All you have to do then is wait for a reply. . . .

Registering Your Nickname

It's a good idea to register your nickname so nobody else can steal it and so people will recognize you the next time you use IRC. In the pane on the left of the window, click the **freenode** item to switch to a welcome channel for

Freenode, the IRC server used by Ubuntu (Figure 21-12). Now, type **/ns register** *password email* into the message box, replacing *email* with your email address and *password* with a good password. For example, typing **/ns register nopeeking jane@example.com** would do the trick if those were your details. Press ENTER to finish the registration.

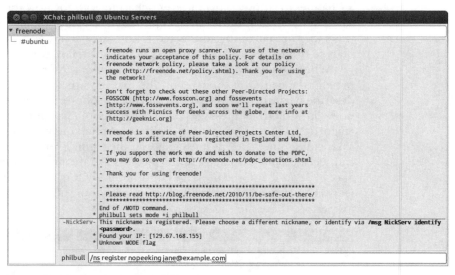

Figure 21-12: Registering your IRC nickname

If everything went according to plan, you'll see a message saying something like An email containing *nickname* activation instructions has been sent to *jane@example.com*. Check your email, and there should be an activation email containing instructions to type something like **/msg NickServ VERIFY REGISTER** *nickname* **jbaxzqxmgzqv** into the Freenode channel you were in earlier. Do this, and you should see a message along the lines of -NickServ- *nickname* has now been verified. That's it, you've registered! Click the *#ubuntu* channel in the left pane to return to where you were before.

If you got a message saying *nickname* is already registered instead of the one about an activation email, someone has already registered the nickname you're using. In this case, type **/nick** *newname*, replacing *newname* with a new choice of nickname, and press ENTER. You'll see a message that says You are now known as *newname*. Ideally, no one else has the same name this time, so try to register again.

The next time you go on IRC, you can retrieve your registered nickname by going to the *freenode* channel, typing **/nick** *nickname*, and pressing ENTER. Then type **/msg NickServ identify** *password* and press ENTER again. Of course, you should replace *nickname* and *password* with your own nickname and password when you do this.

IRC Etiquette

There are rules and social norms to follow on IRC just as there are anywhere else. It goes without saying that you shouldn't go out of your way to offend or harass anyone, just as you wouldn't in the "real world." Here are a few more subtle conventions that you should also be aware of:

Don't shout. Writing in ALL CAPITALS is the IRC equivalent of shouting all the time. There's a special circle of hell for shouters; this is pretty much everyone's pet peeve, and you're bound to get censured for doing it.

Say things only once. Sometimes you won't get a reply for a while, so it can be tempting to keep repeating the same message until someone acknowledges it. Repeating yourself too many times is also considered annoying. Being patient is a necessary skill on IRC because people tend to dip in and out of chats sporadically rather than watching them all the time. It's okay to repeat your message if you don't get a reply after 10 minutes or so, though.

Don't send loads of text. Sending more than a few lines of text at once is called *flooding*. It makes it difficult for other people to have a conversation, so you should avoid doing it. If you have lots of text that you want people to read, use a service like *http://pastebin.com/* to hold the text and simply post a link to it on IRC.

Stay on topic. There are different channels for different purposes, so you should try to stick to the topic for which a particular channel is intended. Advertising is considered to be off-topic in most channels and is particularly frowned upon.

Smile for the camera. Most of the conversations in the public Ubuntu chat rooms are logged and can be viewed at *http://irclogs.ubuntu.com/*. This is useful if you forget a link that someone mentioned last week, but it can be awkward if you said something that you shouldn't have. As a general rule, never post any sensitive or personal information on IRC (especially your password or credit card details), because it could come back to bite you in the posterior.

More Help with IRC

I hope this first expedition into IRC hasn't put you off for life! Lots of people find it confusing at first, but it's a really great way to talk to other Ubuntu users once you're comfortable with it. If you feel you need to hone your IRC skills, the IRC Help website at *http://www.irchelp.org/* is a very useful resource. And if that still doesn't get you into the IRC vibe, you can try a more familiar web interface to the Ubuntu IRC channel, which can be found at *http://webchat .freenode.net/?channels=ubuntu.*

An IRC Alternative: Mailing Lists

If the whole idea of IRC chat has you tearing your hair out, another, gentler option is available in the form of the support mailing lists. All you need to do is send an email to the appropriate list and hope for a reply. Visit *https://lists.ubuntu.com/* to see your options—the *ubuntu-users* list is probably the one you want.

Keeping Up with the News

If you want to find out what's going on in Ubuntu-land, there's no shortage of news outlets. Here are just a few of them (you'll also find additional resources in Appendix D):

Full Circle Magazine (*http://fullcirclemagazine.org/*) Full Circle is an independently produced Ubuntu magazine that is free to download in PDF (you can also get it from the Ubuntu Software Center). It contains everything you might expect to find in a traditional dead-tree magazine, such as reviews, interviews, stories from readers, and handy how-to guides.

Ubuntu Weekly Newsletter (*https://wiki.ubuntu.com/UbuntuWeeklyNewsletter/*) This newsletter aims to provide an overview of the goings-on in the community each week and typically includes notable Ubuntu news stories, interviews with developers, and updates on recent changes to software. It's pitched to the geekier end of the spectrum.

The Fridge (*http://fridge.ubuntu.com/*) The Fridge is a place where people in the community can stick notes and updates on upcoming events. Interviews are sometimes posted here too.

Planet Ubuntu (*http://planet.ubuntu.com/*) This is where you can read the personal blogs of Ubuntu developers. Some of the posts are technical, but if you're interested in cutting-edge developments, this is the place to go.

News and opinion get passed around on microblogging services too. Subscribe to the *#ubuntu* hashtag on Twitter or join the Ubuntu group on Identi.ca (*http://identi.ca/group/ubuntu/*) to join in the tweeting, denting, or whatever you want to call it.

LoCos and LUGs

So far, the whole Ubuntu community thing might seem a bit, well, *virtual* to you. Why shouldn't it? Ubuntu is a very international venture, and communicating online is the most practical way of getting things done. Regardless, there are plenty of opportunities to contact and meet other Ubuntu users in your area through Local Community (LoCo) teams and Linux User Groups (LUGs). These groups often have a membership with diverse computing skills, so they can be a good place to go to get help with Linux, among other things.

LoCos tend to cover reasonably large geographic areas, normally on the scale of whole countries or states. As such, they tend to meet in person less regularly, although many LoCos arrange Ubuntu-related events throughout the year, including "launch parties" around the time of each Ubuntu release. You can find a list of LoCo teams at *http://loco.ubuntu.com/teams/*.

LUGs are much more widespread than LoCos and tend to put a greater emphasis on meeting up. Typically, a LUG will hold regular meetings in a local community center (a pub, if you're lucky) and might organize talks or other Linux-related activities. The best way to find your nearest LUG is to use Google.

Stickers and Other Goodies

If you have a penchant for showing off your Ubuntu addiction, then you're in luck! Free stickers are available from Ubuntu-friendly computer manufacturer system76, and they're just great for replacing the unsightly Windows logo that you probably have hiding somewhere on your computer's case (see Figure 21-13). To order yours, browse to *https://www.system76.com/community/stickers/* and send a stamped, addressed envelope to the relevant address on that page. No club would be complete without a membership badge, would it?

Figure 21-13: My laptop, complete with Ubuntu sticker (I couldn't remove the Windows one)

If stickers leave you cold, other Ubuntu-branded goodies (mugs, T-shirts, backpacks . . . you name it) are available for purchase through the Canonical store (*http://shop.canonical.com/*).

Getting Involved

Lots of people enjoy being part of the Ubuntu community and want to give something back by volunteering to help. Reporting bugs is a great way to make a contribution, but that's only the start of it!

If you talk to existing contributors, you'll soon see that everyone's story is different. I stumbled into contributing to Ubuntu in early 2006, when I started tidying up some bug reports that were missing information. It was something to pass the time and took up about half an hour per day. This was back when Launchpad was new and all the bugs were being transferred from the old system, so the work was pretty fun. The members of the Bug Squad were incredibly encouraging, and I soon found myself spending more and more time doing Ubuntu stuff. As time went on, I started editing help pages on the wiki (*https://help.ubuntu.com/community/*) and eventually found my way to the Documentation Team, where I coauthored a guide on switching from Windows to Ubuntu. Nowadays I'm one of the maintainers of the "upstream" help files at the GNOME project, among other things. Being a contributor has been a great experience—I've met tons of interesting new people, indulged my interests in writing and computers, traveled to conferences around the world, and, most importantly, had tons of fun in the process.

Browse to *http://www.ubuntu.com/community/* to get some ideas on how you might be able to help. You don't need to be a geek to get involved: Artists, writers, multilinguists, marketers . . . the list of ways to participate just goes on. You might even like to attend a conference and have as much fun as the contributors in Figure 21-14! To get started, all you need to do is join the relevant team and introduce yourself on its mailing list. If you are interested, one thing in particular that you should look out for is Ubuntu Open Week, where all of the Ubuntu teams hold talks and tutorials on IRC. Check out *https://wiki.ubuntu.com/UbuntuOpenWeek/* to see when the next one will be.

Ubuntu Accomplishments

If you're not sure how to get involved, or whether getting involved is the right thing for you in the first place, you might like to try out a fun new app called Ubuntu Accomplishments (Figure 21-15). Intended to help you find a way to get involved with Ubuntu, it works a bit like a game. You start out by completing one or two relatively simple community-oriented tasks, like getting a Launchpad account (as you already learned how to do in "Launchpad: Your Passport to the Ubuntu Community" on page 353). For each task you complete, you're awarded a trophy (a digital one, mind; don't expect any engraved plaques through the mail), so you can flaunt your achievements. As you earn more trophies, other "levels" are unlocked, giving you access to more tasks that can earn you even more trophies. Each task comes with instructions on how to complete it, so you learn how things work as you go. In the process, you explore the Ubuntu community, contribute to it a little, and have some fun at the same time. And even if you ultimately decide that contributing to Ubuntu isn't your cup of tea, you'll at least be left with a trophy or two for your troubles.

Figure 21-14: Just a few of Ubuntu's many contributors at a conference (image created by Kenneth Wimer; used under Creative Commons license; original can be found at http://en.wikipedia.org/wiki/File:Uds_karmic.jpg)

You can find more information about Ubuntu Accomplishments, including installation instructions, at *https://wiki.ubuntu.com/Accomplishments/*. It's still in development as this book goes to press, so there are a few rough edges here and there. In particular, some of the tasks seem quite technical in nature. But it's still worth trying it out—go get those trophies!

Figure 21-15: Gain a sense of achievement by finding ways of contributing to Ubuntu.

22

WOUNDED WINGS

Fixing Common Problems

Like death and taxes, computer problems are an inescapable fact of life. Ubuntu suffers from its fair share of annoyances, and although I seem to spend far less time fixing things on Ubuntu than I ever used to on Windows, it's best not to ignore the possibility that you might someday experience a hardware hiccup or sticky software situation.

The purpose of this chapter is to arm you with some general-purpose tips, tricks, and troubleshooting hints. You'll find step-by-step instructions on how to fix several specific problems, but for the most part I've tried to keep the discussion general. This is because the way you resolve some issues will depend heavily on the peculiarities of your setup, and there just isn't a bookshelf big enough for a guide that covers every possible eventuality in suitable detail. Fortunately, the Internet harbors a sizable collection of Ubuntu-related guides, so even if you don't arrive at the exact answer you were looking for here, I hope you'll be able to use some of my tips to help you find the right information on the Web.

If you've run into a problem, flip through this chapter to see whether there's anything that might help. I've covered problems with installation, booting, sound and video, Internet and network connections, hard disks and storage, and displays and graphics cards, along with pesky software issues such as programs freezing or slowing down your computer. If you're not beset by any particular computer quandary, you might like to skim through this chapter to get some idea of what to do if misfortune does befall you in the future. Or, you could take my preferred route: Make yourself a hot beverage and head back to the games chapter (Chapter 17) for some well-deserved R&R.

I Can't Get Ubuntu Installed

Not being able to install Ubuntu is a particularly unhappy problem because it means that you've probably been denied all the fun from the previous 21 chapters of this book! Never fear; there's plenty you can do to convince Ubuntu to install itself on your computer, and if you're still struggling, you can try alternative installation methods like booting from a USB stick, which I cover in Appendix A.

My Computer Won't Boot from the CD

If you tried to start your computer from the Ubuntu installation CD but never even got to the purple boot screen (see "Going for a Dip" on page 12) or if the computer just boots into Windows every time, try one of the following options:

Check the boot order. When your computer starts up (*boots*), it goes through a list of devices in a set order, checking to see whether they have an operating system on them. As soon as it finds an operating system, the computer will boot from that device, and it won't check any of the other devices. This means that if the hard disk comes before the CD drive in the boot order, the computer will boot from the hard disk rather than the CD drive. To boot from the CD, you need to make sure that the CD drive comes first in the boot order. See "Going for a Dip" on page 12 for instructions on setting up the boot order correctly.

Check the integrity of the CD. You could have a faulty or damaged CD that your computer isn't able to boot from. It's possible to check whether a disc has faults on it by doing a *checksum* test. A checksum is sort of like a fingerprint; you take the checksum of your Ubuntu CD and compare it with the checksum of an Ubuntu CD that is known to be free of faults. If there is but one tiny difference between the two discs, the checksums will be different too—the "fingerprints" won't match. Ubuntu uses the MD5SUM program to do its checksums. Go to *https://help.ubuntu.com/community/HowToMD5SUM/* and scroll down to the "MD5SUM on Windows" section to see how you can find the checksum of your disc. If it turns out that the checksums don't match, you'll need to get another CD (for example, by downloading a CD image from *http://www.ubuntu.com/download/desktop/* or by contacting No Starch Press to ask for a replacement).

Make sure you burned the disc correctly.   If you downloaded a disc image (*.iso*) file instead of using the CD that came with this book, make sure that you burned the CD correctly. A common mistake that people make is to just copy the *.iso* file onto a disc, as if it were a normal file. This won't work; you need to use the Burn Disc Image option (or something similar) in your CD-burning software to do it properly. See *https:// help.ubuntu.com/community/BurningIsoHowto/* for instructions.

I Can't Get the Installer to Run

If you can boot from the Ubuntu CD (the purple boot screen in Figure 22-1 is displayed) but when you choose to try or install Ubuntu, something goes wrong and you never get to the installer screen, the computer might be struggling to start some of the software required to run the live CD. You can try the following:

Try some kernel options.   As soon as you get to the purple boot screen, press any key (my favorite is the spacebar) and choose your language from the list that appears by using the arrow keys and ENTER. Then press F6 to open a little menu with a list of cryptic options (Figure 22-2). These *kernel options* can be used to turn off features that sometimes cause problems when you're trying to start the computer. Use the arrow keys to go up and down the list and the ENTER key to select an option (an x will appear next to it). In the first instance, I recommend selecting acpi=off, noapic, nodmraid, and nomodeset. Then press ESC to hide the menu, and then try to boot from the CD normally by selecting one of the options in the main list and pressing ENTER. If that didn't do anything, you might need to apply some good ol' trial and error to the kernel options to find a combination that works for you.

Try an alternative CD/memory stick.   Some computers are simply unable to run the live CD. An alternative text-based installation CD is available from *http://www.ubuntu.com/download/desktop/alternative-downloads/*; you'll have to download the CD image (*.iso*) file yourself and burn it to a disc before you can use it (see *https://help.ubuntu.com/community/BurningIsoHowto/* for details). This installation method isn't as user-friendly as the graphical installation from the live CD, but it's much more likely to work if you're having problems. You could also try installing from a USB memory stick, as described in Appendix A.

Figure 22-1: The purple boot screen is displayed when you first boot from the Ubuntu CD.

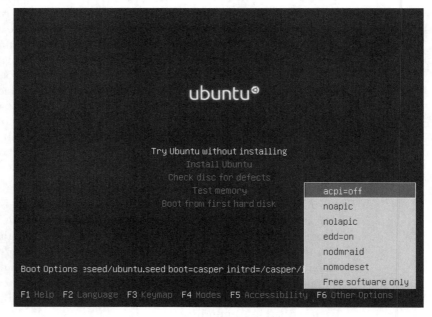

Figure 22-2: Disabling kernel options via the Ubuntu live CD boot menu

The Installer Stops Partway Through

This is probably one of the most annoying problems you can encounter. You boot from the Ubuntu CD, go through all the pages of options described in Chapter 2, and then click **Install** to start installing Ubuntu. But, after all that, the installer doesn't finish and gets stuck a few percent shy of 100.

There are lots of reasons why this might happen, most of which relate to misbehaving hardware. I've briefly described a few of the things you can try in this section, but because the underlying problem might be peculiar to the hardware in your computer, you will probably need to ask for help on the Ubuntu forums.

Wait for a while.   Installation takes longer on some computers than others. There are many reasons why this could happen (such as problems getting hardware to work), but if you give it an extra 20 or 30 minutes, it might finish.

Disconnect from the Internet.   If you are connected to the Internet, the installer might try to fetch extra settings or look for package updates while it is running. If something goes wrong when it tries to do this, it could stall, and the installation won't finish. Restart your computer and boot from the live CD again, but this time make sure you disconnect from the Internet before starting the installer.

Disconnect any unnecessary devices.   Some computer hardware can confuse the installer just by being plugged in. Turn off your computer and disconnect or switch off any devices that you don't absolutely need to have attached. Printers, scanners, USB wireless cards, and external hard disks in particular should be disconnected. Then start the computer and attempt the installation again. Once installation is complete, you should be able to plug everything back in without any problems.

Check the integrity of the CD.   If the CD has a fault on it, the installer might not be able to access something that it needs from the disc. See "My Computer Won't Boot from the CD" on page 374 for advice on how to check the integrity of the disc.

Something Goes Wrong Before Ubuntu Finishes Booting

Boot problems are especially awkward—if Ubuntu won't start, how can you access the software you need to fix the problem? To get around this particular annoyance, you might need to start the computer from a live CD (like the one included with this book) or use some special options to help the process along.

This section covers the two most common classes of boot problems, GRUB errors and kernel problems. There's some general advice for other types of boot problems too, including tips for dual-booters struggling to get Windows to start.

I Get a GRUB Error

When you try to start your computer, you might be left with a black screen, which means that there was a *GRUB error*. This means there is a problem with the GRUB bootloader, which is responsible for telling your computer's hardware how to start Ubuntu. Fixing these errors tends to involve typing a few cryptic-looking commands or booting off a live CD, so be prepared for that. You can find a short guide to handling common GRUB errors at *https:// help.ubuntu.com/community/Grub2#GRUB_Errors*.

I Get a Kernel Panic or the Computer Freezes

Kernel panics have a scary name for a reason. If you get an error message saying that there was a *kernel panic*, something pretty serious went wrong in Linux-land, and you'll probably find that you can't use the computer until you fix the problem. Fortunately, such errors are rare, and even if you do get one, you should be able to fix it without too much work. I should also note that kernel panics are only serious in that they make it difficult to run software on the computer—the physical hardware side of your computer won't be damaged at all, so once you get the software working again, everything will be back to normal. So really, there's no need to panic at all.

Freezes and kernel panics often go hand in hand, but they're not necessarily the same thing. You've probably seen a computer freeze up before—moving the mouse or pressing keys on the keyboard does nothing, and the display stays frozen. If the computer freezes, all you can do is give it a minute or two to see whether it wakes up and, if not, restart the computer or turn it off by holding down the power button for a few seconds.

You can try a few things if you keep getting kernel panics or freezes, detailed in the following sections. If nothing seems to be working, ask for advice in the Ubuntu forums, and, with a bit of luck, you'll soon be up and running again.

Unplug Unnecessary Hardware

A lot of freezes are caused by problems with hardware devices. If you recently bought some new hardware, try unplugging it and see whether you still get the freezes. If you recently installed some system updates, the driver for some hardware could be causing the problem too. It's worth unplugging any unnecessary hardware (such as scanners, printers, external hard drives, and the like) to check whether they're causing the problems.

Disable Restricted Drivers

Some freezes are caused by problems with accelerated graphics drivers (see "Games/Unity Don't Work: Installing Accelerated Graphics Drivers" on page 392) or restricted drivers for other hardware (see "Installing Drivers for Your Network/Wireless Card" on page 388). If you suspect that this might be the case, disable the restricted drivers if you can. To do this, bring up the Dash and open the Hardware Drivers application (Figure 22-3). Select a currently activated driver and click **Remove**. Then restart the computer to see whether you experience any more freezes.

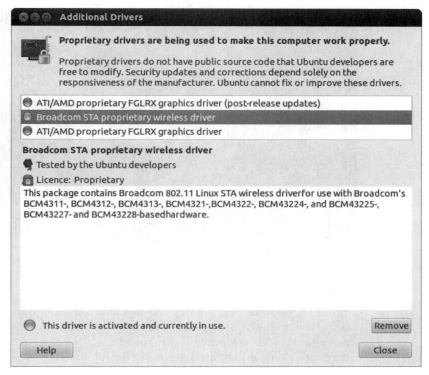

Figure 22-3: Using the Hardware Drivers tool to disable a restricted driver

Check Your System Memory for Defects

Your system memory (also known as RAM) is vital to the operation of your computer. It's where all your programs (and Linux itself) store information when they're running. If a fault develops in your system memory, freezes and crashes can start happening for seemingly no reason.

To check for problems with the system memory, boot from the Ubuntu CD included with this book (see Chapter 2 to remind yourself how to do this). As soon as the purple boot screen appears, press a key and select your language from the gray menu that pops up. Then choose **Test memory** from the main menu and press ENTER. The screen will turn blue, and the Memtest86 program will start running (Figure 22-4).

Memtest86 repeatedly writes things to your system memory and then accesses them a few moments later. It's sort of like a stress test for your RAM. Let it run until the Pass percentage at the top right of the screen has gone past 100 percent once or twice—this might take as long as an hour or two, depending on how much system memory you have. By that time, Memtest86 should have found any faults in the system memory and reported them on the screen. If it does find a problem, you might need to get some of your RAM replaced, because it could be damaged. (If that's the case, it might be time to call in your friendly neighborhood IT technician to take a look at things.)

You can turn off your computer at any time while Memtest86 is running— you don't need to shut it down properly as you usually would.

```
     Memtest86+ v4.20       | Pass  0%
Intel Core 2 2121 MHz       | Test 53% ####################
L1 Cache:    32K    777 MB/s | Test #2  [Moving inversions, ones & zeros]
L2 Cache: 3072K    749 MB/s | Testing:   196K -  512M 512M
L3 Cache:        None        | Pattern:    ffffffff
Memory  :   512M             |-----------------------------------------------
Chipset : Intel i440FX       |                              .

  WallTime    Cached   RsvdMem    MemMap    Cache   ECC   Test   Pass   Errors  ECC Errs
  --------    ------   -------    ------    -----   ---   ----   ----   ------  --------
   0:00:16     512M       0K      e820      on     off   Std     0        0
                                                                  ----------------------




(ESC)Reboot   (c)configuration   (SP)scroll_lock   (CR)scroll_unlock
```

Figure 22-4: Checking for memory faults with Memtest86

Use an Older Kernel

Some freezes occur because of problems with kernel updates or drivers. You can try using an older version of the Linux kernel if you have one installed. Take a look at "If an Update Ruins Your Day . . . or System" on page 86 for instructions on running an older kernel.

Use Rescue Mode

If you've asked for help online, chances are you'll be called upon to type some commands to try to fix your computer. There's no way to enter any commands if you can't get the machine to start up though, so you'll need to use the rescue mode to get yourself to a command line.

Restart your computer and, as quickly as you can, hold down the SHIFT key until a GRUB boot menu like the one in Figure 22-5 appears. If you have a dual-boot setup, you'll be used to seeing this boot menu anyway. Then use the keyboard to select the topmost item with *(recovery mode)* in its name and press ENTER. Text will flash across the screen for a while, and you'll be left at the Recovery Menu screen.

Use the arrow keys to highlight the **netroot** option and press ENTER. After some more text passes by, you'll be dropped to a root command line that says something like root@*rg-laptop*:~# and has a blinking cursor. From here, you can type commands that could help you fix the computer.

In particular, you might like to try updating your system to see whether a subsequent update fixes your problem. (This will work only if you're connected to the Internet.) Type **apt-get update**; press ENTER and wait for the list of packages to be updated. Then type **apt-get dist-upgrade** to see whether any more updates are available for you to install.

NOTE   *Wireless Internet connections are unlikely to work in recovery mode. Plug your computer in with an Ethernet cable if you can.*

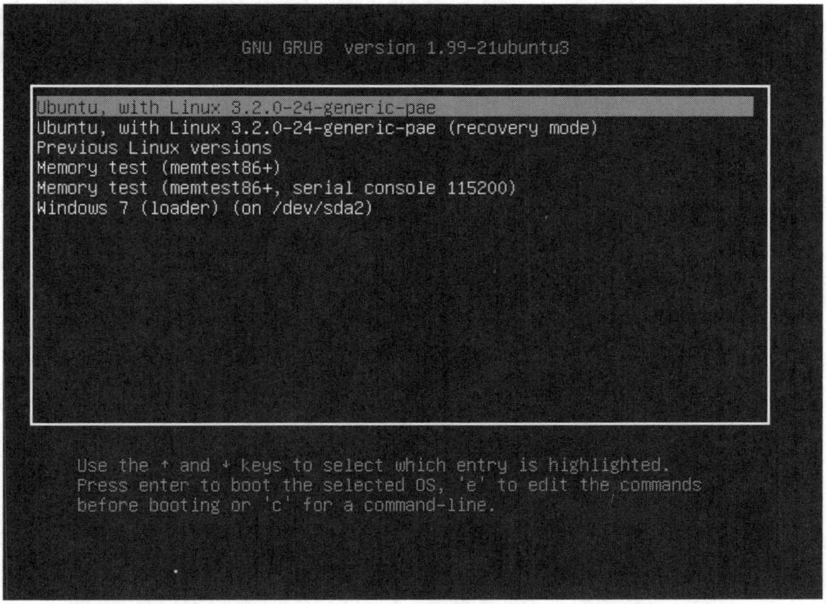

Figure 22-5: The GRUB boot menu

Reinstall Ubuntu

It pains me to say it, but if you just can't fix the problem no matter what you try, it might be worth reinstalling Ubuntu. To do this, follow the instructions in Chapter 2. You might need some of the advice on manual partitioning from Appendix C too.

Before you reinstall, remember to back up any files that you want to keep. You can do this by copying them to an external hard disk or USB memory stick while you're running the live CD—all you need to do to access the files is mount your hard disk as described in "Project 19A: Accessing Files on Your Windows Partition (for Dual-Booters)" on page 322 (but mount your Ubuntu partition rather than your Windows one).

Windows Won't Boot

If you installed Ubuntu in a dual-boot setup, you may find that the computer restarts or displays an error message when you try to boot Windows instead of Ubuntu. Dual-boot Windows setups sometimes have a problem with hibernation and disk checking, so try the following steps to see whether you can get it working again:

1. Boot into Ubuntu and mount your Windows partition (see Chapter 19 for details on how to do this).

2. Find *hiberfil.sys* (it should be in the top-level folder of your Windows partition, as shown in Figure 22-6) and rename it something like *old_hiberfil.sys*. This will cause Windows to ignore all of the hibernation information it has stored.

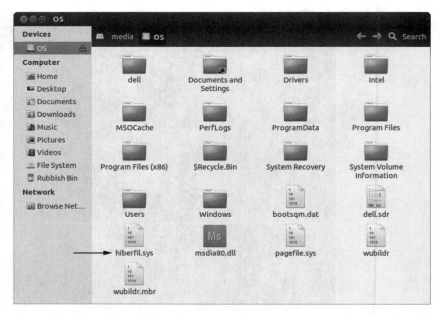

Figure 22-6: The top-level folder of a Windows partition, including the hiberfil.sys *file*

3. Restart your computer and boot into Windows by selecting it from the GRUB boot menu. Ideally, Windows will now boot.

4. If Windows does not boot and you get a blank screen or it restarts, reboot the computer into Windows again but, this time, press the F8 key a few times immediately after choosing to boot Windows from the GRUB menu. A Windows boot menu should appear.

5. Select the **Safe Mode (with Networking)** option and see whether that runs. If it does, perform a disk check in Windows. You can do this by going to (My) Computer, right-clicking your hard disk, and selecting **Properties**. You can find the **Error-checking** option you need on the Tools tab. Once the check is finished, restart the computer to see whether Windows will start normally.

You may need to repeat the rebooting-and-pressing-F8 procedure once or twice for it to stick—let it run a disk check whenever it asks to do so.

Sound and Video Problems

If you're met with silence when you try to watch a movie or play a song, either you've rented a Charlie Chaplin film, or you're having issues with your sound card. Assuming it's the latter, you'll find that most sound-related problems in Ubuntu are caused by using incorrect sound card settings. Unfortunately, the number of these settings tends to be overwhelming, and it's rarely obvious which ones you should change to get things working. Trial and error is the order of the day when it comes to sound problems, I'm afraid, although I've tried to explain as many of the relevant options as possible in this section to help you out.

If the problem has more to do with what you're not seeing than what you're not hearing, then you're possibly in for an easier ride. Video problems tend to be easier to fix—most of the time, all you'll need to do is find the right piece of software to install and then, erm, install it. Skip to the end of the section for more on video issues.

Ubuntu Doesn't Play Any Sounds

There are many reasons why Ubuntu might not be playing any sounds. I'll concentrate on some of the more basic issues in this section, but if none of this helps, you can always try the Ubuntu forums or IRC; both are discussed in detail in Chapter 21.

To start troubleshooting, find a song on your computer and play it in Rhythmbox or the Totem Movie Player. (If you need it, a sample song, called "Josh Woodward - Swansong" is available in the */usr/share/example-content/Ubuntu_Free_Culture_Showcase* folder.) You need to have a sound file playing constantly in the background so that you can tell whether changing any of these settings has worked.

If you are unable to start playing the file, Ubuntu may not have detected your sound card properly. Open a Terminal using the Dash, type `aplay -l` into it, and press ENTER. If the list of playback hardware devices is empty, your sound card hasn't been detected. In this case, you'll definitely need to get some community support—again, see Chapter 21 for more information on using the Ubuntu forums and IRC.

Assuming you can play the file, check that your speakers are turned on, turned up, and plugged into the correct socket on your computer (it's often a light green color). Many times in the past, I've plugged my speakers into the microphone socket and sat there wondering why they were silent. When you're confident that your speakers are okay, try the following steps:

1. Click the speaker icon on the top panel and select **Sound Settings** from the menu that pops up. The Sound window will appear (Figure 22-7).

2. Make sure that the Mute option is not checked and that the Output volume slider at the bottom of the window is pulled all the way to the right.

3. Click the **Applications** tab and make sure that none of the applications in the list is muted or set to a low volume.

4. Click the **Output** tab and make sure that the right connector is chosen. If you're not sure, try choosing different connectors by trial and error until you get one that works. If none of them works, return this option to its original setting (usually *Speakers – Built-in Audio*).

If none of this helped, check out *https://wiki.ubuntu.com/Audio/* or *https://wiki.ubuntu.com/DebuggingSoundProblems/*. The latter is a brief guide to identifying sound problems, which requires a little work in the Terminal. (See

Chapter 8 if you need to refresh your memory on how the Terminal works.) Perhaps its most interesting tip is to try the Ubuntu sound troubleshooter, which you can run by typing `ubuntu-bug audio` into the Terminal, followed by ENTER. It will collect information about your sound card and check for a few common problems that could be the source of your audio woes.

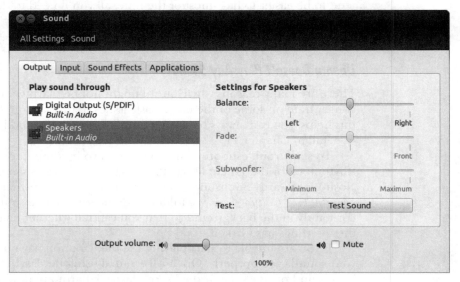

Figure 22-7: The Sound settings window

My Microphone Doesn't Work

As long as your sound card is detected correctly by Ubuntu, any microphone with a standard audio jack connection (similar to the connector on headphones) should work.

To test your microphone, click the speaker icon on the top panel and select Sound Settings from the menu that pops up. In the Sound window that appears, go to the Input tab (Figure 22-8). There you'll see an Input level indicator, which should dance up and down when you make a sound. If nothing happens to the indicator when you make a noise, your microphone isn't being picked up, so try some of the following tips:

Plug it in.   Check that the microphone is plugged in to the correct socket (it should be marked by a small microphone symbol and is often pink). Also, be aware that some sound cards can switch inputs and outputs between different sockets, so what you think is the microphone socket might have actually been assigned to something else. In that case, try plugging the microphone into the other sockets.

Turn it up.   Go back to the Input tab in the Sound window and turn up the Input volume, as high as it will go if necessary. If your sound card or microphone has a volume control, make sure that is turned up too.

Check that it's not muted.   Also on the Input tab, make sure that the Mute option next to the Input volume control is not checked.

Choose the right input.   Ubuntu sometimes detects sound cards as being more than one device. This is often the case for laptops, which might have more than one input (for example, a microphone socket and a built-in microphone). Try choosing a different device from the *Record sound from* list under the Input tab if you can (Figure 22-8). Ensure that the device is unmuted and its volume is turned up.

Test using a different program.   The lack of sound from your microphone could be a problem with the program you're using to record the sound rather than with the way the microphone is set up. Try using a different program to test the microphone. The Sound Recorder (search for it in the Dash) is usually helpful.

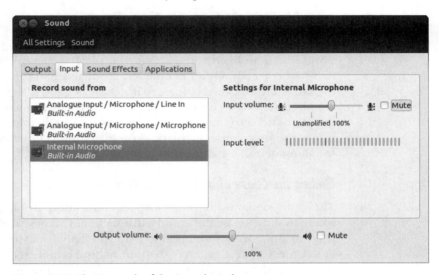

Figure 22-8: The Input tab of the Sound window

NOTE   *One program that seems to suffer from microphone-related problems more frequently than others is Skype. See* https://help.ubuntu.com/community/Skype/ *for some Skype-specific sound troubleshooting tips.*

I Can't Play an Audio or Video File

The most common reason for not being able to play an audio or video file is that you don't have the necessary *codec* installed to play the file. A codec is a small piece of software that adds support for a given audio/video format into a program. Rhythmbox and the Totem Movie Player normally find the right codec for you (for example, see "Installing MP3 Support for Audio Apps" on page 247). However, if they fail, try installing the *Ubuntu restricted extras* package—this package contains a lot of extra codecs. Once the package is installed, close and reopen your audio/video file and see whether it plays.

If it still won't play, you can try using a different program, which might have the right codec built in. Try installing the MPlayer Media Player or VLC media player—both of these programs have support for a wide range of formats.

If you're struggling to play a video on the Web (for example, on YouTube), see "Multimedia Plug-ins" on page 62.

Another reason for your file being unplayable might be that it is damaged. If you downloaded the file, try downloading it again—occasionally, parts of the file are accidentally missed during the download process, so repeating the download should fix this. Similarly, if you ripped the file off a CD, as described in Chapter 14, try ripping it again.

Finally, you might have a problem with your sound card. See "Ubuntu Doesn't Play Any Sounds" on page 383 for advice.

Internet and Network Connection Problems

If you haven't been able to get Ubuntu connected to the Internet (or a network), the most likely cause is that your wireless/network card hasn't been detected correctly. Other people have probably had the same problem with the same network card before, so it's always a good idea to search online to see whether you can find specific instructions on setting up your card. You're not guaranteed to find something useful (or intelligible), however, so I'll provide some general instructions on diagnosing connection problems and installing network and wireless card drivers.

Finding the Cause of a Connection Problem

There are so many different causes of connection problems that knowing where to start can be difficult. In this section, I've provided a few tips on how you can get more information to help you figure out your connection problem. Unfortunately, much of the information is quite technical, so you might find some of the results of these tests confusing. If so, make a note of the results, because the information might be useful to someone in the forums or elsewhere who can help you fix the problem.

Do you have a connection to the Internet?   Open Firefox and try to visit a popular website, like *http://www.google.com/* or *http://www.bbc.co.uk/*. If neither of those pages loads and you get a "Server not found" message or similar, you may not have a link to the Internet, or you might just have a problem with Firefox. To check, open a Terminal using the Dash and then type ping 209.85.227.106 into it, followed by ENTER. This should ping Google's servers—*pinging* a server is a way of checking whether your computer can communicate with it. If you receive a message starting with the text 64 bytes from (as shown in Figure 22-9), you have a working Internet connection. (Press CTRL-C to stop pinging Google.) In this case, the problem might be with your DNS settings or some other software rather than with your connection or your network/wireless card. If you get any other message, you probably aren't connected to the Internet, so you might have a hardware problem.

```
phil@jaguar: ~
phil@jaguar:~$ ping 209.85.227.106
PING 209.85.227.106 (209.85.227.106) 56(84) bytes of data.
64 bytes from 209.85.227.106: icmp_req=1 ttl=51 time=9.29 ms
64 bytes from 209.85.227.106: icmp_req=2 ttl=51 time=9.48 ms
64 bytes from 209.85.227.106: icmp_req=3 ttl=51 time=15.2 ms
64 bytes from 209.85.227.106: icmp_req=4 ttl=51 time=9.41 ms
64 bytes from 209.85.227.106: icmp_req=5 ttl=51 time=10.6 ms
64 bytes from 209.85.227.106: icmp_req=6 ttl=51 time=9.37 ms
^C
--- 209.85.227.106 ping statistics ---
6 packets transmitted, 6 received, 0% packet loss, time 5006ms
rtt min/avg/max/mdev = 9.294/10.581/15.235/2.138 ms
phil@jaguar:~$
```

Figure 22-9: The results of pinging one of Google's servers, if you have a working Internet connection

Is your card recognized?   Open a Terminal, type `lshw -c network -short`, and press ENTER (make sure you put all the spaces and dashes in the right place when you type this, exactly as printed here). A list of the network and wireless cards that were recognized on your computer will be displayed, similar to the one shown in Figure 22-10; check whether any of them has a description matching the make or model of your card. If one does, the card has been recognized, but it may not necessarily have the right drivers needed for it to work properly.

```
phil@jaguar: ~
phil@jaguar:~$ lshw -c network -short
WARNING: you should run this program as super-user.
H/W path       Device  Class        Description
============================================
/0/100/1c.1/0  eth1    network      BCM4312 802.11b/g LP-PHY
/0/100/1c.2/0  eth0    network      88E8040 PCI-E Fast Ethernet Controller
WARNING: output may be incomplete or inaccurate, you should run this program as s
uper-user.
phil@jaguar:~$
```

Figure 22-10: The list of recognized network and wireless cards on my computer

Is your card turned on?   If you have a wireless card, it may have been turned off. See the instructions in "No Wireless Networks Are Found" on page 390 for advice on how to check whether this is the case.

Are you using the right drivers?   Ubuntu sometimes uses the wrong driver for a network/wireless card. To check which driver is being used for your card, open a Terminal and type `lshw -c network` followed by ENTER. Scroll down through all of the text and find the card that has a product or vendor matching that of your card. Then scroll down a few more lines until you get to the `configuration` line. This will tell you which driver is being used and the version number of the driver. You can compare this with the information for your card at *https://wiki.ubuntu.com/HardwareSupportComponentsWiredNetworkCards/* (for wired network cards) or *https://help.ubuntu.com/community/WifiDocs/WirelessCardsSupported/* (for wireless cards).

Have you checked your settings?   Click the Network icon on the top panel, select **Edit Connections** from the menu that pops up, and find the entry for your connection on the appropriate tab (as described in Chapter 4). Then, select the connection and click **Edit**. Check through the settings in the Editing window to see whether any of them are wrong—the usual suspects are your default gateway and DNS servers (if you have a manually configured wired network) and the wireless security key (if you have a wireless connection).

For those of you struggling with a wireless connection, you can find a wireless troubleshooting guide at *https://help.ubuntu.com/community/WifiDocs/WirelessTroubleShootingGuide/*. It's quite technical in places, so you might prefer to ask for help on the Ubuntu forums if you find yourself getting a bit lost.

Installing Drivers for Your Network/Wireless Card

If your network card or wireless card hasn't been recognized or isn't working as expected, you might need to install some different drivers for it. You can try a few methods, and the one that works will very much depend on the make and model of your card. I've included two of the most general ones in the following sections, but some cards need you to follow very specific instructions to get them working. The lists at *https://wiki.ubuntu.com/HardwareSupportComponentsWiredNetworkCards/* (wired cards) and *https://help.ubuntu.com/community/WifiDocs/WirelessCardsSupported/* (wireless cards) should be able to help you figure out which method to use.

Checking for Restricted Drivers

Some wireless cards have *restricted drivers* that you can download to get your card working. These drivers are normally provided by the manufacturer of the card and are "restricted" in the sense that they can't be fixed by Ubuntu developers if something goes wrong with them (in other words, they're not open source).

You need to be connected to the Internet to download restricted drivers. If you don't have a working connection (probably because you're currently in the process of trying to get your card working!), try using an Ethernet cable to plug the computer directly into your wireless router or cable modem (see Chapter 4 for more information). This will work only if you have a functioning wired network card. If your wired network card doesn't work, you won't be able to follow these instructions.

1. Go to the Dash and open Hardware Drivers. Ubuntu will start searching for restricted drivers. If it finds any, they will be displayed in the list at the top of the window (as in Figure 22-3).

2. Check to see whether any of the restricted drivers have anything to do with networks or wireless (it should say in their descriptions). If you find one that does, select it and click **Activate** to download and install it. Some cards require two drivers, so if you find two drivers that look relevant, install them both.

3. Once the installation has finished, you'll probably be told to restart the computer. It's a good idea to do this anyway, so restart.

4. Ideally, after restarting and logging in again, you'll now be able to use your network/wireless connection. See Chapter 4 for details on how to get connected.

Believe it or not, you can sometimes get the Windows drivers for your network/wireless card working in Ubuntu. To do this, you'll need the Windows driver for your card plus a program called *ndiswrapper* that converts the driver into something more Ubuntu-friendly. Full instructions are available at *https://help.ubuntu.com/community/WifiDocs/Driver/Ndiswrapper/*, but here's an outline to help you get started:

1. Find the Windows drivers for your card. These normally come supplied on a CD with your computer, or you may be able to download them from the card manufacturer's website. A list of drivers is available at *http://sourceforge.net/apps/mediawiki/ndiswrapper/*.

2. Find the *.inf* file for the Windows XP version of your card's drivers. The drivers are normally provided as Zip files, which you can open and search inside for the INF file, or in folders on the driver CD. If you can't find the file, you might be able to get more information at the ndiswrapper website mentioned in the previous step.

3. Save the *.inf* file on your desktop or in some other convenient location.

4. Borrow a computer with Internet access and download the *.deb* files from the following links (you'll need to click the link for a nearby location before the file can be downloaded):

   - *http://packages.ubuntu.com/precise/all/ndiswrapper-common/download*
   - *http://packages.ubuntu.com/precise/i386/ndiswrapper-utils-1.9/download*
   - *http://packages.ubuntu.com/precise/i386/ndisgtk/download*

5. Save the three *.deb* files to a memory stick or some other storage device and use it to copy them onto your Ubuntu computer. Again, copying them onto the desktop would be convenient.

6. Now double-click the *ndiswrapper-common* file and install it (see "Project 6C: Installing DEB Packages Not Available via the Ubuntu Repositories—Google Earth" on page 92 to learn how to do this).

7. Once that's installed, install the *ndiswrapper-utils* file.

8. Finally, install the *ndisgtk* file.

NOTE   *The order in which you install these files is important.*

9. Now open Windows Wireless Drivers from the Dash and enter your password if prompted. The Wireless Network Drivers window will open (Figure 22-11).

10. Click **Install New Driver** and then click the **Location** button. Select the *.inf* file you found earlier and click **Open**.

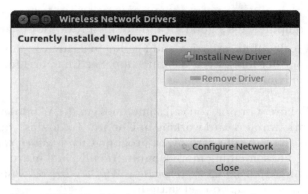

Figure 22-11: The Wireless Network Drivers window

11. Click **Install**. If everything goes according to plan, the Windows driver for your card will be installed.

12. Restart your computer and, once you've logged in again, try to get connected (Chapter 4).

Don't worry if something goes wrong—there are several minor problems that might trip you up during this process. Visit the ndiswrapper website mentioned in Step 1 or ask on the Ubuntu forums for more specific advice.

No Wireless Networks Are Found

If you know that your wireless card is working in Ubuntu but you can't seem to find any networks, try the following steps:

1. Check to make sure that your wireless card is turned on. Many laptops have a keyboard shortcut that toggles the wireless card on and off (on mine it's FN-F2). Some cards have a physical switch that you need to flip instead. If your card has an antenna with a cable, make sure that the cable is firmly secured to the card.

2. Click the Network icon on the top panel and make sure that **Enable Networking** and **Enable Wireless** are checked (Figure 22-12). If they aren't, check them; then wait a minute or two while the wireless card wakes up.

3. If the Enable Wireless option was already checked, try unchecking it, waiting for a minute or so, and then checking it again. Your wireless card might have needed turning off and on again to wake it up. You can also try doing this with the hardware switch/keyboard toggle I mentioned in Step 1.

4. If none of this has any effect, try restarting your computer. Some wireless cards work fine until you hibernate or suspend the computer, after which they fall into a deep sleep. Restarting should be enough to wake up your card.

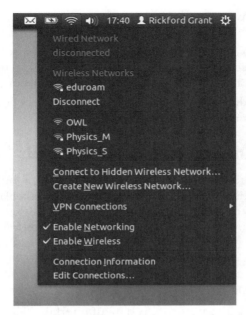

Figure 22-12: Making sure that wireless and network connections are enabled in Network Manager

5. You should also check that the network you want to connect to doesn't have a hidden network name (also called an *SSID*). If it does, it won't appear in Network Manager's list, and you'll have to manually enter the SSID to be able to connect. To do this, click the Network icon, choose **Connect to Hidden Wireless Network** from the menu, and fill out the details in the window that appears.

6. If you're still struggling, are you sure that you're sufficiently close to a wireless base station? If the signal is too weak, your card might not pick up the network at all. It can also be difficult to get a connection if you're in a particularly busy area—a conference venue, for example. Try finding someplace with a little less traffic and see if that helps.

Other Users on My Computer Can't Connect

If you have more than one user account on your computer, you might find that you can connect to the Internet but other users can't. To fix this problem, you need to make your network connection available to all users:

1. While working in your user account, click the Network icon on the top panel and select **Edit Connections** from the pop-up menu.

2. Find the network connection that you use on one of the tabs. For example, if you use a wireless network called "Marconi," you would click the **Wireless** tab and look for *Marconi* in the list there.

3. Select the network and click **Edit**.

4. Check the **Available to all users** option at the bottom of the screen and click **Save**.

5. Type your password when prompted. The network will disconnect, and you may need to reconnect it by using the Network icon on the top panel again (see Chapter 4 for further details on connecting).

6. Log in to a different user account. You should now be able to connect to the network in that user account too.

Problems with the Display and Graphics Cards

Recently, Ubuntu has been doing an excellent job of detecting graphics cards, so it's unlikely that you'll ever be left staring at a blank screen. Things aren't guaranteed to turn out perfectly, however. This section covers such problems as getting 3D acceleration support (if it's missing) and adjusting your screen resolution (if it's looking weird). Just in case, there's something to help you with the dreaded blank screen too.

Games/Unity Don't Work: Installing Accelerated Graphics Drivers

If you can't get Ubuntu's swooshy default interface "Unity" to work or if a certain game doesn't want to run, you might need to install some accelerated graphics drivers. This is because only basic drivers (which can't handle fancy effects and 3D games) are installed for some graphics cards by default, due to the lack of availability of suitable open source alternatives. If accelerated drivers exist for your card, you can install more powerful (but possibly less open source) drivers by opening Hardware Drivers from the Dash, selecting the graphics driver from the list, and then clicking **Activate** to install it. Once it's installed, restart the computer, and the new driver should be enabled.

You can directly download Linux graphics drivers from some manufacturers. These tend to be updated more regularly than the ones that come with Ubuntu, and they may have some extra features too. The next couple of sections cover how to get these drivers from the two biggest manufacturers, ATI/AMD and nVidia.

ATI/AMD Cards

1. Go to *http://support.amd.com/us/gpudownload/Pages/index.aspx*, answer the questions about which model of card you have, and then select **Linux x86** from the list of operating systems (Step 4 on that page).

2. Click **Display Results**, and you'll be taken to a download page for the driver. Click **Download** and, when prompted, click **Save File** to download the driver.

3. When the download finishes, find the driver file. It will probably be saved in your *Downloads* folder, and its name should end with *.run*.

4. Open a Terminal and type `cd Downloads` (followed by ENTER) to change to your Downloads folder (if it's stored in there).

5. Now type `chmod +x amd-driver*.run` and press ENTER to make it possible to run the file as a program.

6. To start the installer, type **sudo ./amd-driver** and then press the TAB key. This should complete the name of the installer file for you, so you can press ENTER and run the installer.

7. Enter your password. Then follow the instructions on the screen to install the driver.

nVidia Cards

1. Go to *http://www.nvidia.com/object/unix.html* and click the link for the latest version under the "Linux x86/IA32" heading (or the "Linux x86_64" heading if you're running the 64-bit version of Ubuntu).

NOTE *Depending on how old your graphics card is, you might have to download the* latest legacy GPU version *rather than the plain old latest version. Click the link for the latest version and check the list of supported products on the download page; if your card isn't listed, try the legacy version instead.*

2. Click **Download** and then **Agree & Download**. When prompted, click **Save File** to download the driver.

3. Find the driver file; it will probably be in your *Downloads* folder, with a name ending with *.run*.

4. Open a Terminal, type **cd Downloads**, and press ENTER to change to your *Downloads* folder (if it's stored in there).

5. Now type **chmod +x NVIDIA-Linux*.run** and press ENTER to be able to run the file as a program.

6. To start the installer, type **sudo ./NVIDIA-Linux** and then press the TAB key. This should complete the name of the installer file for you, so you can press ENTER and run the installer.

7. Enter your password and then follow the instructions on the screen to install the driver.

NOTE *Because they're not open source, the quality of some of the graphics drivers can vary, and problems can't be fixed by the Ubuntu developers (as they can be with open source ones). As such, some accelerated graphics drivers can cause problems, most often when you try to hibernate or suspend your computer. If you do run into problems, consider uninstalling the driver so that you revert to the default open source one.*

The Screen Looks Stretched or the Wrong Size

If your screen doesn't look quite right, the screen resolution has probably been detected incorrectly. To fix this problem, click the power button at the far right of the top panel and select Displays from the menu that appears. Then, change the Resolution setting to match the default resolution of your screen (trial and error will suffice if you don't know what the default is). Click **Apply**; if everything looks okay, click **Keep This Configuration**. If your screen goes blank, don't worry—just wait for 30 seconds, and the resolution will be returned to its original setting.

If the correct resolution for your monitor isn't available from the list, you might have to use a different display driver. See "Games/Unity Don't Work: Installing Accelerated Graphics Drivers" on page 392.

The Screen Is Blank

One possible cause of a blank screen is that something went wrong with your graphics card or its drivers. Thankfully, this is a reasonably rare occurrence, and it's much more likely that something minor (and easy to fix) happened. Peruse the following tips before you start worrying about some sort of graphics card apocalypse:

Check that the display cable is connected.   Most desktop computers have a separate monitor that plugs into the back of the computer box. Look at the back of the monitor and make sure both of the cables coming out of the back are firmly plugged in at both ends. You might also want to check that the display is switched on and that its power cable hasn't fused.

Try to wake up the computer.   Your computer may have gone into a power-saving (sleep) mode; you can wake it up by moving your mouse or pressing keys on the keyboard. If that doesn't work, try pressing the power button on your computer once. This sometimes wakes up a computer from its sleep when just "tickling" it doesn't.

Switch to a command line.   The part of Ubuntu that's responsible for displaying things on the screen is called *X11*, *Xorg*, or just *X*. Sometimes X fails to start. To see whether this has happened, press CTRL-ALT-F2. You should see a `login:` prompt if everything but X is working properly. You can type your username and password (pressing ENTER after typing each one) to access a command line, just like the Terminal you met in Chapter 8. While you're using the command line, try typing **sudo startx**, followed by ENTER; type your password again if prompted. This will try to start X—it might work, or it might give you an error message telling you what the problem is. Alternatively, type **sudo reboot** to restart your computer. (If you're wondering what happened here, pressing CTRL-ALT-F2 switched you to a different *virtual terminal*. Ubuntu starts a few virtual terminals and uses them for different things; pressing CTRL-ALT-F7 will switch you back to the virtual terminal used by X to display everything.)

Restart the computer.   Some computers occasionally start up without turning on the graphics card or the monitor. (This tends to be more of a problem on older computers.) As a last resort, try turning the computer off and then on again by pressing the power button. If the computer doesn't turn off at first, hold down the power button for a few seconds until it does.

Hard Disks and Storage Problems

I never really understood how you could completely fill up your hard disk until I bought a digital video camera. If you have a similarly expensive disk-usage habit, this section is for you. We'll cover a few tips on how to free up some disk space and, worst-case scenario, how to deal with a *completely* full disk.

My Disk Is Almost Full

If your hard disk is almost full, Ubuntu will pop up a warning message similar to the one in Figure 22-13. Click the **Examine** button to start the Disk Usage Analyzer—it will scan your disk and display a color chart showing you what is using most of the disk space. You can use this information to hunt down the files and folders that are taking up most of your disk's capacity. If you're wondering exactly how much disk space you have left, open the System Monitor from the Dash and look on the File Systems tab to see how much space remains on each disk.

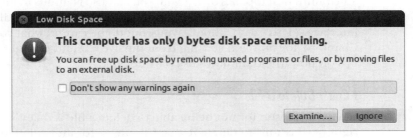

Figure 22-13: A message warning you that your disk is almost full

Apart from rooting through your Home folder and deleting unwanted files, you can try a few other things to free up some disk space:

Empty your Trash.   When you delete files, they get moved to the *Trash* folder in case you change your mind about having removed them. To empty the *Trash* folder (thus permanently removing all the files in it), click the **Trash** icon at the bottom of the Launcher and then click the **Empty Trash** button in the Nautilus window that appears.

Clean up unwanted packages.   When you remove a package using the Ubuntu Software Center, it sometimes leaves other packages that were installed at the same time on the system, even though they're not needed anymore. To remove them, open a Terminal, type `sudo apt-get autoremove`, and then press ENTER. Type your password when prompted, followed by ENTER, and see whether there are any leftover packages that can be removed. If there are, type **y** and press ENTER to remove them.

Empty the package cache.   When the Ubuntu Software Center installs a program, it keeps the package used to install it for a little while in case it's needed again. These cached files can take up quite a bit of disk space, but it's fine to delete them (the program won't be uninstalled or anything like that). Open a Terminal and type `sudo apt-get clean` followed by ENTER. Type your password if prompted and then press ENTER to empty the cache.

My Disk Is Completely Full

If your hard disk is completely full, you may not be able to start Ubuntu at all, and all you'll get is a blank screen. If this happens, press CTRL-ALT-F2 to change to a Terminal login prompt. Type your username, followed by ENTER, followed by your password, followed by ENTER again, to access a command line. Once there, try clearing some disk space by typing some of the commands recommended in the previous section, "My Disk Is Almost Full." You can also use the rm command to remove some files in your Home folder, but be careful: There's no undo when using rm.

Once you've cleared a little disk space, type **sudo reboot** to restart the computer. With any luck, there will be enough disk space for you to be able to log in now.

If all this seems a bit tedious and technical to you, you could always try booting from the Ubuntu Live CD included with this book. Once you have an Ubuntu desktop in front of you, you can use Nautilus to mount your hard disk, allowing you to find and delete files using a more friendly graphical interface. (This goes without saying, but do be careful what you delete!) See Chapter 2 for more on starting from the live CD and Chapter 19 for some tips on how to mount hard-disk partitions.

I Can't Delete a File

The usual reason for not being able to delete a file is that you don't have the right permissions to delete it (see Chapter 7 for an explanation of file permissions). Right-click a blank area of the folder in which the file is stored, choose **Properties**, and select the **Permissions** tab. If you are listed as the owner, make sure that your Folder Access permissions are set to Create and delete files. Click **Close** and then try to delete the file again.

If you are not the owner of the folder, you'll have to gain ownership of it before you can delete the file. This is where you need to ask yourself, "Should I really be deleting someone else's file?" Sometimes file permissions get messed up, and so the file might be yours—in that case, it's okay to delete it. If it's someone else's file, though, ask for his permission first.

If you're convinced that deleting the file is a good idea, open a Terminal and use the **chown** command to change the owner of the folder. Here's how it works: If I wanted to delete a file called *cats.jpg* from the *Pets* folder in the *Shared* folder, I would type **sudo chown phil ~/Shared/Pets**, followed by the ENTER key (remember, ~ means "my Home folder"). After typing my password and pressing ENTER again, I would become the owner of the *Pets* folder and could delete *cats.jpg* as normal. Of course, you should substitute the name of the folder and your username in place of mine for this to work for you.

NOTE   *Don't use this method to delete system files (in other words, files that aren't stored in the /home folder) unless you're sure you know what you're doing. There's a good reason why you don't have permission to delete system files by default; you could really screw up your system if you remove something vital.*

Software Installation Problems

Ubuntu's software management tools tend to operate pretty smoothly these days. Nevertheless, I've included some troubleshooting tips for two or three problems that used to be common (but seem to be getting rarer with each release). If you're having a problem with installing, removing, or updating packages, this section is for you.

I Get an Error About Unauthenticated Packages

If you get an error message about unauthenticated packages when you try to install a program, try the following:

1. Open the Update Manager from the Dash.
2. Click the **Check** button and, if prompted, enter your password. The package list will be updated, along with all the files that are used to check whether your packages are "authentic."
3. When the Update Manager has finished updating the package list, close it and try to install your program again.

If you're still getting the error message, you may have added a software repository without adding its GPG key. The *GPG key* is required to do the authentication stuff that the error message is talking about. If this is the case, look at "Adding Extra Software Repositories" on page 88 for instructions on how to add the GPG key for a repository.

I Get a dpkg Error

There are a couple of common reasons why you might get an error message related to dpkg when you try to install, update, or remove a software package.

If you get an error saying E: Sub-process /usr/bin/dpkg returned an error code (1), you could have a broken package on your system. Here are some techniques you can try to fix a broken package:

1. Open the Terminal by searching for it in the Dash.
2. Type `sudo apt-get install --fix-broken` and press ENTER. Type your password when prompted and press ENTER again. This command looks for broken packages and tries to fix them.
3. With any luck, this will fix the problem; try installing a package via the Ubuntu Software Center to see whether you still get the dpkg error message.
4. If you still get the error message, type `sudo dpkg --configure -a` into the Terminal and press ENTER. This command tries to fix half-installed packages if there are any.
5. Try installing a package from the Ubuntu Software Center again. At this point, if you're still getting an error message, ask for help on the Ubuntu forums.

If you get an error message saying E: Could not get lock /var/lib/dpkg/lock - open (11: Resource temporarily unavailable) or E: Unable to lock the administration directory (/var/lib/dpkg/), you might be running more than one package manager (APT frontend) at the same time. For example, if you are installing a package using the apt-get command in a Terminal while simultaneously trying to install a program with the Ubuntu Software Center, you will get this error message.

Wait until one of the package managers finishes what it's doing, and then close it and try to use the other one again. If no other package managers are running, you won't get this error message. If you don't think you have any other package managers running, the Update Manager could be running in the background and causing the problem. Wait for a few minutes for the Update Manager to finish what it's doing and then try again.

NOTE   *You might also receive these error messages if you are using the* apt-get *command in the Terminal without prefixing it with* sudo. *See Chapter 8 for the correct commands to use.*

I Have a Broken Update

If you update your computer using Update Manager but receive an error message saying that you have a broken update, try the instructions in "I Get a dpkg Error" on page 397 to try to fix the problem. If that doesn't work, try asking on the Ubuntu forums for help—there may be a bug in the package that was being updated when the error occurred.

A Software Repository/PPA That I Added Doesn't Show Up in the Software Center

"Adding Extra Software Repositories" on page 88, I mentioned that it might take a while for any repository that you add to show up in the Ubuntu Software Center. This is because APT is updating its list of software sources in the background but, infuriatingly, doesn't let you know when it has finished. If you've been waiting for a while and have already tried closing and then reopening the Software Center (as suggested in Chapter 6) to no effect, then it might be time to break out the big guns and *force* the Software Center to take notice of the new repository.

To do this, first close the Ubuntu Software Center. Then bring up the Dash, open up a Terminal, and type **sudo apt-get update**. Enter your password when prompted and wait for APT to update its list of software sources. Now open the Software Center again and click the arrow immediately to the right of the All Software button to see if the software repository/PPA has finally appeared.

If that still hasn't done the trick, there could be a problem with the repository itself. If this is the case, you may have seen an error message when you typed the apt-get command in the Terminal. For example, if the repository no longer exists, you would have seen an error message starting with W: Failed to fetch. There's nothing much you can do if the repository has vanished, I'm afraid!

Alternatively, there could have been a problem with the GPG key for the repository, which will prevent the Software Center from recognizing it. Follow the instructions in "Adding Extra Software Repositories" on page 88 to manually download and add the correct GPG key for the repository if you suspect that this is the problem.

Common Problems with Applications

So many applications are available for Ubuntu that it would be impossible to go through each one and point out what might possibly, someday, go wrong. Instead, in this section I've chosen to provide some general advice on how to deal with misbehaving programs, plus I've given you a sneaky little section on a common Firefox problem. If you need to handle something specific, it's never a bad idea to try looking at the help files for a given program. Selecting **Help ▸ Contents** should get you to a manual for most software. Failing that, a Google search often does the trick for me.

Firefox Says It's Already Running

When you exit Firefox, it sometimes takes a while to close itself down properly—the window will disappear, but Firefox could still be running somewhere in the murky depths of your computer. When you try to open Firefox again, you may receive a message that Firefox is running in the background so you can't open a new window. This is no good because you want a Firefox window that you can see! If this happens, open a Terminal, type **killall firefox**, and press ENTER. (The command is case sensitive, so be sure you're typing in all lowercase.) This will force Firefox to shut down immediately. With that done, try to open Firefox again, and the window should pop up as normal. If it still isn't working, try following the advice at *http://support .mozilla.org/en-US/kb/Firefox%20is%20already%20running%20but%20is %20not%20responding/*.

A Program Always Crashes

If you have a program that keeps crashing, try running it in a Terminal to see what's going wrong. You'll have to get the name of the command needed to run the program first—see "Reporting a Bug" on page 355 for information on how you can find it. Once you have the command, type it into the Terminal and press ENTER. The program should run as normal, so keep using it until it crashes. When it does, look at the Terminal to see whether it left any clues as to what's going wrong in there. Error messages in the Terminal can be cryptic, so you might want to ask someone on the forums or IRC (both of which are discussed in Chapter 21) if she knows what it means.

If the messages in the Terminal are no help, you should report a bug. See "Bugs, Bugs, Glorious Bugs" on page 354 for details.

A Program Won't Start

If a program doesn't start when you click it in the Dash, try running it in the Terminal, as described in the previous section. It could be crashing soon after starting and might leave some information about the crash in the Terminal.

My Computer Is Running Slowly

Certain tasks take up lots of computing power and cause your computer to run slowly. Burning a CD, installing software, and converting music files to a different format all tend to strain your system, so you shouldn't be surprised if things feel a little sluggish when something like that is running. But what if your computer is running slowly even if you're not doing anything intensive? You can investigate the cause of the slowdown by opening the System Monitor with the Dash. Select the Resources tab and check your CPU (processor) usage—if it's around 100 percent, then a program running in the background is probably responsible for the problem (for example, the one in Figure 22-14). Choose the Processes tab and click the % CPU column heading once or until it has a down arrow next to it. This will sort the list of programs in order of how much of the processor they are using. The one that's using all of the CPU should appear at the top of the list.

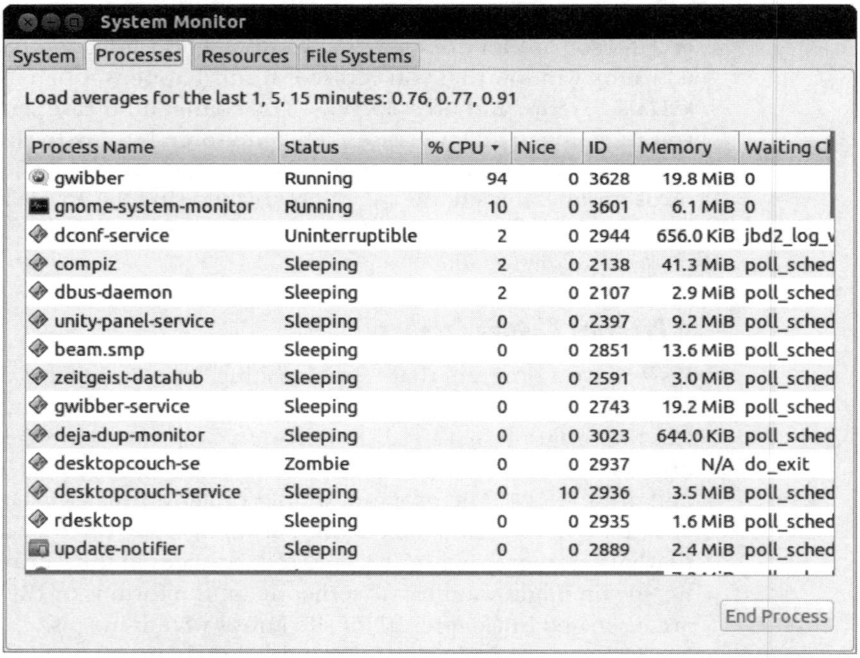

Process Name	Status	% CPU ▾	Nice	ID	Memory	Waiting CH
gwibber	Running	94	0	3628	19.8 MiB	0
gnome-system-monitor	Running	10	0	3601	6.1 MiB	0
dconf-service	Uninterruptible	2	0	2944	656.0 KiB	jbd2_log_v
compiz	Sleeping	2	0	2138	41.3 MiB	poll_sched
dbus-daemon	Sleeping	2	0	2107	2.9 MiB	poll_sched
unity-panel-service	Sleeping	0	0	2397	9.2 MiB	poll_sched
beam.smp	Sleeping	0	0	2851	13.6 MiB	poll_sched
zeitgeist-datahub	Sleeping	0	0	2591	3.0 MiB	poll_sched
gwibber-service	Sleeping	0	0	2743	19.2 MiB	poll_sched
deja-dup-monitor	Sleeping	0	0	3023	644.0 KiB	poll_sched
desktopcouch-se	Zombie	0	0	2937	N/A	do_exit
desktopcouch-service	Sleeping	0	10	2936	3.5 MiB	poll_sched
rdesktop	Sleeping	0	0	2935	1.6 MiB	poll_sched
update-notifier	Sleeping	0	0	2889	2.4 MiB	poll_sched

System Monitor — System, Processes, Resources, File Systems

Load averages for the last 1, 5, 15 minutes: 0.76, 0.77, 0.91

End Process

Figure 22-14: The System Monitor, showing the Gwibber service program using an unhealthy 94 percent of the processor for a long period of time

It's normally best to wait a few minutes and see whether the program reduces its CPU usage by itself. After all, maybe some system software is running a scan or dealing with some other maintenance operation. If the CPU usage stays high, the program might have gotten stuck, so select it and click **End Process** to force it to close. Your system should return to its usual speed within a few seconds.

If you didn't notice high CPU usage on the Resources tab, then it's possible that something is overusing your hard disk instead. Programs that do this almost always finish what they're doing within 5 or 10 minutes, so you should probably ride it out. If the sluggishness persists, the easiest way to fix the problem is to restart the computer.

Lost Files

Losing an important file is one of those uniquely frustrating experiences in life. If you've already looked in all of the most likely locations (like your Home folder) and have tried searching in the Dash, see if one of the following options works instead:

Recent Documents   Open the Dash and click the Files & Folders lens at the bottom of the screen to see whether the missing file is in the Recent list of recently edited files. If it was an Office document, try the **File ▸ Recent Documents** menu in LibreOffice too.

Basic search   The basic Search for Files tool is useful only if you can remember part of the file's name. Bring up the Dash and open the Search for Files tool. In the window that appears, type part of the file's name in the Name contains box and click **Find**. It might turn up in the list of search results.

Heavy-duty search   The more advanced Tracker search tool can look inside documents, which is handy if you don't remember the file's name but you do remember some of its contents. Install the Desktop Search application from the Software Center. Once installed, Tracker will start building its search index. This should take about 15 to 20 minutes, so you might want to wander off and do something else for a while. When you come back to the computer, open the Desktop Search app from the Dash and search for your lost file there. (Note that you may want to play with the Tracker search settings to make sure that all of the relevant locations are being searched. You can do this using the Search and Indexing tool, which you can open from the Dash.)

Look in the Trash   It's possible that you accidentally deleted the file. Click the Trash icon on the Launcher and look for it in there.

Another explanation for the lost file might be that it was saved in a temporary folder. This happens when you open an email attachment, for example—the file is put in a temporary folder by your email client and then opened using the default application for that type of file. Unfortunately, some programs don't realize that the file is temporary, and they let you save it in the temporary directory . . . which is periodically wiped clean. If you suspect that this may have happened and you have restarted your computer since you last saved the file, then it's probably gone forever.

If you haven't restarted, there may still be hope; try opening the (unmodified, original) file again to see which folder it gets stored in by selecting **File ▸ Save As** (or similar) in the program you're using. Then check which folder the Save window opens up to. For example, the Thunderbird mail client temporarily stores attachments that you open in the */tmp* folder (see Figure 22-15 for an example). Note the name of the folder and open your Home folder in Nautilus. Then, select **Go ▸ Location**, type the name of the temporary folder in the box that appears, and try to find your file in the folder that opens. It's hardly convenient, but if you find an important file, it's worth it.

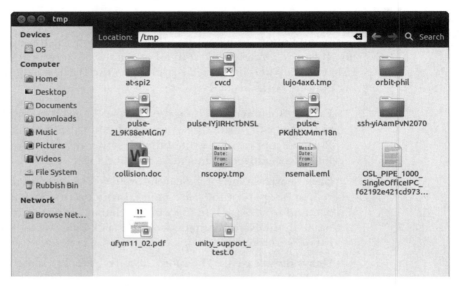

Figure 22-15: Looking for a file that was saved in a temporary folder by Thunderbird

Where Can I Go to Get More Help?

Many of the instructions in this chapter are quite general, so they might leave out the specifics that you need to get your computer behaving properly. If you suspect that this is the case or if nothing in this chapter seemed to help with your problem, then seeking help elsewhere is a good idea. Ubuntu has a large and thriving online support community that prides itself on being friendly and helpful. There are quite a few options for you to choose from:

- Visit *https://help.ubuntu.com/* and use the search to find help guides and tutorials.

- Ask a question on the #ubuntu IRC channel (see "Chatting on IRC" on page 364).

- Ask a question on a mailing list (see "An IRC Alternative: Mailing Lists" on page 368).

- Ask a question on the Ask Ubuntu website (see "Ask Ubuntu" on page 363).

- Post a question on the Ubuntu forums (see "The Ubuntu Forums" on page 361).

From here on out, it's up to you and the Ubuntu community to figure out what's going on. Good luck fixing your problem!

A

INSTALLING UBUNTU FROM A USB FLASH DRIVE

If you have a netbook, ultrabook, or some other computer that doesn't come with a CD drive, don't worry: You can still install Ubuntu by using a USB flash drive instead. Booting from a USB drive can be a little more involved than booting from a CD or using Wubi, but once the installer is up and running, the installation process is identical. I'm going to assume that you're using Windows for the rest of this appendix, but it's possible to create a USB install disk with other operating systems too; see *https://help.ubuntu.com/community/Installation/FromUSBStick/* for instructions.

NOTE *Some older computers don't have the ability to boot from USB disks. If this is the case, you won't be able to use this method to install Ubuntu. Other alternative installation methods are available, such as downloading Wubi directly; see* https://help.ubuntu.com/community/Installation/ *for a list of options.*

Preparing the Installer Files

First, you're going to need a flash drive with sufficient capacity to hold the Ubuntu installer: About 2GB should do it. Make sure that you don't have any files on the flash drive, either—you'll be formatting the drive shortly, so any files on it will be permanently deleted. Next, you'll need to download an Ubuntu CD image. If you're feeling clever, you can use your CD-burning software to make an *.iso* image from the CD provided with the book, but otherwise head over to *http://www.ubuntu.com/download/desktop/* and click **Start download** to download an Ubuntu CD image. The image is large at around 700MB, so it might take a while to squeeze its way through your Internet connection.

Sometimes, large downloads don't finish properly, and you could be left with an incomplete CD image. An easy (though not foolproof) way to check whether the image downloaded correctly is to open the folder where you saved it, right-click the image, and select **Properties**. Check that the size of the image file is *almost* 700MB (690MB, say). If it's much lower than this, it probably didn't download properly, so you'll have to try again.

The final thing you'll need is the software used to put the installer onto the USB drive. Use your web browser to download the Universal USB Installer from *http://www.pendrivelinux.com/universal-usb-installer-easy-as-1-2-3/* (click the Download link near the bottom of the page).

Creating a Bootable Installer Disk

With the installation files downloaded, you'll now be able to make a bootable Ubuntu flash disk. Plug your USB drive into the computer and follow these instructions:

1. Double-click the *Universal-USB-Installer-<XYZ>.exe* file you just downloaded to run it (*XYZ* will be replaced by the current version number of the Universal USB Installer).

2. A License Agreement screen will appear. Click **I Agree**, and you'll be taken to the Setup Your Selections page.

3. Where it says *Step 1*, choose **Ubuntu 12.04 Desktop** from the list.

4. Click the **Browse** button under *Step 2* and find the Ubuntu CD *.iso* image that you downloaded earlier. Click once to select it and then click **Open**.

5. Under *Step 3*, select your flash drive from the list (make sure it's the right one; otherwise, you could wipe a bunch of important files from some other disk!) and check the box next to it to say that you want to format the drive. Your screen should now look like the one in Figure A-1.

6. Click **Create** and wait for a few minutes while the installer is put on the disk.

Once the process has finished, close the Universal USB Installer window and safely eject your flash drive, as you normally would.

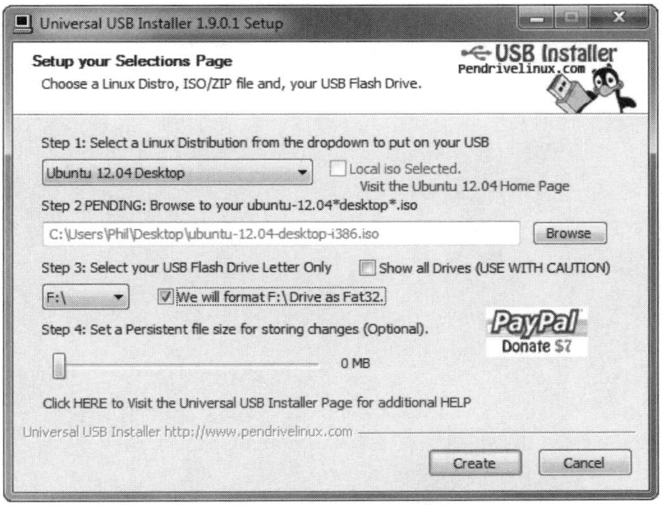

Figure A-1: Creating a bootable USB install disk

Booting from the USB Disk

Now plug the flash drive back in and restart the computer. This is where you find out whether you're set up to boot from USB drives—if you get a purple Ubuntu boot screen, you're all ready to go! The rest of the process will be the same as the usual installation from a CD, which you can read about in Chapter 2. If the computer just boots back into Windows (or whatever operating system you're using), you'll need to change some settings to get it to boot from the flash drive. Restart the computer again and look on the screen for text related to the boot order or BIOS settings for your computer. You'll normally have to press a key (such as DELETE, ESC, or F2) to access these settings, but this very much depends on the make and model of your computer. More information on accessing your BIOS is given in Chapter 2.

Once you've found the settings screen, find the option that lets you choose to boot from a USB drive (that is, make the USB drive the first boot device), save your changes, and restart. Ideally, you'll now be taken to a purple Ubuntu boot screen. In that case, head over to Chapter 2 and continue the installation as normal.

If you run into any problems, take a look at *https://help.ubuntu.com/ community/Installation/FromUSBStickQuick/* for hints and tips or head over to the forums (*http://www.ubuntuforums.org/*) for advice.

B

UBUNTU DESKTOP
64-BIT DISCS

As I mentioned in Chapter 1, the version of the Ubuntu Desktop CD that comes with this book is designed to work with i386 processors, in either PCs or Intel-based Macs. It will also work with AMD64 or Intel Core 2 processors, albeit not in 64-bit mode. In order to use Ubuntu with these processors (or any other machine based on AMD64 or EM64T architecture) in 64-bit mode, you must get a different disc on your own. There are a few ways to do this: downloading an ISO (disc image) and then burning it to disc yourself or ordering the disc from an online Linux disc provider.

Downloading and Burning Ubuntu Desktop CD ISOs to Disc

To download an ISO of the 64-bit version of the Ubuntu Desktop disc, go to the Ubuntu website at *http://www.ubuntu.com/*, find the link to the download page, and then select and download the 64-bit version. Remember that the ISO file you will be downloading is a heavyweight, weighing in at 700MB, so the download will take a bit of time. Don't count on getting it all downloaded and done before dinner . . . or, if you happen to be using a dial-up Internet connection, before dinner tomorrow. Yikes!

Burning the ISO to Disc in Windows

Once the Ubuntu Desktop CD ISO has been downloaded, you need to burn it to CD before you can use it. Although Windows has built-in disc-writing capabilities, not all versions have the built-in ability to burn ISOs. To burn an ISO to disc in Windows 7, just right-click the ISO file, select **Burn disc image**, and then click the **Burn** button in the window that appears. In all other versions of Windows, however, you must use a third-party commercial application, such as Nero. If you don't have a commercial disc-burning utility installed on your system, try the free and handy ISO Recorder.

To get ISO Recorder, visit *http://isorecorder.alexfeinman.com/isorecorder.htm*. Once the download is complete, double-click the *ISORecorderSetup.msi* file on your hard disk to install it. After the installation is finished, burn your ISO to disc by right-clicking the Ubuntu ISO file on your machine and selecting **Open with ▸ ISO Recorder** in the pop-up menu. A wizard window will appear. Using ISO Recorder is pretty intuitive, but if you like your directions clearly laid out, a set is available online at *http://isorecorder.alexfeinman.com/HowTo.htm*.

One thing to bear in mind when making your installation discs is that it is generally best to burn installation or live discs at a lower speed than the maximum speed allowed by your drive in order to reduce the chance of error (with 2X to 4X speeds considered optimal). To do so, make your choice from the Recording speed drop-down menu. Next, pop a blank disc into the drive and click the **Next** button. The CD-burning process should begin. Once it's done, the CD should pop out of the drive, and if all goes well, you'll have yourself an AMD64-compatible live CD. You can then use it by following the directions at the beginning of Chapter 2 for using the live CD that comes with this book.

NOTE *If your CD does not seem to work, there could be a problem with the ISO file you downloaded. Find out by doing an integrity check as explained at* https://help.ubuntu.com/community/HowToMD5SUM/.

Burning the ISO to Disc in OS X

Although Ubuntu no longer comes in PowerPC editions, the i386 editions can be installed and run on Intel-based Macs. You can also, of course, download ISOs for other architectures on your Mac and then burn them to CD for use on other machines.

To burn an ISO file to CD in OS X, first check to make sure the ISO image is not mounted by opening a Finder window and checking the disc in the area at the top portion of the left pane. If the disc is mounted, a drive icon will appear in that location. If the drive icon is there, click the arrow next to that entry to eject, or *unmount*, it.

After that, click **Applications** in the same Finder window and then look for and open the **Utilities** folder. In that folder, find and then double-click **Disk Utility**. If the ISO is not listed in the left pane of the Disk Utility window when it opens, go back to the Finder window, locate the Ubuntu Live CD ISO you just downloaded, and drag it to the left pane of the Disk Utility window, just below the listings for your current drives. Once the ISO file appears in that list, click it once to highlight it.

To complete the process, click the **Burn** icon in the Disk Utility window's toolbar and, when prompted to do so, insert a blank CD into your drive. Once the blank disc is inserted and recognized, you will be able to adjust the burn speed from the drop-down menu next to the word *Speed*. Select as low a speed as your hardware will allow, which, depending on the age of your Mac, will probably be 4X to 8X. Finally, click the **Burn** button in that same window, and the burning process will begin.

Ordering an Install Disc from Other Online Sources

While it is possible to buy Ubuntu Desktop CDs from the Ubuntu store (*https://shop.canonical.com/*), only the 32-bit version is available, which is the same version that comes with this book. You can, however, order a 64-bit version from an independent online source, such as OSDisc.com (*http://www.osdisc.com/*).

C

MANUALLY PARTITIONING YOUR HARD DISK

When you're partitioning your hard disk with the Ubuntu installer, the first two options (use the whole disk and resize an existing partition) should cover most eventualities. They're both discussed in Chapter 2. But if you're in a geekier mood, you can carve up your disk space in a few fancy ways. For example, you can create a shared data partition so your files can be shared between Windows and Ubuntu, or you can make a separate partition for your */home* directory so you can reinstall Ubuntu (or install a different Linux distro) without having to fully back up all of your files.

When you get to the Installation type screen of the installer, choose **Something else** and click **Continue**. You'll be presented with a colored-bar view of your current partition setup (Figure C-1) and a list of your partitions below that. None of the changes that you make in this window will be applied until you click **Install Now**, and you can click the **Back** button if you want to forget about making the manual changes altogether. (There is one exception: Changes are made immediately and irreversibly when you resize a partition. See "Editing Existing Partitions" on page 414 for more on this.)

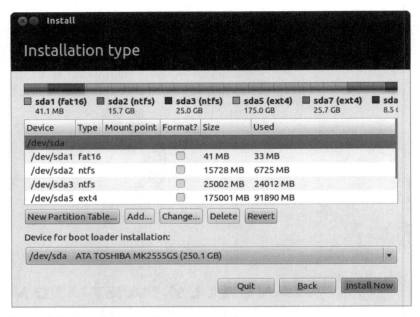

Figure C-1: Using the manual partitioning tool

Creating and Deleting Partitions

You can create new partitions only if you have some "free space" to put them in. This is free space in the sense that there's not already a partition on that part of the disk, not that there are no files there. One way of creating free space is to delete an existing partition; to do this, click the list item for the partition and click **Delete**. After a few seconds, it'll change into free space in the list (Figure C-2). Alternatively, if you're planning to completely change your partition setup, select the hard disk you want to modify and click **New Partition Table**. You'll be left with a completely blank slate where all you need to do is add new partitions.

NOTE *You can identify which items in the list are hard disks by checking whether there is a number after the entry in the Device column; anything that does not have a number (for example, /dev/sda) is a hard disk, and everything else is a partition.*

Select any free space and click **Add** to put a new partition in it. You'll be presented with a Create partition window (Figure C-3), which will ask how big you want to make the partition in megabytes (1GB is roughly 1,000MB). See "Varieties of Partitions" on page 414 for advice on how big to make your partitions.

The Use as option lets you specify the filesystem type you want to use. A *filesystem* tells your operating system how to store files on the partition. You can choose from a number of different filesystems, but not all of them will be understood by Windows and Mac OS. Ext4 is the best choice for a partition that will be used solely by Linux, but FAT32 is the one you need if you want to share files with Windows or Mac OS.

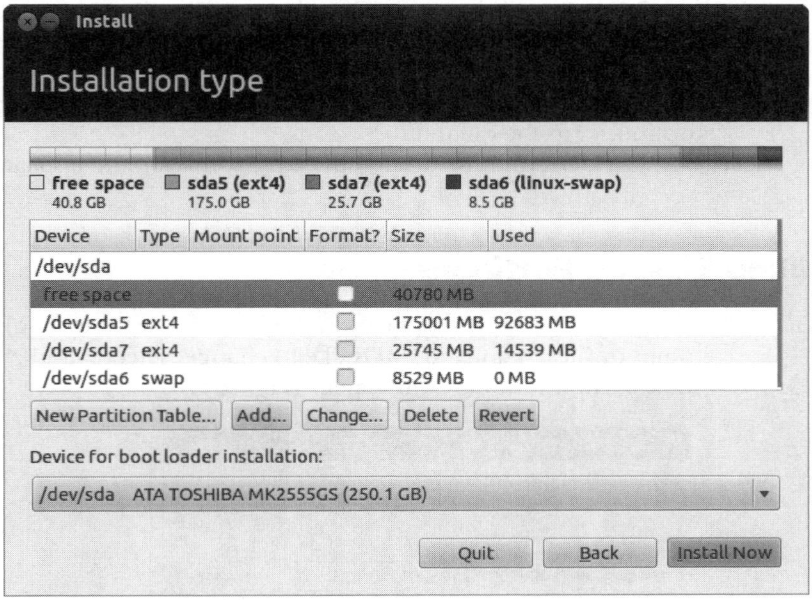

Figure C-2: Creating some free space

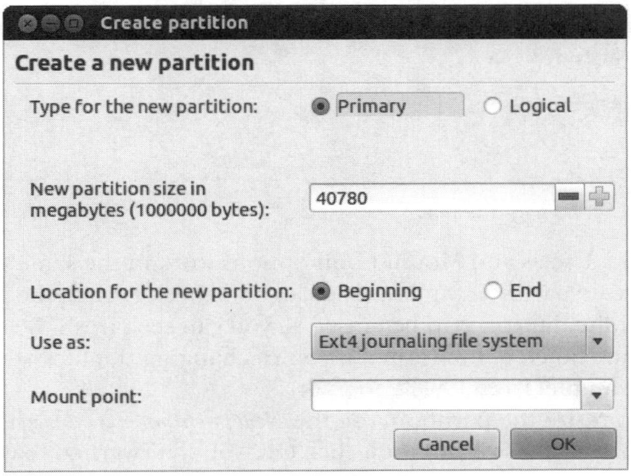

Figure C-3: Creating a new partition

You can also select the *mount point*, which is where Ubuntu will put the folder that corresponds to this partition (see Chapter 7 if you're not familiar with how Linux organizes folders). For example, you would mount the home partition as the */home* folder. More detail on mount points is given in "Varieties of Partitions" on page 414.

There are two more options in the Create partition window, both of them rather technical and boring in my opinion. The Type for the new partition option gives you a choice between creating a *primary* or *logical* partition. You can have a maximum of four primary partitions on a disk but lots of logical partitions—the disk partitioner will choose the right option for you, so there's no need to alter this setting (it doesn't affect how you use the partition in any way). The other option, Location for the new partition, lets you choose where on the disk to put the new partition. It doesn't really matter, so leave this option set to the default too.

Click **OK** to finish adding the partition; it should appear in the list after a second or two.

Editing Existing Partitions

If you have an existing partition that you'd like to resize or whose mount point or filesystem type you'd like to change, select it and click **Change**. An Edit partition window will appear (Figure C-4).

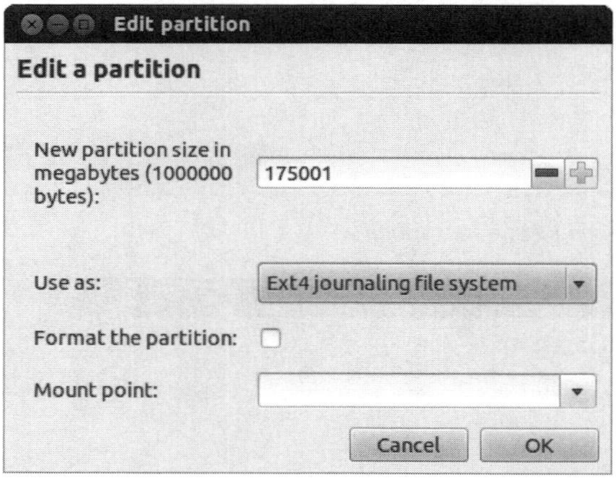

Figure C-4: Editing a partition

The Use as and Mount point options work in the same way as those in the Create partition window. You can also check **Format the partition** if you'd like all the data on it to be erased so you can start fresh. Be aware that you have no choice but to format if you're changing the filesystem of a partition (for example, from FAT32 to Ext4).

To resize the partition, use the *New partition size in megabytes* option. If you change the size and then click **OK**, you'll be warned that the changes will be written to disk. Click **Continue**, and the partitioner will start to resize the partition immediately—you can't undo this change, so think carefully about whether you've chosen the right options before clicking Continue.

Varieties of Partitions

You'll need to be familiar with a few varieties of partitions when you manually partition your disk. I've summarized these in the following sections and provided some tips on choosing their size, mount points, and filesystems.

Root Partition

You must have a root partition; it's where important system files are stored and software is installed. I recommend making it at least 10GB in size, but aim for 12GB to 15GB, if you can, to leave room for installing new programs. If you're not going to have a separate home partition (described in a moment), all of your files will be stored in the root partition too, so in that case you should make it as big as possible to accommodate all your stuff. The mount point should be set to / and the filesystem to *ext4*.

Swap Partition

You must have a swap partition. The swap partition is like an extra area of system memory (RAM); if your computer's system memory gets full, it will start using this partition to handle the overspill. It's also used to store the contents of your system memory (like all of your open files and programs) when you hibernate the computer. See *https://help.ubuntu.com/community/SwapFaq/* for more details on swap.

As a rough guide, your swap partition should be a little larger than the amount of RAM that your computer has. For example, if you have 2GB of RAM, make a 2.2GB swap partition. The filesystem should be set to *swap area*, and there's no need to set a mount point.

NOTE   *It's possible to get away without a swap partition by creating a* swap file *after you've installed Ubuntu, but the method for doing this is beyond the scope of this book.*

Home Partition

The */home* folder (see Chapter 7 for a description) can be put in a separate partition. You don't need to do this, but it's useful if anything ever goes wrong and you need to reinstall Ubuntu—all your personal files and configuration settings will be left intact on the home partition while Ubuntu is reinstalled on the root partition. This can save a lot of work when restoring your system. If you don't have a separate home partition, the */home* folder will be put in your root partition with everything else. The way you access your Home folder (for example, through the Launcher) will be exactly the same whether you put it on a separate partition or not.

The home partition is where all your files and settings are stored, so you'll want to make it as big as possible. (For various perspectives on how big is big enough, see "Example Partition Layouts" on page 416.) The filesystem should be *ext4*, and the mount point should be set to */home*.

Windows Partition

If you have Windows installed, you will need to resize the Windows partition to make room for Ubuntu. When you do this, be sure to leave at least enough disk space for Windows to function properly. Windows XP needs a partition at least 2GB in size, and for Vista and Windows 7 you should leave at least 16GB. You will probably want to leave more space than this so that you can install programs and save files when using Windows, and remember to leave space for your existing Windows files too. The Used column in the main partitioning window will tell you how much space your Windows files are currently taking up.

Windows partitions will be of type NTFS or FAT32. Remember not to format the Windows partition, or your current installation of Windows will be erased.

Shared Partition

If you want an easy way to share files between Windows and Ubuntu, create a shared partition. In both operating systems, it will appear as a separate hard disk, which you can use to store whatever you like.

Make the partition as big as you think you'll need: If you only ever copy small files between Ubuntu and Windows, then 1GB to 2GB should be plenty; if you want to permanently store all your Windows and Ubuntu files in there (sort of like a shared Home folder), make it as big as possible (see the next section for an example). You should choose FAT32 as the filesystem, but you can use almost anything for the mount point—*/windows* will be one of the default suggestions, but you could type something like */shared* or */wormhole* into the Mount point box if you liked. Just make sure you use a name without any spaces in it.

Example Partition Layouts

Partitioning can be confusing if you've never done it before, so I've provided a few example partition layouts that should make things clearer. In all of these examples, I've used a 100GB hard disk, but you can scale all the partition sizes up or down for your disk according to the advice in "Varieties of Partitions" on page 414.

Standard Ubuntu-Only Installation

Only Ubuntu will be installed on the disk, so only the root and swap partitions are needed (Figure C-5). Since I have 4GB of RAM, I made the swap partition 4.2GB. The root partition filled up the rest of the disk space to give me as much room for files and programs as possible. (There was no need to partition the disk manually in this case; the Ubuntu installer's Erase disk and install Ubuntu, or Replace Windows with Ubuntu options, would have achieved the same result.)

Ubuntu-Only with a Separate Home Partition

Only Ubuntu will be installed, but there will be a separate home partition to keep my data safe in case I ever need to reinstall (Figure C-6). I'm planning to store home movies on this one, which means lots of very large files, so I went for a smallish 12GB root partition and a slightly undersized 4GB swap partition. This leaves lots more space for the home partition (and my videos), which takes up the remaining 84GB of the disk.

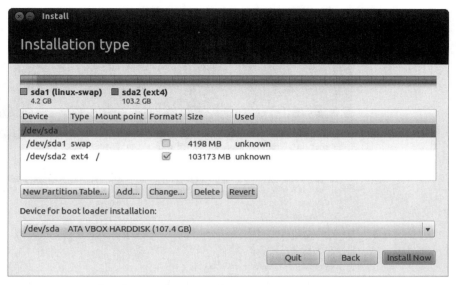

Figure C-5: A simple, Ubuntu-only partition layout

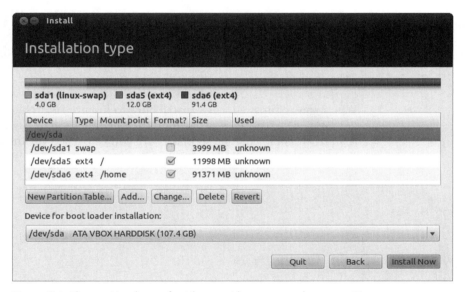

Figure C-6: The partition layout for Ubuntu with a separate home partition

Ubuntu and Windows with a Shared Partition

Ubuntu will be installed alongside Windows XP, and I want a shared partition so that I can copy files between the two operating systems (Figure C-7). My existing Windows installation was using 6.7GB of the disk because I had files and programs installed on it. I resized the Windows installation to 15GB, leaving 8.3GB of space free for future expansion. Note that the Windows partition will *not* be formatted, so Windows and all my files on that partition remain intact. I created a 40GB Ubuntu root partition and a 4.2GB swap partition and then created a shared FAT32 partition in the remaining 40GB or so of disk space.

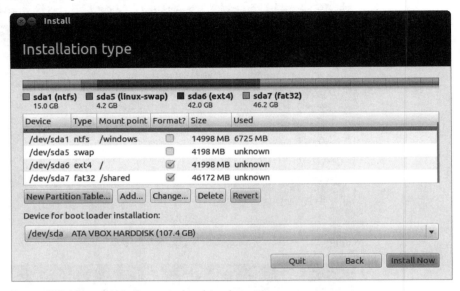

Figure C-7: Ubuntu, Windows, and a shared partition

Finishing Up

When you've finished, click **Install Now** to finalize your changes. If you're deleting or formatting any partitions, the changes will be written to disk. This is an irreversible change, so make sure you've backed up any valuable data that is on the affected partitions!

D

RESOURCES

Because Linux owes much of its growth and development to the Internet, it should come as no surprise that a wealth of information about the various flavors of Linux, including Ubuntu, is available online. In addition to the usual news, how-to, and download sites, you will find a variety of tutorials, forums, blogs, and other sources of useful information—all of which you can turn to as you use and learn more about your system.

Forums

When you are looking for advice, trying to solve a particular problem, or just looking for some general tips, online forums are the way to go. Fortunately, Ubuntu has a forum all its own, and since Ubuntu is primarily a desktop-oriented Linux distro, you are likely to find many fellow newbies and newbie-friendly posters there (rather than the hard-core geeks you might find on some other sites). There are, of course, other newbie-friendly forums, which, although not Ubuntu-specific, should also be able to provide you with lots of helpful information.

Regardless of which forum you are posting in, just be sure to mention that you are using Ubuntu, which version you have (Precise Pangolin, in case you forgot), and that you are new to Linux. And remember always to seek clarification when you get an answer you don't understand. The same poster will usually come back and restate things for you. You should feel right at home at most of these sites, though you will probably come to like one or two more than the others.

http://ubuntuforums.org/   This is the official Ubuntu community forum, which was covered in detail in Chapter 21. This is always a good place to start when you're in a fix, have a question, or just want to find out what's going on.

http://www.ubuntux.org/forum/   You may find this slightly smaller Ubuntu-specific forum a good place to turn if you find UbuntuForums.org a bit too much to wade through.

http://askubuntu.com/   This is a truly problem-solving and how-to oriented forum, so it is yet another great place to turn when you have problems, questions, or doubts.

http://www.kubuntuforums.net/   This forum is dedicated to Kubuntu, an official Ubuntu edition based on the KDE desktop environment.

http://www.justlinux.com/ and *http://www.linuxquestions.org/*   If you can't find what you want in the previously mentioned forums, you can try these forums dealing with general Linux issues. You are sure to find many Ubuntu users on them.

Linux References

You can learn more about using Ubuntu or Linux in general at these sites, many of which are geared toward newbies:

http://www.ubuntu.com/ubuntu/   An overview of Ubuntu and its features.

http://ubuntuguide.org/wiki/ubuntu:precise   An unofficial Ubuntu startup guide.

https://help.ubuntu.com/   Official documentation for the current release of Ubuntu.

http://www.tuxfiles.org/   Lots of tutorials and information for Linux newbies.

http://www.linuxcommand.org/   Where you can learn to use commands in Linux.

http://www.linux.org/   News, book reviews, downloads, and all sorts of other stuff—all about Linux.

http://www.libreoffice.org/get-help/   A number of help resources for users of Ubuntu's LibreOffice office suite.

Blogs

You can also find a lot of great information in blogs. In these blogs, you can discover the findings of fellow users as they try new things, share tips, and offer solutions to problems:

http://www.ubuntux.org/blog/   A mostly Ubuntu-oriented news blog.

http://www.ubuntugeek.com/   Despite having the word *geek* in the name, this is a pretty accessible set of mostly useful Ubuntu system and software tweaks.

http://www.omgubuntu.co.uk/   A very interesting and useful Ubuntu blog that is almost like a magazine, containing news, reviews, tips, and interviews.

http://www.webupd8.org/   A useful news blog focusing on, but not limited to, Ubuntu and other distros based on Ubuntu.

Hardware Compatibility Issues

If you want to find out whether or not your hardware is compatible with Linux or if you want to read up on other matters related to hardware support, take a look at the following sites:

http://www.ubuntu.com/certification/   Contains official Ubuntu-specific hardware compatibility information.

https://wiki.ubuntu.com/HardwareSupport/   Also provides Ubuntu-specific hardware compatibility information.

http://www.linuxcompatible.org/compatdb/   Offers numerous compatibility lists, arranged by distribution.

http://www.linuxfoundation.org/   A great spot for reading up on printer compatibility issues.

http://www.linmodems.org/   Find out if your modem is supported.

http://www.sane-project.org/   Check to see if your scanner is Linux compatible and look for fixes if it isn't.

http://www.linux-laptop.net/   Have laptop, want Linux? Check it out here.

http://www.tuxmobi Provides information for using Linux with anything that isn't stuck to your desk (laptops, PDAs, phones, and so on).

Wireless Connections

If you use a wireless card to connect to the Internet and have trouble getting your card to work, or if you just want to know where all the free wireless hotspots are, the following sites should help:

https://help.ubuntu.com/community/WifiDocs/

http://www.linuxwireless.org/

http://www.hpl.hp.com/personal/Jean_Tourrilhes/Linux/

http://www.ezgoal.com/hotspots/wireless/

Free Downloads

If you find yourself looking for more goodies to play with, you should be able to find plenty of free stuff to download at one of these sites. You can start with the Ubuntu Apps Directory and then branch out from there.

Applications and Other Packages

https://apps.ubuntu.com/cat/

http://www.getdeb.net/

http://sourceforge.net/

http://www.freecode.com/

http://www.gnomefiles.org/

Free Fonts

http://www.fontfreak.com/

http://www.fontparadise.com/

http://fonts.tom7.com/

News and Information

These sites are mainly informational, keeping you abreast of what's going on in the Linux world as a whole (I covered some Ubuntu-specific ones in Chapter 21). DistroWatch focuses on the various distributions available, whereas Linux Today, LinuxPlanet, and Phoronix fit better in the online magazine/newspaper genre.

http://www.distrowatch.com/

http://www.linuxtoday.com/

http://www.linuxplanet.com/

http://www.phoronix.com/

Magazines

If you are more of a tactile type who enjoys the feel of paper pressed between your fingers, then you might want to turn to some of the Linux magazines available at most major newsstands. All have a good deal of online content as well, so even if you're not interested in the pleasures of holding a magazine in your hand, their sites are worth checking out.

http://www.linux-magazine.com/   (European)

http://www.linux-mag.com/   (US)

http://www.linuxformat.com/

http://www.linuxjournal.com/

http://www.ubuntu-user.com/

http://fullcirclemagazine.org/

Note that two (unrelated) magazines share almost the same name: One of these is from the United States; the other is from Europe. Newbies who want some pizzazz in their reading materials, plus some useful tips and things to play around with, should go for the European version. The US version is targeted toward business users and power geeks, not newbies.

Books

Once you've finished working through this book, you should be able to do just about whatever you want in Ubuntu. Still, your interest may have been piqued enough that you want to find out a bit more about Linux. Here are some books that might help in that quest:

The Debian System: Concepts and Techniques by Martin F. Krafft (No Starch Press, 2005)

How Linux Works: What Every Superuser Should Know by Brian Ward (No Starch Press, 2004)

The Linux Command Line: A Complete Introduction by William E. Shotts Jr. (No Starch Press, 2012)

The Linux Cookbook: Tips and Techniques for Everyday Use (2nd edition), by Michael Stutz (No Starch Press, 2004)

Linux Multimedia Hacks: Tips & Tools for Taming Images, Audio, and Video by Kyle Rankin (O'Reilly Media, 2006)

Linux Pocket Guide (2nd edition) by Daniel J. Barrett (O'Reilly Media, 2012)

Running Linux (5th edition) by Matthias Kalle Dalheimer and Matt Welsh (O'Reilly Media, 2006)

Ubuntu CDs

To order an AMD64 version of the Ubuntu Desktop CD, get a replacement for the i386 version that comes with this book, or get the next version of Ubuntu when it comes out (if you don't want to or can't download it), just place an order with any of the following sites. (CDs from most suppliers will cost $5 to $10 or so.)

http://shop.canonical.com/

http://www.osdisc.com/

NOTE   *The Ubuntu Shop* (http://shop.canonical.com/) *sells only 32-bit discs.*

INDEX

The Electronic Frontier Foundation (EFF) is the leading organization defending civil liberties in the digital world. We defend free speech on the Internet, fight illegal surveillance, promote the rights of innovators to develop new digital technologies, and work to ensure that the rights and freedoms we enjoy are enhanced — rather than eroded — as our use of technology grows.

PRIVACY EFF has sued telecom giant AT&T for giving the NSA unfettered access to the private communications of millions of their customers. eff.org/nsa

FREE SPEECH EFF's Coders' Rights Project is defending the rights of programmers and security researchers to publish their findings without fear of legal challenges. eff.org/freespeech

INNOVATION EFF's Patent Busting Project challenges overbroad patents that threaten technological innovation. eff.org/patent

FAIR USE EFF is fighting prohibitive standards that would take away your right to receive and use over-the-air television broadcasts any way you choose. eff.org/IP/fairuse

TRANSPARENCY EFF has developed the Switzerland Network Testing Tool to give individuals the tools to test for covert traffic filtering. eff.org/transparency

INTERNATIONAL EFF is working to ensure that international treaties do not restrict our free speech, privacy or digital consumer rights. eff.org/global

EFF.ORG
ELECTRONIC FRONTIER FOUNDATION
Protecting Rights and Promoting Freedom on the Electronic Frontier

EFF is a member-supported organization. Join Now! www.eff.org/support